Hands-On Data Preprocessing in Python

Learn how to effectively prepare data for successful data analytics

Roy Jafari

BIRMINGHAM—MUMBAI

Hands-On Data Preprocessing in Python

Copyright © 2022 Packt Publishing

Group Product Manager: Gebin George

Publishing Product Manager: Ali Abidi

Senior Editor: Roshan Kumar

Content Development Editor: Priyanka Soam

Technical Editor: Sonam Pandey

Copy Editor: Safis Editing

Project Coordinator: Aparna Ravikumar Nair

Proofreader: Safis Editing

Indexer: Pratik Shirodkar

Production Designer: Nilesh Mohite

Marketing Coordinator: Shifa Ansari

First published: January 2022

Production reference: 1161221

Published by Packt Publishing Ltd.

Livery Place

35 Livery Street

Birmingham

B3 2PB, UK.

978-1-80107-213-7

www.packt.com

تقدیم به پدر و مادرم

صغری بیاتی

و

جهانفر جعفری

To my parents,

Soqra Bayati

and

Jahanfar Jafari.

Contributors

About the author

Roy Jafari, Ph.D. is an assistant professor of business analytics at the University of Redlands.

Roy has taught and developed college-level courses that cover data cleaning, decision making, data science, machine learning, and optimization.

Roy's style of teaching is hands-on and he believes the best way to learn is to learn by doing. He uses active learning teaching philosophy and readers will get to experience active learning in this book.

Roy believes that successful data preprocessing only happens when you are equipped with the most efficient tools, have an appropriate understanding of data analytic goals, are aware of data preprocessing steps, and can compare a variety of methods. This belief has shaped the structure of this book.

About the reviewers

Arsia Takeh is a director of data science at a healthcare company and is responsible for designing algorithms for cutting-edge applications in healthcare. He has over a decade of experience in academia and industry delivering data-driven products. His work involves the research and development of large-scale solutions based on machine learning, deep learning, and generative models for healthcare-related use cases. In his previous role as a co-founder of a digital health start-up, he was responsible for building the first integrated -omics platform that provided a 360 view of the user as well as personalized recommendations to improve chronic diseases.

Sreeraj Chundayil is a software developer with more than 10 years of experience. He is an expert in C, C++, Python, and Bash. He has a B.Tech from the prestigious National Institute of Technology Durgapur in electronics and communication engineering. He likes reading technical books, watching technical videos, and contributing to open source projects. Previously, he was involved in the development of NX, 3D modeling software, at Siemens PLM. He is currently working at Siemens EDA (Mentor Graphics) and is involved in the development of integrated chip verification software.

I would like to thank the C++ and Python communities who have made an immense contribution to molding me into the tech lover I am today.

Table of Contents

3

Data – What Is It Really?

4

Databases

Part 2: Analytic Goals

5

Data Visualization

6

Prediction

7
Classification

8
Clustering Analysis

Part 3: The Preprocessing

9
Data Cleaning Level I – Cleaning Up the Table

10

Data Cleaning Level II – Unpacking, Restructuring, and Reformulating the Table

11

Data Cleaning Level III – Missing Values, Outliers, and Errors

12

Data Fusion and Data Integration

13

Data Reduction

14

Data Transformation and Massaging

Part 4: Case Studies

15

Case Study 1 – Mental Health in Tech

16

Case Study 2 – Predicting COVID-19 Hospitalizations

17

Case Study 3: United States Counties Clustering Analysis

18

Summary, Practice Case Studies, and Conclusions

Index

Other Books You May Enjoy

Preface

Data preprocessing is the first step in data visualization, data analytics, and machine learning, where data is prepared for analytics functions to get the best possible insights. Around 90% of the time spent on data analytics, data visualization, and machine learning projects is dedicated to performing data preprocessing.

This book will equip you with the optimum data preprocessing techniques from multiple perspectives. You'll learn about different technical and analytical aspects of data preprocessing – data collection, data cleaning, data integration, data reduction, and data transformation – and get to grips with implementing them using the open source Python programming environment. This book will provide a comprehensive articulation of data preprocessing, its whys and hows, and help you identify opportunities where data analytics could lead to more effective decision making. It also demonstrates the role of data management systems and technologies for effective analytics and how to use APIs to pull data.

By the end of this Python data preprocessing book, you'll be able to use Python to read, manipulate, and analyze data; perform data cleaning, integration, reduction, and transformation techniques; and handle outliers or missing values to effectively prepare data for analytic tools.

Who this book is for

Junior and senior data analysts, business intelligence professionals, engineering undergraduates, and data enthusiasts looking to perform preprocessing and data cleaning on large amounts of data will find this book useful. Basic programming skills, such as working with variables, conditionals, and loops, along with beginner-level knowledge of Python and simple analytics experience, are assumed.

What this book covers

Chapter 1, Review of the Core Modules of NumPy and Pandas, introduces two of three main modules used for data manipulation, using real dataset examples to show their relevant capabilities.

Chapter 2, Review of Another Core Module – Matplotlib, introduces the last of the three modules used for data manipulation, using real dataset examples to show its relevant capabilities.

Chapter 3, Data – What Is It Really?, puts forth a technical definition of data and introduces data concepts and languages that are necessary for data preprocessing.

Chapter 4, Databases, explains the role of databases, the different kinds, and teaches you how to connect and pull data from relational databases. It also teaches you how to pull data from databases using APIs.

Chapter 5, Data Visualization, showcases some analytics examples using data visualizations to inform you of the potential of data visualization.

Chapter 6, Prediction, introduces predictive models and explains how to use **Multivariate Regression** and a **Multi-Layered Perceptron** (**MLP**).

Chapter 7, Classification, introduces classification models and explains how to use **Decision Trees** and **K-Nearest Neighbors** (**KNN**).

Chapter 8, Clustering Analysis, introduces clustering models and explains how to use **K-means**.

Chapter 9, Data Cleaning Level I – Cleaning Up the Table, introduces three different levels of data cleaning and covers the first level through examples.

Chapter 10, Data Cleaning Level II – Unpacking, Restructuring, and Reformulating the Table, covers the second level of data cleaning through examples.

Chapter 11, Data Cleaning Level III – Missing Values, Outliers, and Errors, covers the third level of data cleaning through examples.

Chapter 12, Data Fusion and Data Integration, covers the technique for mixing different data sources.

Chapter 13, Data Reduction, introduces data reduction and, with the help of examples, shows how its different cases and versions can be done via Python.

Chapter 14, Data Transformation and Massaging, introduces data transformation and massaging and, through many examples, shows their requirements and capabilities for analysis.

Chapter 15, Case Study 1 – Mental Health in Tech, introduces an analytic problem and preprocesses the data to solve it.

Chapter 16, Case Study 2 – Predicting COVID-19 Hospitalizations, introduces an analytic problem and preprocesses the data to solve it.

Chapter 17, Case Study 3 – United States Counties Clustering Analysis, introduces an analytic problem and preprocesses the data to solve it.

Chapter 18, Summary, Practice Case Studies, and Conclusions, introduces some possible practice cases that users can use to learn in more depth and start creating their analytics portfolios.

To get the most out of this book

The book assumes basic programming skills such as working with variables, conditionals, and loops, along with beginner-level knowledge of Python. Other than that, you can start your journey from the beginning of the book and start learning.

The Jupyter Notebook is an excellent UI for learning and practicing programming and data analytics. It can be downloaded and installed easily using Anaconda Navigator. Visit this page for installation: `https://docs.anaconda.com/anaconda/navigator/install/`.

Software/hardware covered in the book	Operating system requirements
Python using the Jupyter Notebook	Windows or macOS

While Anaconda has most of the modules that the book uses already installed, you will need to install a few other modules such as Seaborn and Graphviz. Don't worry; when the time comes, the book will instruct you on how to go about these installations.

If you are using the digital version of this book, we advise you to type the code yourself or access the code from the book's GitHub repository (a link is available in the next section). Doing so will help you avoid any potential errors related to the copying and pasting of code.

While learning, keep a file of your own code from each chapter. This learning repository can be used in the future for deeper learning and real projects. The Jupyter Notebook is especially great for this purpose as it allows you to take notes along with the code.

Download the example code files

You can download the example code files for this book from GitHub at `https://github.com/PacktPublishing/Hands-On-Data-Preprocessing-in-Python`. If there's an update to the code, it will be updated in the GitHub repository.

We also have other code bundles from our rich catalog of books and videos available at `https://github.com/PacktPublishing/`. Check them out!

Download the color images

We also provide a PDF file that has color images of the screenshots and diagrams used in this book. You can download it here: `https://static.packt-cdn.com/downloads/9781801072137_ColorImages.pdf`.

Conventions used

There are a number of text conventions used throughout this book.

`Code in text`: Indicates code words in text, database table names, folder names, filenames, file extensions, pathnames, dummy URLs, user input, and Twitter handles. Here is an example: "To create this interactive visual, we have used the `interact` and `widgets` programming objects from the `ipywidgets` module."

A block of code is set as follows:

```
from ipywidgets import interact, widgets
interact(plotyear,year=widgets.
IntSlider(min=2010,max=2019,step=1,value=2010))
```

When we wish to draw your attention to a particular part of a code block, the relevant lines or items are set in bold:

```
Xs_t.plot.scatter(x='PC1',y='PC2',c='PC3',sharex=False,
                  vmin=-1/0.101, vmax=1/0.101,
                  figsize=(12,9))
x_ticks_vs = [-2.9*4 + 2.9*i for i in range(9)]
```

Bold: Indicates a new term, an important word, or words that you see on screen. For instance, words in menus or dialog boxes appear in **bold**. Here is an example: "The missing values for the attributes from **SupportQ1** to **AttitudeQ3** are from the same data objects."

> **Tips or Important Notes**
> Appear like this.

Get in touch

Feedback from our readers is always welcome.

General feedback: If you have questions about any aspect of this book, email us at customercare@packtpub.com and mention the book title in the subject of your message.

Errata: Although we have taken every care to ensure the accuracy of our content, mistakes do happen. If you have found a mistake in this book, we would be grateful if you would report this to us. Please visit www.packtpub.com/support/errata and fill in the form.

Piracy: If you come across any illegal copies of our works in any form on the internet, we would be grateful if you would provide us with the location address or website name. Please contact us at copyright@packt.com with a link to the material.

If you are interested in becoming an author: If there is a topic that you have expertise in and you are interested in either writing or contributing to a book, please visit authors.packtpub.com.

Share Your Thoughts

Once you've read *Hands-On Data Preprocessing in Python*, we'd love to hear your thoughts! Scan the QR code below to go straight to the Amazon review page for this book and share your feedback.

https://packt.link/r/1-801-07213-2

Your review is important to us and the tech community and will help us make sure we're delivering excellent quality content.

Part 1: Technical Needs

After reading this part of the book, you will be able to use Python to effectively manipulate data.

This part comprises the following chapters:

1

Review of the Core Modules of NumPy and Pandas

NumPy and Pandas modules are capable of meeting your needs for the majority of data analytics and data preprocessing tasks. Before we start reviewing these two valuable modules, I would like to let you know that this chapter is not meant to be a comprehensive teaching guide to these modules, but rather a collection of concepts, functions, and examples that will be invaluable, as we will cover data analytics and data preprocessing in proceeding chapters.

In this chapter, we will first review the Jupyter Notebooks and their capability as an excellent coding **User Interface** (**UI**). Next, we will review the most relevant data analytic resources of the NumPy and Pandas Python modules.

The following topics will be covered in this chapter:

- Overview of the Jupyter Notebook
- Are we analyzing data via computer programming?
- Overview of the basic functions of NumPy
- Overview of Pandas

Technical requirements

The easiest way to get started with Python programming is by installing Anaconda Navigator. It is open source software that brings together many useful open source tools for developers. You can download Anaconda Navigator by following this link: `https://www.anaconda.com/products/individual`.

We will be using Jupyter Notebook throughout this book. Jupyter Notebook is one of the open source tools that Anaconda Navigator provides. Anaconda Navigator also installs a Python version on your computer. So, following Anaconda Navigator's easy installation, all you need to do is open Anaconda Navigator and then select **Jupyter Notebook**.

You will be able to find all of the code and the dataset that is used in this book in a GitHub repository exclusively created for this book. To find the repository, click on the following link: `https://github.com/PacktPublishing/Hands-On-Data-Preprocessing-in-Python`. Each chapter in this book will have a folder that contains all of the code and datasets that were used in the chapter.

Overview of the Jupyter Notebook

The **Jupyter Notebook** is becoming increasingly popular as a successful **User Interface (UI)** for Python programing. As a UI, the Jupyter Notebook provides an interactive environment where you can run your Python code, see immediate outputs, and take notes.

Fernando Pérezthe and *Brian Granger*, the architects of the Jupyter Notebook, outlines the following reasons in terms of what they were looking for in an innovative programming UI:

- Space for individual exploratory work
- Space for collaboration
- Space for learning and education

If you have used the Jupyter Notebook already, you can attest that it delivers all these promises, and if you have not yet used it, I have good news for you: we *will be using Jupyter Notebook for the entirety of this book.* Some of the code that I will be sharing will be in the form of screenshots from the Jupyter Notebook UI.

The UI design of the Jupyter Notebook is very simple. You can think of it as one column of material. These materials could be under code chunks or Markdown chunks. The solution development and the actual coding happens under the code chunks, whereas notes for yourself or other developers are presented under Markdown chunks. The following screenshot shows both an example of a Markdown chunk and a code chunk. You can see that the code chunk has been executed and the requested print has taken place and the output is shown immediately after the code chunk:

Figure 1.1 – Code for printing Hello World in a Jupyter notebook

To create a new chunk, you can click on the + sign on the top ribbon of the UI. The newly added chunk will be a code chunk by default. You can switch the code chunk to a Markdown chunk by using the drop-down list on the top ribbon. Moreover, you can move the chunks up or down by using the correct arrows on the ribbon. You can see these three buttons in the following screenshot:

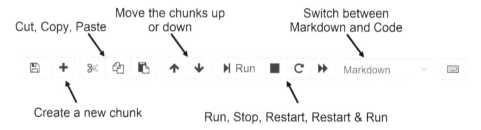

Figure 1.2 – Jupyter Notebook control ribbon

You can see the following in the preceding screenshot:

- The ribbon shown in the screenshot also allows you to **Cut**, **Copy**, and **Paste** the chunks.

- The **Run** button on the ribbon is to execute the code of a chunk.

- The **Stop** button is to stop running code. You normally use this button if your code has been running for a while with no output.

- The **Restart** button wipes the slate clean; it removes all of the variables you have defined so you can start over.

- Finally, the **Restart & Run** button restarts the kernel and runs all of the chunks of code in the Jupyter Notebook files.

There is more to the Jupyter Notebook, such as useful short keys to speed up development and specific Markdown syntax to format the text under Markdown chunks. However, the introduction here is just enough for you to start meaningfully analyzing data using Python through the Jupyter Notebook UI.

Are we analyzing data via computer programming?

To benefit most from the two modules that we will cover in this chapter, we need to understand what they really are and what we are really doing when we use them. I am sure whoever is in the business of content development for data analytics using Python, including me (guilty as charged), would tell you that when you use these modules to manipulate your data, you are analyzing your data using computer programming. However, what you are actually doing is not computer programming. The computer programming part has already been done for the most part. In fact, this has been done by the top-notch programmers who put together these invaluable packages. What you do is use their code made available to you as programming objects and functions under these modules. Well, if I am being completely honest, you are doing a tad bit of computer programming, but just enough to access the good stuff (these modules). Thanks to these modules, you will not experience any difficulty in analyzing data using computer programming.

So, before embarking on your journey in this chapter and this book, remember this: for the most part, our job as data analysts is to connect three things – *our business problem*, *our data*, and *technology*. The technology could be commercial software such as Excel or Tableau, or, in the case of this book, these modules.

Overview of the basic functions of NumPy

In short, as the name suggests, **NumPy** is a Python module brimming with useful functions for dealing with numbers. The *Num* in the first part of the name NumPy stands for *numbers*, and *Py* stands for *Python*. There you have it. If you have numbers and you are in Python, you know what you need to import. That is correct; you need to import NumPy, simple as that. See the following screenshot:

```
In [2]:   ▶  import numpy as np
```

Figure 1.3 – Code for importing the NumPy module

As you can see, we have given the alias np to the module after importing it. You can actually assign any alias that you wish and your code would function; however, I suggest sticking with np. I have two compelling reasons for doing so:

- First, everyone else uses this alias, so if you share your code with others, they know what you are doing throughout your project.

- Second, a lot of the time, you end up using code written by others in your projects, so consistency will make your job easier. You will see that most of the famous modules also have a famous alias, for example, pd for Pandas, and plt for matplotlib.pyplot.

Good practice advice

NumPy can handle all types of mathematical and statistical calculations for a collection of numbers, such as **mean**, **median**, **standard deviation** (**std**), and **variance** (**var**). If you have something else in mind and are not sure whether NumPy has it, I suggest googling it before trying to write your own. If it involves numbers, chances are NumPy has it.

The following screenshot shows the mean, for example, applied to a collection of numbers:

```
In [3]:  ▶ lst_nums = [2,5,7,11,13,17,23,31,37,41,43,47]
            np.mean(lst_nums)

   Out[3]: 23.083333333333332

In [4]:  ▶ lst_nums = [2,5,7,11,13,17,23,31,37,41,43,47]
            ary_nums = np.array(lst_nums)
            ary_nums.mean()

   Out[4]: 23.083333333333332
```

Figure 1.4 – Example of using the np.mean() NumPy function and the .mean() NumPy array function

As shown in *Figure 1.4*, there are two ways to do this. The first one, portrayed in the top chunk, uses np.mean(). This function is one of the properties of the NumPy module and can be accessed directly. The great aspect of using this approach is that you do not need to change your data type most of the time before NumPy honors your request. You can input lists, Pandas series, or DataFrames. You can see on the top chunk that np.mean() easily calculated the mean of lst_nums, which is of the list type. The second way, as shown in the bottom chunk, is to first use np.array() to transform the list into a NumPy array and then use the .mean() function, which is a property of any NumPy array. Before continuing to progress with this chapter, take a moment and use the Python type() function to see the different types of lst_numbs and ary_nums, as shown in the following screenshot:

```
In [5]:  ▶ type(lst_nums)
    Out[5]: list

In [6]:  ▶ type(ary_nums)
    Out[6]: numpy.ndarray
```

Figure 1.5 – The application of the type() function

Next we will learn about four NumPy functions: np.arange(), np.zeros(), np.ones(), and np.linspace().

The np.arange() function

This function, as shown in the following screenshot, produces a sequence of numbers with equal increments. You can see in the figure that by changing the two inputs, you can get the function to output many different sequences of numbers that are required for your analytic purposes:

```
In [7]:  ▶ np.arange(15)
    Out[7]: array([ 0,  1,  2,  3,  4,  5,  6,  7,  8,  9, 10, 11, 12, 13, 14])

In [8]:  ▶ np.arange(5,15)
    Out[8]: array([ 5,  6,  7,  8,  9, 10, 11, 12, 13, 14])

In [9]:  ▶ np.arange(-7.1,7)
    Out[9]: array([-7.1, -6.1, -5.1, -4.1, -3.1, -2.1, -1.1, -0.1,  0.9,  1.9,  2.9,
                    3.9,  4.9,  5.9,  6.9])
```

Figure 1.6 – Examples of using the np.arange() function

Pay attention to the three chunks of code in the preceding figure to see the default behavior of np.arange() when only one or two inputs are passed.

- When only one input is passed, as in the first chunk of code, the default of np.arange() is that you want a sequence of numbers from zero to the input number with increments of one.

- When two inputs are passed, as in the second chunk of code, the default of the function is that you want a sequence of numbers from the first input to the second input with increments of one.

The np.zeros() and np.ones() functions

np.ones() creates a NumPy array filled with ones, and np.zeros() does the same thing with zeros. Unlike np.arange(), which takes the input to calculate what needs to be included in the output array, np.zeros() and np.ones() take the input to structure the output array. For instance, the top chunk of the following screenshot specifies the request for an array with four rows and five columns filled with zeros. As you can see in the bottom chunk, if you only pass in one number, the output array will have only one dimension:

```
In [10]:  ▶ np.zeros([4,5])

Out[10]:  array([[0., 0., 0., 0., 0.],
                 [0., 0., 0., 0., 0.],
                 [0., 0., 0., 0., 0.],
                 [0., 0., 0., 0., 0.]])

In [11]:  ▶ np.ones(7)

Out[11]:  array([1., 1., 1., 1., 1., 1., 1.])
```

Figure 1.7 – Examples of np.zeros() and np.ones()

These two functions are excellent resources for creating a placeholder to keep the results of calculations in a loop. For instance, review the following example and observe how this function facilitated the coding.

Example – Using a placeholder to accommodate analytics

Given the grade data of 10 students, create a code using NumPy that calculates and reports their grade average.

The data of the 10 students and the solution to this example are provided in the following screenshots. Please review and try this code before progressing:

```
In [12]: Names = ['Jevon', 'Dawn', 'Kayleigh', 'Jadene', 'Kennedy', 'Kaydee',
                  'Ansh', 'Flynn', 'Kier', 'Clarence']
         Math_grades = [80, 50, 60, 70, 60, 100, 70, 70, 60, 70]
         Science_grades = [90, 80, 50, 50, 60, 50, 90, 70, 80, 80]
         History_grades = [60, 90, 50, 90, 100, 100, 100, 100, 90, 70]
```

Figure 1.8 – Grade data for the example

Now that you've had a chance to engage with this example, allow me to highlight a few matters about the provided solution presented in *Figure 1.9*:

- Notice how np.zeros() facilitated the solution by streamlining it significantly. After the code is done, all of the average grades are calculated and saved already. Compare the printed values before and after the for loop.

- The enumerate() function in the for loop might sound strange to you. What that does is help the code to have both an index (i) and the item (name) from the collection (Names).

- The .format() function is an invaluable property of any string variable. If there are any symbols such as { } in the string, this function will replace them with what has been input sequentially.

- # `better-looking report` is a comment in the second chunk of the code. Comments are not compiled and their only purpose is to communicate something with whoever reads the source code.

```
In [13]: Average_grades = np.zeros(10)
         print(Average_grades)

         for i, name in enumerate(Names):
             Average_grades[i] = np.mean([Math_grades[i],Science_grades[i],
                                          History_grades[i]])

         print(Average_grades)

         [0. 0. 0. 0. 0. 0. 0. 0. 0. 0.]
         [76.66666667 73.33333333 53.33333333 70.          73.33333333 83.33333333
          86.66666667 80.          76.66666667 73.33333333]
```

```
In [14]: # better-looking report

         for i, name in enumerate(Names):
             print("Average for {} : {}".format(name,Average_grades[i]))

         Average for Jevon : 76.66666666666667
         Average for Dawn : 73.33333333333333
         Average for Kayleigh : 53.333333333333336
         Average for Jadene : 70.0
         Average for Kennedy : 73.33333333333333
         Average for Kaydee : 83.33333333333333
         Average for Ansh : 86.66666666666667
         Average for Flynn : 80.0
         Average for Kier : 76.66666666666667
         Average for Clarence : 73.33333333333333
```

Figure 1.9 – Solution to the preceding example

The np.linspace() function

This function returns evenly spaced numbers over a specified interval. The function takes three inputs. The first two inputs specify the interval, and the third shows the number of elements that the output will have. For example, refer to the following screenshot:

```
In [15]: np.linspace(0,1,21)

Out[15]: array([0.  , 0.05, 0.1 , 0.15, 0.2 , 0.25, 0.3 , 0.35, 0.4 , 0.45, 0.5 ,
                0.55, 0.6 , 0.65, 0.7 , 0.75, 0.8 , 0.85, 0.9 , 0.95, 1.  ])
```

```
In [16]: np.linspace(10,1000,100)

Out[16]: array([  10.,   20.,   30.,   40.,   50.,   60.,   70.,   80.,   90.,
                 100.,  110.,  120.,  130.,  140.,  150.,  160.,  170.,  180.,
                 190.,  200.,  210.,  220.,  230.,  240.,  250.,  260.,  270.,
                 280.,  290.,  300.,  310.,  320.,  330.,  340.,  350.,  360.,
                 370.,  380.,  390.,  400.,  410.,  420.,  430.,  440.,  450.,
                 460.,  470.,  480.,  490.,  500.,  510.,  520.,  530.,  540.,
                 550.,  560.,  570.,  580.,  590.,  600.,  610.,  620.,  630.,
                 640.,  650.,  660.,  670.,  680.,  690.,  700.,  710.,  720.,
                 730.,  740.,  750.,  760.,  770.,  780.,  790.,  800.,  810.,
                 820.,  830.,  840.,  850.,  860.,  870.,  880.,  890.,  900.,
                 910.,  920.,  930.,  940.,  950.,  960.,  970.,  980.,  990.,
                1000.])
```

Figure 1.10 – Solution to the preceding example

In the first code block, 19 numbers are evenly spaced between 0 and 1, altogether creating an array with 21 numbers. The second gives another example. After trying out the two examples in the screenshot, try np.linspace(0,1,20) and after investigating the results, think about why I chose 21 over 20 in my example.

np.linspace() is a very handy function for situations where you need to try out different values to find the one that best fits your needs. The following example showcases a simple situation like that.

Example – np.linspace() to create solution candidates

We are interested in finding the value(s) that holds the following mathematical statement: $x^2 - 5x + 6 = 0$.

Imagine that we don't know that the statement can be simplified easily to ascertain that either 2 or 3 will hold the statement:

$$x^2 - 5x + 6 = (x - 2)(x - 3)$$

So we would like to use NumPy to try out any whole numbers between -1000 and 1000 and find the answer.

The following screenshot shows Python code that provides a solution to this problem:

```
In [16]:  ▶  Candidates = np.linspace(-1000,1000,2001)
             #print(Candidates)

             for candidate in Candidates:
                 if(candidate**2 - 5*candidate +6 ==0):
                     print("Just found a possible answer: {}".format(candidate))

          Just found a possible answer: 2.0
          Just found a possible answer: 3.0
```

Figure 1.11 – Solution to the preceding example

Please review and try this code before moving on.

Now that you've had a chance to engage with this example, allow me to highlight a couple of things:

- Notice how smart use of np.linspace() leads to an array with all of the numbers that we were interested in trying out.

- Uncomment #print(Candidates) and review all of the numbers that were tried out to establish the desired answers.

This concludes our review of the NumPy module. Next, we will review another very useful Python module, Pandas.

Overview of Pandas

In short, **Pandas** is our main module for working with data. The module is brimming with useful functions and tools, but let's get down to the basics first. The greatest tool of Pandas is its data structure, which is known as a **DataFrame**. In short, a DataFrame is a two-dimensional data structure with a *good interface* and *great codability*.

The DataFrame makes itself useful to you right off the bat. The moment you read a data source using Pandas, the data is restructured and shown to you as a DataFrame. Let's give it a try.

We will use the famous adult dataset (`adult.csv`) to practice and learn the different functionalities of Pandas. Refer to the following screenshot, which shows the importing of Pandas and then reading and showing the dataset. In this code, `.head()` requests that only the top five rows of data are output. The `.tail()` code could do the same for the bottom five rows of the data.

```
In [17]:    ▶  import pandas as pd

               adult_df = pd.read_csv('adult.csv')
               adult_df.head()
```

Out[17]:

	age	workclass	fnlwgt	education	education-num	marital-status	occupation	relationship	race	
0	39	State-gov	77516	Bachelors	13	Never-married	Adm-clerical	Not-in-family	White	
1	50	Self-emp-not-inc	83311	Bachelors	13	Married-civ-spouse	Exec-managerial	Husband	White	
2	38	Private	215646	HS-grad	9	Divorced	Handlers-cleaners	Not-in-family	White	
3	53	Private	234721	11th	7	Married-civ-spouse	Handlers-cleaners	Husband	Black	
4	28	Private	338409	Bachelors	13	Married-civ-spouse	Prof-specialty	Wife	Black	F

Figure 1.12 – Reading the adult.csv file using pd.read_csv() and showing its first five rows

The adult dataset has six continuous and eight categorical attributes. Due to print limitations, I have only been able to include some parts of the data; however, if you pay attention to *Figure 1.12*, the output comes with a scroll bar at the bottom that you can scroll to see the rest of the attributes. Give this code a try and study its attributes. As you will see, all of the attributes in this dataset are self-explanatory, apart from `fnlwgt`. The title is short for final weight and it is calculated by the *Census Bureau* to represent the ratio of the population that each row represents.

Good practice advice

It is good practice to always get to know the dataset you are about to work on. This process always starts with making sure you understand each attribute, the way I just did now. If you have just received a dataset and you don't know what each attribute is, ask. Trust me, you will look more like a pro than not.

There are other steps to get to know a dataset. I will mention them all here and you will learn how to do them by the end of this chapter.

Step one: Understand each attribute as I just explained.

Step two: Check the shape of the dataset. How many rows and columns does the dataset have? This one is easy. For instance, just try `adult_df.shape` and review the result.

Step three: Check whether the data has any missing values.

Step four: Calculate summarizing values for numerical attributes such as mean, median, and standard deviation, and compute all the possible values for categorical attributes.

Step five: Visualize the attributes. For numerical attributes, use a histogram or a boxplot, and for categorical ones, use a bar chart.

As you just saw, before you know it, you are enjoying the benefits of a Pandas DataFrame. So it is important to better understand the structure of a DataFrame. Simply put, a DataFrame is a collection of series. A **series** is another Pandas data structure that does not get as much credit, but is useful all the same, if not more so.

To understand this better, try to call some of the columns of the adult dataset. Each column is a property of a DataFrame, so to access it, all you need to do is to use `.ColumnName` after the DataFrame. For instance, try running `adult_df.age` to see the column age. Try running all of the columns and study them, and if you come across errors for some of them, do not worry about it; we will address them soon if you continue reading. The following screenshot shows how you can confirm what was just described for the adult dataset:

```
In [18]:  ▶  type(adult_df.age)

   Out[18]:  pandas.core.series.Series

In [19]:  ▶  type(adult_df)

   Out[19]:  pandas.core.frame.DataFrame
```

Figure 1.13 – Checking the type of adult_df and adult_df.age

It gets more exciting. Not only is each attribute a series, but each row is also a series. To access each row of a DataFrame, you need to use .loc[] after the DataFrame. What comes between the brackets is the index of each row. Go back and study the output of df_adult.head() in *Figure 1.12* and you will see that each row is represented by an index. The indices do not have to be numerical and we will see how indices of a Pandas DataFrame can be adjusted, but when reading data using pd.read_csv() with default properties, numerical indices will be assigned. So give it a try and access some of the rows and study them. For instance, you can access the second row by running adult_df.loc[1]. After running a few of them, run type(adult_df.loc[1]) to confirm that each row is a series.

When accessed separately, each column or row of a DataFrame is a series. The only difference between a column series and a row series is that the index of a column series is the index of the DataFrame, and the index of a row series is the column names. Study the following screenshot, which compares the index of the first row of adult_df and the index of the first column of adult_df:

```
In [20]:  ▶  adult_df.loc[0].index

  Out[20]:  Index(['age', 'workclass', 'fnlwgt', 'education', 'education-num',
                    'marital-status', 'occupation', 'relationship', 'race', 'sex',
                    'capitalGain', 'capitalLoss', 'hoursPerWeek', 'nativeCountry',
                    'income'],
                   dtype='object')

In [21]:  ▶  adult_df.age.index

  Out[21]:  RangeIndex(start=0, stop=32561, step=1)
```

Figure 1.14 – Investigating the index for a column series and a row series

Now that we have been introduced to Pandas data structures, next we will cover how we can access the values that are presented in them.

Pandas data access

One of the greatest advantages of both Pandas series and DataFrames is the excellent access they afford us. Let's start with DataFrames, and then we will move on to series as there are lots of commonalities between the two.

Pandas DataFrame access

As DataFrames are two-dimensional, this section first addresses how to access rows, and then columns. The end part of the section will address how to access each value.

DataFrame access rows

The only two keywords you will ever need to access the rows of a DataFrame are `.loc[]` and `.iloc[]`. To understand the difference between them, you need to know that each Pandas series or DataFrame carries two types of indices: **default indices** or **assigned indices**. The default indices are the integer numbers that are automatically assigned to your dataset upon reading. However, Pandas allows you to update them. The function that you can use to do so is `.set_index()`. For instance, we would like to make sure all of the indices in `adult_df` have five digits, so instead of indices between 0 and 32651 (run `len(adult_df)` to see that this is the number of rows `adult_df` has), we want indices to be from 10000 to 42651. The following screenshot uses `np.arange()` and `.set_index()` to do this. In this code, `inplace=True` indicates to the `.set_index()` function that you want the change to be applied to the DataFrame itself.

Why is it that when `inplace=True` is incorporated, there is no output, and when it is included, Jupyter Notebook shows the updated DataFrame?

The answer is that the `.set_index()` function, by default, outputs a new DataFrame that has the requested index unless `inplace=True` is specified, which requests the change to be applied to the original DataFrame.

```
In [22]:  ▶  adult_df.set_index(np.arange(10000,42561),inplace=True)

In [23]:  ▶  adult_df.set_index(np.arange(10000,42561))
   Out[23]:
```

	age	workclass	fnlwgt	education	education-num	marital-status	occupation	relationship	ra
10000	39	State-gov	77516	Bachelors	13	Never-married	Adm-clerical	Not-in-family	Whi
10001	50	Self-emp-not-inc	83311	Bachelors	13	Married-civ-spouse	Exec-managerial	Husband	Whi
10002	38	Private	215646	HS-grad	9	Divorced	Handlers-cleaners	Not-in-family	Whi

Figure 1.15 – Updating the index of adult_df as described

Now, each row of the DataFrame can be accessed by specifying the index in between the brackets of `.loc[]`. For instance, running `adult_df.loc[10001]` will give you the second row. This is how you would always access the DataFrame using the assigned indices. If you started missing the default indices, as you often do when you go about preprocessing your data, Pandas has you covered.

You can use .iloc[] to access the data using the default integer indices. For instance, running adult_df.iloc[1] will also return the second row. In other words, Pandas will change the index to your liking, but behind the scenes, it will also keep its integer default index and also lets you use it if you so wish.

DataFrame access columns

As there are two ways to access each row, there are also two ways to access each column. The easier and better way to access your columns is to know that each column is coded to be a property of a DataFrame. So, you can access each column by using .ColumnName. For instance, run adult_df.age, adult_df.occupation, and so on to see how easy it is to access the columns in this way.

If you happened to run adult_df.education-number, you have already seen that this gives you an error. If you haven't, go ahead and do so to study the error. Why does this error happen?

```
In [24]:  ▶  adult_df.education-num

-----------------------------------------------------------------------
NameError                                 Traceback (most recent call last)
<ipython-input-24-a83283968914> in <module>
----> 1 adult_df.education-num

NameError: name 'num' is not defined
```

Figure 1.16 – Running adult_df.education-number and its error

If you study the error message, it is prompting that 'num' is not defined. That is true; we do not have anything named 'num'. That is the key to use this error to answer my question.

Python deciphers dashes as subtraction operators unless presented inside a quotation. So it all comes down to this. Because of the way this variable is named, you cannot use the .ColumnName method to access the variable. You either need to change the name of the variable or use the second method to access the columns.

The second method passes the name as a string, or, in other words, inside a quotation. Try running adult_df['education-num'] and this time you will not get an error.

> **Good practice advice**
>
> If you are new to programming, one of the pieces of advice that I have for you is not to be intimidated by errors, and not only that, welcome errors with open arms because they are an excellent opportunity to learn. I just used an error to teach you something.

DataFrame access values

Imagine you want to access the education value for the third row of `adult_df`. There are so many ways you can go about this. You can start from the column and once you get a column series, access the value, or you can go from the row, and once you get a row series, access the value. Study the following screenshot; the first three chunks of code show different possibilities of doing that. However, my favorite way to access the values is to use `.at []`, shown in the last chunk.

```
In [25]:   ▶  adult_df.iloc[2].loc['education']

Out[25]:   'HS-grad'


In [26]:   ▶  adult_df.education.loc[10002]

Out[26]:   'HS-grad'


In [27]:   ▶  adult_df['education'].iloc[2]

Out[27]:   'HS-grad'


In [28]:   ▶  adult_df.at[10002,'education']

Out[28]:   'HS-grad'
```

Figure 1.17 – Four different methods of accessing the records of a Pandas DataFrame

Accessing values with .at [] is my favorite for two reasons. First, it is much neater and more straightforward. Second, you can treat the DataFrame like a matrix as it is one, at least visually.

Pandas series access

Access to the values of series is very similar to that of DataFrames, just simpler. You can access the values of a series using all of the methods mentioned for DataFrames, except for .at []. You can see all of the possibilities in the following screenshot. If you were to try the last line of the second chunk of code, Python would generate a syntax error as numbers cannot be the name of programming objects. To use this method, you have to make sure that the series indices are of the string type.

```
In [29]:    row_series = adult_df.loc[10002]
            print(row_series.loc['education'])
            print(row_series.iloc[3])
            print(row_series['education'])
            print(row_series.education)

            HS-grad
            HS-grad
            HS-grad
            HS-grad


In [30]:    columns_series = adult_df.education
            print(columns_series.loc[10002])
            print(columns_series.iloc[2])
            print(columns_series[10002])
            # print(row_series.10002)   This will give syntax error!

            HS-grad
            HS-grad
            HS-grad
```

Figure 1.18 – Different methods of accessing the values of a Pandas series

Slicing

Slicing applies to both NumPy and Pandas; however, since this is a book about data preprocessing, we will use it more often with a Pandas DataFrame. Let's begin by slicing NumPy arrays to understand slicing and then apply it to a Pandas DataFrame.

Slicing a NumPy array

We slice a NumPy array when we need access to more than one value of the data. For instance, consider the code in the following screenshot:

```
In [31]:  ▶ my_array = np.array([[2,3,5,7],[11,13,17,19],
                                [23,29,31,37,], [41,43,47,49]])
            my_array

Out[31]: array([[ 2,  3,  5,  7],
                [11, 13, 17, 19],
                [23, 29, 31, 37],
                [41, 43, 47, 49]])


In [32]:  ▶ my_array[1,1]

Out[32]: 13


In [33]:  ▶ my_array[1,:]

Out[33]: array([11, 13, 17, 19])


In [34]:  ▶ my_array[:,1]

Out[34]: array([ 3, 13, 29, 43])
```

Figure 1.19 – Examples of slicing NumPy arrays

Here, my_array, which is a 4 x 4 matrix, has been sliced in different ways. The second chunk of code is not slicing; as you can see, only one value is accessed. What separates normal access from slicing access is the presence of a colon (:) in any of the index inputs. For instance, a colon in the third chunk of code means you are requesting all of the columns, and the output includes all of the columns, but since only the second row (index 1) is specified, the entirety of the second row is output. The fourth chunk of code is the opposite; one column is specified and the whole rows are requested, so the entirety of the second column is output.

You can also use a colon (:) to only specify access from a certain index to another one. For instance, in the second chunk of the following code, while all the columns are requested, only the second to fourth rows (1:3) are requested. The third chunk of code shows that both columns and rows can be sliced at the same time. Finally, the last chunk of code shows that you can pass a list of indices that you want to include in your slice.

```
In [35]:  ▶ my_array

Out[35]: array([[ 2,  3,  5,  7],
                [11, 13, 17, 19],
                [23, 29, 31, 37],
                [41, 43, 47, 49]])

In [36]:  ▶ my_array[1:3,:]

Out[36]: array([[11, 13, 17, 19],
                [23, 29, 31, 37]])

In [37]:  ▶ my_array[1:3,0:2]

Out[37]: array([[11, 13],
                [23, 29]])

In [38]:  ▶ my_array[1:3,[0,2]]

Out[38]: array([[11, 17],
                [23, 31]])
```

Figure 1.20 – More complex examples of slicing

Slicing a Pandas DataFrame

Just like NumPy arrays, Pandas DataFrames can also be sliced both on the columns and rows. However, the slicing function can only be done inside either .loc[] or .iloc[]. The access method, .at[], and the other ways of accessing data do not support slicing. For instance, the following code slices adult_df to show all of the rows, but only the columns from education to occupation. Running adult_df.iloc[:,3:6] will result in the same output.

```
In [39]:  ▶ adult_df.loc[:,'education':'occupation']

Out[39]:
```

	education	education-num	marital-status	occupation
10000	Bachelors	13	Never-married	Adm-clerical
10001	Bachelors	13	Married-civ-spouse	Exec-managerial
10002	HS-grad	9	Divorced	Handlers-cleaners

Figure 1.21 – Example of slicing a Pandas DataFrame

You want to become comfortable with slicing a Pandas DataFrame. It is a very useful way to access your data. See the following example, which showcases one practical way in which you could use slicing.

Practical example of slicing

Run `adult_df.sort_values('education-num')`. You will see this code sort the DataFrame based on the `education-num` column. In Jupyter Notebook output, you only see the first five and the last five rows of this sorting. Slice the output of the rows from across the DataFrame instead of just from the beginning and the end.

The following screenshot shows how slicing the DataFrame can make this happen:

```
In [40]:  ▶ adult_df.sort_values('education-num').reset_index().iloc[1:32561:3617]
     Out[40]:
```

	index	age	workclass	fnlwgt	education	education-num	marital-status	occupation	relationsh
1	23248	68	Private	168794	Preschool	1	Never-married	Machine-op-inspct	Not-in-fam
3618	19607	25	Private	251854	11th	7	Never-married	Adm-clerical	Own-chi
7235	38845	31	Private	272856	HS-grad	9	Never-married	Craft-repair	Own-chi
10852	32759	56	Private	182273	HS-grad	9	Married-civ-spouse	Machine-op-inspct	Husbar
14469	10419	34	State-gov	240283	HS-grad	9	Divorced	Transport-moving	Unmarri
18086	31532	25	Self-emp-inc	98756	Some-college	10	Divorced	Adm-clerical	Own-chi
21703	17245	37	Federal-gov	40955	Some-college	10	Never-married	Other-service	Own-chi
25320	40595	43	Private	342567	Bachelors	13	Married-spouse-absent	Adm-clerical	Unmarri
28937	15200	43	Federal-gov	144778	Bachelors	13	Never-married	Exec-managerial	Not-in-fami
32554	27308	55	Self-emp-not-inc	53566	Doctorate	16	Divorced	Exec-managerial	Not-in-fami

Figure 1.22 – Solution to the practical example of slicing a Pandas DataFrame

Let's go over this code step by step:

- The first part, `.sort_values('education-num')`, as mentioned, sorts the DataFrame by `education-num`. I hope you have given this a try before reading on. Pay attention to the indices of the sorted `adult_df`. They look jumbled up, as they should. The reason is that the DataFrame is now sorted by another column.

- If we want to have a new index that matches this new order, we can use `.reset_index()`, as it has been used in the preceding screenshot. Go ahead and give this a try as well. Run `adult_df.sort_values('education-num').reset_index()`. You will see that the old index is presented as a new column and that the new index looks as ordered as any newly read dataset.

- Adding `.iloc[1:32561:3617]` achieves what this example is asking. This specific slice requests the first row and every 3,617th row after that until the end of the DataFrame. The number 32561 is the number of rows in `adult_df` (run `len(adult_df)`), and 3617 is the quotient of the division of 32561 by 9. This division calculates the equal jumps that take us from row one to nearly the end of `adult_df`. Pay attention if the division of 32561 by 9 didn't have a remainder; the code would take you all the way to the end of the DataFrame.

> **Good practice advice**
>
> Being able to slice DataFrames this way is advantageous in the initial stages of getting to know a dataset. One of the disadvantages of data manipulations using programming instead of spreadsheet software such as Excel is that you cannot scroll through the data as you would in Excel. However, slicing the data this way can allow you to somehow mitigate this shortcoming.

Now that we have learned how to access and slice a dataset, we need to learn how to filter the data based on our needs. To do that, next we will learn about Boolean masking, which is a powerful filtering technique.

Boolean masking for filtering a DataFrame

One of the simplest and yet most powerful tools of working with data is **Boolean masking**. When you want to filter a DataFrame using a Boolean mask, you need a one-dimensional collection of Boolean values (True or False) that has as many Boolean values as the number of rows of DataFrames you want to filter.

The following screenshot shows an example of Boolean masking:

```
In [41]:  ▶ twopowers_sr = pd.Series([1,2,4,8,16,32,64,128,256,512,1024])
            BM = [False,False,False,True,False,False,False,True,True,True,True]
            twopowers_sr[BM]

  Out[41]:  3         8
            7       128
            8       256
            9       512
            10     1024
```

Figure 1.23 – Example of Boolean masking

The code portrays Boolean masking in three steps:

1. The code first creates the Pandas series `twopowers_sr`, which contains the values of 2 to the power of 0 through 10 (2^0, 2^1, 2^2, ..., 2^{10}).

2. Then, a Boolean mask is set up. Pay attention as `twopowers_sr` has 11 numerical values, while BM also has 11 Boolean values. From now on in this book, every time you see BM, you can safely assume it stands for *Boolean mask*.

3. The last line of code filters the series using the mask.

The way a Boolean mask works is straightforward. If the counterpart of the numerical value from `twopowers_sr` in the Boolean mask (BM) is **False**, the mask blocks the number, and if it is **True**, the mask lets it through. Check whether that has been the case regarding the output of the preceding code. This is shown in the following figure:

1	2	4	8	16	32	64	128	256	512	1024
False	False	False	True	False	False	False	True	True	True	True
●	●	●	○	●	●	●	○	○	○	○
			8				128	256	512	1024

Figure 1.24 – Depiction of Boolean masking

What is great about Pandas is that you can use the DataFrame or series themselves to create useful Boolean masks. You can use any of the mathematical comparison operators to do this. For instance, the following screenshot first creates a Boolean mask that would only include **True** for numbers greater than or equal to 500. Then, the Boolean mask is applied to `twopowers_sr` to filter out the numbers in two ways.

Both of these ways are legitimate, correct, and they work. On the first one, you still give the Boolean mask a name. We use the name BM to do this as mentioned earlier. Then, we use BM to apply the Boolean mask. On the second one, you create and use the Boolean mask *on the fly*, as programmers say. That means you do everything in one line of code. I use the first one more often than not as I believe it makes the code more readable.

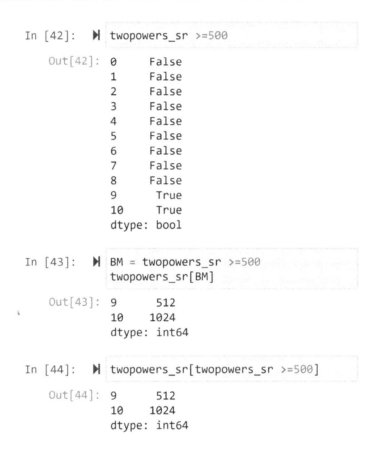

Figure 1.25 – Example of Boolean masking to filter data

You might be asking from the preceding code, so what if we can filter the data using Boolean masking? That is a legitimate question. Boolean masks come into their own when you use them on DataFrames for analytics. The following two examples will clarify this for you.

Analytic example 1 that uses Boolean masking

We are interested in calculating the mean and median age of people with preschool education in `adult_df`.

This can be easily done using Boolean masking. The following screenshot first creates BM using the series `adult_df.education`.

```
In [45]:   ▶  BM = adult_df.education == 'Preschool'
              print('Mean: {}'.format(np.mean(adult_df[BM].age)))
              print('Median: {}'.format(np.median(adult_df[BM].age)))

              Mean: 42.76470588235294
              Median: 41.0
```

Figure 1.26 – Solution to the preceding example

Since the BM series has as many elements as the `adult_df` DataFrame (why?), BM can be applied to filter it. Once the DataFrame is filtered using `adult_df[BM]`, it only contains rows that their `education` is `'Preschool'`. So now you can easily use `np.mean()` and `np.median()` to calculate the mean and median of age for these filtered rows.

Analytic example 2 that uses Boolean masking

We are interested in comparing the *Capital Gain* of individuals with less than 10 years' education with individuals with more than 10 years' education.

```
In [46]:   ▶  BM1 = adult_df['education-num'] > 10
              BM2 = adult_df['education-num'] < 10

              print('More than 10 years of education - Capital Gain: {}'
                    .format(np.mean(adult_df[BM1].capitalGain)))
              print('Less than 10 years of education - Capital Gain: {}'
                    .format(np.mean(adult_df[BM2].capitalGain)))

              More than 10 years of education - Capital Gain: 2230.9397109166985
              Less than 10 years of education - Capital Gain: 492.25532059102613
```

Figure 1.27 – Solution to the preceding example

Again, Boolean masks can help us immensely here. Two of them, BM1 and BM2, are first created based on what we are interested in calculating. Then, two calculations and reports show the mean of the capital gain for people with more than, and less than, 10 years of education.

Pandas functions for exploring a DataFrame

When you compare spreadsheet software such as Excel with coding, one of the stark disadvantages of coding is that you cannot create as tangible a relationship with your data as you would with Excel. That is a fair comparison as Excel lets you scroll up and down on your data and so allows you to get to know it. While coding does not grant you this privilege, Pandas has a handful of useful functions that help you to familiarize yourself with the data.

Getting to know a dataset has two aspects. The first is to get to know the structure of the data, such as the number of rows, columns, and the name of columns. The second one is to get to know the values under each column. So we first cover getting to know the structure of the dataset and then we will focus on the values under each column.

Getting to know the structure of a dataset

You can use three useful properties of a Pandas Dataframe to study the structure of a dataset. These are .shape, .columns, and .info(). In the following sections, we will go over them one by one.

The .shape property

.shape is the property of any Pandas DataFrame. It tells you how many rows and columns the DataFrame has. So, once you apply this to adult_df, as executed by the code in the following screenshot, you can see that the DataFrame has **32,561** rows and **15** columns:

```
In [47]:   ▶ adult_df.shape

  Out[47]: (32561, 15)
```

Figure 1.28 – Example of using the .shape property of a DataFrame to get to know the dataset

The .columns property

.columns allows you to see and edit the column names in your DataFrame. In the following code, you can see that adult_df.columns resulted in the output of all the column names of adult_df. Of course, you could have scrolled to see all of the columns when you read the dataset; however, this is not possible when the data has more than 20 columns.

```
In [48]:  ▶ adult_df.columns

  Out[48]:  Index(['age', 'workclass', 'fnlwgt', 'education', 'education-num',
                    'marital-status', 'occupation', 'relationship', 'race', 'sex',
                    'capitalGain', 'capitalLoss', 'hoursPerWeek', 'nativeCountry',
                    'income'],
                   dtype='object')
```

Figure 1.29 – Example of using the .columns property of a DataFrame to get to know the dataset

Furthermore, `.columns` can be used to update the columns' names. This has been shown in the following screenshot. After running the following code, you can safely use `adult_df.education_num` to access the relevant attribute. We just change the attribute name from `'education-num'` to `'education_num'` and now the attribute can be accessed using the `.columnName` method. Refer to *Figure 1.16*, which showed the error you'd get if you were to run `adult_df.education-num`.

```
In [49]:  ▶ adult_df.columns = ['age', 'workclass', 'fnlwgt', 'education',
                    'education_num', 'marital_status', 'occupation',
                    'relationship', 'race', 'sex', 'capitalGain',
                    'capitalLoss', 'hoursPerWeek', 'nativeCountry',
                    'income']
```

Figure 1.30 – Example of updating the column titles of a DataFrame

The `.info()` function

This function provides information about both the shape and the columns of the DataFrame. If you run `adult_df.info()`, you will see other information, such as the number of non-null values and also the type of data under each column that will be reported.

Getting to know the values of a dataset

The functions that Pandas has to get to know the numerical columns are different than those of categorical columns. The difference between numerical and categorical columns is that categorical columns are not represented by numbers or, more accurately, do not carry numerical information.

To get to know numerical columns, the `.describe()`, `.plot.hist()`, and `.plot.box()` functions are very useful. On the other hand, the `.unique()` and `.value_counts()` functions are instrumental for categorical columns. We will cover these one by one.

The .describe() function

This function outputs many useful statistical metrics that are meant to summarize data for each column. These metrics include Count, Mean, Standard Deviation (std), Minimum (min), first quartile (25%), second quartile (50%) or median, third quartile (75%), and Maximum (max). The following screenshot shows the execution of the function for `adult_df` and its output:

```
In [50]:  ▶  adult_df.describe()
```

Out[50]:

	age	fnlwgt	education_num	capitalGain	capitalLoss	hoursPerWee
count	32561.000000	3.256100e+04	32561.000000	32561.000000	32561.000000	32561.00000
mean	38.581647	1.897784e+05	10.080679	1077.648844	87.303830	40.43745
std	13.640433	1.055500e+05	2.572720	7385.292085	402.960219	12.34742
min	17.000000	1.228500e+04	1.000000	0.000000	0.000000	1.00000
25%	28.000000	1.178270e+05	9.000000	0.000000	0.000000	40.00000
50%	37.000000	1.783560e+05	10.000000	0.000000	0.000000	40.00000
75%	48.000000	2.370510e+05	12.000000	0.000000	0.000000	45.00000
max	90.000000	1.484705e+06	16.000000	99999.000000	4356.000000	99.00000

Figure 1.31 – Example of using the .describe() function to get to know a dataset

The metrics that the `.describe()` function outputs are very valuable summarizing tools, especially if these metrics are meant to be used for algorithmic analytics. However, studying them all at once still overwhelms our human comprehension. To summarize data for human comprehension, there are more effective tools, such as visualizing data using histograms and boxplots.

Histograms and boxplots to visualize numerical columns

Pandas makes drawing these visuals very easy. Each Pandas series has a very useful collection of plot functions. For instance, the following screenshot shows how easy it is to draw the histogram for the `age` column. To create the boxplot for the `age` column, all you need to change is the last part of the code: `adult_df.age.plot.box()`. Give it a try. Also, draw the boxplot and histogram for all of the other numerical attributes and see for yourself how much easy it is to understand each column using visualization.

```
In [51]:    ▶ adult_df.age.plot.hist()

Out[51]:   <matplotlib.axes._subplots.AxesSubplot at 0x29b11f8d8b0>
```

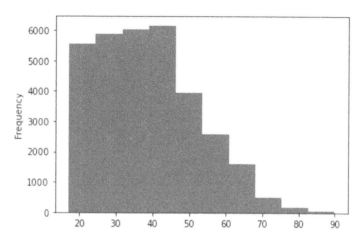

Figure 1.32 – Drawing the histogram of the adult_df.age column

Let's move on to the functions that we will use for categorical attributes. We will start with .unique().

The .unique() function

If the column is categorical, our approach to get to know it would be completely different. First, we need to see what are all the possibilities for the column. The .unique() function does just that. It simply returns all the possible values of the columns. See the following screenshot, which is an example of all the possible values of the relationship column in adult_df:

```
In [52]:    ▶ adult_df.relationship.unique()

Out[52]:   array(['Not-in-family', 'Husband', 'Wife', 'Own-child', 'Unmarried',
                  'Other-relative'], dtype=object)
```

Figure 1.33 – Example of using the .unique() function to get to know a dataset

Now that we have covered the .unique() function, we will cover the .value_counts() function next.

The .value_counts() function

The next step in getting to know a categorical column is realizing how often each possibility happens. The `.value_counts()` function does exactly that. The following screenshot shows the outcome of this function on the column's relationship:

```
In [53]:  ▶  adult_df.relationship.value_counts()

Out[53]:  Husband           13193
          Not-in-family      8305
          Own-child          5068
          Unmarried          3446
          Wife               1568
          Other-relative      981
          Name: relationship, dtype: int64
```

Figure 1.34 – Example of using the .value_counts() function to get to know a dataset

The output of the `.value_counts()` function is also known as the **frequency table**. There is also the **relative frequency table**, which shows the ratio of occurrences instead of the number of occurrences for each possibility. To get the relative frequency table, all you need to do is to specify that you want the table to be normalized: `.value_counts(normalize=True)`. Give it a try!

Barcharts for visualizing numerical columns

To draw the bar chart of a categorical attribute, even though you might be tempted to try out something like `adult_df.relationship.plot.bar()`, it won't work. Give it a try and study the error.

To create the bar chart, you would have to first create the frequency table. As the frequency table is a Pandas series itself, you can then draw the bar chart using that. The following screenshot shows how we can draw the bar chart for the relationship column using the functions `.value_counts()` and `.plot.bar()`:

```
In [54]:   ▶| adult_df.relationship.value_counts().plot.bar()
```

Out[54]:   <matplotlib.axes._subplots.AxesSubplot at 0x2341fcf2f40>

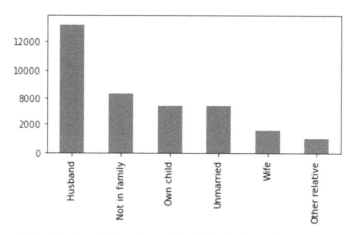

Figure 1.35 – Drawing the bar chart of the adult_df.relationship column

In this part, we learned how we can take advantage of Pandas resources to get to know new datasets. Next, we will learn about a Pandas function that is a game-changer in analyzing and preprocessing data using programming.

Pandas applying a function

There are a lot of instances where we will want to do the same calculations for each row in a dataset. The traditional approach to going about such calculations is to loop through the data and, on every iteration of the loop, perform and save the calculations. Python and Pandas have changed this paradigm by introducing the concept of applying a function. When you apply a function to a DataFrame, you request Pandas to run it for every row.

You can apply a function to a series or a DataFrame. Since applying a function to a series is somewhat easier, we will learn about that first and then we will move on to apply a function to a DataFrame.

Applying a function to a series

Let's say we want to multiply the series `adult_df.age` by 2. First, you need to write a function that assumes one input as a number, multiply the input by 2, and then output the result. The following screenshot shows this. First, the `MutiplyBy2()` function is defined, and then, using `adult_df.age.apply(MutiplyBy2)`, is applied to the series.

```
In [55]:  ▶  def MultiplyBy2(n):
                 return n*2

             adult_df.age.apply(MultiplyBy2)

Out[55]: 10000     78
         10001    100
         10002     76
         10003    106
         10004     56
                 ...
         42556     54
         42557     80
         42558    116
         42559     44
         42560    104
```

Figure 1.36 – Example of using the .apply() function

Now, let's see an analytic example where the `.apply()` function can be instrumental.

Applying a function – Analytic example 1

Not only does the series `adult_df.fnlwgt` not have an intuitive name, but also its values are not easily relatable. As mentioned earlier, the values are meant to be the ratio of the population that each row represents. As the numbers are neither percentages nor the actual number of people that each row represents, these values are neither intuitive nor relatable.

Now that we know how to do a calculation for each value in a series, let's fix this with a simple calculation. How about we divide every value by the sum of all the values in the series?

The following screenshot shows the steps for going about this:

1. First, `total_fnlwgt`, which is the sum of all the values in the `fnlwgt` column, is calculated.

2. Second, the `CalculatePercentage` function is defined. This function outputs the input values divided by `total_fnlwgt` and multiplied by 100 (to develop a percentage).

3. Third, the `CalculatePercentage` function is applied to the series
    `adult_df.fnlwgt`.

Now, pay attention! Instead of just seeing the results of the calculations, the following code
has assigned the result to `adult_df.fnlwgt` itself, which substitutes the original values
with the newly calculated percentages. The following code does not show the output of the
code, but give it a try on your Jupyter notebook and study the output on your own:

```
total_fnlwgt = adult_df.fnlwgt.sum()
def CalculatePercentage(v):
    return v/total_fnlwgt*100
adult_df.fnlwgt = adult_df.fnlwgt.apply(
CalculatePercentage)
adult_df
```

Applying a Lambda function

A **lambda function** is a function that is expressed in one line. So, a lot of the time,
applying a lambda function may make coding easier and perhaps help our code become
a bit more readable at times. For instance, if you wanted to answer the preceding
calculations "on the fly," you could simply apply a lambda function instead of an explicit
function. See the following code and compare the simplicity and conciseness of using a
lambda function instead of an explicit function:

```
total_fnlwgt = adult_df.fnlwgt.sum()
adult_df.fnlwgt = adult_df.fnlwgt.apply(lambda v: v/total_
fnlwgt*100)
adult_df
```

It is important to understand that the right choice between a lambda function or an explicit
function depends on the situation. Sometimes, having to jam a perhaps complicated
function into a line causes coding to become more difficult and renders the code less
readable. This will be the case if the function has more than one conditional statement.

Applying a function to a DataFrame

The major difference between applying a function to a DataFrame and a series is when
you are defining the function. While, for a series, we had to assume that one value would
be input in the function, for a DataFrame, we have to assume that a row series will be
input. So, when you are defining a function to apply to a DataFrame, you can engage any
column that you need.

For instance, the following code has defined and applied a function that subtracts education_num from age for every column. Pay attention to three aspects:

1. First, when defining the CalcLifeNoEd() function, the input row was assumed to be a row series of adult_df. In other words, the CalcLifeNoEd() function is tailored just for application to adult_df or any DataFrame that has age and eduction_num as columns.

2. Second, the .apply() function comes right after the DataFrame itself instead of after any columns. Compare the code for applying a function to a DataFrame to that of a series. Compare the last two code snippets with the following code snippet.

3. Third, the inclusion of axis=1 is necessary, and what this means is that you want to apply the function to every row and not every column. You could also apply a function to every column. That almost never happens for analytics, but if you ever needed to, you would have to change it to axis=0.

I have not included the output of this executed code. Give the code a try and study its output:

```
def CalcLifeNoEd(row):
    return row.age - row.education_num
adult_df.apply(CalcLifeNoEd,axis=1)
```

This could have easily been done using the lambda function as well. The code that you will need to run is the following. Give it a try:

```
adult_df.apply(lambda r: r.age-r.education_num,axis=1)
```

Applying a function – Analytic example 2

Which one is more important in terms of your financial success: education or life experience?

To answer this question, we could use adult_df as a sample dataset and extract some insight from the population of people in 1966. The code in the following screenshot first creates two new columns in the data:

*   lifeNoEd: The number of years for which you have lived without formal education
*   capitalNet: The subtraction of capitalLoss from capitalGain

To answer this question, we can check which one of `education_num` or `lifeNoEd` has a higher correlation with `capitalNet`. Doing this is very easy using Pandas, as each Pandas DataFrame comes with a function, `.corr()`, which calculates the Pearson correlation coefficient for all the combinations of the numerical attributes in the DataFrame. As we are only interested in the correlations between `education_num`, `lifeNoEd`, and `capitalNet`, the last line of the code has removed other columns before running the `.corr()` function.

```
In [60]:   ▶ adult_df['lifeNoEd'] = adult_df.apply(
                  lambda r: r.age-r.education_num,axis=1)

             adult_df['capitalNet'] = adult_df.apply(
                  lambda r: r.capitalGain - r.capitalLoss,axis=1)

             adult_df[['education_num','lifeNoEd','capitalNet']].corr()
Out[60]:
```

	education_num	lifeNoEd	capitalNet
education_num	1.000000	-0.150452	0.117891
lifeNoEd	-0.150452	1.000000	0.051490
capitalNet	0.117891	0.051490	1.000000

Figure 1.37 – Solution to the preceding example

From the output, you can see that while the correlation between `lifeNoEd` and `capitalNet` is 0.051490, the correlation between `education_num` and `capitalNet` is higher, at 0.117891. So we have some evidence that education has a more effective role in financial success than just life experience.

Now that you've learned how to effectively apply a function for analytics purposes, we can move on to learn about another very powerful and useful function in Pandas that is invaluable for data analytics and preprocessing.

The Pandas groupby function

This is one of the most useful analytics and preprocessing tools of Pandas. As the name *Groupby* suggests, it groups your data by something. Normally, you would want to group your data by categorical attributes.

If you are familiar with SQL queries, Pandas groupby is almost identical to SQL groupby. For both SQL queries and Pandas queries, grouping your data by itself will not have any added value or any output, unless it is accompanied by an aggregate function.

For instance, if you want to count the number of rows per `marital_status` category, you can use the Groupby function. See and try the following code:

```
adult_df.groupby('marital_status').size()
```

You can group the DataFrame by more than one column as needed. To do so, you will have to introduce the columns you are grouping the DataFrame by in the form of a list of column names. For instance, the following code groups the data based on both the `marital_status` and `sex` columns:

```
adult_df.groupby(['marital_status','sex']).size()
```

Pay attention that the two columns are introduced to the function as a list of string values.

The only aggregate function that works without having to specify a column of interest is `.size()`, as seen above. However, once you specify the column of interest that you want to aggregate the data of, you could use any aggregate function that you can use on a Pandas series or DataFrame. The following table shows a list of all the aggregate functions that you can use:

Function	Description	Function	Description
`.count()`	Number of non-null observations	`.median()`	Arithmetic median of values
`.sum()`	Sum of values	`.min()`	Minimum of values
`.mean()`	Mean of values	`.max()`	Maximum of values
`.mad()`	Mean absolute deviation	`.mode()`	Mode of values
`.std()`	Unbiased standard deviation	`.Var()`	Unbiased variance
`.sem()`	Unbiased standard error of the mean	`.Describe()`	Count(), mean(), std(), and so on
`.skew()`	Unbiased skewness	`.kurt()`	Unbiased kurtosis

Figure 1.38 – List of Pandas aggregate functions

For instance, the following shows the code to group `adult_df` by `martial_status` and `sex`, and calculates the median of each group:

```
adult_df.groupby(['marital_status','sex']).age.median()
```

As you study the code and its output, you can start appreciating the analytic value of the `.groupby()` function. Next, we will look at an example that will help you appreciate this valuable function even further.

Analytic example using Groupby

Were the race and gender of individuals in 1966 influential in their financial success?

Incidentally, `adult_df` was collected in 1966, so we can use it to provide some insight into this question. You may take different approaches in going about this. One approach, as depicted in the following screenshot, is to group the data by `race` and `sex` and then calculate the mean of `capitalNet` for the groups and study the differences.

```
In [62]:  ▶  adult_df.groupby(['race','sex']).capitalNet.mean()

Out[62]:  race                sex
          Amer-Indian-Eskimo  Female     530.142857
                              Male       628.864583
          Asian-Pac-Islander  Female     727.583815
                              Male      1707.440115
          Black               Female     471.142765
                              Male       627.268324
          Other               Female     218.385321
                              Male      1314.438272
          White               Female     508.219857
                              Male      1266.413112
```

Figure 1.39 – Solution to the preceding example

Another approach would be to group the data based on `race`, `sex`, and `income` and then calculate the mean of `fnlwgt`. Give this one a try and see whether you come to a different conclusion.

Pandas multi-level indexing

Let's first understand what **multi-level indexing** is. If you look at the output of grouping a DataFrame by more than one column, the indexing of the output looks different than normal. Although the output is a Pandas series, it looks different. The reason for this dissimilarity is multi-level indexing. The following screenshot shows you the index of the .groupby() output for the previous screenshot. You can see that the index of the series has two levels, specifically, race and sex:

```
In [63]:    grb_result =adult_df.groupby(['race','sex']).capitalNet.mean()

            print(grb_result.index)

            MultiIndex([('Amer-Indian-Eskimo',  'Female'),
                        ('Amer-Indian-Eskimo',    'Male'),
                        ('Asian-Pac-Islander',  'Female'),
                        ('Asian-Pac-Islander',    'Male'),
                        (              'Black',  'Female'),
                        (              'Black',    'Male'),
                        (              'Other',  'Female'),
                        (              'Other',    'Male'),
                        (              'White',  'Female'),
                        (              'White',    'Male')],
                       names=['race', 'sex'])
```

Figure 1.40 – An example of multi-level indexing

Now, let's learn a few useful and relevant functions that can help us with data analytics and preprocessing. These functions are .stack() and .unstack().

The .unstack() function

This function pushes the outer level of the multi-level index to the columns. If the multi-level index only has two levels, after running .unstack(), it will become single-level. Likewise, if the .unstack() function is run for a series with a multi-level index, the output will be a DataFrame whose columns are the outer level index that was pushed. For instance, the following screenshot demonstrates the change in appearance and structure of the output when the .unstack() function is executed:

```
In [64]:  ▶  grb_result =adult_df.groupby(['race','sex']).capitalNet.mean()
              grb_result
```

```
Out[64]:  race                sex
          Amer-Indian-Eskimo  Female     530.142857
                              Male       628.864583
          Asian-Pac-Islander  Female     727.583815
                              Male      1707.440115
          Black               Female     471.142765
                              Male       627.268324
          Other               Female     218.385321
                              Male      1314.438272
          White               Female     508.219857
                              Male      1266.413112
          Name: capitalNet, dtype: float64
```

```
In [65]:  ▶  grb_result.unstack()
```

Out[65]:

sex	Female	Male
race		
Amer-Indian-Eskimo	530.142857	628.864583
Asian-Pac-Islander	727.583815	1707.440115
Black	471.142765	627.268324
Other	218.385321	1314.438272
White	508.219857	1266.413112

Figure 1.41 – Example of the .unstack() function

If there are more than two levels, executing .unstack() more than once will, one by one, push the outer level of the index to the columns. For instance, you can see in the following screenshot that the code in the first chunk results in grb_result, which is a series with a three-level index. The second chunk of code executes .unstack() once and the outer level of the index in grb_result, which is income, is pushed to the columns. The third chunk of code, however, executes .unstack() twice, and the second outer level of the index in grb_result, which is sex, joins income in the columns.

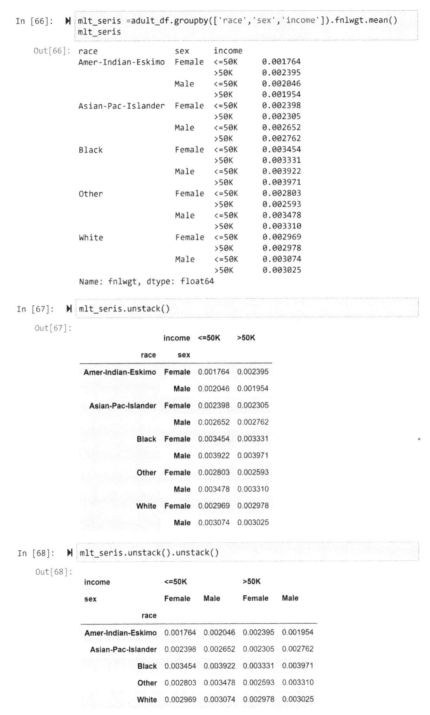

```
In [66]:   ▶ mlt_seris =adult_df.groupby(['race','sex','income']).fnlwgt.mean()
              mlt_seris
```

```
Out[66]: race                sex     income
         Amer-Indian-Eskimo  Female  <=50K    0.001764
                                     >50K     0.002395
                             Male    <=50K    0.002046
                                     >50K     0.001954
         Asian-Pac-Islander  Female  <=50K    0.002398
                                     >50K     0.002305
                             Male    <=50K    0.002652
                                     >50K     0.002762
         Black               Female  <=50K    0.003454
                                     >50K     0.003331
                             Male    <=50K    0.003922
                                     >50K     0.003971
         Other               Female  <=50K    0.002803
                                     >50K     0.002593
                             Male    <=50K    0.003478
                                     >50K     0.003310
         White               Female  <=50K    0.002969
                                     >50K     0.002978
                             Male    <=50K    0.003074
                                     >50K     0.003025
         Name: fnlwgt, dtype: float64
```

```
In [67]:   ▶ mlt_seris.unstack()
```

Out[67]:

	income	<=50K	>50K
race	**sex**		
Amer-Indian-Eskimo	**Female**	0.001764	0.002395
	Male	0.002046	0.001954
Asian-Pac-Islander	**Female**	0.002398	0.002305
	Male	0.002652	0.002762
Black	**Female**	0.003454	0.003331
	Male	0.003922	0.003971
Other	**Female**	0.002803	0.002593
	Male	0.003478	0.003310
White	**Female**	0.002969	0.002978
	Male	0.003074	0.003025

```
In [68]:   ▶ mlt_seris.unstack().unstack()
```

Out[68]:

income		<=50K		>50K	
sex		**Female**	**Male**	**Female**	**Male**
	race				
Amer-Indian-Eskimo		0.001764	0.002046	0.002395	0.001954
Asian-Pac-Islander		0.002398	0.002652	0.002305	0.002762
Black		0.003454	0.003922	0.003331	0.003971
Other		0.002803	0.003478	0.002593	0.003310
White		0.002969	0.003074	0.002978	0.003025

Figure 1.42 – Another example of the .unstack() function with two levels of indexing

As an index can be multi-level in Pandas, columns can also have multiple levels. For instance, in the first chunk of the following screenshot, you can see that the output DataFrame has two levels. The second chunk of code outputs the columns of the DataFrame. You can see that the columns have the two levels that were pushed from the index using .unstack():

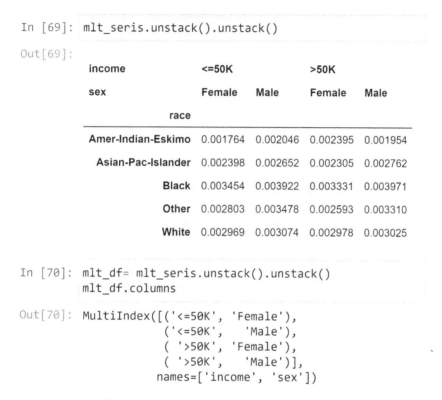

```
In [69]: mlt_seris.unstack().unstack()
Out[69]:
```

income		<=50K		>50K	
sex		Female	Male	Female	Male
race					
Amer-Indian-Eskimo		0.001764	0.002046	0.002395	0.001954
Asian-Pac-Islander		0.002398	0.002652	0.002305	0.002762
Black		0.003454	0.003922	0.003331	0.003971
Other		0.002803	0.003478	0.002593	0.003310
White		0.002969	0.003074	0.002978	0.003025

```
In [70]: mlt_df= mlt_seris.unstack().unstack()
         mlt_df.columns

Out[70]: MultiIndex([('<=50K', 'Female'),
                      ('<=50K',   'Male'),
                      ( '>50K', 'Female'),
                      ( '>50K',   'Male')],
                     names=['income', 'sex'])
```

Figure 1.43 – An example of multi-level columns

The .stack() function

The opposite of .unstack() is .stack(), where the outer level of the columns is pushed to be added as the outer level of the index. For example, in the following screenshot, you can see that mlt_df, which we saw has two-level columns, has undergone .stack() twice. The first .stack() function pushed the income level to the index, and the second .stack() function pushed the sex level to the index. This made the data be presented as a series as there is only one column of data.

```
In [71]: mlt_df.stack()
```

Out[71]:

	income	<=50K	>50K
race	**sex**		
Amer-Indian-Eskimo	**Female**	0.001764	0.002395
	Male	0.002046	0.001954
Asian-Pac-Islander	**Female**	0.002398	0.002305
	Male	0.002652	0.002762
Black	**Female**	0.003454	0.003331
	Male	0.003922	0.003971
Other	**Female**	0.002803	0.002593
	Male	0.003478	0.003310
White	**Female**	0.002969	0.002978
	Male	0.003074	0.003025

```
In [72]: mlt_df.stack().stack()
```

```
Out[72]: race                sex      income
         Amer-Indian-Eskimo  Female   <=50K     0.001764
                                      >50K      0.002395
                             Male     <=50K     0.002046
                                      >50K      0.001954
         Asian-Pac-Islander  Female   <=50K     0.002398
                                      >50K      0.002305
                             Male     <=50K     0.002652
                                      >50K      0.002762
         Black               Female   <=50K     0.003454
                                      >50K      0.003331
                             Male     <=50K     0.003922
                                      >50K      0.003971
         Other               Female   <=50K     0.002803
                                      >50K      0.002593
                             Male     <=50K     0.003478
                                      >50K      0.003310
         White               Female   <=50K     0.002969
                                      >50K      0.002978
                             Male     <=50K     0.003074
                                      >50K      0.003025
         dtype: float64
```

Figure 1.44 – Example of the .stack() function

Multi-level access

The value access in series or DataFrames with multi-level indexes, or DataFrames with multi-level columns, is slightly different. *Exercise 2* at the end of this chapter is designed to help you learn that.

In this subsection, we gathered sizable exposure to multi-level indexing and columns. Now we are moving on to another set of functions that are somewhat similar to the `.stack()` and `.unstack()` functions, but different at the same time. These functions are `.pivot()` and `.melt()`.

Pandas pivot and melt functions

In a nutshell, `.pivot()` and `.melt()` help you to switch between two forms of two-dimensional data structures: **wide form** and **long form**. The following figure depicts the difference between the two forms. The wide form is what you are typically used to if you are a spreadsheet user. The wide form uses many columns to introduce new dimensions in the dataset. The long form, however, uses a different logic of data structure and uses one index column to include all the relevant dimensions. The `.melt()` function, as you may picture it in your mind based on the meaning of the word *melt*, can easily reshape a dataset from the wide form to the long form. The `.pivot()` function can do the opposite.

To practice and learn these two functions, we will read `wide.csv` using Pandas into `wide_df`, and read `long.csv` using Pandas into `long_df`.

	ReadingDateTime	Species	Value
0	01/01/2017 00:00	NO	3.5
1	01/01/2017 01:00	NO	3.6
2	01/01/2017 02:00	NO	2.2
3	01/01/2017 00:00	NO2	30.8
4	01/01/2017 01:00	NO2	31.5
5	01/01/2017 02:00	NO2	27.3
6	01/01/2017 00:00	NOX	36.2
7	01/01/2017 01:00	NOX	37.0
8	01/01/2017 02:00	NOX	30.7
9	01/01/2017 00:00	PM10	35.7
10	01/01/2017 01:00	PM10	28.5
11	01/01/2017 02:00	PM10	22.7
12	01/01/2017 00:00	PM2.5	31.0
13	01/01/2017 01:00	PM2.5	31.0
14	01/01/2017 02:00	PM2.5	31.0

long_df

	ReadingDateTime	NO	NO2	NOX	PM10	PM2.5
0	01/01/2017 00:00	3.5	30.8	36.2	35.7	31.0
1	01/01/2017 01:00	3.6	31.5	37.0	28.5	31.0
2	01/01/2017 02:00	2.2	27.3	30.7	22.7	31.0

wide_df

Figure 1.45 – Comparison of the long and wide forms

To switch between the long and the wide format, all you need to do is to provide the right input to these functions. The following screenshot shows the application of .melt() on wide_df, reshaping it into a long format. In the second chunk of code, you can see that .melt() requires four inputs:

- id_vars: This input takes the identifying columns.

- value_vars: This input takes the columns that hold the values.

- var_name: This input takes the name you would like to give to the identifying column that will be added to the long format.

- value_name: This input takes the name you would like to give to the new value column that will be added to the long format.

The following screenshot shows an example of using the .melt() function to switch the data from wide format to long format:

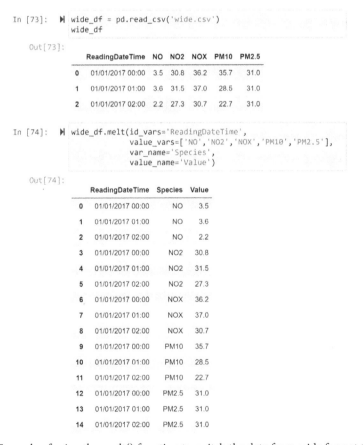

Figure 1.46 – Example of using the .melt() function to switch the data from wide format to long format

The `.pivot()` function reshapes a DataFrame from the long form to the wide form. For instance, the following screenshot shows the application of the function on `long_df`. Unlike, `.melt()`, which requires four inputs, `.pivot()` needs three:

- `index`: This input takes what will be the index of the wide form.

- `columns`: This input takes the columns of the long form that will be expanded to create the columns for the wide form.

- `values`: This input takes the column in which the long form keeps the values.

```
In [75]:    ▶  long_df = pd.read_csv('long.csv')
               long_df
```

Out[75]:

	ReadingDateTime	Species	Value
0	01/01/2017 00:00	NO	3.5
1	01/01/2017 01:00	NO	3.6
2	01/01/2017 02:00	NO	2.2
3	01/01/2017 00:00	NO2	30.8
4	01/01/2017 01:00	NO2	31.5
5	01/01/2017 02:00	NO2	27.3
6	01/01/2017 00:00	NOX	36.2
7	01/01/2017 01:00	NOX	37.0
8	01/01/2017 02:00	NOX	30.7
9	01/01/2017 00:00	PM10	35.7
10	01/01/2017 01:00	PM10	28.5
11	01/01/2017 02:00	PM10	22.7
12	01/01/2017 00:00	PM2.5	31.0
13	01/01/2017 01:00	PM2.5	31.0
14	01/01/2017 02:00	PM2.5	31.0

```
In [76]:    ▶  long_df.pivot(index='ReadingDateTime',
                             columns='Species',
                             values='Value')
```

Out[76]:

Species	NO	NO2	NOX	PM10	PM2.5
ReadingDateTime					
01/01/2017 00:00	3.5	30.8	36.2	35.7	31.0
01/01/2017 01:00	3.6	31.5	37.0	28.5	31.0
01/01/2017 02:00	2.2	27.3	30.7	22.7	31.0

Figure 1.47 – Example of using the .pivot() function to switch the data from the long format to the wide format

Summary

Congratulations on your excellent progress so far! In this chapter, you first learned about the Jupyter Notebook, which is the UI we will be using throughout this book. Then, you learned about the most important functions of the two Python core modules for data analytics and data preprocessing. In the next chapter, you will learn about the functions of another core module: Matplotlib. This module will be our core module for visualization needs.

Before moving on to the next chapter, I highly encourage you to spend some time and meaningfully engage with the following exercises.

Exercises

1. Use the `adult.csv` dataset and run the code shown in the following screenshots. Then, answer the questions that follow:

Figure 1.48 – Exercise 1

a) Use the output to answer what is the difference in behavior of `.loc` and `.iloc` when it comes to slicing?

b) Without running, but just by looking at the data, what will be the output of `adult_df.loc['10000':'10003', 'relationship':'sex']`?

c) Without running, but just by looking at the data, what will be the output of `adult_df.iloc[0:3, 7:9]`?

2. Use Pandas to read `adult.csv` into `adult_df` and then use the `.groupby()` function to run the following code and create the multi-index series `mlt_sr`:

```
import pandas as pd
adult_df = pd.read_csv('adult.csv')
mlt_seris =adult_df.groupby(['race','sex','income']).
fnlwgt.mean()
mlt_seris
```

a) Now that you have created a multi-index series, run the following code, study the outputs, and answer the following questions:

Run the following code first and then answer this question: When we use `.iloc[]` for a multi-index series or DataFrame, what should we expect?

```
print(mlt_seris.iloc[0])
print(mlt_seris.iloc[1])
print(mlt_seris.iloc[2])
```

b) Run the following code first and then answer this question: When we use `.loc[]` to access the data of one of the innermost index levels of the multi-index series, what should we expect?

```
mlt_seris.loc['Other']
```

c) Run the following code first and then answer this question: When we use `.loc[]` to access the data of one of the non-innermost index levels of a multi-index series, what should we expect?

When you run either line of the following code, you will get an error, and that is the point of this question. Study the error and try to answer the question:

```
mlt_seris.loc['Other']
mlt_seris.loc['<=50K']
```

d) Run the following code first and then answer this question: How does the use of `.loc[]` or `.iloc[]` differ when working with a multi-index series or a DataFrame?

```
print(mlt_seris.loc['Other']['Female']['<=50K'])
print(mlt_seris.iloc[12])
```

3. For this exercise, you need to use a new dataset: `billboard.csv`. Visit `https://www.billboard.com/charts/hot-100` and see the latest song rankings of the day. This dataset presents information and rankings for 317 song tracks in 80 columns. The first four columns are `artist`, `track`, `time`, and `date_e`. The first columns are intuitive descriptions of song tracks. The `date_e` column shows the date that the songs entered the hot 100 list. The rest of the 76 columns are song rankings at the end of each week from "w1" to "w76". Download and read this dataset using Pandas and answer the following questions:

    a) Write one line of code that gives you a great idea of how many null values each column has. If any columns have no non-null values, drop them.

    b) With a `for` loop, draw and study the values in each of the remaining W columns.

    c) The dataset is in wide format. Use an appropriate function to switch to a long format and name the transformed DataFrame `mlt_df`.

    d) Write code that shows `mlt_df` every 1,200 rows.

    e) Run the following code first and answer this question: Could this also have been done by using Boolean masking?

    ```
    mlt_df.query('artist == "Spears, Britney"')
    ```

    f) Use either the approach in e or the Boolean mask to extract all the unique songs that Britney Spears has in this dataset.

    g) In `mlt_df`, show all of the weeks when the song "Oops!.. I Did It Again" was in the top 100.

4. We will use `LaqnData.csv` for this exercise. Each row of this dataset shows an hourly measurement recording of one of the following five air pollutants: NO, NO2, NOX, PM10, and PM2.5. The data was collected in a location in London for the entirety of the year 2017. Read the data using Pandas and perform the following tasks:

    a) The dataset has six columns. Three of them, named `'Site'`, `'Units'`, and `'Provisional or Ratified'` are not adding any informational values as they are the same across the whole dataset. Use the following code to drop them:

    ```
    air_df.drop(columns=['Site','Units','Provisional or
    Ratified'], inplace=True)
    ```

    b) The dataset is in a long format. Apply the appropriate function to switch it to the wide format. Name the transformed Dataframe `pvt_df`.

    c) Draw and study the histogram and boxplots for columns of `pvt_df`.

5. We will continue working with LaqnData.csv:

a) Run the following code, see its output, and then study the code to answer what each line of this code does:

```
air_df = pd.read_csv('LaqnData.csv')
air_df.drop(columns=['Site','Units','Provisional or
Ratified'], inplace=True)
datetime_df = air_df.ReadingDateTime.str.split('
',expand=True)
datetime_df.columns = ['Date','Time']
date_df = datetime_df.Date.str.split('/',expand=True)
date_df.columns = ['Day','Month','Year']
air_df = air_df.join(date_df).join(datetime_df.Time).
drop(columns=['ReadingDateTime','Year'])
air_df
```

b) Run the following code, see its output, and then study the code to answer what this line of code does:

```
air_df = air_df.set_
index(['Month','Day','Time','Species'])
air_df
```

c) Run the following code, see its output, and then study the code to answer what this line of code does:

```
air_df.unstack()
```

d) Compare the output of the preceding code with pvt_df from Exercise 4. Are they the same?

e) Explain what the differences and similarities are between the pair .melt()/.pivot() and the pair .stack()/.unstack()?

f) If you were to choose one counterpart for .melt() between .stack()/.unstack(), which one would you choose?

2
Review of Another Core Module – Matplotlib

Matplotlib is our go-to module for creating visualizations from data. Not only can this module draw many different plots, but it also gives us the capability to design and tailor the plots to our needs. Matplotlib will serve our data analytics and data preprocessing journey by providing a great number of functions for effective visualizations.

Before we start reviewing this valuable module, I would like to let you know that this chapter is not meant to be a comprehensive teaching guide for Matplotlib, but rather a collection of concepts, functions, and examples that will be invaluable as we cover data analytics and data preprocessing in future chapters.

We have actually started using this module in the previous chapter. The **Pandas** plot functions that we introduced in *Chapter 1, Review of the Core Modules of NumPy and Pandas,* under the *Pandas functions to explore a DataFrame* are section, actually Matplotlib visuals that Pandas uses internally.

In this chapter, I will first introduce the main plots that Matplotlib can draw. Following that, I will cover some design and altering functionalities of the visuals. Then, we will learn about the invaluable subplotting capability of Matplotlib that will allow us to create more complex and effective visualizations.

The following topics will be covered in this chapter:

- Main plots
- Modifying the visuals
- Subplots
- Resizing visuals and saving them

Technical requirements

You will be able to find all of the code and the dataset that is used in this chapter in this book's GitHub repository:

`https://github.com/PacktPublishing/Hands-On-Data-Preprocessing-in-Python`

Each chapter in this book will have a folder that contains all of the code and datasets used.

Drawing the main plots in Matplotlib

Drawing visuals with Matplotlib is easy. All you need is the right input and a correct understanding of the data. The main five visuals that we use in Matplotlib to draw are **histograms**, **boxplots**, **bar charts**, **line plots**, and **scatterplots**. Let's introduce them with the following examples.

Summarizing numerical attributes using histograms or boxplots

We already draw histograms using Pandas, which we learned about in the *Pandas functions to explore a DataFrame* section in the previous chapter. However, the same plot can also be drawn using Matplotlib. The following screenshot shows the best and most common way to import Matplotlib. There are two points here:

1. First, you want to use the `plt` alias, as everyone else uses that.
2. Second, you want to import `matplotlib.pyplot` instead of just `matplotlib`, as everything we will need from `matplotlib` is under `.pyplot`.

The second chunk of code in the following screenshot shows how easy it is to draw a *histogram* using Matplotlib. All you need to do is input the data you want to be plotted into `plt.hist()`. The last line of code, `plt.show()`, is what I always add to force `Jupyternotebook` to only show the plot I want without the rest of the outputs that come with the plot. Run `plt.hist(adult_df.age)` by itself to see the difference.

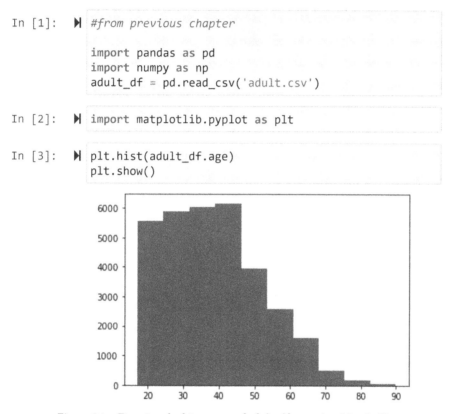

Figure 2.1 – Drawing the histogram of adult_df.age using Matplotlib

The following screenshot, in turn, shows the *boxplot* of the same data using `plt.boxplot()`. I have also requested the boxplot to be drawn horizontally by specifying `vert=False` so the boxplot and the preceding histogram can be compared visually.

```
In [4]:  ▶  plt.boxplot(adult_df.age, vert=False)
            plt.show()
```

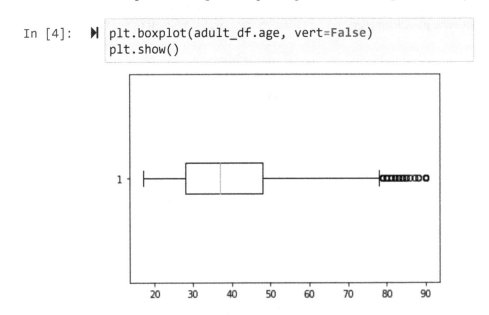

Figure 2.2 – Drawing the box plot of adult_df.age using Matplotlib

So far, we've learned two of the main plots of the Matplotlib module. Next, we will cover the line plot.

Observing trends in the data using a line plot

A *line plot*, not exclusively, but very often, is applied to time series data to show trends. A great example of time series data is stock prices. For instance, the stock price of the company **Amazon** changes minute by minute, and if someone is interested to see the trend of changes in these stock prices, they can use a line plot to do that.

We are going to use Amazon and **Apple** stock prices to showcase the application of line plots in illustrating trends. The following code shows the loading of that data with the `Amazon Stock.csv` and `Apple Stock.csv` files using the `pd.read_csv()` function. These files contain the stock prices of Amazon and Apple from 2000 to 2020:

```
amz_df = pd.read_csv('Amazon Stock.csv')
apl_df = pd.read_csv('Apple Stock.csv')
```

The following screenshot shows us using the `plt.plot()` function to draw the line plot of the closing prices of the stocks:

```
In [6]:  ▶ plt.plot(amz_df.Close)
           plt.plot(apl_df.Close)
           plt.show()
```

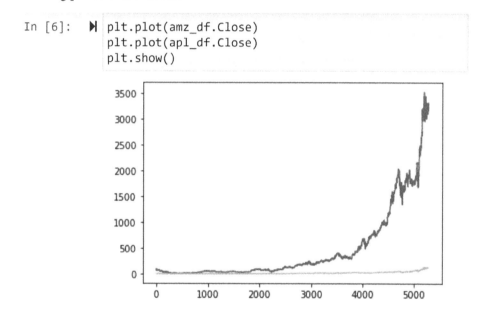

Figure 2.3 – Drawing the line plots of Amazon and Apple stock trends

Next, we are going to learn about scatterplots.

Relating two numerical attributes using a scatterplot

Scatterplots can be drawn using the plt.scatter() function. This function is great for examining the relationship between numerical attributes. For instance, the following screenshot shows us the relationship between the prices of Amazon and Apple stocks in the years from 2000 to 2020. Each dot in this scatterplot represents one trading day from 2000 to 2020.

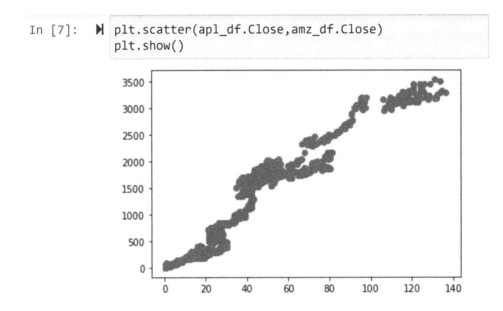

Figure 2.4 – Drawing the scatterplots of Amazon and Apple stock trends

So far in this chapter, we have been introduced to the main plots of Matplotlib and their analytics functionalities. Next, we will learn how to edit the visuals in simple but effective ways.

Modifying the visuals

The Matplotlib module is great at allowing you to modify the plots so that they serve your needs. The first thing you need before modifying a visual is to know the name of the part of the visual that you are intending to modify. The following figure shows you the anatomy of these visuals and is a great reference to find the name of the part you intend to modify.

In the following examples, we will see how to modify the title and markers of the visuals, and the labels and the ticks of the axes of the visuals. These are the most frequent modifications that you will need. If you found yourself in situations where you need to modify other parts too, how you would go about those are very similar, and so long as you know the name of what you plan to modify, you are one **Google** search away from finding how it is done.

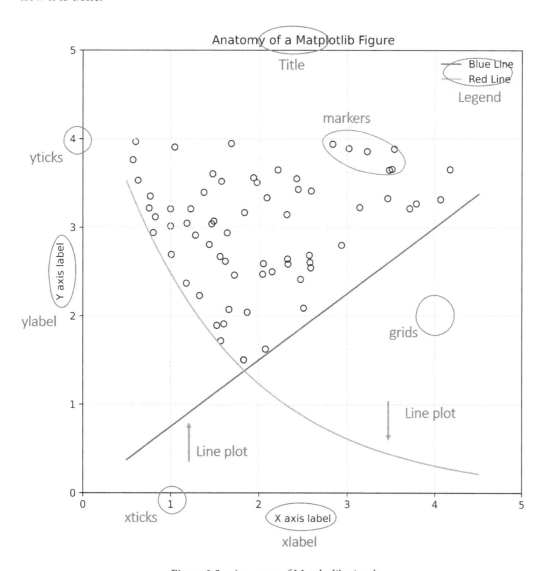

Figure 2.5 – Anatomy of Matplotlib visuals

Adding a title to visuals and labels to the axis

To modify any part of a Matplotlib visual, you need to execute a function that can do the modifying trick. For instance, to add a title to a visual, you need to use `plt.title()` after a visual is executed. Also, to add a label to the *x* axis or the *y* axis, you can employ `plt.xlabel()` or `plt.ylabel()`.

The following screenshot shows the application of `plt.title()` and `plt.ylabel()` to add a title to the visual and add a label to the *y* axis respectively:

```
In [8]:  ▶ plt.plot(amz_df.Close)
            plt.plot(apl_df.Close)
            plt.title('Line plots of Amazon and Apple stock prices from 2000 to 2020')
            plt.ylabel('Closing Price')
            plt.show()
```

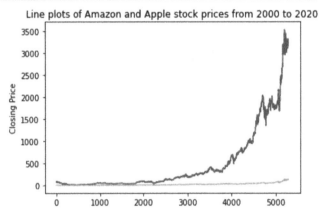

Figure 2.6 – Example of adding a title and label to a Matplotlib visual

Having learned how to add titles and labels, we will now turn our attention to learn how to add and modify legends.

Adding legends

For adding *legends* to a Matplotlib visual, there are two steps:

1. First, you need to add a relevant label as you introduce each segment of the data to Matplotlib.

2. Second, after executing the visuals, you need to execute `plt.legend()`.

The following screenshot depicts how these two steps are taken to add a legend to the line plot:

```
In [9]:  ▶  plt.plot(amz_df.Close, label='Amazon')
            plt.plot(apl_df.Close, label='Apple')
            plt.title('Line plots of Amazon and Apple stock prices from 2000 to 2020')
            plt.ylabel('Closing Price')
            plt.legend()
            plt.show()
```

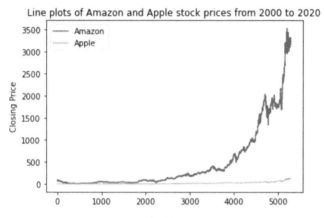

Figure 2.7 – Example of adding a legend to a Matplotlib visual

Next, we will learn about how to edit the *xticks* or the *yticks*.

Modifying ticks

Modifying the *ticks* is perhaps the most complex of all modifications of Matplotlib visuals. Let's discuss how this is done as it pertains to a line plot, and you can extrapolate that to the other visuals easily.

You need to know a little about the workings of the plt.plot() function before you can successfully modify the ticks. When a line plot is first introduced, you either explicitly introduce the *x* axis to the plt.plot() function, or the function assumes integer values starting from zero to the number values inputted for plotting minus one. As we did not explicitly introduce the x values in the past couple of line plots (see previous), the plt. plot() function has assumed the integer values for the *x* axis. However, pay attention to the outputted visuals where only x values of 0, 1000, 2000, 3000, 4000, and 5000 are being represented.

The following screenshot shows how instead of representing all the trading days with six integers, you could represent them with as many as you want. The integers you want to be represented in the ticks are simply introduced to the plt.xticks() function. Also, you can use the property rotation to change the angle of the ticks, so they are more legible.

```
In [10]:   ▶ plt.plot(amz_df.Close, label='Amazon')
             plt.plot(apl_df.Close, label='Apple')
             plt.title('Line plots of Amazon and Apple stock prices from 2000 to 2020')
             plt.ylabel('Closing Price')
             plt.xticks([0,500,1000,1500,2000,2500,3000,3500,4000,4500,5000,5500],
                         rotation=90)
             plt.legend()
             plt.show()
```

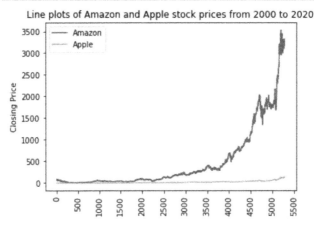

Figure 2.8 – Example of modifying the ticks of a Matplotlib visual – level 1

How about if we want to re-represent these integers that represent trading days with their trading day's actual dates? This can easily be done using the plt.xticks() function. After introducing the integers that you want to be represented, you need to also introduce the replacing counterparts of these integers to the function.

The code in the following screenshot provides an example of how this can be done:

1. First, the integers that we want represented are inputted as np.arange(0,len(amz_df),250). Pay attention to the fact that instead of typing the integers, the code has used the np.arange() function to produce those integers. Run np.arange(0,len(amz_df),250) separately and study the output.

2. Second, the replacing counterparts, which are the dates of these trading days, are also introduced to `plt.xticks()`. They are introduced using the column `Date` in `amz_df`. The `amz_df.Date[0:len(amz_df):250]` code ensures that the replacing representations are their relevant counterparts in the integer representation. Pay attention – we have used `amz_df`, as we know the column date for `amz_df` and `apl_df` are identical.

In [11]: ▶
```
plt.plot(amz_df.Close, label='Amazon')
plt.plot(apl_df.Close, label='Apple')
plt.title('Line plots of Amazon and Apple stock prices from 2000 to 2020')
plt.ylabel('Closing Price')
plt.legend()
plt.xticks(np.arange(0,len(amz_df),250),amz_df.Date[0:len(amz_df):250],
          rotation=90)
plt.show()
```

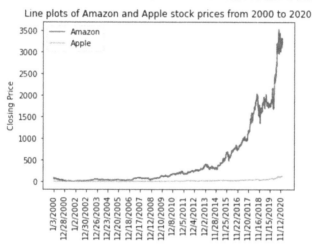

Figure 2.9 – Example of modifying the ticks of a Matplotlib visual – level 2

Pay attention to the fact that the number 250 in the preceding code had been reached by trial and error. We were looking for an increment that would not make the xticks too crowded or too sparse. Try running the code with alternative increments and study the behavior of the visual.

Modifying markers

The only visuals that we presented here that use markers are scatterplots. To modify the color and the shape of the markers, all you need to do is specify them when executing `plt.scatter()`. This function takes two inputs that it uses to draw the visual the way you would like. The `marker` input takes the shape of the marker you intend to draw, and the `color` input takes its color. The following screenshot shows how to change the default blue dots of Matplotlib scatterplots to green crosses by inputting `marker='x'` and `color='green'`. You cannot see the change of the colors in print as the book is printed in grayscale, but you will see the change in color if you try out the code yourself. The code also shows another example of using `plt.title()`, `plt.xlabel()`, and `plt.ylabel()` to modify the title of the visual and the labels of its axes.

In [12]: ▶
```
plt.scatter(apl_df.Close,amz_df.Close, marker = 'x', color='green')
plt.title('Amazon and Apple stock prices in 2000 to 2020')
plt.xlabel('Apple price ($)')
plt.ylabel('Amazon price ($)')
plt.show()
```

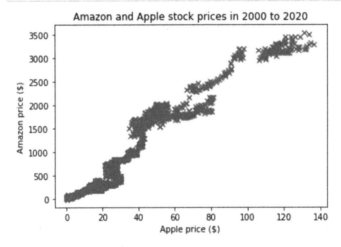

Figure 2.10 – Example of modifying the markers in a Matplotlib visual

There are many marker shapes and marker color options that you can use. To study these options, visit the following web pages from the Matplotlib official website:

- **Markers**: `https://matplotlib.org/stable/api/markers_api.html`
- **Colors**: `https://matplotlib.org/stable/gallery/color/named_colors.html`

So far, we have learned how to create visuals and modify them using Matplotlib. Next, we will learn another useful function that allows us to organize multiple visuals next to one another.

Subplots

Drawing a **subplot** can be a very useful data analytics and data preprocessing tool. We use subplots when we want to populate more than one visual and organize them next to one another in a specific way.

The following screenshot shows an example of subplotting. The logic of creating subplots in Matplotlib is unique and interesting. To draw a subplot, you first need to plan and decide the number of visuals you intend to have and their matrix-like organization. For instance, the following example has two visuals, and the visuals are organized in a matrix with two rows and one column. Once you know that, you can start coding.

Let's do this together step by step:

1. The logic of Matplotlib subplots is that you use a line of code to announce you are about to start giving the code for each specific visual. The `plt.subplot(2,1,1)` line says that you want to have a subplot with two rows and one column, and you are about to run the code for the first visual.

2. Once you are done with the first visual, you run another `plt.subplot()`, but this time you announce your intention to start another visual. For instance, by running `plt.subplot(2,1,2)`, you are announcing that you are done with the first visual, and you are about to start introducing the second visual.

Pay attention to the fact that the first two inputs of `plt.subplot()` stay the same throughout subplotting, as they specify the matrix-like organization of the subplots and they should be the same throughout.

The `plt.tight_layout()` function is best used after you are done with all the visuals and are about to show the whole subplots. This function makes sure that each visual fits within its own boundaries and there are no overlaps. Run the following code block without `plt.tight_layout()` and study the differences:

```
In [13]:    ▶  plt.subplot(2,1,1)
               plt.hist(adult_df.age)
               plt.title('Histogram')
               plt.ylabel('Age')

               plt.subplot(2,1,2)
               plt.boxplot(adult_df.age, vert=False)
               plt.title('Boxplot')
               plt.yticks([1],['Age'])

               plt.tight_layout()
               plt.show()
```

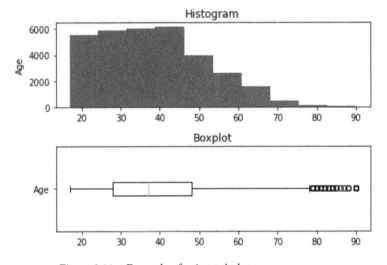

Figure 2.11 – Example of using subplots

So far, we have learned how to draw and design the visuals and then modify them. However, we have yet to learn how to resize them so we can fit them for our needs. Next, we will learn how to resize and save them on our computers.

Resizing visuals and saving them

It is very simple to save Matplotlib visuals with any resolution that you would like. However, before adjusting the resolution and saving the visuals, you might want to resize the visual. Let's first take a look at how we can resize the visuals and then see how we can save the visuals with specific resolutions.

Resizing

Matplotlib uses a default visual size (6x4 inches) for all its visual output, and from time to time, you may want to adjust the size of the visuals (especially if you have subplots as you may need a larger output). To adjust the visual size, the easiest way is to run `plt.figure(figsize=(6,4))` before starting to request any visuals. Of course, adding the mentioned code will not change the size as the inputted values are the same as the Matplotlib default size. To observe the difference, add `plt.figure(figsize=(9,6))` to the code in the previous screenshot and run it to study the differences. Also, change the values a few times to find the values that work best for you.

Saving

All you need to use to save and adjust the resolution of the output figures is the `plt.savefig()` function. This function takes the name of the file you would like to create for saving the visual and also its resolution in terms of **dots per inch** (**DPI**). The higher the DPI value of a figure, the higher its resolution. For instance, running `plt.savefig('visual.png',dpi=600)` saves the visual in a file named `visual.png` in your computer under the same directory where your **Jupyter Notebook** file is located. Of course, the DPI resolution of the saved visual will be `600`.

Example of Matplotilb assisting data preprocessing

A great way to get to know a new dataset is to visualize its columns. The numerical columns are best visualized using either histograms or boxplots. However, the combination of the two is the best, especially when the boxplot is drawn vertically. Use the subplot function of Matplotlib to draw the histogram and boxplot of all the numerical columns of adult_df in a 2x5 matrix-like visual. Make sure that the histogram and the boxplot of each column are in the same subplot column. Also, save the visual in a file named `ColumnsVsiaulization.png` with a resolution of `900` DPI.

The following code shows the solution for this example:

```
Numerical_colums = ['age', 'education_num', 'capitalGain',
'capitalLoss', 'hoursPerWeek']
plt.figure(figsize=(20,5))
for i,col in enumerate(Numerical_colums):
    plt.subplot(2,5,i+1)
    plt.hist(adult_df[col])
    plt.title(col)
for i,col in enumerate(Numerical_colums):
    plt.subplot(2,5,i+6)
    plt.boxplot(adult_df[col],vert=False)
    plt.yticks([])
plt.tight_layout()
plt.savefig('ColumnsVsiaulization.png', dpi=900)
```

After running the code, if it is successfully executed, check the directory that your Jupyter Notebook file is in, and the ColumnsVisualization.png file must be added there. Open the file and enjoy the high-quality visual that was created by Matplotlib.

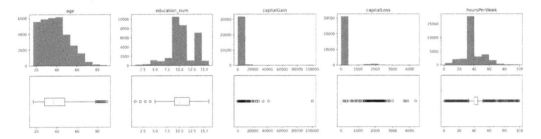

Figure 2.12 – Histogram and boxplot of the numerical attributes of adult_df

Congratulations on successfully finishing this chapter! Now you are equipped with visualization tools that will prove very handy for data analytics and data preprocessing.

Summary

In this chapter, you learned how to create the five main Matplotlib visuals and design them for your needs. You also learned how to create more complex visuals by organizing them in one visual using the Matplotlib subplot functionality. Ultimately, you also learned how to resize the visuals and save them with your desired resolution for later use.

In the next chapter, you will be given some essential lessons about data, along with concepts that are necessary for successful data preprocessing. However, before moving on to the next chapter, take some time and solidify and improve your learning using the following exercises.

Exercises

1. Use `adult.csv` and *Boolean masking* to answer the following questions:

   a. Calculate the mean and median of `education-num` for every race in the data.

   b. Draw one histogram of `education-num` that includes the data for each race in the data.

   c. Draw a comparative boxplot that compares the `education-num` for each race.

   d. Create a subplot that puts the visual from *b)* on top of the one from *c)*.

2. Repeat the analysis on *1, a)*, but this time use the `groupby` function.

   a. Compare the runtime of using Boolean masking versus groupby (hint: you can import the module time and use the `.time()` function).

3. If you have not already done so, solve *Exercise 4* in the previous chapter. After you have created `pvt_df` for *Exercise 4*, run the following code:

```
import seaborn as sns
sns.pairplot(pvt_df)
```

The code outputs what is known as a *scatter matrix*. This code takes advantage of the **Seaborn** module, which is another very useful visualization module. To practice subplots and resizing, recreate what Seaborn was able to do with `sns.pairplot()` using Matplotlib (hint: doing this with `plt.subplot()` might be a bit too challenging for you. First, give it a try and figure out what the challenge is, and then Google `plt.subplot2grid()`).

Pay attention – if you have never used the Seaborn module before, you may have to install it on your **Anaconda** first. It is easy – just run the following code in your Jupyter notebook:

```
conda install seaborn
```

3
Data – What Is It Really?

This chapter presents a conceptual understanding of data and introduces data concepts, definitions, and theories that are essential for effective data preprocessing. First, the chapter demystifies the word "data" and presents a definition that best serves data preprocessing. Next, it puts forth the universal data structure, table, and the common language everyone uses to describe it. Then, we will talk about the four types of data values and their significance for data preprocessing. Finally, we will discuss the statistical meanings of the terms *information* and *pattern* and their significance for data preprocessing.

The following topics will be covered in this chapter:

- What is data?
- The most universal data structure: a table
- Types of data values
- Information versus pattern

Technical requirements

You will be able to find all of the code examples that are used in this chapter, as well as the dataset, in *Chapter 3*'s GitHub repository:

```
https://github.com/PacktPublishing/Hands-On-Data-
Preprocessing-in-Python/tree/main/Chapter03
```

What is data?

What is the definition of data? If you ask this question of different professionals in various fields, you will get all kinds of answers. I always ask this at the beginning of my data-related courses, and I always get a wide range of answers. The following are some of the common answers that my students have given when this question was asked:

- Facts and statistics

- Collections of records in databases

- Information

- Facts, figures, or information that's stored in or used by a computer

- Numbers, sounds, and images

- Records and transactions

- Reports

- Things that computers operate on

All of the preceding answers are correct, as the term data in different situations could be used to refer to all of the preceding. So, next time someone says we came to XYZ conclusions after analyzing the data, you know what your first question should be, right? Yes, the next question would be to understand exactly what they mean by "data."

So, let me try and answer this question, *What is meant by data?*, with regards to this book, *Hands-On Data Preprocessing Using Python*.

From a data preprocessing perspective, we need to step back and provide a more general and all-encompassing definition. Here, we define data as symbols or signs representing a measurement or model of reality. These symbols and signs are in themselves useless until used with regard to **higher-level conventions and understandings** (HLCUs).

I like two things about the previous definition:

- First, the definition is universal and encompasses all of the kinds of data you can imagine, including the ones my students offered.

- Second, it verbalizes an implicit assumption in all the other definitions – the existence of HLCUs.

Without HLCUs, data is a pile of meaningless symbols and signs.

> **Note:**
>
> A quick note before moving forward – I am going to use "HLCU" a lot in this chapter, so maybe read its definition a few more times to commit it to memory.

Before the advent of AI, we could safely say the HLCU is almost always human language and comprehension. However, now algorithms and computers are becoming a legitimate, and in some aspects more powerful, HLCU of data.

Why this definition?

For data preprocessing, the very first thing you want to decide is the HLCU you will be using. That is, what HLCU are you preparing your data for? If the data is being prepared for human comprehension, the result will be very different than when the data is prepared for computers and algorithms. Not only that, the HLCU might be different from one algorithm to another.

One of the stark differences between human comprehension and computers as HLCUs is that humans cannot digest more than two to three dimensions at a time. Being able to process data with larger dimensions and size is the hallmark of algorithms and computers.

There is an important and distinctive relationship between the two HLCUs that needs to be understood for effective data preprocessing. Let's learn about the DIKW pyramid first, and I will use this to discuss that distinction.

DIKW pyramid

Data, Information, Knowledge, and Wisdom (**DIKW**), also known as the wisdom hierarchy or data pyramid, shows the relative importance and abundance of each of these four elements. The following figure shows transactional steps between the stages, namely processing, cognition, and judgment. Moreover, the figure specifies that only wisdom, which is the rarest and most important element, is of the future, and the three other elements, namely knowledge, information, and data, are of the past.

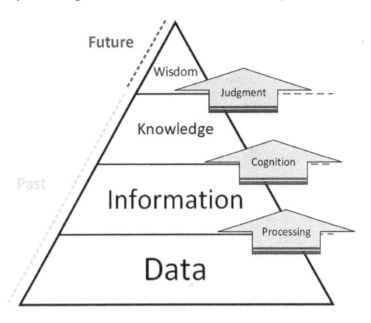

Figure 3.1 – DIKW pyramid

The definition of the four elements is presented as follows:

- **Data**: A collection of symbols – cannot answer any questions.

- **Information**: Processed data – can answer the questions *who, when, where, and what*.

- **Knowledge**: Descriptive application of *Information* – can answer the question *how*.

- **Wisdom**: Embodiment of *Knowledge* and appreciation of *why*.

While the DIKW pyramid is referenced again and again in many data analytics books and articles, you can see that the pyramid's HLCU is human language and comprehension. That is why even though the pyramid makes a lot of sense, it is still not completely applicable to data analytics.

An update to DIKW for machine learning and AI

I have updated the DIKW pyramid to **Data**, **Dataset**, **Pattern**, and **Action** (**DDPA**) as I believe it pertains better to **Machine Learning** (**ML**) and **artificial intelligence**.

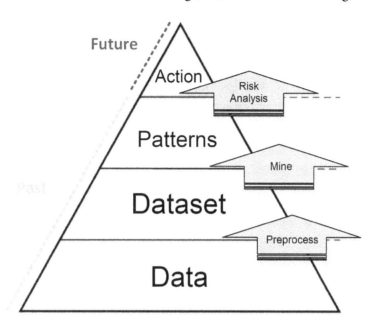

Figure 3.2 – DDPA pyramid

The definitions of all four elements of DDPA are presented as follows:

- **Data**: All possible data from across all the data resources

- **Dataset**: A relevant collection of data selected from all the available data sources, cleaned and organized for the next step

- **Patterns**: The interesting and useful trends and relationships within the dataset

- **Action**: The decision made, which is informed by the recognized patterns

Let's go through the three transactional steps between the four elements of the DDAP pyramid:

1. **Preprocess** is to select the relevant data and prepare it for the next step.

2. **Mine** is applying data mining algorithms to the data in search of patterns.

3. Lastly, **risk analysis** is the step to consider the uncertainty of the recognized patterns and arrive at a decision.

The DDPA pyramid shows the pivotal role of data preprocessing as the goal of being able to drive action from data. Preprocessing of the data is perhaps the most important step from *D* to *A* (*Data* to *Action*). Not all the data in the world will be useful for driving action in specific cases, and the data mining algorithms that are developed are not capable of finding patterns in all types of data.

An update to DIKW for data analytics

It is important to remember that data preprocessing in no way pertains only to ML and artificial intelligence. When analyzing data using data visualization, data preprocessing also has a pivotal but slightly different role.

Neither the DIWK nor the DDPA pyramid can be applied well to data analytics. As mentioned earlier, DIWK was designed for human language and comprehension, and I created DDPA for algorithms and computers, so it is better suited for machine learning and artificial intelligence. However, data analytics falls between the two ends of this spectrum, where both humans and computers are involved.

I have designed another pyramid specifically for data analytics and its unique HLCUs. As the HLCUs of data analytics are both humans and computers, the **Data**, **Dataset**, **Visualization**, and **Wisdom** (**DDVW**) pyramid is a combination of the other two pyramids.

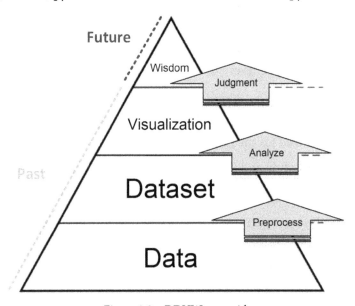

Figure 3.3 – DDVW pyramid

The definitions of all four elements of DDVW are presented as follows:

- **Data**: All possible data from across all the data resources

- **Dataset**: A relevant collection of data selected from all the available data sources and organized for the next step

- **Visualization**: The comprehensible presentation of what has been found in the dataset (similar to *Knowledge* in DIKW – descriptive application of *Information*)

- **Wisdom**: Embodiment of *Knowledge* and appreciation of *why* (the same as *Wisdom* in DIKW)

While the first transactional step of DDVW is similar to that of DDPA (both are preprocessing), the second and third are different. The second transactional step of DDVW is to *analyze*. That is what a data analyst does – use technology to do the following:

1. Explore the dataset.

2. Test the hypothesis.

3. Report the relevant findings.

The most understandable way to report the findings for the decision-maker is visualization. A decision-maker will understand the visualization and use judgment (the third transaction step of DDVW) to develop wisdom.

Data preprocessing for data analytics versus data preprocessing for machine learning

Data preprocessing is a pivotal step for both data analytics and machine learning. However, it is important to recognize the preprocessing that is done for data analytics is very different from that of machine learning.

As seen in DDPA, the only HLCU for machine learning is computers and algorithms. However, as shown in DDVW, the HLCU of data analytics is first computers and then it switches over to humans. So, in a sense, the data preprocessing that is done for machine learning is simpler, as there is only one HLCU to consider. However, when the data is preprocessed for data analytics, both HLCUs need to be considered.

Now that we have a good understanding of what we mean by data, let's switch gears and learn some important concepts surrounding data. The next concept we will discuss helps us distinguish between data analytics and machine learning even further.

The three Vs of big data

A very useful concept that helps to distinguish between machine learning and data analytics is the **three Vs of big data**. The three Vs are **volume, variety**, and **velocity**.

The general rule of thumb is that when your data has high volume, high variety, and high velocity, you want to consider machine learning and AI over data analytics. As a general rule, this could be true, but if and only if you have high volume, high variety, and high velocity *after appropriate data preprocessing*. So, data preprocessing plays a major role, and that will be explained in more detail after going over the three Vs:

- **Volume**: The number of data points that you have. You can roughly think of data points as rows in an Excel spreadsheet. So, if you have many occurrences of the phenomena or entities that you have collected, your data is of high volume. For example, if **Facebook** was interested in studying its users in the US, the volume of this data would be the number of Facebook users in the US. Pay attention – the data point in this study of Facebook is US users of the platform.

- **Variety**: The number of different sources of data you have that give you fresh new information and perspective about the data points. You can roughly think of the variety of your data as the number of columns you have in an Excel spreadsheet. Continuing the Facebook example – Facebook has information such as the name, date of birth, and email of its users. But Facebook could also add variety to this data by including behavior columns, such as the number of visits in the last week, the number of posts, and many more. The variety does not stop there for Facebook, as it also owns other services that users may be using, such as **Instagram** and **WhatsApp**. Facebook could add variety by including the behavior data of the same users from the other services.

- **Velocity**: The rate at which you are getting new data objects. For instance, the velocity of Facebook US users' data is much higher than the velocity of Facebook's employees' data. But the velocity of Facebook US users' data is much lower than Facebook's US post's data. Pay attention to what changes the velocity of data – it is how often the phenomena or the entities you are collecting happen.

The importance of the three Vs for data preprocessing

Data analytics that heavily involves human comprehension cannot accommodate data that has high volume, high variety, and high velocity. However, sometimes the high Vs are happening due to the lack of proper data preprocessing. One important element of successful data preprocessing is to include data that is relevant to the analysis. Just because you have to dig through data with high Vs to prepare a dataset, that is not enough of a reason to give up on data analytics in favor of machine learning.

Next, we will move on from pure concepts to begin talking about the data itself and the way we normally organize it.

The most universal data structure – a table

Regardless of the complexity and high Vs of your data, and even regardless of you wanting to do data visualization or machine learning, successful data preprocessing always leads to one table. At the end of successful data preprocessing, we want to create a table that is ready to be mined, analyzed, or visualized. We call this table a dataset. The following figure shows you a table with its structural elements:

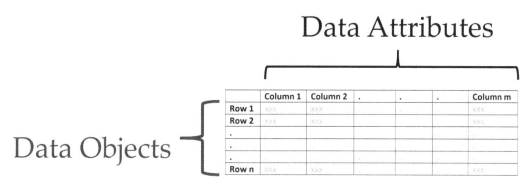

Figure 3.4 – Table data structure

As shown in the figure, for data analytics and machine learning, we use specific keywords to talk about the structure of a table: **data objects** and **data attributes**.

Data objects

I'm sure you have seen and successfully made sense of so many tables and created so many of them as well. I bet many of you would have never paid attention to the conceptual foundations of the table that allows you to create them and make sense of them. The conceptual foundation of a table is its definition of the *data object*.

Data objects are known by many different names, such as data points, rows, records, examples, samples, tuples, and many more. However, as you know for a table to make sense, you need the conceptual definition of data objects. You need to know for what phenomena, entity, or event the table is presenting values.

The definition of the data object is the entity, concept, phenomena, or event that all of the rows share. For instance, the entity that holds a table of information about customers together is the concept of the "customer." Each row of the table represents a customer and gives you more information about them.

The definition of the data object for some tables is straightforward, but not always. The very first concept you want to figure out when reading a new table is what the assumed definition of data objects for the table is. The best way you can go about this is to ask the following question: *what is the one entity that all of the columns in the table describe?* Once you have found that one entity, bingo! You have found the definition of the data object.

Emphasizing the importance of data objects

For data preprocessing, the definition of the data objects becomes more important. A lot of the time, the data analyst or machine learning engineer is the one that needs to first envision the end table that data needs to be preprocessed into. This table needs to be both realistic and useful. In the following two paragraphs I will address what I mean by realistic and useful:

- **Realistic**: The table needs to be realistic in the sense that you have the data, technology, and access to create the table. For instance, I can imagine if I had a table of data about newly married couples, with columns for the first month of their marriage such as the number of times they kissed, or the number of times they were passive-aggressive toward each other, I could build a universal model that could tell couples whether their marriage was going to be successful or not. In this case, the definition of data objects is newly married couples, and all of the imagined columns describe this entity. However, realistically coming up with such a table is very difficult. Incidentally, John Gottman from the University of Washington and James Murry from Oxford University did create this model, but only with 700 couples who were willing to be recorded while they were discussing contentious topics and were willing to share the updates on their relationship with the researchers.

- **Useful**: The imagined table also needs to be useful for analytics goals. For instance, suppose that somehow we have access to the video recordings of the first month of all of the newly married couples. These recordings are stored in separate files, organized by day. So, we set out to preprocess the data and count the number of kisses and the number of passive-aggressive incidents for each recording and store them in a table. This table's data object definition is *the video recording of one day of a newly married couple*. Is this data object definition useful for the analytics goals of predicting the success of couples? No, *the data needs to be collated differently so the data objects are the newly married couples*.

Data attributes

As shown in *Figure 3.4*, the columns of a table are known as attributes. Different names such as columns, variables, features, and dimensions might be used instead of attributes. For example, in math, you are more likely to refer to "variables" or "dimensions," whereas, in programming, you more often refer to "variables."

Attributes are describers of the data objects in a table. Each attribute describes something about all of the data objects. For instance, in the table we envisioned for the newly married couples, the number of kisses and the number of passive-aggressive incidents are the attributes of that table.

Types of data values

For successful data preprocessing, you need to know the different types of data values from two different standpoints: analytics and programming. I will review the types of data values for both standpoints and then share with you their relationships and their connections.

Analytics standpoint

There are four major types of values from analytics standpoints: **nominal**, **ordinal**, **interval-scaled**, and **ratio-scaled**. In the literature, these four types of values are under four types of data attributes. The reason is that the types of values for each attribute must remain the same, therefore, you can extrapolate value types to attribute types.

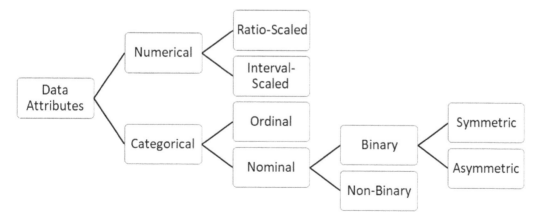

Figure 3.5 – Types of data attributes

The preceding figure shows the tree of attribute types. The four mentioned types are in the middle. As you can see in the tree, **Nominal** and **Ordinal** attributes are called **Categorical** (or **qualitative**) attributes, whereas **Interval-Scaled** and **Ratio-Scaled** attributes are called **Numerical** (or **quantitative**).

Nominal attributes

As the name suggests, this type of attribute refers to the *naming* of objects. There is no other information that this attribute describes apart from a simple set of letters and symbols that act as a name of the object or a category of the object.

A prominent example of a nominal attribute is gender when data objects are individuals. While this attribute may be shown differently, the information it contains is a simple name for two categories of humans. I have seen this information represented in many ways. The following table shows all the different ways the nominal attribute gender can be presented. Regardless of how the categories are presented, the information that is gathered by this category is that an individual is either male or female.

Male	M	0	1	1
Female	F	1	0	2

Figure 3.6 – Different presentations of the nominal attribute gender

Other examples of nominal attributes when the data objects are individuals are hair color, skin color, eye color, marital status, or occupation. What is important to remember about nominal attributes is that they do not contain any other information than just names.

Ordinal attributes

On the other hand, ordinal attributes, as the name suggests, contain more information that pertains to some types of order. For instance, when the data objects are individuals, the level of education is a prime example of an ordinal attribute. While high school, bachelor's, master's, and doctoral are names that refer to the names of education degrees, there is a well-recognized order between all of them.

No one could logically give any order to the importance, value, or recognition between the values of a nominal attribute such as gender. However, it is quite acceptable to assume the number of resources (time, money, energy) someone has spent to get a bachelor's degree is more than a high school degree.

Other examples of ordinal attributes are course letter grades (A, B, C, D), professional rankings (Assistant Professor, Associate Professor, and Full Professor), and survey rates (highly agree, agree, neutral, disagree, highly disagree).

So far, we know that ordinal attributes can contain more information than nominal attributes. At the same time, ordinal attributes are themselves limited in the sense that they do not contain how much each possible value of an ordinal attribute is different from the other. For instance, we know that *Individual A*, who has a doctorate, might be able to deal with research projects better than *Individual B*, who has a bachelor's degree. However, we cannot say Individual A will finish a research task 20 hours faster than Individual B. Simply put, ordinal attributes do not contain information that allows for interval comparison between data objects.

Interval-scaled attributes

These attributes contain more information than ordinal attributes, as they allow for interval comparison between data objects. By moving from ordinal attributes to interval attributes, we also move from symbols and categories to numbers (categorical attributes to numerical attributes). With numbers comes the capability to know how much difference exists between data objects. For instance, when data objects are individuals, height is an interval attribute. For instance, Roger Federer's height is 6'1", and everyone will agree that he is shorter than Juan Martín del Potro by 5", as del Potro's height is 6'6".

Another example of an interval attribute when the data objects are individuals is weight. The measurement of temperature in Fahrenheit or Celcius when the data objects are days is also an example of an interval-scaled attribute.

The limitation of interval attributes is that we cannot use them for a ratio-based comparison. For instance, will we ever be able to say an individual is twice as tall as the other individual? You might be thinking yes. But the answer is no. The reason is that there is no meaningful *zero* for the concept of human tallness. That is to say, there is no individual whose height is zero.

The shortest man in the world is documented to have been Chandra Bahadur Dangi and his height was 1'10". Also, Robert Wadlow, with a height of 8'3", is reported to have been the tallest man in the world. To put things into perspective, consider the following figure, where you can compare the average heights with the recorded extremes:

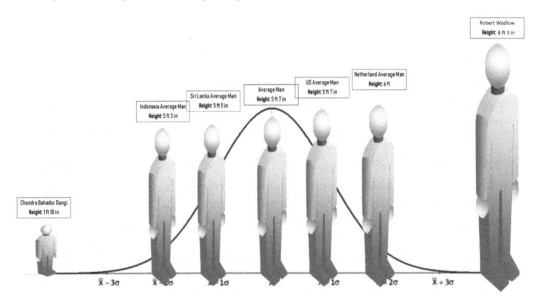

Figure 3.7 – The spectrum of men's heights

Looking at the two extremes might challenge our preconceptions about height. However, if you remove the two extremes, you will start feeling more comfortable. The reason for this discomfort is that tallness is an interval attribute for our brain. We do not come across very tall people or very short people in our daily lives. Although it will completely make sense to most people if you say you are 2 inches taller than another person, it would not make sense if you were to claim you are more than 3 times taller than the shortest man in the world.

For instance, since I am 6'3", you will believe I am 3.41 times taller than the shortest man in the world. While the mathematics of this calculation is correct ((6*12+3) / (6*1+10) = 3.41), you cannot say I am 3.41 times taller than the shortest man in the world, because the shortest man in the world is the zero in the concept of human tallness. At best, you can say I am 3.41 times taller an object than Chandra Bahadur Dangi. But to be able to do that, you had to change the definition of the data object from an individual to an object.

Even if you have a roommate that is a very short person and you see him every day, mathematically, it does not make sense to have a multiplication of tallness as there is no absolute zero. There is no individual you could ascribe the value zero to for their tallness.

Ratio-scaled attributes

When we move to ratio-scaled attributes, the last limitation, which was the incapability to multiply or divide values for interval-scaled attributes, is also removed, as we can find an inherent zero for them. For instance, when our data objects are individuals, monthly income is an example of a ratio-scaled attribute. We can imagine an individual with no monthly income. For instance, it completely makes sense if you were to report that your dad makes twice what you make every month. Another example of a ratio-scaled attribute is the temperature in kelvin when the definition of data object is a day.

Binary attributes

Binary attributes are nominal attributes with only two possibilities. For instance, the gender you are assigned at birth is either male or female, so **Sex Assigned At Birth** (**SAAB**) is a binary attribute.

There are two types of binary attributes: **symmetric** and **asymmetric**. Symmetric binary attributes, such as SAAB, are where either of the two possibilities happens as frequently and carries the same level of importance for our analysis.

However, one of the two possibilities of asymmetric binary attributes happens less frequently and is normally more important. For instance, the result of a COVID test is an asymmetric binary attribute, where the positive results happen less often but are more important in our analysis.

You might think that symmetric binary attributes are more common than asymmetric binary attributes, however, that is far from the reality. Try to think of other symmetric binary attributes, and email them to me if you find a few good ones.

Conventionally, the rarer possibility of a binary attribute is denoted by a positive (or one), whereas the more common possibility is denoted by a negative (or zero).

Understanding the importance of attribute types

As analytic methods become more complex, it will become easier to make mistakes and never know about them. For instance, you might inadvertently input an integer-coded nominal attribute into an algorithm that regards these values as real numbers. What you have done is to input randomly assumed relationships between the data objects that have no basis in reality to a model that cannot think for itself. See *Exercise 5* for an example of this.

Programming standpoint

By and large, values are either known as numbers, strings, or Booleans for computers. Numbers might be recognized as integers or floating points, but that is it.

Integers are whole numbers from zero to infinity. For instance, 0, 1, 2, 3, and so on are all integer values. Floating points are numbers. They can be positive or negative and have decimal points. For instance, 1.54, -25.1243, and 0.1 are all floating points.

I hope you see the challenge here – from an analytics perspective, you may have nominal or ordinal attributes but computers can only show them as strings. Similarly, from an analytics perspective, you may have ratio-scaled or interval-scaled attributes but computers can only show them as numbers. The only complete match between programming value types and analytics value types is binary attributes that can be presented completely with Boolean values.

The following table presents a mapping of attribute (value) types between analytics and programming perspectives. As you are developing skills to effectively preprocess data, this mapping should become second nature to you. For instance, you want to understand your options of presenting an ordinal attribute with Booleans, strings, or integers, and what each option would entail (see *exercise 6* in the *Exercise* section).

Analytic Perspective		Programming Perspective
Nominal attributes	Binary	Booleans or strings
	Non-binary	
Ordinal attributes		Integers
Interval-scaled attributes		Integers or floating points
Ration-scaled attributes		

Figure 3.8 – Mapping of value types between analytics and programming

So far in this chapter, we covered the definition of data and also the types of data attributes. Now, we are going to talk about two high-level and important concepts that are essential for successful data preprocessing: information and pattern.

Information versus pattern

Before finishing this chapter, which aims to arm you with all the necessary definitions and concepts needed for data preprocessing, we need to cover two more concepts: *information* and *pattern*.

Understanding everyday use of the word "information"

First, I need to bring your attention to two specific and yet very different functions of the term *information*. The first one is the everyday use of "information," which means "facts or details about somebody or something." This is how the Oxford English Dictionary defines information. However, while statisticians also employ this function of the word, sometimes the term information serves another purpose.

Statistical use of the word "information"

The term "*information*" could also refer to the value variation of one attribute across the population of a data object. In other words, information is used to refer to what an attribute adds to space knowledge of a population of data objects. Let's explore an example dataset, `customer_df`, as shown in the following screenshot. The dataset is pretty small and has 10 data objects and 4 attributes. The definition of the data object for the following dataset is *customers*.

```
In [1]:   ▶  import pandas as pd
             customer_df = pd.read_excel('Customers Dataset.xlsx')
             customer_df
```

Out[1]:

	Customer Name	Store	Last week number of visits	Last week Purchase $
0	Abu Irvine	Starbuck - Claremont Village	5	33.43
1	Colleen Melendez	Starbuck - Claremont Village	4	11.32
2	Lyla-Rose Ruiz	Starbuck - Claremont Village	1	9.48
3	Riley-Jay Manning	Starbuck - Claremont Village	2	15.50
4	Ieuan Carroll	Starbuck - Claremont Village	4	17.96
5	Renesmae Lawson	Starbuck - Claremont Village	5	19.84
6	Lawrence Medina	Starbuck - Claremont Village	3	23.21
7	Ben O'Connor	Starbuck - Claremont Village	1	6.12
8	Adnaan Kim	Starbuck - Claremont Village	6	36.16
9	Abbigail Dunlap	Starbuck - Claremont Village	2	6.88

Figure 3.9 – Reading Customer Dataset.xlsx and seeing its records

We will talk about this dataset as we go over the following subsections.

Statistical information for categorical attributes

`Customer Name` is a nominal attribute, and the value variation this attribute adds to the space knowledge of this dataset is the maximum possible for a nominal attribute. Each data object has a completely different value under this attribute. Statistically speaking, the amount of information this attribute has is very high.

The case of the attribute store is the opposite. This attribute adds the minimal possible information a nominal attribute may add – that is, the value for every data object under this attribute is the same. When this happens, you should remove the attribute and see whether you can perhaps update the definition of the data objects. If we change the definition of the data objects to `Starbucks customers of Claremont Village store`, we have retained the information and we can safely remove the attribute.

Statistical information for numerical attributes

The matter of statistical information for numerical attributes is a little bit different. For numerical attributes, you can calculate a metric called *variance* to drive how much information each numerical attribute has. Variance is a statistical metric that captures the spread between a collection of numbers. It is calculated by the summation of the squared distances of each number from the mean of all the numbers. The higher the variance of an attribute, the more information the attribute has. For instance, the variance for the `Last week number of visits` attribute is 3.12, and the variance for the `Last week Purchase $` attribute is $109.63. Calculating the variance using **Pandas** is very easy. See the following screenshot:

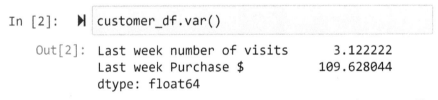

Figure 3.10 – Calculating the variance for the numerical attributes of customer_df

We would be able to say the `Last week Purchase $` attribute has more information than the `Last week number of visits` attribute if the attributes had a similar range. However, the attributes have a completely different range of values, and it makes the two variance values incomparable. There is a way to get around this issue – we can normalize both the attributes and then calculate their variance. **Normalization** is a concept that we will cover later in this book.

Data redundancy – attributes presenting similar information

We call an attribute redundant if the variation of its value across the data objects of a dataset is too similar to that of another attribute. To check data redundancy, you can draw a scatterplot for the variables you suspect are presenting similar information. For instance, the following screenshot has drawn the scatterplot of the two numerical attributes of customer_df:

```
In [3]:  ▶  import matplotlib.pyplot as plt
            customer_df.plot.scatter(x='Last week number of visits',
                                     y='Last week Purchase $')
            plt.show()
```

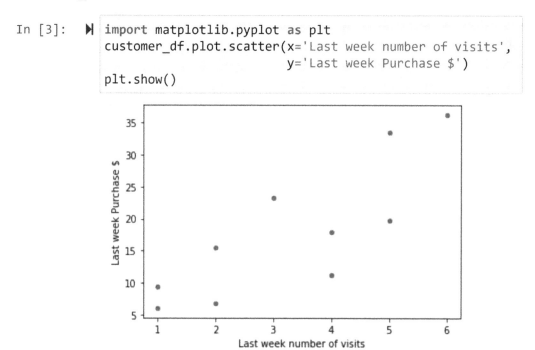

Figure 3.11 – Drawing the scatterplots for the two attributes, Last week number of visits and Last week Purchase $

You can see that it seems that with the increase in the number of visits, the purchase has also increased.

Correlation coefficient to investigate data redundancy

You can also use the correlation coefficient to investigate data redundancy. A **correlation coefficient** value falls between -1 and 1. When the value is close to zero, it means the two attributes are not showing similar information. When the correlation coefficient between two numerical attributes is closer to both ends of the spectrum (-1 or +1), it shows that the two attributes are showing similar statistical information and perhaps one of them is redundant. When two attributes have a significant and positive correlation coefficient (greater than 0.7), that means if the value of one attribute increases the value of the other attribute will also increase. On the other hand, when two attributes have a significant and negative correlation coefficient (smaller than -0.7), that means the increase of one attribute leads to the decrease of the other.

The following screenshot has used .corr() to calculate the correlation coefficient between the numerical attributes in customer_df:

```
In [4]:    ▶ customer_df.corr()

    Out[4]:
```

	Last week number of visits	Last week Purchase $
Last week number of visits	1.000000	0.821282
Last week Purchase $	0.821282	1.000000

Figure 3.12 – Finding the correlation coefficients for the pairs of numerical attributes in customer_df

The correlation coefficient is 0.82, which is considered high, indicating one of the two numerical attributes might be redundant. The cut-off rule of thumb for high correlation is 0.7 – that is, if the correlation coefficient is higher than 0.7 or lower than -0.7, there might be a case of data redundancy.

Now that we have a good understanding of the term *information*, let's turn our attention to the term *pattern*.

Statistical meaning of the word "pattern"

While the statistical meaning of "information" is the value variation of *one* attribute across the data objects of a dataset, the statistical meaning of "*pattern*" is about the value variation of *more than one* attribute across the data objects. Every specific value variation of more than one attribute across the data objects of a dataset is called a *pattern*.

It is important to understand that most patterns are neither useful nor interesting. It is the job of a data analyst to find interesting and useful patterns from the data and present them. Also, it is the job of an ML engineer to streamline a model that collects the expected and useful patterns from the data and makes calculated decisions based on the collected patterns.

Example of finding and employing a pattern

The relationship we found between the two numerical attributes of `customer_df` in the following situation could be considered as useful.

The manager of the Starbucks store in Claremont Village made a huge blunder and accidentally removed the values of `Last week Purchase $` for 10 customers from the records, but luckily she knows about the power of data analytics, and the `Last week number of visits` attribute is intact. The following screenshot shows the second part of this data:

```
In [5]:   ▶  customer2_df = pd.read_excel('Customers Dataset 2.xlsx')
              customer2_df
```

Out[5]:

	Customer Name	Store	Last week number of visits	Last week Purchase $
0	Nelson Rivera	Starbuck - Claremont Village	3	NaN
1	Abbigail Felix	Starbuck - Claremont Village	1	NaN
2	Kelly North	Starbuck - Claremont Village	2	NaN
3	Aneesa Moran	Starbuck - Claremont Village	5	NaN
4	Ammara Ritter	Starbuck - Claremont Village	7	NaN
5	Elise Valenzuela	Starbuck - Claremont Village	1	NaN
6	Jaidan Gay	Starbuck - Claremont Village	4	NaN
7	Alejandro Mercer	Starbuck - Claremont Village	3	NaN
8	Arisha Whittaker	Starbuck - Claremont Village	5	NaN
9	Mehmet Power	Starbuck - Claremont Village	2	NaN

Figure 3.13 – Reading Customer Dataset 2.xlsx and seeing its records

The manager of the store, after having seen the high correlation between `Last week number of visits` and `Last week Purchase $`, can use simple linear regression to extract, formulate, and package the pattern from the 10 customers with all of the data. After the regression model is *trained*, the manager can use it to estimate the purchase $ for the customers that have missing values.

Simple linear regression is a statistical method where the values of one numerical attribute (X) are linked to the values of another numerical attribute (Y). In statistical terms, when we observe a close relationship between two numerical attributes, we may investigate to see whether X can predict Y.

The following screenshot illustrates the application of .regplot() from the **Seaborn** module to visualize the linear regression line that has fitted to the data of the first 10 customers in customer_df:

```
In [6]:   ▶  import seaborn as sns
             sns.regplot(x='Last week number of visits',
                         y='Last week Purchase $',data=customer_df)
             plt.show()
```

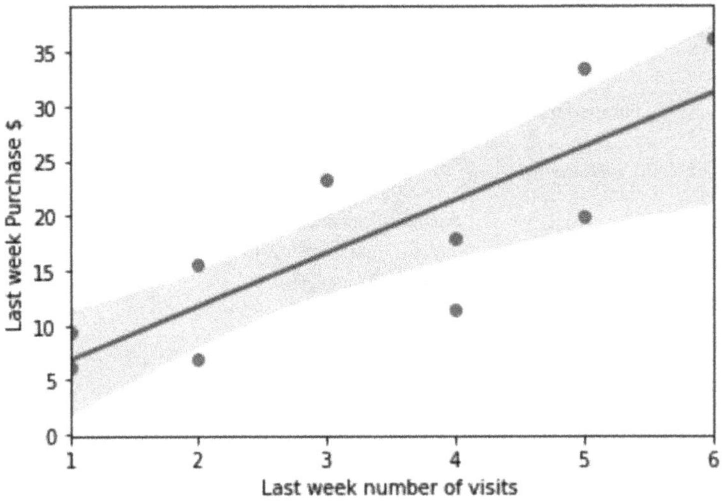

Figure 3.14 – Using .regplot() to show the regression line between the two attributes, Last week number of visits and Last week Purchase $

Installation of the Seaborn module

If you have never used the Seaborn module, you have to install it first.
Installing it on **Anaconda** is very simple. Open a chunk of code in your **Jupyter notebook** and run the following line of code:

```
conda install seaborn
```

The equation of the fitted regression model is shown as follows:

$$Last\ Week\ Purchase\ \$ = 1.930 + 4.867 \times Last\ Week\ number\ of\ visits$$

Now, this equation allows us to estimate the missing values of customer2_df. The following screenshot shows the preceding equation is applied to customer2_df to calculate the missing values:

```
In [7]:   ▶  customer2_df['Last week Purchase $'] = customer2_df[
              'Last week number of visits'].apply(lambda v:1.930 + 4.867 *v)
          customer2_df
```

Out[7]:

	Customer Name	Store	Last week number of visits	Last week Purchase $
0	Nelson Rivera	Starbuck - Claremont Village	3	16.531
1	Abbigail Felix	Starbuck - Claremont Village	1	6.797
2	Kelly North	Starbuck - Claremont Village	2	11.664
3	Aneesa Moran	Starbuck - Claremont Village	5	26.265
4	Ammara Ritter	Starbuck - Claremont Village	7	35.999
5	Elise Valenzuela	Starbuck - Claremont Village	1	6.797
6	Jaidan Gay	Starbuck - Claremont Village	4	21.398
7	Alejandro Mercer	Starbuck - Claremont Village	3	16.531
8	Arisha Whittaker	Starbuck - Claremont Village	5	26.265
9	Mehmet Power	Starbuck - Claremont Village	2	11.664

Figure 3.15 – Using the extracted pattern (regression equation) and .apply() function to estimate and replace the missing values

So, this way the manager of the Starbucks store in Claremont Village was able to save the day and replace the missing values with estimated values that are based on a reliable pattern found in the data.

Before moving on, let me acknowledge that we have not yet covered *linear regression* in this book (we will do this in *Chapter 6, Prediction*). However, in this example, we used linear regression to showcase an instance of extracting and using the pattern in a dataset for an analytic situation. We did this in the interest of understanding what we mean by "useful patterns," and extracting and packaging patterns for later use.

Summary

Congratulations on finishing this chapter. You have now equipped yourself with an essential understanding of data, data types, information, and pattern. Your understanding of these concepts will be vital in your journey to successful data preprocessing.

In the next chapter, you will learn about the important roles databases play for data analytics and data preprocessing. However, before moving on to the next chapter, take some time and solidify and improve your learning using the following exercises.

Exercises

1. Ask five colleagues or classmates to provide a definition for the term data.

    a) Record these definitions and notice the similarities among them.

    b) In your own words, define the all-encompassing definition of data put forth in this chapter.

    c) Indicate the two important aspects of the definition in *b)*.

    d) Compare the five definitions of data from your colleagues with the all-encompassing definitions and indicate their similarities and differences.

2. In this exercise, we are going to use `covid_impact_on_airport_traffic.csv`. Answer the following questions. This dataset is from **Kaggle.com** – use this link to see its page:

    `https://www.kaggle.com/terenceshin/covid19s-impact-on-airport-traffic`

    The key attribute of this dataset is `PercentOfBaseline`, which shows the ratio of air traffic in a specific day compared to a pre-pandemic time range (February 1 to March 15, 2020).

    a) What is the best definition of the data object for this dataset?

    b) Are there any attributes in the data that only have one value? Use the `.unique()` function to check. If there are, remove them from the data and update the definition of the data object.

    c) What type of values do the remaining attributes carry?

    d) How much statistical information does the `PercentOfBaseline` attribute have?

3. For this exercise, we are going to use US_Accidents.csv. Answer the following questions. This dataset is from Kaggle.com – use this link to see its page:

    https://www.kaggle.com/sobhanmoosavi/us-accidents

    This dataset shows all the car accidents in the US from February 2016 to December 2020.

    a) What is the best definition of the data object for this dataset?

    b) Are there any attributes in the data that only have one value? Use the .unique() function to check. If there are, remove them from the data and update the definition of the data object.

    c) What type of values do the remaining attributes carry?

    d) How much statistical information do the numerical attributes of the dataset carry?

    e) Compare the statistical information of the numerical attributes and see whether any of them are a candidate for data redundancy.

4. For this exercise, we are going to use fatal-police-shootings-data.csv. There are a lot of debates, discussions, dialogues, and protests happening in the US surrounding police killings. The Washington Post has been collecting data on all fatal police shootings in the US. The dataset available to the government and the public alike has date, age, gender, race, location, and other pieces of situational information related to these fatal police shootings. You can download the last version of the data from https://github.com/washingtonpost/data-police-shootings.

    a) What is the best definition of the data object for this dataset?

    b) Are there any attributes in the data that only have one value? Use the .unique() function to check. If there are, remove them from the data and update the definition of the data object.

    c) What type of values do the remaining attributes carry?

    d) How much statistical information do the numerical attributes of the dataset carry?

    e) Compare the statistical information of the numerical attributes and see whether any of them are a candidate for data redundancy.

5. For this exercise, we will be using `electricity_prediction.csv`. The following screenshot shows the five rows of this dataset and a linear regression model created to predict electricity consumption based on the weekday and daily average temperature:

```
In [1]: import pandas as pd

        electricity_df = pd.read_csv('electricity_prediction.csv')
        electricity_df.head()
```

Out[1]:

	Date	Weekday	Consumption	Average Temperature
0	1/1/2016	4	2581914	80
1	1/2/2016	5	2663011	77
2	1/3/2016	6	2725351	78
3	1/4/2016	0	3092978	80
4	1/5/2016	1	3231827	81

```
In [2]: from sklearn.linear_model import LinearRegression

        X = electricity_df[['Weekday', 'Average Temperature']]
        y = electricity_df['Consumption']

        lrm = LinearRegression()
        lrm.fit(X, y)

        print('intercept ', lrm.intercept_)
        print(pd.DataFrame({'Predictor': X.columns, 'coefficient': lrm.coef_}))
```

```
intercept  3074181.4950158806
                  Predictor    coefficient
0                   Weekday  -55710.145405
1       Average Temperature   -3476.377056
```

Figure 3.16 – Screenshot for Exercise 5

a) The regression model that is derived from the data is presented as follows:

$$Consumption = 3074181.5 - 55710.1 \times Weekday - 3476.4 \times Average\ Temperature$$

b) What is the fundamental mistake in this analysis? Describe it and provide possible solutions for it.

6. For this exercise, we will be using `adult.csv`. We used this dataset extensively in *Chapter 1, Review of the Core Modules NumPy and Pandas* and *Chapter 2, Review of Another Core Module – Matplotlib*. Read the dataset using **Pandas** and call it `adult_df`.

    a) What type of values does the `education` attribute carry?

    b) Run `adult_df.education.unique()`, study the results, and explain what the code does.

    c) Based on your understanding, order the output of the code you ran for *b)*.

    d) Run `pd.get_dummies(adult_df.education)`, study the results, and explain what the code does.

    e) Run `adult_df.sort_values(['education-num'])`. `iloc[1:32561:1200]`, study the results, and explain what the code does.

    f) Compare your answer to *c)* and what you learned from *e)*. Was the order you came up with in *c)* correct?

    g) The `education` attribute is an ordinal attribute – translating an ordinal attribute from an analytic perspective to a programming perspective involves choosing between Boolean representation, string representation, and integer representation. Choose which choice has been made for the three following representations of the `education` attribute:

    `adult_df.education`

    `pd.get_dummies(adult_df.education)`

    `adult_df['education']`

    h) Each choice has some advantages and some disadvantages. Select which programing data representation each following statement describes:

    If an ordinal attribute is presented using this programming value representation, no bias or assumptions are added to the data, but algorithms that work with numbers cannot use the attribute.

    If an ordinal attribute is presented using this programming value representation, the data can be used by algorithms that only take numbers, but the size of the data becomes bigger and there may be concerns for computational costs.

    If an ordinal attribute is presented using this programming value representation, there will be no size or computational concerns, but some statistical information that may not be true is assumed and it may create bias.

References

John M. Gottman, James D. Murray, Catherine C. Swanson, Rebecca Tyson, and Kristin R. Swanson. *The Mathematics of Marriage: Dynamic Nonlinear Models*. MIT Press, 2005.

4

Databases

Databases play a major technological role in data preprocessing and data analytics. However, time and again, I have seen plenty of misunderstandings surrounding their role in analytics. While it is possible to do simple analytics and data preprocessing using databases themselves, these tasks are not what databases are designed for. In contrast, databases are technological solutions to record and retrieve data effectively and efficiently.

In this chapter, we will first discuss the technological role of databases in effective analytics and preprocessing. We will then enumerate and understand the different types of databases. Finally, we will cover five different methods of connecting to, and pulling data from, databases.

The following topics will be covered in this chapter:

- What is a database?
- Types of databases
- Connecting to, and pulling data from, databases

Technical requirements

You will be able to find all of the code and the dataset that is used in this book in a GitHub repository exclusively created for this book. To find the repository, click on this link, `https://github.com/PacktPublishing/Hands-On-Data-Preprocessing-in-Python`, find *chapter 04* in this repository, and download the code and the data for better learning.

What is a database?

There may be a handful of different definitions of a database, all of which might be correct, but there is one definition that best serves the purpose of data analytics. A **database** is a technological solution to store and retrieve data both effectively and efficiently.

While it is true that databases are the technological foundations of data analytics, effective analytics do not happen inside them and that is a great thing. We want databases to be good at what they are meant to do: the effective and efficient storage and retrieval of data. We want a database to be fast, accurate, and secure. We also want a database to be able to serve our needs as regards quick sharing and synching.

When we want to get some data from databases for analytics purposes, it is easy to forget that databases are not designed to serve our analytics purposes. So, it should not be a surprise that the data in the database is organized in a way that serves its functions – the effective and efficient storage and retrieval of data – rather than being organized for our analytics purposes.

One of the very first steps of data analytics is to locate and collect data from various databases and sources, and reorganize it into a dataset that has the potential to answer questions about our decision-making environment. The following diagram illustrates this important step of data analytics:

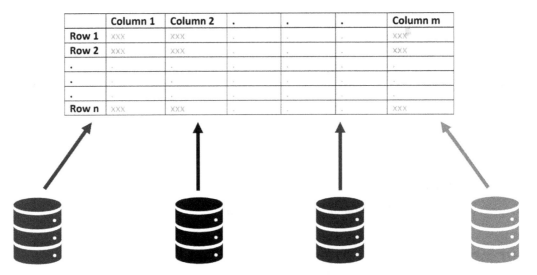

Figure 4.1 – From databases to a dataset

At times, the data might be coming from one database but, all the same, the data needs to be reorganized into a dataset that is designed for our analytics needs. When we are reorganizing the data into a dataset, we need to pay close attention to the dataset's definition of the data objects. We define the data object of a dataset so that the dataset serves the needs of our analytics.

Understanding the difference between a database and a dataset

A database and dataset are not the same concepts, but are often and incorrectly used interchangeably. We did define a database as a technological solution for storing and retrieving data both effectively and efficiently. However, a **dataset** is a specific organization and presentation of some data for a specific reason.

For data analytics, while the data comes from databases, it is eventually reorganized into a dataset. The "*specific reason*" for such a dataset is the analytics goals and the "*specific organization and presentation*" of that dataset is to support those goals.

For instance, we want to use weather data such as temperature, humidity, and wind speed to predict the hourly electricity consumption of the city of Redlands. For such analytics, we need a dataset whose definition of the data object is an hour in the city of Redlands. The attributes will be average temperature, average humidity, average wind speed, and electricity consumption. Pay attention that all of these attributes describe the data object – an hour in the city of Redlands. That is the design of the dataset that supports the analytical goal of predicting hourly electricity consumption in the city of Redlands based on weather data.

In the city of Redlands, the weather data and electricity data come from different databases. The weather data comes from 5 databases that collect data from 5 locations across the city, and each database records the weather data of its surroundings every 15 minutes. The electricity data comes from the city's only electricity supplier and its database records the amount of electricity consumption in the city every 5 minutes.

The data in these six databases needs to be collated and reorganized into the described dataset so that the prediction of hourly electricity consumption based on weather is possible.

Types of databases

Mainly there are four types of databases:

- **Relational databases** (or SQL databases)

- **Unstructured databases** (NoSQL)

- **Distributed databases**

- **Blockchain**

The distinctions between these databases are not cut and dried technologically and in practice. For instance, distributed databases are essentially a combination of different types of databases in multiple locations. Here, we will discuss these types of databases to develop a better appreciation for the way databases organize data according to a situation's needs. We will also briefly talk about the differences and similarities, as well as the advantages and disadvantages, of the types of databases.

Why do we need to know the types of databases for data preprocessing?

Each of the four types of databases organizes and stores the data differently. As our data analytics journey always involves locating and collecting data from various databases, knowing different kinds of databases serves two important purposes.

First, by knowing what is possible, we may be able to envision what could be out there when we look for data.

Second, and more importantly, as we want to reorganize the relevant data into our designed dataset, we need to understand the organization and structure of its source first.

The differentiating elements of databases

Before discussing the four types of databases, let's first talk about what are the elements that may require using various kinds of databases. These elements are the level of structure, storage location, and authority.

Level of data structure

Data with no structure is a pile of signs and symbols with no use or meaning. So do not let the term "unstructured databases" fool you since every piece of usable data needs at least some structure. The more data is structured, the less processing it will need when using it. However, structuring data is expensive and not always sensible.

When data is structured, not only does it potentially take up more space, but it also needs resources to preprocess and handle data before it is recorded. On the other hand, when the data is sufficiently structured on one occasion, it can then be used again and again. So, the way to determine how much structure data needs is to factor in the costs and benefits of structuring.

For example, while the benefits of structuring the basic customer data that is the core asset of many businesses easily outweigh its costs, in many cases, the costs of structuring customer emails, voice, and social media data may seem too overwhelming for small and medium organizations.

The following diagram shows the interaction between costs and benefits of structuring data. As the data is more structured, naturally, the cost of structuring it goes up. But in return, the cost of having to deal daily with unstructured data goes down until the benefits of structuring the data plateau. By considering the costs and benefits, we can find the appropriate level of data structure.

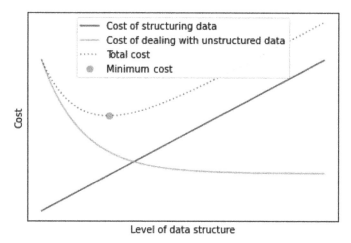

Figure 4.2 – Interaction between costs and benefits of structuring data – a general case

The best level of structuring data will vary from situation to situation and also from data to data. For instance, some data, such as video, sound, and social media data, may need specific preprocessing every time it is used for different purposes. That means every time it is used, it needs to go through data restructuring in any case, so structuring the data will not bestow any benefit and it does not make economical sense. Furthermore, these types of data tend to be large, and only a unique segment of them are needed to be structured from time to time without us not knowing which segment in advance. In such cases, structuring the whole data in advance does not make economical sense as we do not know what segment of the data we will need to be structured in the future. The following diagram shows this specific situation:

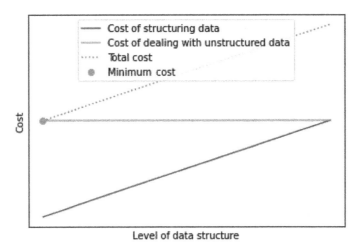

Figure 4.3 – Interaction between costs and benefits of structuring data – a specific situation

Storage location

The geographical location that the databases are located in is also important for a variety of reasons, including data security, data availability, data accessibility, and, of course, operation costs.

Authority

There are two key questions under authority that are very important to consider when choosing what type of database is appropriate:

1. Who does that data belong to?
2. Who should have the authority to update it?

Relational databases (SQL databases)

Relational databases, or **structured databases**, are an ecosystem of data collection and management in which both the collected data and the incoming data must conform with a pre-defined set of relationships between the data. For relational databases, if incoming data is not expected in a relational database, the data cannot be stored. Until the database ecosystem is updated in such ways, those types of incoming data are expected in the new ecosystem.

Some types of data are so different that updating the ecosystem of the database so that they are expected will only impede the database's goals. Furthermore, for some types of data, we may not be certain if we want to invest in them enough to change the ecosystem for them. This is often the case for video, voice, text, and social media data that tends to have a large size. For these types of data, we give up on changing the relational databases to accommodate them and store them in types of databases that do not require as much structuring.

Unstructured databases (NoSQL databases)

NoSQL, or **unstructured databases**, are precisely the solution for the problem of wanting to store data that we are unable to structure, or are ambivalent to do so. Furthermore, unstructured databases can be used as an interim house for data we do not have the resources to structure just now.

The term "unstructured databases" is not literal of course. Fully unstructured data is a pile of signs and symbols with no values. The term "unstructured databases" comes up against relational databases to create a distinction. The following example demonstrates a practical distinction between structured and unstructured data and their different applications for a law firm.

A practical example that requires a combination of both structured and unstructured databases

Seif and Associates law firm has been active in the area of civil and criminal law since 1956. Back in the day, the firm kept a paper copy of every legal document, every memo, every appeal, every invoice, and so on. In 1998, the firm went through a major IT overhaul and created a relational database that keeps track of all of the legal and business activities. The relational database that supports the firm is highly structured and allows the firm four different types of reports, that only such a highly structured database would allow. For instance, the database could report the monthly assigned legal tasks of every paralegal.

All of the documents that are sent out to the courts and the invoices that are sent to customers are not data objects in the database, but are produced on demand from the database. For instance, an invoice is produced every time by checking the invoice number in the database reading the items and prices associated with the invoice. Once all this data is found in the database, a piece of software puts them together and prints out an invoice every time.

As the major IT overhaul in 1998 was a significant undertaking by itself, the firm never had the chance to digitalize the paper copies from 1956 to 1998. However, 1 year ago, the firm decided to unburden itself from having to carry all those physical copies. Now, the firm keeps a scanned version of these documents on an unstructured database. Even though the data is all in the unstructured database, detailed reports from this database are not possible.

An AI company has recently approached the firm and suggested that they have the technology to go through the digital copies of the documents from 1956 to 1998 and include them in the structured database. The firm concluded that the cost of structuring that data (the AI company's price quote) does not meet or exceed the possible benefits of structuring it. Therefore, the firm decided that an unstructured database for those records will suffice as they are only recorded for legal purposes and if any of those documents are needed, the unstructured database has enough indexing, so the documents are found in 5 to 10 minutes.

Distributed databases

When we think of structured or unstructured databases, we normally assume that each database is located physically at one site or one computer. However, this can easily be an incorrect assumption. There are many reasons for having multiple locations/sites/computers for a database, such as higher data availability, lower operational costs, and superior data safety. Simply put, a distributed database is a collection of databases (structured, unstructured, or a combination of the two) whose data is physically stored in multiple locations. To the end user, however, it feels like just one database.

The foundation of cloud computing is distributed databases. For instance, Amazon Web Services (AWS) is a masterfully connected web of distributed databases across the world that offers database space with high availability and safety and bills its customers based on their actual usage.

Blockchain

We normally assume that a database is owned by one person or one organization. While this is a correct assumption in many cases, Blockchain is the solution when central ownership and authority are not advantageous.

For instance, this is one of the many reasons that Bitcoin has become a competitive option for digital money. While banks' central authority of the databases provides some assurances for data safety, the banks will also have the technological authority to cut customers off from their money if they deem this necessary. However, Blockchain is a database alternative that does not have a central authority while providing data safety.

The downside of Blockchain is that all of its data is stored in blocks and each block can only hold a small amount of information. Furthermore, the complex and detailed reports that are easily produced by relational databases cannot be created by Blockchain.

So far, we have covered some important topics:

- What are databases?

- Different types of databases

- Why we need various types of databases

Now, we turn our attention to how we can create and connect to databases and get the data we want.

Connecting to, and pulling data from, databases

For data analytics and data preprocessing, we need to have the skillset to connect to databases and pull the data we want from them. There are a few ways you can go about this. In this section, we will cover these ways, share their advantages and disadvantages, and, with the help of examples, we will see how this is done.

We will cover five methods of connecting to a database: **direct connection**, **web page connection**, **API connection**, **request connection**, and **publicly shared**.

Direct connection

When you are allowed access to a database directly, it means you can pull any data you want from the database. This is a great method of pulling data from databases, but there are two major disadvantages. First, you are rarely given direct access to databases unless you are completely trusted by the owner of the database. Second, you need to have the skillset to interact with a database to pull the data from it. The script you need to know for connecting to relational databases is called **Structured Query Language (SQL)**. In SQL, every time you want to pull data from a database, you write a query using the SQL language. A great resource for learning SQL is available for free at W3Schools.com: https://www.w3schools.com/sql/.

> **Advice to beginners about learning SQL**
>
> If you are not familiar with SQL, make certain to at least know the following concepts: SQL table, primary keys, and foreign key, and the following operators: SELECT, DISTINCT, WHERE, AND, OR, ORDER BY, LIKE, JOIN, GROUP BY, COUNT(), MIN(), MAX(), AVE(), SUM(), HAVING, and CASE. https://www.w3schools.com/sql/ can help you learn the topics mentioned.

When you have written a correct query, you need to somehow send it to the database and be able to get back the results, and for that, you need a connection to the database. There is no one way to create a connection to the database. There is software with an interactive **User Interface** (UI) that can do that for you. Examples of such software are Microsoft Access, **SQL Server Management Studio** (**SSMS**), and SQLite.

The good news is that we can also create a connection to a database using the Python module `sqlite3`. We will be using the Chinook sample database to practice connecting to databases using Python and the module `sqlite3`. The following diagram shows the Chinook database using the **Unified Modeling Language** (**UML**). This sample database has 11 tables that are connected to one another by their primary keys to create a database that is designed to support a small/medium-sized business that sells music tracks. The UML of a database helps to understand the connections between tables and to design queries to pull data from a database.

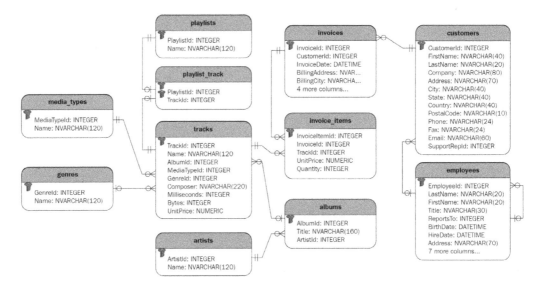

Figure 4.4 – UML of the Chinook database (source: sqlitetutorial.net)

The following screenshot shows the combined use of `pandas` and `sqlite3` modules to create a connection to a database and read the data from the database into a pandas DataFrame. The code employs the function `pd.read_sql_query()` for this purpose. This function requires two inputs: a query in the form of a string and a connection. The code uses the `sqlite3.connect()` function to create a connection, and then passes `Connection` and `query_txt` into `pd.read_sql_query()` to have the requested data in a DataFrame.

```
In [1]:  ▶  import sqlite3
            import pandas as pd


In [2]:  ▶  Connection = sqlite3.connect('chinook.db')
            query_txt = "SELECT * FROM customers;"

            df_customers = pd.read_sql_query(query_txt,Connection)
```

Figure 4.5 – Creating a connection to chinook.db using the sqlite3 module

So far, we have covered one of the five methods of connecting to databases: direct connection. Next, we will look at the four remaining methods: web page connection, API connection, request connection, and publicly shared.

Web page connection

Sometimes, the owner of the database only wishes to give you controlled access to their database. As these types of access are controlled, data sharing happens on the owner's terms. For instance, the owner might wish to give you access to a certain part of their database. Furthermore, the owner might not wish you to be able to pull all the data you need at once, but in timed portions.

A web page connection is one of the methods that database owners can use when offering controlled access to their database. A great example of a web page connection can be seen and interacted with at `londonair.org.uk/london/asp/datadownload.asp`. After you open this page, you can either pick a specific location or a specific measurement. Regardless of your choice, the page takes you to another page and takes more input from you before showing you a graph and providing you with a CSV dataset. Go to this web page and try different inputs and download some datasets before reading on.

API connection

The second method for giving out controlled access to databases is providing an API connection. However, unlike the web page connection method, where a web page would navigate and respond to your request, with API connections, a web server handles your data requests. A great example of data sharing through an API connection is data of the stock market. Different web services provide free and or subscription-based APIs for users to get access to live stock market data.

An example of connecting and pulling data using an API

The Finnhub Stock API (finnhub.io) is a great example of such a web service. Finnhub provides both free and subscription-based access to its databases. You can access and use their basic stock market data, such as daily, hourly, and minute by minute, of US stock prices. With their free version access, you can request their basic data, such as stock prices and you may send up to 60 requests per minute. If you need to process more than 60 requests per minute, or you want data that is not included in the free access, you will have to subscribe.

The Finnhub free version is enough for us to practice accessing data through APIs. First, on the first page of finnhub.io, click on *Get a Free API Key* and get yourself an API key. Second, type the following code into your Jupyter notebook and change API_Key from the arbitrary 'abcdefghijklmnopq' to the free API key you got from finnhub.io. If you have done every step correctly, you will get *<Response [200]>* printed out, which means everything went well. Via this code, you connected to the Finnhub web server and collected some data:

```
import requests
stk_ticker = 'AMZN'
data_resolution = 'W'
timestamp_from = 1577865600
timestamp_to = 1609315200
API_Key = 'abcdefghijklmnopq'
Address_template = 'https://finnhub.io/api/v1/stock/
candle?symbol={}&resolution={}&from={}&to={}&token={}'
API_address = Address_template.format(stk_ticker, data_
resolution, timestamp_from, timestamp_to, API_Key)
r = requests.get(API_address)
print(r)
```

Now, let's dissect this code together. Every API request needs to be expressed in a web address. This is universally true; the way you should translate your request into a web address might be somewhat different for different web servers, but they are very similar. If you have already run the proceeding code, when you execute print(API_address), as realized in the following screenshot, you will see the web address that claims to have the API key of abcdefghijklmnopq and requests the weekly Amazon stock price from January 1 to December 30, 2020. Study the web address and find out each segment of the address before reading on.

```
In [4]:  ▶  print(API_address)

            https://finnhub.io/api/v1/stock/candle?symbol=AMZN&resolution=W&from=157786
            5600&to=1609315200&token=bsiqli7rh5rc8orbnkqg
```

Figure 4.6 – Printing API_address

The following bullet points list and explain the different parts of the web address:

- symbol=AMZN specifies that you want the prices with the stock ticker AMZN, which indicates Amazon.

- resolution=W specifies that you want the weekly prices. You could request minute by minute, every 5 minutes, every 15 minutes, every half an hour, hourly, daily, weekly, and monthly prices by using, respectively, 1, 5, 15, 30, 60, D, W, and M.

- from=1577865600 specifies the time from which you want data. The weird-looking number is a timestamp for January 1, 2020.

- to=1609315200 specifies the time up to which you want data. The weird-looking number is a timestamp for December 30, 2020.

- token=abcdefghijklmnopq specifies the API key for this address.

What is next?

Now that you understand the preceding code and you have got the <Response [200]> message, we need to access and use the data. Let's do this step by step. First, run and study the output of the following code:

```
print(r.json())
```

The output is a JSON formatted string that has the following structure: {'c': a list with 51 numbers, 'h': a list with 51 numbers, 'l': a list with 51 numbers, 'o': a list with 51 numbers, 's': 'okay', 't: a list with 51 numbers, 'v': a list with 51 numbers}.

The output basically shows the 51-week data of Amazon stock prices. The following list shows what each letter stands for.

- 'c': the closing price for the period
- 'h': the highest price during the period
- 'l': the lowest price during the period
- 'o': the opening price for the period
- 's': the status of the stock
- 't': the timestamp showing the end of the period
- 'v': the trading volume in the period

Working with the stock data when presented with this format is not easy. However, transforming it to a format that you are used to is easy. Run the following code and study the output:

```
AMZN_df = pd.DataFrame(r.json())
AMZN_df
```

After running the code, the data will be presented in AMZN_df, which is a pandas DataFrame. A pandas DataFrame is a data structure that we like as we know how to manipulate the data using multiple pandas functions.

Putting it all together

The following screenshot shows all the preceding code that created AMZN_df and another six lines of code that are added to restructure the data into a more presentable and codeable format:

```
In [7]:   ▶  from datetime import datetime
             import requests
             import pandas

             stk_ticker = 'AMZN'
             data_resolution = 'W'
             timestamp_from = 1577865600
             timestamp_to = 1609315200
             API_Key = 'bsiqli7rh5rc8orbnkqg'
             Address_template = 'https://finnhub.io/api/v1/stock/candle?symbol={}&resolut:

             API_address = Address_template.format(stk_ticker,data_resolution,
                                                  timestamp_from,timestamp_to,API_Key)

             AMZN_df = pd.DataFrame(r.json())
             AMZN_df.drop(columns=['s'],inplace=True)
             AMZN_df.t = AMZN_df.t.apply(datetime.fromtimestamp)
             AMZN_df.t = AMZN_df.t.apply(lambda v:v.date())
             AMZN_df.set_index('t',drop=True,inplace=True)
             AMZN_df.columns = ['Closing','High','Low','Opening','Volume']
             AMZN_df.head()
```

Out[7]:

t	Closing	High	Low	Opening	Volume
2020-01-01	1891.97	1913.89	1860.00	1875.00	19514188
2020-01-08	1862.02	1917.82	1855.09	1909.89	15160738
2020-01-15	1887.46	1902.50	1857.25	1882.99	13580875
2020-01-22	1858.00	1894.99	1815.34	1885.11	14688733
2020-01-29	2039.87	2071.02	1850.61	1858.00	37459327

Figure 4.7 – An example of using an API connection to connect and pull data

The following list indicates how each added line of code contributes to this goal.

- `inplace=True`: When this is added to a pandas function, you mean to specify that you want the requested change to be applied to the DataFrame itself. The alternative is to have the function output a new DataFrame that has the requested change. This code is added to two of the following lines of code.

- `AMZN_df.drop(columns=['s'],inplace=True)`: This line of code drops the column s as this column only has one value across all the data objects.

- `AMZN_df.t = AMZN_df.t.apply(datetime.fromtimestamp)`: This line of code applies the `datetime.fromtimestamp` function from the `datatime` module to the column `t`. This function takes a timestamp and transforms it into a `DateTime` object. Run `datetime.fromtimestamp(1609315200)` to see the workings of this function.

- `AMZN_df.t = AMZN_df.t.apply(lambda v:v.date())`: This line of code applies a lambda function to only keep the date part of a `DataTime` object as the time for all the data objects is 16:00.

- `AMZN_df.set_index('t',drop=True,inplace=True)`: This line of code sets the column `t` as the index of the DataFrame. The part `drop=True` indicates that you want the original index to be dropped.

- `AMZN_df.columns = ['Closing','High','Low','Opening','Volume']`: This line of code changes the name of `AMZN_df` columns.

- `AMZN_df.head()`: This line of code outputs a DataFrame with only the first five rows of the `AMZN_df` DataFrame.

So far, we have covered three of the five methods of connecting to databases: direct connection, web page connection, and API connection. Next, we will look at the remaining two methods: request connection and publicly shared.

Request connection

This type of connection to a database happens when you do not have any access to the database of interest under any of the three preceding methods, but you know someone who has access and is authorized to share some parts of the data with you. In this method, you need to clearly explain what data you need from the database. This method of accessing the database has some pros and cons. See *Exercise 4* to figure out what they are.

Publicly shared

This method of connecting to databases is the least flexible. Under the publicly shared method, the owner of the database has extracted one dataset out of the databases they owned and has provided access to that one dataset. For instance, almost all of the datasets that you find on `kaggle.com` fall under this method of connecting to a database. Furthermore, most of the data access that is provided under `data.gov` also falls under this inflexible access to the databases.

Summary

Congratulations on successfully finishing this chapter! Now you are equipped with a powerful understanding of databases and it will pay dividends in your quest for effective data preprocessing.

In this chapter, you learned the technological role of databases in data analytics and data preprocessing. You also learned about different kinds of databases and how they should be chosen for different situations. Specifically, you understood how you would decide about the level of data structures in their databases. Last but not least, you learned the five different methods of connecting to, and pulling data from, databases.

This chapter concludes your learning of part 1 of this book: `Technical needs`. Now you are ready to start learning about analytics goals, which is the second part of this book. The technical needs will empower you to use technology to effectively read and manipulate data. The analytics goals will give you a foundational understanding so that you know for what purposes you will need to manipulate the data.

The next part of the book will be an exciting one as we will see examples of what can be done with data. However, before moving on to the next part, take some time and solidify and improve your learnings by completing the following exercises.

Exercises

1. In your own words, describe the difference between a dataset and a database.

2. What are the advantages and disadvantages of structuring data for a relational database? Mention at least two advantages and two disadvantages. Use examples to elucidate.

3. In this chapter, we were introduced to four different types of databases: relational databases, unstructured databases, distributed databases, and Blockchain.

    a. Use the following table to specify a ranking for each of the four types of databases based on the criteria presented in the table.

    b. Provide reasoning for your selections.

The table already has some of the rankings to get you started. *N/A* stands for *Not applicable.* Study the ranking provided and give your reasoning as to why they are correct.

	Relational Databases	Unstructured Databases	Distributed databases	Blockchain
Ease of loading new data to the database	2	1	1 or 2	N/A
Ease of introducing new types of data to the database				
Data access reliability	2	2	1	N/A
Decentralized authority				
Ease of creating more detailed reports				
Ease of recording larger sizes of data				
Better manageability of operational costs				
Prone to political considerations	N/A	N/A	1	2
The need for more preprocessing for analytic purposes				

Figure 4.8 – Database type ranking

4. In this chapter, we were introduced to five different methods for connecting to databases: direct connection, web page connection, API connection, request connection, and publicly shared. Use the following table to indicate a ranking for each of the five methods of connecting to databases based on the specified criteria. Study the rankings and provide reasoning as to why they are correct.

	Direct Connection	Web page Connection	API Connection	Request Connection	Publicly Shared
Flexibility of access	1	2	2	4	5
Prone to human miscommunications	5	5	5	1	5
Need for a high level of technical skillset	1	3	2	4	5
Need for knowing the database tables	1	5	5	5	5
Fastest access to the desired data	1	2	2	5	4
More code-friendly	1	5	2	5	5
Awareness of the possibilities in the database	1	3	3	2	5
Least time-consuming data pulling	1	3	2	5	4
Highest database security	4	2	2	3	1

Figure 4.9 – Ranking of database connection methods

5. Using the Chinook database as an example, we want to investigate and find an answer to the following question: Do tracks that are titled using positive words sell better on average than tracks that are titled with negative words. We would like to focus solely on the following words in the investigations:

List of negative words: ['Evil', 'Night', 'Problem', 'Sorrow', 'Dead', 'Curse', 'Venom', 'Pain', 'Lonely', 'Beast']

List of positive words: ['Amazing', 'Angel', 'Perfect', 'Sunshine', 'Home', 'Live', 'Friends']

a. Connect to the Chinook database using Sqlite3 and execute the following query:

```
SELECT * FROM tracks join invoice_items on tracks.TrackId
= invoice_items.TrackId
```

b. Use the skills you learned in previous chapters (applying a function, `group by function`, and so on) to come up with a table that lists the average total sales for tracks containing good words and the same for tracks containing bad words. Here is what the table will look like:

	TotalSale
MusicTitleTyple	
Negative	1.110000
Neither	1.174550
Positive	1.188667

Figure 4.10 – Table report from the Chinook database for Exercise 5

c. Report your conclusions.

6. In the year 2020, which of the following 12 stocks experienced the highest growth.

Stocks: ['Baba', 'NVR', 'AAPL', 'NFLX', 'FB', 'SBUX', 'NOW', 'AMZN', 'GOOGL', 'MSFT', 'FDX', and 'TSLA']

For a good estimate of growth, use both formula 1 and formula 2 on the weekly closing stock prices. (a) `Formula1: (a-b)`, and (b) `Formula2: (a-b)/c`

In these formulas, a, b, and c are, respectively, the stock closing price for 2020, the median of stock prices during 2020, and the mean of stock prices during 2020.

Based on each formula, what is the stock with the highest growth, and what is the difference between the outcome of each formula?

Part 2:
Analytic Goals

After reading this part, you will be able to perform popular analytics using cleaned and issue-free data.

This part comprises the following chapters:

5
Data Visualization

Being able to visualize data is the backbone of data analysis. The area of data visualization is very exciting, as there are endless possibilities for novelty and creativity in drawing visualizations that tell better stories about your data. However, the core mechanisms of even the most innovative graphs are similar. In this chapter, we will cover these fundamental mechanisms of visualizations that give life to the data and allow us to compare, analyze, and see patterns in it.

As you will learn these fundamental mechanisms, you will also be developing a better backbone/skillset for your data preprocessing goals. If you can fully understand the connection between the data and its visualizations, you will be more effective at preprocessing data for effective visuals. In this chapter, you will work with the data that I have already preprocessed, but in later chapters, we will cover the concepts and techniques that lead to these preprocessed datasets.

This chapter will cover the following main topics:

- Summarizing a population
- Comparing populations
- Investigating the relationship between two attributes
- Adding visual dimensions
- Showing and comparing trends

Technical requirements

You will be able to find the codes and dataset for this chapter in the book's GitHub repository in the `Chapter05` folder:

`https://github.com/PacktPublishing/Hands-On-Data-Preprocessing-in-Python`

Summarizing a population

You can use simple tools such as the **histogram, boxplot**, or **bar chart** to visualize the variations in the values of one column of a dataset across the populations of the data object. These visualizations are immensely useful, as they help you to see the values of one attribute at a glance.

One of the most common reasons for using these visuals is to familiarize yourself with a dataset. The term *getting to know your data* is famous among data scientists and is said time and again to be one of the most necessary steps for successful data analytics and data preprocessing.

What we mean by getting to know a dataset is understanding and exploring the statistical information for each attribute of the dataset. That is, we want to know what types of values each attribute has and how the values vary across the population of the datasets.

For this purpose, we use data visualization tools to summarize the data object population per attribute. Numerical and categorical attributes require different tools for each type of attribute. For numerical attributes, we can use either the histogram or boxplot to summarize the attribute, whereas for categorical attributes, it is best to use bar charts. The following examples walk you through how this can be done all at once for any dataset.

Example of summarizing numerical attributes

Write some code that does the following:

1.   Reads the `adult.csv` dataset into the `adult_df` pandas DataFrame

2.   Creates a histogram and boxplots for the numerical attributes of `adult_df`

3.   Saves the figure for each attribute with a 600 mpi resolution in a separate file

Give the preceding example a try before looking at the following code:

1. First, we will import the modules that we will use throughout this chapter:

```
import pandas as pd
import matplotlib.pyplot as plt
import numpy as np
```

2. Then, we start working on the problem:

```
adult_df = pd.read_csv('adult.csv')
numerical_attributes = ['age', 'fnlwgt', 'education-num',
'capitalGain', 'capitalLoss', 'hoursPerWeek']
for att in numerical_attributes:
    plt.subplot(2,1,1)
    adult_df[att].plot.hist()
    plt.subplot(2,1,2)
    adult_df[att].plot.box(vert=False)
    plt.tight_layout()
    plt.show()
    plt.savefig('{}.png'.format(att), dpi=600)
```

When you run this code, the **Jupyter notebook** will show you all 12 charts. Each numerical attribute will have one histogram and one boxplot. The code will also save a .png file on your computer for each attribute that saves the histogram and boxplot of the attribute. For example, the following figure shows the education-num.png file that was saved on my computer after running the preceding code:

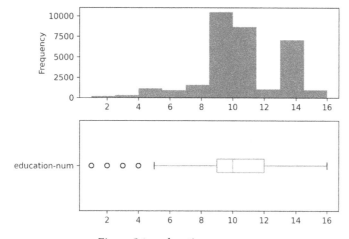

Figure 5.1 – education-num.png

> **Where Are the Files on My Computer?**
>
> If you have difficulty finding the files on your computer, you need to understand the difference between an *absolute file path* and a *relative file path*. The absolute file path includes the root element and the complete directory path. However, the relative path is given with an understanding that you are already in a specific directory.
>
> In the preceding code, we did not include the root element in the file path when using `plt.savefig()`, so **Python** correctly read this as a relative path and assumed that you want the files to be saved in the same directory as the one you have in your Jupyter notebook file.

In this example, you saw the application of boxplots and histograms to summarize the numerical attributes of a dataset. Now, let's look at another example that shows you similar steps for categorical attributes. For categorical attributes, we always use bar charts.

Example of summarizing categorical attributes

Write some code that does the following:

1. Creates bar charts for the categorical attributes of `adult_df`

2. Saves the figure for each attribute with a `600 mpi` resolution in a separate file

Give the preceding example a try before looking at the following code:

```python
categorical_attributes = ['workclass', 'education',
'marital-status', 'occupation', 'relationship', 'race',
'sex','nativeCountry','income']
for att in categorical_attributes:
    adult_df[att].value_counts().plot.barh()
    plt.title(att)
    plt.tight_layout()
    plt.savefig('{}.png'.format(att), dpi=600)
    plt.show()
```

When you run this code, the Jupyter notebook will show you all nine charts. Each categorical attribute will have one bar chart. The code will also save a `.png` file on your computer for each attribute that saves the bar chart of the attribute. For example, the following figure shows the `education.png` file that was saved on my computer after running the preceding code:

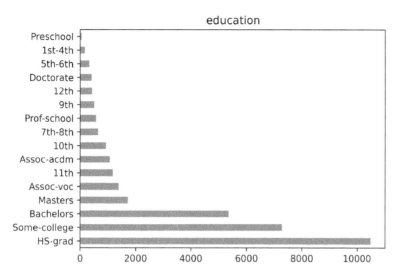

Figure 5.2 – education.png

> **Good Practice Advice**
>
> Technically, you could also use a pie chart to summarize a categorical attribute. However, I advise against it. The reason is that pie charts are not as easily digested by our human brains as bar charts. It has been shown we do much better in appreciating differences in length than the difference in chunks of pies.

So far, you were able to create visualizations that are meant to summarize a population. There are other advantages of being able to do this. Now that we can create these visualizations, we can also create more than one of them and put them next to one another for comparison. The next section will teach you how to do this.

Comparing populations

Putting these kinds of summarizing visualizations of different populations next to one another will be useful to create visuals that help us compare those populations. This can be done with histograms, boxplots, and bar charts. Let's see how this is done using the following three examples.

Example of comparing populations using boxplots

Write some code that creates the following two boxplots next to one another:

- A boxplot of education-num for data objects with an income value that is <=50K

- A boxplot of education-num for data objects with an income value that is >50K

Give the preceding example a try on your own before looking at the following code:

```
income_possibilities = adult_df.income.unique()
for poss in income_possibilities:
    BM = adult_df.income == poss
    plt.hist(adult_df[BM]['education-num'], label=poss,
    histtype='step')

plt.boxplot(dataForBox_dic.values(),vert=False)
plt.yticks([1,2],income_possibilities)
plt.show()
```

Once you run this code, the Jupyter notebook will display the following figure:

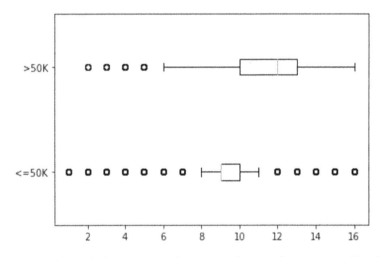

Figure 5.3 – Boxplots of education-num for two populations of income <=50K and >50K

Let's first go through the code before discussing the preceding visual. To completely understand the functioning of the preceding code, you will need to understand three concepts:

1. The code first loops through all the populations that we want to be included in the visual. Here, we have two populations: data objects with an `income` **<=50K** and data objects with an `income` **>50K**. In each iteration of the loop, the code uses Boolean masking to extract each specific population from `adult_df`.

2. The code uses `dataForBox_dic`, which is a dictionary data structure, as a placeholder. On each iteration of the loop, the code adds a new key and its specific value. In the case of this code, there are two iterations. The first iteration adds `'<=50K '` as the first key and all the `education-num` values of the specific population as the value of the key. All those values are assigned to each key as a **Pandas Series**. On the second iteration, the code does the same thing for `'>50K '`.

3. After the loop is completed, the `dataForBox_dic` is full with the necessary data, so `plt.boxplot()` can be applied to create the visuals with two boxplots. The reason that `dataForBox_dic.values()` is passed instead of `dataForBox_dic` is that `plt.boxplot()` requires the dictionary that is passed for drawing only has strings as keys and lists of numbers as values of the keys. Add `print(dataForBox_dic)` and `print(dataForBox_dic.values())` before and after the loop to see all these differences on your own.

Now, let's bring our attention to the merit of the output of the preceding code, which is shown in *Figure 5.3*. As you can see, the visual clearly tells the story of how *education* is important for *higher income*.

Example of comparing populations using histograms

Write some code that creates the following two histograms in the same plot:

*   A histogram of `education-num` for data objects with an `income` value that is <=50K

*   A histogram of `education-num` for data objects with an `income` value that is >50K

Give the preceding example a try on your own before looking at the following code:

```
income_possibilities = adult_df.income.unique()
for poss in income_possibilities:
    BM = adult_df.income == poss
```

```
    plt.hist(adult_df[BM]['education-num'],
             label=poss, histtype='step')
plt.legend()
plt.show()
```

Once you run this code, the Jupyter notebook will display the following figure:

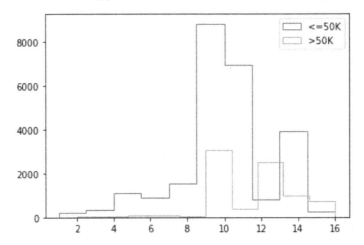

Figure 5.4 – Histograms of education-num for two populations of income <=50K and >50K

The code for creating histograms is less complicated than the code for creating boxplots. The major difference is that for histograms, you do not need to use a placeholder to prepare the data for plt.boxplot(). With plt.hist(), you can just call it as many times as you need and Matplotlib will put these visuals on top of one another. The code, however, uses two of the plt.hist() properties: label=poss and histtype='step'. The following explains the necessity of both:

- label=poss is added to the code so that plt.legend() can add the legends to the visual. Remove label=poss from the code and study the warning that running the update code gives you.

- histtype='step' is setting the type of histogram. There are two different histograms that you can choose from: 'bar' or 'step'. Change histtype='step' to histtype='bar' and run the code to see the difference between them.

The following figure is created by using plt. subplot() to put *Figure 5.3* and *Figure 5.4* together. I have not shared the code here, so challenge yourself to create it before reading on:

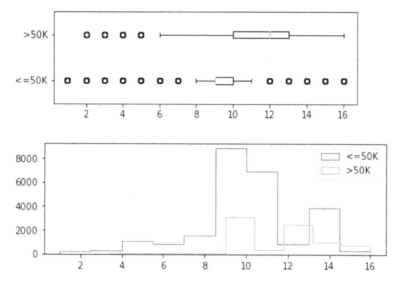

Figure 5.5 – Histograms and boxplots of education-num for two populations of income
<=50K and >50K

These two visuals next to one another can help us see the differences and similarities between the two populations easily, and that is the value we get from creating them and meaningfully organizing them together.

So far, we have learned how to compare populations that are described by numerical attributes. Now, let's look at an example that will teach us how we can compare populations that are described by categorical attributes. For this purpose, we will use bar charts.

Example of comparing populations using bar charts

Create a visualization that uses bar charts to compare the categorical attribute `race` for the two following populations:

- Data objects with an `income` value that is <=50K
- Data objects with an `income` value that is >50K

Give this a try on your own before reading on.

You can do this in six different but meaningful ways. Let's go through all of the possible ways that this can be done.

The first way of solving the problem

The following screenshot shows the code and its output for the first way. In this way of solving the problem, we have used `plt.subplot()` to put the bar charts of the two populations on top of one another:

```
In [8]:  ▶  income_possibilities = adult_df.income.unique()

            for i,poss in enumerate(income_possibilities):
                plt.subplot(2,1,i+1)
                BM = adult_df.income == poss
                adult_df[BM].race.value_counts().plot.barh()
                plt.xlim([0,22000])
                plt.ylabel(poss)
```

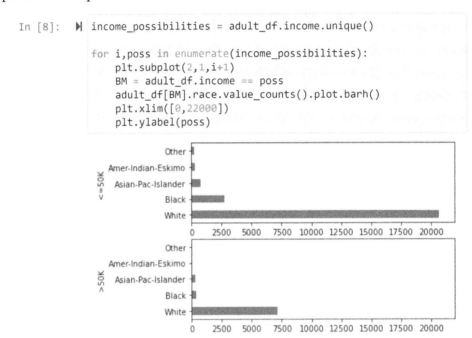

Figure 5.6 – The first way of solving the problem (screenshot of the code and its output)

While this way of solving the problem is legitimate and valuable, bar chats are capable of fusing the chart of the two populations at different levels. The five other ways show these levels.

The second way of solving the problem

The following screenshot shows the code and its output for the second way. In this way of coding it, we have merged the two visuals we saw in *Figure 5.6* and we only have one bar chart that contains all the information. However, this merging has come at the price of having to make the y-ticks of the chart more complicated. Take a moment to compare *Figure 5.6* and *Figure 5.7* before reading on:

```
In [9]:    ▶ adult_df.groupby(['income','race']).size().plot.barh()
             plt.show()
```

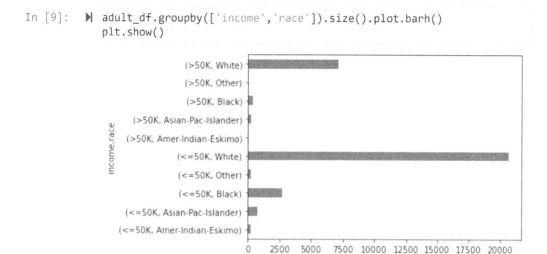

Figure 5.7 – The second way of solving the problem (screenshot of the code and its output)

So far, we have managed to somewhat fuse the bar charts of the two populations. Let's take another step by using a legend and colors to make the resulting chart a bit stronger.

The third way of solving the problem

The following screenshot shows the code and its output for the third way. In this way, we have used a legend and different colors to represent each possibility under the race attribute. Compared to the fusion in *Figure 5.7*, the fusion in the following figure is more effective:

```
In [10]:    ▶ adult_df.groupby(['income','race']).size().unstack().plot.barh()
              plt.show()
```

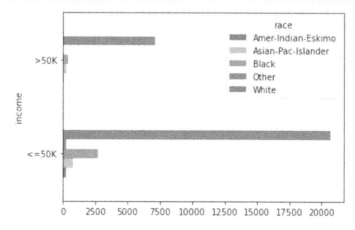

Figure 5.8 – The third way of solving the problem (screenshot of the code and its output)

While the comparison of the two populations based on income is possible with all three preceding figures, the comparison of each possibility of the race attribute is not easily done. The next three ways of solving this problem will highlight visualizations that make that easier.

The fourth way of solving the problem

The following screenshot shows the code and its output for the fourth way. In this approach, we have coded the visual so that the two possibilities of the income attribute are next to one another for each possibility of the race attribute. This way allows us to compare both income group populations (*income <=50K* and *income >50K*) against each race attribute.

```
In [11]:  ▶  adult_df.groupby(['race','income']).size().plot.barh()
              plt.show()
```

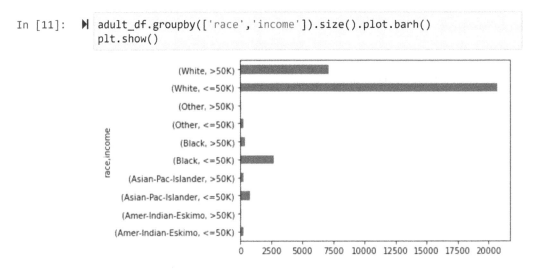

Figure 5.9 – The fourth way of solving the problem (screenshot of the code and its output)

The fusion level of the preceding visual can be improved, and the next way of solving this problem will do this.

The fifth way of solving the problem

The following screenshot shows the code and its output for the fifth way. The only difference between this and the previous way is the use of a legend and colors to make the visual more presentable and neater. Without reservations, we can claim that *Figure 5.10* is more effective in solving this problem than *Figure 5.9*. Why?

```
In [12]:    ▶ adult_df.groupby(['race','income']).size().unstack().plot.barh()
              plt.legend(loc=4)
              plt.show()
```

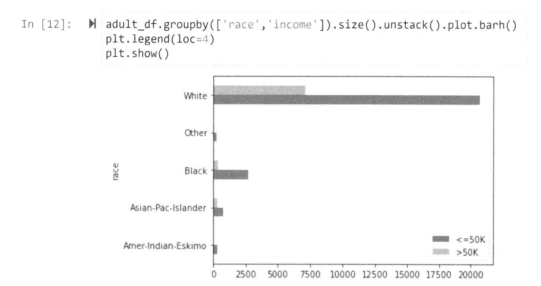

Figure 5.10 – The fifth way of solving the problem (screenshot of the code and its output)

The last way of presenting this data is to stack the two bars under each `race` category, instead of having them next to one another. The next way of solving the problem will show how that can be done.

The sixth way of solving the problem

The following screenshot shows the code and its output for the sixth way. The visual created from this code is called a **stacked bar chart**.

```
In [13]:  ▶  adult_df.groupby(['race','income']).size().unstack().plot.barh(stacked=True)
             plt.legend(loc=4)
```

```
Out[13]:  <matplotlib.legend.Legend at 0x2ac034b4970>
```

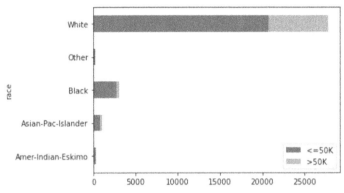

Figure 5.11 – The sixth way of solving the problem (screenshot of the code and its output)

We prefer a stacked bar chart to a typical bar chart when we know the total number of data objects under each possibility is more important than the comparison between populations. In this case, as we are creating this visual to compare the two income group populations, using a stacked bar chart is not very wise.

So far in this chapter, we have learned how we can summarize and compare populations of data objects based on one attribute. Next, we are going to learn how we can see if two or more attributes have specific relationships with one another.

Investigating the relationship between two attributes

The best way to investigate the relationships between attributes visually is to do it in pairs. The tools we use for investigating the relationship between a pair of attributes depends on the type of attributes. In what follows, we will cover these tools based on the following pairs: *numerical-numerical*, *categorical-categorical*, and *categorical-numerical*.

Visualizing the relationship between two numerical attributes

The best tool for portraying the relationship between two numerical attributes is the **scatter plot**. In the following example, we will use a tool called **scatter matrix** that creates a matrix of scatterplots for a dataset with numerical attributes.

Example of using scatterplots to investigate relationships between numerical attributes

In this example, we will use a new dataset, `Universities_imputed_reduced.csv`. This dataset's definition of data objects is `Universities in the USA`, and these data objects are described using the following attributes: `College Name`, `State`, `Public/Private`, `num_appli_rec`, `num_appl_accepted`, `num_new_stud_enrolled`, `in-state tuition`, `out-of-state tuition`, `% fac. w/PHD`, `stud./fac. Ratio`, and `Graduation rate`. The naming of these attributes is very intuitive and does not need further description.

To practice, apply the techniques that you have learned so far to get to know this new dataset before reading on. It will help your understanding immensely.

The following code uses the `pariplot()` function of the `seaborn` module to create a scatter plot for every pair combination of the numerical attributes in the `uni_df` DataFrame. If you have never used the `seaborn` module before, you need to install it first. How to install `seaborn` is shown in *Chapter 4, Databases,* in the *Statistical meaning of the word pattern* section:

```
import seaborn as sns
uni_df = pd.read_csv('Universities_imputed_reduced.csv')
sns.pairplot(uni_df)
```

After running the preceding code, the Jupyter notebook will show you *Figure 5.12.* Using this figure, you can investigate the relationship between any two attributes in `uni_df`. For instance, you can see that there is a strong relationship between `num_appl_accepted` and `num_new_stud_enrolled`, which makes sense. As the number of accepted applications increases, we would expect the number of new enrollments to increase.

Furthermore, by studying the last column or the last row of the scatter matrix in the following figure, you can study the relationship between graduation and all the other attributes one by one. After doing so, you can see that, surprisingly and interestingly, the `graduation rate` attribute's strongest relationship is with `in-state tuition` and `out-of-state tuition`. Interestingly, graduation does not have a strong relationship with other attributes, such as `num_new_stud_enrolled`, `% fac. w/PHD`, and `stud./fac. Ratio`.

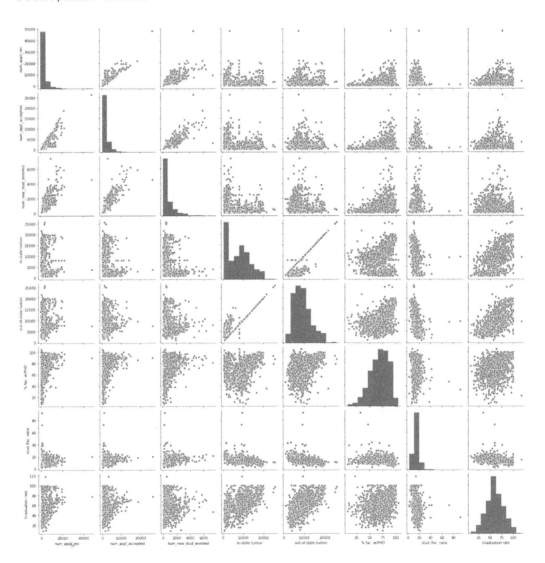

Figure 5.12 – Scatter matrix of the uni_df DataFrame

Now that we have practiced making visuals to investigate the relationship between numerical attributes, next, we will do the same for categorical attributes.

Visualizing the relationship between two categorical attributes

The best visual tool for examining the relationship between two categorical attributes is the color-coded **contingency table**. A contingency table is a matrix that shows the frequency of data objects in all the possible value combinations of two attributes. While you could create a contingency table for numerical attributes, doing so in most cases will not lead to effective visualizations; contingency tables are almost always used for categorical attributes.

Example of using a contingency table to examine the relationship between two categorical (binary) attributes

In this example, we are interested to see if there is a relationship between two categorical attributes, sex and income, among the data objects in adult_df. To examine this relationship, we will use a contingency table. The following screenshot shows how this can be done using the pd.crosstab() pandas function. This function gets two attributes and outputs the contingency table for them:

```
In [15]:  ▶ contingency_tbl = pd.crosstab(adult_df.income,adult_df.sex)
             contingency_tbl
```

Out[15]:

sex	Female	Male
income		
<=50K	9592	15128
>50K	1179	6662

Figure 5.13 – The code and output of creating a contingency table for two categorical attributes, adult_df.sex and adult_df.income

You can see in the outputted contingency table in the preceding screenshot that, while around 11% of female data objects have an income >50K, around 30% of male data objects have an income >50K. To derive such conclusions from a contingency table we normally do some simple calculations, such as the one we did just now; we calculated the relative percentages of the income totals for each gender. However, we could color code the contingency table so that these extra steps are not be needed. The following screenshot displays a two-step process for doing this by using the sns.heatmapt() function from the seaborn module:

```
In [16]:  ▶ probablity_tbl = contingency_tbl/ contingency_tbl.sum()
            sns.heatmap(probablity_tbl, annot=True, center=0.5 ,cmap="Greys")
            plt.show()
```

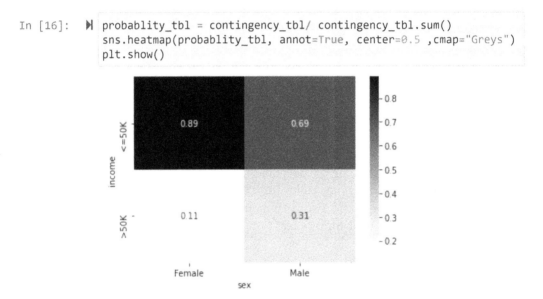

Figure 5.14 – Transforming the contingency table from Figure 5.13 into a heatmap

The two steps to create the color-coded contingency table from the original contingency table are as follows:

1. Create a probability table from the contingency table by dividing the values of each column by the sum of all the values in the column.

2. Use sns.heatmap() to create the color-coded contingency table. Apart from inputting the calculated probability table (probablity_tbl) from the previous step, three more inputs are added: annot=True, center=0.5, and cmap="Greys". Remove them one by one and run the same code shown in the preceding screenshot to understand what each addition does.

Now, by simply looking at the color-coded contingency table in the preceding screenshot, we can see that while among both males and females, more data objects earn <=50K, data objects that are male are more likely to earn >50K than female data objects. Therefore, we can conclude that `sex` and `income` do have a meaningful and visualizable relationship with one another.

This example examines the relationship between two binary attributes. When the attributes are not binary, the steps we take to create a color-coded contingency table are identical. Let's see this in an example.

Example of a using contingency table to relationship between two categorical (non-binary) attributes

Create a visualization that examines the relationship between the `race` and `occupation` attributes for the data objects in `adult_df`.

Give this a try on your own before reading on.

The following screenshot displays the code and the correct output for this example:

```
In [17]:  ▶ contingency_tbl = pd.crosstab(adult_df.occupation,adult_df.race)
            probablity_tbl = contingency_tbl/ contingency_tbl.sum()
            sns.heatmap(probablity_tbl, annot=True, center=0.5 ,cmap="Greys")
            plt.show()
```

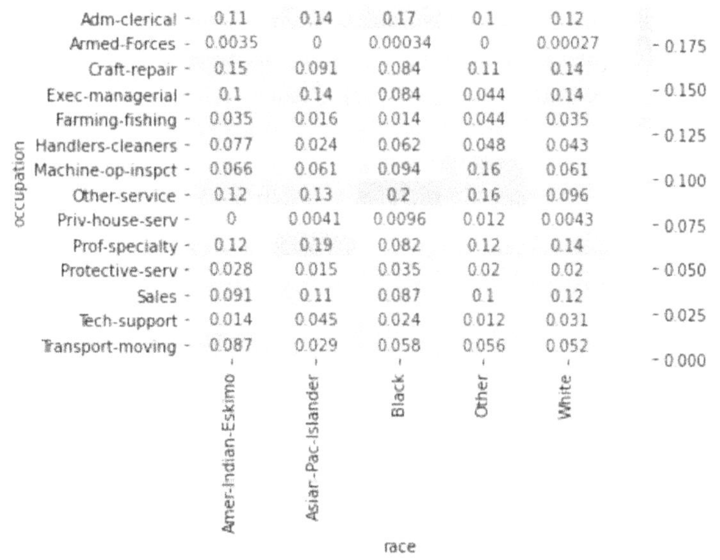

occupation	Amer-Indian-Eskimo	Asian-Pac-Islander	Black	Other	White
Adm-clerical	0.11	0.14	0.17	0.1	0.12
Armed-Forces	0.0035	0	0.00034	0	0.00027
Craft-repair	0.15	0.091	0.084	0.11	0.14
Exec-managerial	0.1	0.14	0.084	0.044	0.14
Farming-fishing	0.035	0.016	0.014	0.044	0.035
Handlers-cleaners	0.077	0.024	0.062	0.048	0.043
Machine-op-inspct	0.066	0.061	0.094	0.16	0.061
Other-service	0.12	0.13	0.2	0.16	0.096
Priv-house-serv	0	0.0041	0.0096	0.012	0.0043
Prof-specialty	0.12	0.19	0.082	0.12	0.14
Protective-serv	0.028	0.015	0.035	0.02	0.02
Sales	0.091	0.11	0.087	0.1	0.12
Tech-support	0.014	0.045	0.024	0.012	0.031
Transport-moving	0.087	0.029	0.058	0.056	0.052

race

Figure 5.15 – Creating a contingency heatmap for the two categorical attributes, adult_df.race and adult_df.occupation

In the color-coded table, you can clearly see the following patterns:

- Data objects with the `race` attribute value of `white` are more likely to have the `occupation` attribute values of `Craft-repair`, `Exec-managerial`, or `Prof-specialty`

- Data objects with the `race` attribute value of `black` are more likely to have the `occupation` attribute values of `Adm-clerical` and `Other-service`

- Data objects with the `race` attribute value of `Asian-Pac-Islander` are more likely to have the `occupation` attribute value of `Prof-specialty`

- Data objects with the `race` attribute value of `Amer-Indian-Eskimo` are more likely to have the `occupation` attribute value of `Craft-repair`.

Again, using the contingency table we can see that there is a visualizable and meaningful relationship between `race` and `occupation` among the data object in `adult_df`.

So far, we have learned how to visualize the relationships between pairs of attributes of the same type, namely, *numerical-numerical* and *categorical-categorical*. Next, we will tackle visualizing the relationship for the non-matching pairs, specifically, numerical-categorical.

Visualizing the relationship between a numerical attribute and a categorical attribute

What makes this situation more challenging is obvious: the types of the attributes are different. To be able to visualize the relationship between a categorical attribute and a numeric attribute, one of the attributes has to be transformed into the other type of attribute. Almost always, it is best to transform the numerical attribute into a categorical one, and then use a contingency table to examine the relationship between the two attributes. The following example shows how this can be done.

Example of examining the relationship between a categorical attribute and a numerical attribute

First, create a visualization that examines the relationship between the `race` and `age` attributes for the data objects in `adult_df`.

The `Age` attribute is numerical and the `race` attribute is categorical. So first, we need to transform `age` into a categorical attribute. Then, we can use a contingency table to visualize their relationship. The following screenshot shows these steps:

```
In [18]:  ▶  age_discretized = pd.cut(adult_df.age, bins = 5)
             contingency_tbl = pd.crosstab(age_discretized,adult_df.race)
             probablity_tbl = contingency_tbl/ contingency_tbl.sum()
             sns.heatmap(probablity_tbl, annot=True, center=0.5 ,cmap="Greys")
             plt.show()
```

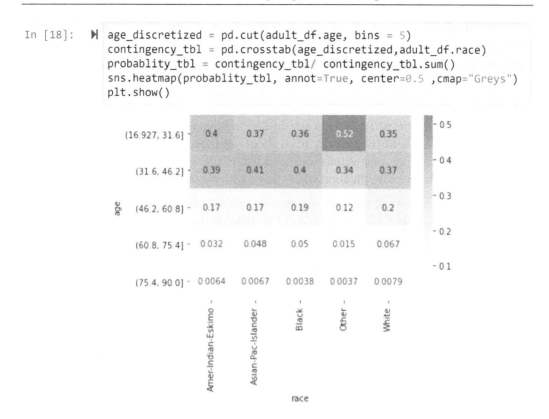

Figure 5.16 – Creating a contingency heatmap for a categorical attribute (adult_df.race) and a numerical attribute (adult_df.age)

The solution showed in the preceding screenshot has the following three steps:

1. Use the pd.cut() pandas function to transform adult_df.age into a categorical attribute with five possibilities. Choosing 5 bins is arbitrary, but it is a good number unless there are good reasons to group the data into a different number of bins. **Discretization** is what we call the transformation of a numerical attribute into a categorical one; that is why we have used age_discretized as the name for the transformed adult_df.age attribute.

2. Create a contingency table for age_discretized and adult_df.race using the pd.crosstab() pandas function.

3. Create a probability table using the contingency table created in the previous step and then use sns.heatmap() to create the color-coded contingency table.

The output visual shows that there is a meaningful and visualizable relationship between the two attributes. Specifically, the data objects that have other for the race attribute are younger than the data objects where the race attributes are white, black, asian-Pac-Islander, and Amer-Indian-Eskimo.

This example demonstrated the common scenario where the numerical attribute will be transformed into a categorical attribute to examine its relationship with another categorical attribute. While this is will be the best way to go about this in almost all cases, there are cases where it is advantageous to transform the categorical attribute into a numerical one. The following example shows a rare situation where this transformation is preferred.

Another example of examining the relationship between a categorical attribute and a numerical attribute

First, create a visualization that examines the relationship between the education and age attributes for the data objects in adult_df.

Again, we have a categorical attribute and a numerical attribute. However, this time, the categorical attribute has two characteristics that make it possible for us to choose the less common way to approach this situation. These two characteristics are as follows:

- Education is an *ordinal* categorical attribute and not a *nominal* categorical attribute.
- The attribute can be made into a numeric attribute with a few reasonable assumptions.

The default method to transform an ordinal attribute to a numerical one is **ranking transformation**. For instance, you can perform a ranking transformation on the education attribute and replace each of the possibilities under adult_df.education with an integer number. Interestingly, the adult_df dataset already has another attribute that is the rank transformation of the education attribute, and that transformed attribute is called education-num. The following figure shows the one-to-one relationship between these two attributes:

education	Preschool	1st-4th	5th-6th	7th-8th	9th	10th	11th	12th	HS-grad	Some-college	Assoc-voc	Assoc-acdm	Bachelors	Masters	Prof-school	Doctorate
education-num		1	2	3	4	5	6	7	8	9	10	11	12	13	14	15	16

Figure 5.17 – The one-to-one relationship between the education and education-num attributes in adult_df

You can see the relationship between the two attributes portrayed in the preceding figure yourself by running the following code:

```
adult_df.['education','education-num']).size()
```

When you run this code, you will see that the .groupy() function does not split per possibilities of education-num for education; the reason for this is that there is a one-to-one relationship between these two attributes.

Now that we have the numerical version of the education attribute, we can use a scatter plot to visualize the relationship between education and age. The following screenshot shows the code and the visualization:

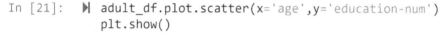

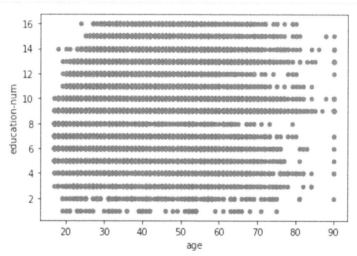

Figure 5.18 – Creating a scatter plot for a categorical attribute (adult_df.education) and a numerical attribute (adult_df.age)

Using the visualized relationship, we can see that the two attributes, age and education, are not related. For the sake of practice, let's also do this analysis the other way around; let's discretize age and create a contingency table to see if we will get to the same conclusion. The following screenshot shows the code and the output visual for this analysis:

In [22]:   ▶

```
age_discretized = pd.cut(adult_df['age'], bins = 5)
contingency_tbl = pd.crosstab(adult_df.education,age_discretized)
probablity_tbl = contingency_tbl/ contingency_tbl.sum()
sns.heatmap(probablity_tbl, annot=True, center=0.5 ,cmap="Greys")
plt.show()
```

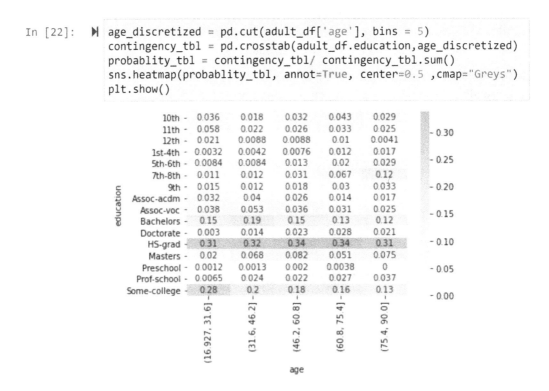

Figure 5.19 – Creating a contingency heatmap for a categorical attribute (adult_df.education) and a numeric attribute (adult_df.age)

We can see that this visual also gives the impression that the two attributes, age and education, are not related to one another.

So far in this chapter, we have learned how to summarize a population, compare populations, and just now, we learned how to visualize the relationship between all kinds of attributes. Now, let's begin another data visualization aspect – next, we will learn about adding dimensions to our visualizations.

Adding visual dimensions

The visualizations that we have created so far have only two dimensions. When using data visualization as a way to tell a story or share findings, there are many good reasons not to add too many dimensions to your visuals. For instance, visuals that have too many dimensions may overwhelm your audience. However, when the visuals are used as exploratory tools to detect patterns in the data, being able to add dimensions to the visuals might be just what a data analyst needs.

There are many ways to add dimensions to a visual, such as using *color*, *size*, *hue*, *line styles*, and more. Here, we will cover the three most applied approaches by adding dimensions using *color*, *size*, and *time*. In this case, we will show adding the dimensions for the case of scatter plots, but the techniques shown can be easily extrapolated to other visuals if applicable. The following example demonstrates how adding extra dimensions to the scatter plot could be of significant value.

Example of a five-dimensional scatter plot

Use `WH Report_preprocessed.csv` to create a visualization that shows the interaction of the following five columns in this dataset:

- `Healthy_life_expectancy_at_birth`
- `Log_GDP_per_capita`
- `Year`
- `Continent`
- `Population`

To solve this problem, we are going to have to do it step by step. So, please stay with me throughout.

The dataset we use for this example is taken from *The World Happiness Report*, which includes the data of 122 countries from 2010 to 2019. Before starting to engage with the solutions given for this example, take some time and familiarize yourself with the dataset.

> **Advice for Better Learning**
>
> As we learn more and more complex analyses, algorithms, and code, we may
> not have space in these pages to *get to know* every new dataset we cover in the
> book. Every time a new dataset is introduced throughout this book, I strongly
> recommend that you take the steps that were laid out in the *Pandas functions to*
> *explore a DataFrame* section in *Chapter 1, Review of the Core Modules NumPy*
> *and Pandas*. Of course, this applies here. Take the time to get to know the WH
> `Report_preprocessed.csv` dataset before reading on.

The following code uses `plt.subplot()` and `plt.scatter()` to bring three
dimensions together: `Healthy_life_expectancy_at_birth`, `Log_GDP_per_`
`capita`, and `year`:

```
country_df = pd.read_csv('WH Report_preprocessed.csv')
plt.figure(figsize=(15,8))
year_poss = country_df.year.unique()
for i,yr in enumerate(year_poss):
    BM = country_df.year == yr
    X= country_df[BM].Healthy_life_expectancy_at_birth
    Y= country_df[BM].Log_GDP_per_capita
    plt.subplot(2,5,i+1)
    plt.scatter(X,Y)
    plt.title(yr)
    plt.xlim([30,80])
    plt.ylim([6,12])
plt.show()
plt.tight_layout()
```

The output of the preceding code is shown in *Figure 5.20*. The visual manages to achieve
the following important things:

- The figure visualizes the three dimensions all at once.

- The figure shows the upward and rightward movement of the countries in both
  X and Y dimensions. This movement has the potential to tell the story of global
  success improving on both dimensions, `Healthy_life_expectancy_at_`
  `birth` and `Log_GDP_per_capita`.

However, the visual is choppy and sloppy at showing the movement of the countries in the years between 2010 and 2019, so we can do better.

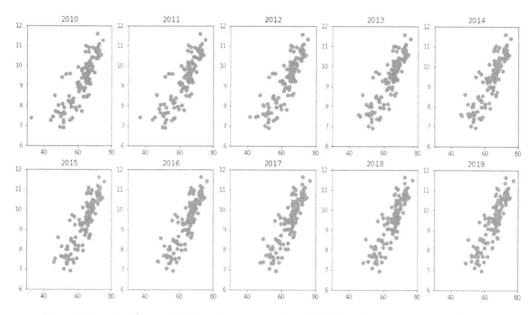

Figure 5.20 – One figure with three dimensions of the WH Report_preprocessed.csv dataset

Now, we want to improve the preceding figure by seamlessly incorporating time in one visual instead of having to use subplots. The following figure (*Figure 5.21*) shows our end goal in this segment. The figure is interactive, and by sliding the control bar on the top widget, we can change the year for the visual and therefore see the movement of countries under the two dimensions of Healthy_life_expectancy_at_birth and Log_GDP_per_capita. Of course, we cannot do that on paper, but I will share the code that can make this happen right here. But, we have to do this in two steps:

1.   Create a function that outputs the relevant visual for the inputted year.

2.   Use new modules and programing objects to create the slide bar.

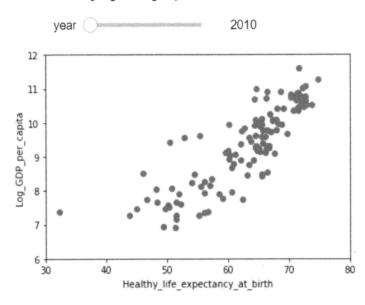

Figure 5.21 – One figure with three dimensions of the WH Report_preprocessed.csv dataset using a slide bar widget

The following code creates the function that we need for the interactive visual:

```
def plotyear(year):
    BM = country_df.year == year
    X= country_df[BM].Healthy_life_expectancy_at_birth
    Y= country_df[BM].Log_GDP_per_capita
    plt.scatter(X,Y)
    plt.xlabel('Healthy_life_expectancy_at_birth')
    plt.ylabel('Log_GDP_per_capita')
    plt.xlim([30,80])
    plt.ylim([6,12])
    plt.show()
```

After creating this function and before moving forward, put the function in use by calling it a few times – for instance, run `plotyear(2011)`, `plotyear(2018)`, and `plotyear(2015)`. If everything is working well, you'd get a new scatter plot on every run.

After you have a well-functioning `plotyear()`, writing and running the following code gives you the interactive visual showed in the preceding figure (*Figure 5.21*). To create this interactive visual, we have used the `interact` and `widgets` programming objects from the `ipywidgets` module:

```
from ipywidgets import interact, widgets
interact(plotyear,year=widgets.
IntSlider(min=2010,max=2019,step=1,value=2010))
```

After you have managed to create the interactive visual, go ahead and put the control bar to use and enjoy the upward movement of the countries. Before your eyes, you will see the history of global success from 2010 to 2019.

The fourth dimension

So far, we have only been able to include three dimensions in our visuals: `Healthy_life_expectancy_at_birth`, `Log_GDP_per_capita`, and `year`. We have two more dimensions to go.

We used a scatter plot to include the first two dimensions, and we used the time to include the third dimension, `year`. Now, let's use color to include the fourth dimension, `Continent`.

The following code adds color to what we've already built. Pay close attention to how a `for` loop has been used to iterate over all the continents and add the data of each continent one by one to the visual and thus separate them:

```
Continent_poss = country_df.Continent.unique()
colors_dic={'Asia':'b', 'Europe':'g', 'Africa':'r',
'South America':'c', 'Oceania':'m', 'North America':'y',
'Antarctica':'k'}
def plotyear(year):
    for cotinent in Continent_poss:
        BM1 = (country_df.year == year)
        BM2 = (country_df.Continent ==cotinent)
        BM = BM1 & BM2
        X = country_df[BM].Healthy_life_expectancy_at_birth
        Y= country_df[BM].Log_GDP_per_capita
        plt.scatter(X,Y,c=colors_dic[cotinent], marker='o',
        linewidths=0.5, edgecolors='w', label=cotinent)
```

```
      plt.xlabel('Healthy_life_expectancy_at_birth')
      plt.ylabel('Log_GDP_per_capita')
      plt.xlim([30,80])
      plt.ylim([6,12])
      plt.legend()
      plt.show()
   interact(plotyear,year=widgets.
   IntSlider(min=2010,max=2019,step=1,value=2010))
```

After successfully running the preceding code, you will get another interactive visual. The following figure shows the visual when the **year** control bar is set to 2015.

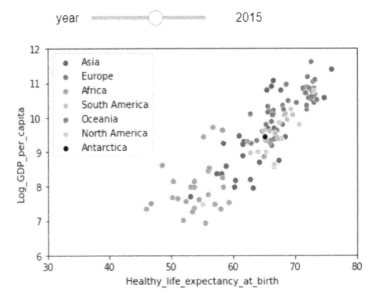

Figure 5.22– One figure with four dimensions of the WH Report_preprocessed.csv dataset using a slide bar widget and color

Contemplating and interacting with the preceding visual not only adds extra dimensions to the visual before our eyes, but it also adds further dimensions to the story we have been developing. We can see the clear disparity between the continents in the world, but also, we see the same upward movement to a higher GDP and life expectancy for all countries.

The fifth dimension

So far, we have only been able to include the following four dimensions in one visual: `Healthy_life_expectancy_at_birth`, `Log_GDP_per_capita`, `year`, and `Continent`. Now, let's add the fifth dimension, which is `population`, using the size of the markers to represent this. The following code adds the dimension of the population as the size of the markers:

```
Continent_poss = country_df.Continent.unique()
colors_dic={'Asia':'b', 'Europe':'g', 'Africa':'r',
'South America':'c', 'Oceania':'m', 'North America':'y',
'Antarctica':'k'}
country_df.sort_values(['population'],inplace = True,
ascending=False)
def plotyear(year):
    for cotinent in Continent_poss:
        BM1 = (country_df.year == year)
        BM2 = (country_df.Continent ==cotinent)
        BM = BM1 & BM2
        size = country_df[BM].population/200000
        X = country_df[BM].Healthy_life_expectancy_at_birth
        Y= country_df[BM].Log_GDP_per_capita
        plt.scatter(X,Y,c=colors_dic[cotinent], marker='o',
        s=size, inewidths=0.5, edgecolors='w', label=cotinent)
    plt.xlabel('Healthy_life_expectancy_at_birth')
    plt.ylabel('Log_GDP_per_capita')
    plt.xlim([30,80])
    plt.ylim([6,12])
    plt.legend(markerscale=0.5)
    plt.show()
interact(plotyear,year=widgets.
IntSlider(min=2010,max=2019,step=1,value=2010))
```

After successfully running the preceding code, you will get another interactive visual. The following figure shows the visual when the **year** control bar is set to 2019.

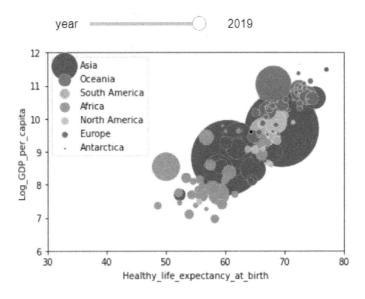

Figure 5.23 – One figure with five dimensions of the WH Report_preprocessed.csv dataset, using a slide bar widget, color, and size

There are three parts of the preceding code that might be confusing for you. Let's go over them together:

```
country_df.sort_values(['population'], inplace = True,
ascending=False)
```

The preceding code is included so the countries with higher populations are added to the visual first, therefore, their markers will go to the background and will not cover up the countries with lower populations.

```
size = country_df[BM].population/200000
```

The preceding code is added to scale down the big population numbers for creating the visual. The number was found purely after some trial and error.

```
plt.legend(markerscale=0.5)
```

The markerscale=0.5 is added to scale the markers shown in the legend, as without this they would be too big. Remove markerscale=0.5 from the code to see this for yourself.

Voila! We are done. We were able to learn how to create a five-dimensional scatter plot.

So far in this chapter, you have been able to learn useful visualization techniques and concepts, such as summarizing and comparing populations, investigating the relationships between attributes, and adding visual dimensions. Next, we will cover how we can use **Python** to display and compare trends in data.

Showing and comparing trends

Trends can be visualized when the data objects are described by attributes that are highly related to one another. A great example of such datasets is **time series data**. Time series datasets have data objects that are described by time attributes and with an equal duration of time between them. For instance, the following dataset is a time series dataset that shows the daily closing prices of **Amazon** and **Apple** stocks for the first 10 trading days of 2020. In this example, you can see that all of the attributes of the dataset have a time nature and they have an equal duration of a day between them:

Date	1/2/2020	1/3/2020	1/6/2020	1/7/2020	1/8/2020	1/9/2020	1/10/2020	1/13/2020	1/14/2020	1/15/2020
Amazon	1898.01	1874.97	1902.88	1906.86	1891.97	1901.05	1883.16	1891.3	1869.44	1862.02
Apple	74.3335	73.6108	74.1974	73.8484	75.0364	76.6302	76.8035	78.4443	77.3851	77.0534

Figure 5.24 – Time series data example (daily stock prices of Amazon and Apple)

The best way to visualize time series data is using **line plots**. *Figure 2.9* from *Chapter 2, Review of Another Core Module – Matplotlib,* is a great example of using line plots to show and compare trends.

Line plots are very popular in stock market analysis. If you search for any stock ticker, you will see that **Google** will show you a line plot of the price trends. It also gives you the option to change the duration of time over which you want the line plot to visualize the price trends. Give this a try – for example, try some searches: Amazon stock, Google stock, and Walmart stock.

Line plots are popular in stock market analysis; however, they are very useful in other areas, too. Any dataset that has time series data could potentially take advantage of line plots for showing trends. The following example illustrates another instance of applying line lots to visualize and compare trends.

Example of visualizing and comparing trends

Use WH Report_preprocessed.csv to create a visualization that shows and compares the trend of the Perceptions_of_corruption attribute for all continents between the years 2010 and 2019. To be clear, we want the data for only the two years – 2010 and 2019.

Give this example a try before reading on.

This example can be easily solved by all the programming and visualization tools that we have learned so far. The following code creates the requested visualization:

```
country_df = pd.read_csv('WH Report_preprocessed.csv')
continent_poss = country_df.Continent.unique()
byContinentYear_df = country_df.groupby(['Continent','year']).
Perceptions_of_corruption.mean()
Markers_options = ['o', '^','P', '8', 's', 'p', '*']
for i,c in enumerate(continent_poss):
    plt.plot([2010,2019], byContinentYear_
    df.loc[c,[2010,2019]], label=c, marker=Markers_options[i])
plt.xticks([2010,2019])
plt.legend(bbox_to_anchor=(1.05, 1.0))
plt.title('Aggregated values per each continent in 2010 and
2019')
plt. label('Perceptions_of_corruption')
plt.show()
```

Before going over the different parts of this code, let's enjoy seeing, analyzing, and appreciating the story the following visual tells us. These are the following five points that the visual clearly shows:

- For most continents, namely, Africa, North America, Asia, and Europe, Perceptions_of_corruption have declined.

- Between all these improving continents, Europe has had the fastest decrease in Perceptions_of_corruption.

- Asia has had a faster improvement than North America, thereby placing Asia in a better place than North America in 2019 compared to 2010.

- The two continents that have had an increase in Perceptions_of_corruption are South America and Antarctica.

- The Perceptions_of_corruption values for Oceania have not changed, and because of that, the continent has achieved the status of having the lowest Perceptions_of_corruption among all continents.

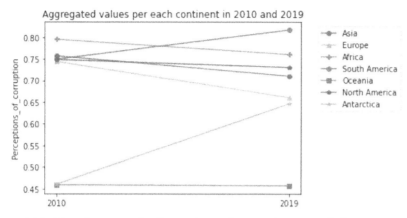

Figure 5.25 – Line plot comparing Perceptions_of_corruption across different continents
in 2010 and 2019

Now, let's go through different elements of the preceding code:

1. The following line of code groups the data based on the two attributes, Continent
    and year, and then calculates the aggregate function .mean() for the
    Perceptions_of_corruption attribute. The result of this grouping is recorded
    in byContinentYear_df, which is a DataFrame.

    ```
    byContinentYear_df = country_df.groupby(
    ['Continent','year']
    ).Perceptions_of_corruption.mean()
    ```

    The rest of the solution uses numbers in this DataFrame to draw different elements
    of the visual. Separately, run print(byContinentYear_df) to see this. That
    will help your understanding of the solution.

2. To better separate the continents, the code has used markers. First, the code creates
    a list of possible markers for later use. The following line of code has done this:
    Markers_options = ['o', '^','P', '8', 's', 'p', '*']. Then,
    within the loop through all the continents and when each line is introduced using
    the plt.plot() function, the code uses marker=Markers_options[i] to
    assign one of those possible markers.

3. The code has incorporated box_to_anchor=(1.05, 1.0) for plt.
    legend() to place the legend box outside the visual. Change the numbers a few
    times and run the code to see how this functionality of Matplotlib works.

Now, we are completely done with this example. We first appreciated the visual's
storytelling values, then we also discussed each important element of the code we used
to create the visual.

Summary

Congratulations on your excellent progress in this chapter. Together, we learned the fundamental data visualization paradigms, such as summarizing and comparing populations, examining the relationships between attributes, adding visual dimensions, and comparing trends. These visualization techniques are very useful in effective data analytics.

All of the data we used in this chapter had been cleaned and preprocessed so we could focus on learning the visualization goals of data analytics. Now that you are on your way toward learning about effective data preprocessing in the next chapters, this deeper understanding of data visualization will help you become more effective in data preprocessing, and in turn, become more effective in data visualization and analytics.

In the next two chapters, we will continue learning about other data analytics goals, namely, prediction, classification, and clustering, before we start introducing effective preprocessing techniques.

Before moving forward and starting your journey in understanding those goals, spend some time on the following exercises to practice what you have learned.

Exercise

1. In this exercise, we will be using `Universities_imputed_reduced.csv`. Draw the following visualizations:

    a) Use boxplots to compare the student/faculty ratio (`stud./fac. ratio`) for the two populations of public and private universities.

    b) Use a histogram to compare the student/faculty ratio (`stud./fac. ratio`) for the two populations of public and private universities.

    c) Use subplots to put the results of *a)* and *b)* on top of one another to create a visual that compares the two populations even better.

2. In this exercise, we will continue using `Universities_imputed_reduced.csv`. Draw the following visualizations:

    a) Use a bar chart to compare the private/public ratio of all the states in the dataset. In this example, the populations we are comparing are the states.

    b) Improve the visualizations by sorting the states on the visuals based on the total number of universities they have.

    c) Create a stacked bar chart that shows and compares the percentages of public and private schools across different states.

3. For this example, we will be using WH Report_preprocessed.csv. Draw the following visualizations:

    a) Create a visual that compares the relationship between all the happiness indices.

    b) Use the visual you created in *a)* to report the happiness indices with strong relationships and describe those relationships.

    c) Confirm the relationships you found and described by calculating their correlation coefficients and adding these new pieces of information to your description to improve them.

4. For this exercise, we will continue using WH Report_preprocessed.csv. Draw the following visualizations:

    a) Draw a visual that examines the relationship between two attributes, Continent and Generosity.

    b) Based on the visual, is there a relationship between the two attributes? Explain why.

5. For this exercise, we will be using whickham.csv. Draw the following visualizations:

    a) What is the numerical attribute in this dataset? Draw two different plots that summarize the population of data objects for the numerical attribute.

    b) What are the categorical attributes in this dataset? Draw a plot per attribute that summarizes the population of the data object for each attribute.

    c) Draw a visual that examines the relationship between outcome and smoker. Do you notice anything surprising about this visualization?

    d) To demystify the surprising relationship you observed on *c)*, run the following code, and study the visual it creates:

    ```
    person_df = pd.read_csv('whickham.csv')
    person_df['age_discretized'] = pd.cut(person_df.age, bins
    = 4, labels=False)
    person_df.groupby(['age_discretized','smoker']).outcome.
    value_counts().unstack().unstack().plot.bar(stacked=True)
     plt.show()
    ```

    Using the visual that was created for the preceding code, explain the surprising observation made for *c)*.

    e) How many dimensions does the visual that was created for *d)* have? How did we manage to add dimensions to the bar chart?

6. For this exercise, we will be using WH Report_preprocessed.csv.

    a) Use this dataset to create a five-dimensional scatter plot to show the interactions between the following five attributes: year, Healthy_life_expectancy_at_birth, Social_support, Life_Ladder, and population. Use a control bar for year, marker size for population, marker color for Social_support, the x-axis for Healthy_life_expectancy_at_birth, and the y-axis for Life_Ladder.

    b) Interact with and study the visual you created for *a)* and report your observations.

7. For this exercise, we will continue using WH Report_preprocessed.csv.

    a) Create a visual that shows the trend of change for the Generosity attribute for all the countries in the dataset. To avoid making the visual overwhelming, use a gray color for the line plots of all the countries, and don't use a legend.

    b) Add three more line plots to the previous visual using a blue color and a thicker line (linewidth=1.8) for the three countries, United States, China, and India. Work out the visual so it only shows you the legend of these three countries. The following screenshot shows the visual that is being described:

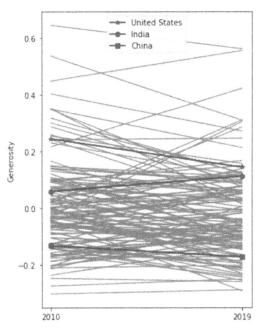

Figure 5.26 – Line plot comparing Generosity across all countries in 2010 and 2019 with an emphasis on the United States, India, and China

c) Report your observations from the visual. Make sure to refer to all of the line plots (gray and blue) in your observations.

6
Prediction

Being able to predict the future using data is becoming increasingly possible. Not only that; soon, being able to perform successful predictive modeling will not be a competitive advantage anymore—it will be a necessity to survive. To improve the effectiveness of predictive modeling, many focus on the algorithms that are used for prediction; however, there are many meaningful steps you can take to improve the success of prediction by performing more effective data preprocessing. That is the end goal in this book: learning how to preprocess data more effectively. However, in this chapter, we are going to take a very important step toward that goal. In this chapter, we are going to learn the fundamentals of predictive modeling. When we learn the concepts and the techniques of data preprocessing, we will rely on these fundamentals to make better data preprocessing decisions.

While many different algorithms can be applied for predictive modeling, the fundamental concepts of these algorithms are all the same. After covering those fundamentals in this chapter, we will cover two of these algorithms that are distinct from one another in terms of complexity and transparency: **linear regression** and **multi-layer perceptron** (**MLP**).

These are the main topics that this chapter will cover:

- Predictive models
- Linear regression
- MLP

Technical requirements

You will be able to find all of the code and the datasets that are used in this book in a GitHub repository exclusively created for this book. To find the repository, click on this link: `https://github.com/PacktPublishing/Hands-On-Data-Preprocessing-in-Python`. In this repository, you will find a folder titled `Chapter06`, from which you can download the code and the data for better learning.

Predictive models

Using data to predict the future is exciting and doable using data analytics. In the realm of data analytics, there are two types of future predictions, outlined as follows:

- Predict a numerical value—for example, predict next year's price of Amazon's stock market.

- Predict a label or a class—for example, predict whether a customer is likely to stop purchasing your services and switch to your competition.

By and large, when we use the term **prediction**, we mean predicting a numerical value. To predict a class or a label, the term that is used is **classification**. In this chapter, we will focus on the prediction goal of data analytics, and the next chapter will cover classification.

The prediction of future numerical values also falls into two major overarching types: **forecasting** and **regression analysis**. We will briefly explain forecasting, before turning our attention to regression analysis.

Forecasting

In data analytics, forecasting refers to techniques that are used to predict the future numerical values of time-series data. Where forecasting is distinct is in its application to time-series data—for instance, the simplest forecasting method is the **simple moving average** (**SMA**). Under this method, you would forecast the numerical value of a future data point in your time-series data using the most recent data points.

Example of using forecasting to predict the future

Let's look at an example that features the **moving average (MA)** for forecasting. The following table shows the number of student applications that **Mississippi State University (MSU)** received from **2006** to **2021**:

Year	2006	2007	2008	2009	2010	2011	2012	2013	2014	2015	2016	2017	2018	2019	2020	2021
N_Applications	5778	5140	6141	7429	7839	9300	9864	10449	11117	10766	12701	13930	13817	17363	18269	16127

Figure 6.1 – Number of MSU applications from 2006 to 2021

The following screenshot visualizes the data presented in the preceding table using a line plot:

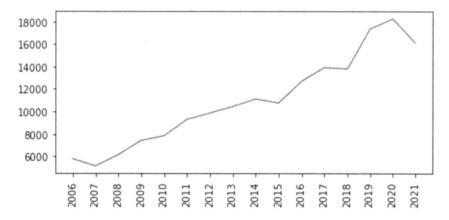

Figure 6.2 – Line plot for the number of MSU applications from 2006 to 2021

MSU, for planning purposes, would like to have some ideas of how many new applications they will receive in 2022. One way to go about this would be to use the MA method. For this method, you need to specify the number of data points you want to use for forecasting. This is often denoted by n. Let's use five data points ($n=5$). In that case, you would use the data from 2017, 2018, 2019, 2020, and 2021 in your prediction. Simply, you calculate the average number of applications for these years and use that as the estimated forecast for the next year. The average value of 13,930, 13,817, 17,363, 18,269, and 16,127 is 15,901.2, which can be used as an estimate for the number of applications for 2022.

The following screenshot depicts the application of MA with *n=5*:

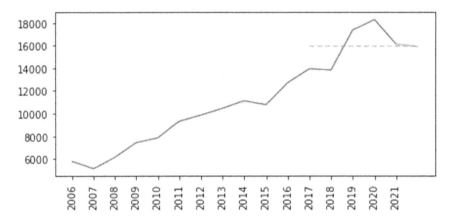

Figure 6.3 – Application of a simple MA forecasting method on the number
of MSU applications from 2006 to 2021

There are more complicated methods for forecasting using time-series data such
as weighted MA, exponential smoothing, double exponential smoothing, and more.

We do not cover these methods in this book as the data preprocessing that is needed for
all time-series data is the same. However, what you'd want to remember from forecasting
is that the methods work on single-dimensional time-series data for prediction.
For instance, in the MSU example, the only dimension of data we had was the N_
Applications attribute.

This single dimensionality is in stark contrast to the next prediction methodology we will
cover. Regression analysis, in contrast to forecasting, finds relationships between multiple
attributes to estimate numerical values of one of the attributes.

Regression analysis

Regression analysis tackles the task of predicting numerical values using the relationship
between **predictor attributes** and the **target attribute**.

The target attribute is the attribute whose numerical values we are interested in
predicting. The term **dependent attribute** is another name that is used for the same
idea. The meaning of dependent attribute comes from the fact that the value of the
target attribute is dependent on other attributes; we call those attributes **predictors**
or **independent attributes**.

Many different methods could be used for regression analysis. As long as the methods seek to find relationships between the independent attributes and the dependent attribute for predicting the dependent attribute, we categorize the methods under regression analysis. **Linear regression**, which is one of the simplest and yet widely used methods of regression analysis is, of course, one of these methods. However, other techniques such as **MLP** and **regression tree** are also categorized under regression analysis.

Example of designing regression analysis to predict future values

For example, the prediction of the number of MSU applications in the next year can also be modeled using regression analysis. The following figure shows two independent attributes that have the potential to predict the **Number of Applications** dependent attribute. You can see in this example that the prediction model engages more than one dimension; we have three dimensions—two independent attributes and one dependent attribute.

The first independent attribute, **Previous year football performance**, is the MSU football team ratio of winning games. The second independent attribute is **Average number of applications from last two years**:

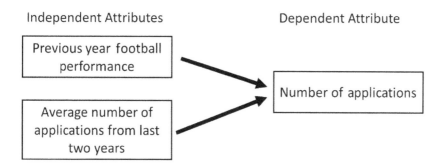

Figure 6.4 – Example of regression analysis

The second independent attribute is interesting as it depicts that you can interface forecasting methods with regression analysis by including the value of forecasting methods as independent attributes of regression analysis. The average number of applications from the last 2 years is the value of the SMA method with *n=2*.

How Do We Find Possible Independent Attributes?

You can see the vital role of having appropriate independent attributes for predicting the attribute of interest (dependent attribute) in regression analysis. Envisioning and collecting possible predictors (independent attributes) is the most important part of performing successful regression analysis.

So far, you have learned valuable skills in this book that can help you in the quest to envision possible predictors. The understanding you amassed in *Chapter 4, Databases*, will allow you to imagine what is possible and search for and collect that data.

In one of the future chapters, *Chapter 12, Data Fusion and Integration*, you will learn all the skills you will need to go about integrating data from different sources to support your regression analysis.

Once the independent and dependent attributes are identified, we have completed and modeled our regression analysis. Next, we will need to employ the appropriate algorithms to find relationships between these attributes and use those relationships for prediction. In this chapter, we will cover two very different algorithms that can do this: linear regression and MLP.

Linear regression

The name **linear regression** will tell you all you need to know about it—the *regression* part tells you this method performs regression analysis, and the *linear* part tells you the method assumes linear relationships between attributes.

To find a possible relationship between attributes, linear regression assumes and models a universal equation that relates the target (the dependent attribute) to the predictors (the independent attributes). This equation is depicted here:

$$target = \beta_0 + \beta_1 \times predictor1 + \beta_2 \times predictor2 + \cdots + \beta_N \times predictorN$$

This equation uses a parameter approach. In this equation N stands for the number of predictors shows the linear regression universal equation.

The working of linear regression is very simple. The method first estimates the βs so that the equation fits the data best, and then uses the estimated βs for prediction.

Let's learn this method with an example. We will continue solving the number of MSU applications in the following example.

Example of applying linear regression to perform regression analysis

We have so far identified our independent and dependent attributes, so we can show the linear regression equation for this example. The equation is shown here:

$$N\_Applications = \beta_0 + \beta_1 \times P\_Football\_Performance + \beta_2 \times SMA2$$

The MSU applications.csv dataset has all the attributes we need to estimate the βs. Let's first read this data and take a look at it. The following screenshot shows the code we run to read the data and the whole dataset:

```
In [1]:    import pandas as pd
           msu_df = pd.read_csv('MSU applications.csv')
           msu_df.set_index('Year',drop=True,inplace=True)
           msu_df
```

Out[1]:

Year	P_Football_Performance	SMAn2	N_Applications
2006	0.273	5778.0	5778
2007	0.273	5778.0	5140
2008	0.250	5459.0	6141
2009	0.615	5640.5	7429
2010	0.333	6785.0	7839
2011	0.417	7634.0	9300
2012	0.692	8569.5	9864
2013	0.538	9582.0	10449
2014	0.615	10156.5	11117
2015	0.538	10783.0	10766
2016	0.769	10941.5	12701
2017	0.692	11733.5	13930
2018	0.462	13315.5	13817
2019	0.692	13873.5	17363
2020	0.615	15590.0	18269
2021	0.462	17816.0	16127

Figure 6.5 – Reading MSU applications.csv and showing the dataset

In this dataset, we have the following attributes:

- `P_Football_Performance`: This attribute is the overall winning ratio of the MSU football team during the previous academic year.

- `SMAn2`: This attribute is the calculated value of the SMA with *n=2*. For instance, `SMAn2` for row **2009** is the average of the `N_Applications` attribute in 2008 and 2007. Confirm this calculation before reading on.

- `N_Applications`: This is the same data as what we saw in *Figure 6.1* and *Figure 6.2*. This is the dependent attribute that we are interested in predicting.

We are going to use the `scikit-learn` module to estimate these *βs* using `msu_df`, so first, we need to install this module on our **Anaconda** platform. Running the following code will install the module:

```
conda install scikit-learn
```

Once installed, you need to import the module to start using it every time, just as with the other module we have been using. However, since `scikit-learn` is rather large, we will import exactly what we want to use each time. For instance, the following code only imports the `LinearRegression` function from the module:

```
from sklearn.linear_model import LinearRegression
```

Now, we have at our disposal a function that can seamlessly calculate the *βs* of our model using `msu_df`. We now only need to introduce the data to the `LinearRegression()` function in the appropriate way.

We can do this in four steps, as follows:

1. First, we will specify our independent and dependent attributes, by specifying the X and y list of variables. See the following code snippet:

   ```
   X = ['P_Football_Performance','P_2SMA']
   Y = 'N_Applications'
   ```

2. Second, we will create two separate datasets from `msu_df` using the list X and Y: `data_X` and `data_y`. `data_X` is a DataFrame with all the independent attributes, and `data_y` is a Series that is the dependent attribute. The following code shows this:

   ```
   data_X = msu_df[X]
   data_y = msu_df[y]
   ```

This step and the previous step could have been merged with the next steps; however, it is best to keep your code clean and tidy, and I highly recommend using my guidelines, at least in the beginning.

3. Next, we will create the model and introduce the data. The following code will do that. We create a linear regression model and call it `lm`, and introduce the data to it:

```
lm = LinearRegression()
lm.fit(data_X, data_y)
```

When you run the following code almost nothing happens, but don't worry—the model has done its bit, and we only need to access the estimated βs in the next step.

4. As indicated, the estimated βs are within the trained `lm` model. We can use `lm.intercept_` to access $\beta 0$, and `lm.coef_` will show you $\beta 1$, and $\beta 2$. The following code prints out an organized report with all the $\beta 0$ instances:

```
print('intercept (b0) ', lm.intercept_)
coef_names = ['b1','b2']
print(pd.DataFrame({'Predictor': data_X.columns,
                    'coefficient Name':coef_names,
                    'coefficient Value': lm.coef_}))
```

After running these four steps successfully, you will have estimated the βs. I did show the code for this step by step, but all this is normally done in one chunk of code. The following screenshot shows the preceding lines of code and a small report from *Step 4*:

```
In [2]:    from sklearn.linear_model import LinearRegression

           X = ['P_Football_Performance','SMAn2']
           y = 'N_Applications'

           data_X = msu_df[X]
           data_y = msu_df[y]

           lm = LinearRegression()
           lm.fit(data_X, data_y)

           print('intercept (b0) ', lm.intercept_)
           coef_names = ['b1','b2']
           print(pd.DataFrame({'Predictor': data_X.columns,
                               'coefficient Name':coef_names,
                               'coefficient Value': lm.coef_}))

           intercept (b0)   -890.7106225983407
                          Predictor coefficient Name   coefficient Value
           0   P_Football_Performance              b1         5544.961933
           1                    SMAn2              b2            0.907032
```

Figure 6.6 – Fitting msu_df data to LinearRegression() and reporting the βs

Now that we have estimated the βs of the regression model, we can introduce our trained model. The following equation shows the trained regression equation:

$$N\_Applications = -890.71 + 5544.96 \times P\_Football\_Performance + 0.91 \times SMAn2$$

Next, we will learn how the trained regression equation can be used for prediction.

How to use the trained regression equation for prediction

To use the equation to predict the number of MSU applications in 2022, MSU needs to put together the P_Football_performance and SMAn2 attributes for 2022. Here, we describe the process of finding these values:

- P_Football_performance: At the time of writing this chapter (April 2021), the college football season of 2020-21 had ended and MSU achieved 4 wins out of 11 games, reaching 0.364 winning ratios.

- SMAn2: The N_Applications values for 2021 and 2020 are 18,269 and 16,127, respectively. The average value of these numbers is 17,198.

Here is the calculation to predict N_Applications values in 2022:

$$N_{Applications} = -890.71 + 5544.96 \times 0.364 + 0.91 \times 17198 = 16777.83$$

We do not have to do the preceding calculations ourselves; we did this for learning purposes. We can use the .predict() function that comes with all of the scikit-learn predictive models. The following screenshot shows how this can be done:

```
In [3]:  ▶  newData = pd.DataFrame({'P_Football_Performance':0.364,'SMAn2':17198},
                                    index=[2022])
            newData

Out[3]:
                    P_Football_Performance   SMAn2

            2022                     0.364   17198


In [4]:  ▶  lm.predict(newData)

Out[4]:  array([16726.78787061])
```

Figure 6.7 – Calculating the number of applications for 2022 using the .predict() function

There is some difference between the preceding equation calculation and programming calculation. One reached 16777.82 and the other arrived at 16726.78. The difference is due to the rounding-ups we did to present the regression equation. The value that the .predict() function came to, 16726.78, is more accurate.

Pay Attention!

Linear regression, and regression analysis in general, is a very established field of analytics. There are many evaluative methods and procedures to ensure the model we have created is of good quality. In this book, we will not cover those concepts, as the goal of this chapter is to introduce techniques that may need data preprocessing. By knowing the mechanism of these techniques, you will be able to perform data preprocessing more effectively.

Now that we have completed this prediction, look back and examine the working of linear regression. Here, linear regression achieved the following two objectives:

1. Linear regression used its universal and linear equation to find the relationship between the independent and dependent attributes. The β coefficient of each independent attribute tells you how the independent attributes relate to the dependent attribute—for instance, the coefficient of *SMAn2*, $\beta2$, came out to be 0.91. This means that even if the MSU football team loses all of its games (which makes the value of N_Football_Performance zero), next year, the number of applications will be an equation of *-890.71 + 0.91×SMAn2*.

2. The linear regression equation has packaged the estimated relationship in an equation that can be used for future observations.

These two matters, extraction and estimation of the relationships and packaging the estimated relationship for future data objects, are essential for the proper working of any predictive model.

What is great about linear regression is that the simplicity of these matters can be seen and appreciated. This simplicity helps in understanding the working of linear regression and comprehending the patterns it extracts. However, the simplicity works against the method as far as its reach to estimate and package a more complex and non-linear relationship between the independent and dependent attributes.

Next in this chapter, we will be briefly introduced to another prediction algorithm that is at the other end of the spectrum. MLP is a complex algorithm that is capable of finding and packaging more complex patterns between independent and dependent attributes, but it lacks the transparency and intuitiveness of linear regression.

MLP

MLP is a very complex algorithm with many details, and going over its functioning and different parts abstractly will be difficult to follow. So, let's dive in with an example. We will continue using the number of MSU applications in this section.

While linear regression uses an equation, MLP uses a network of neurons to connect the independent attributes to the dependent attribute. An example of such a network is shown in the following screenshot:

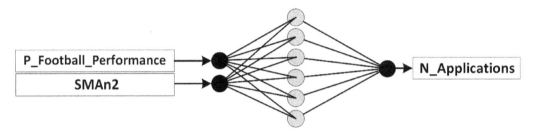

Figure 6.8 – An MLP network example for the number of MSU applications problem

Every MLP network has six distinct parts. Let's go through these parts using *Figure 6.8*, as follows:

- **Neurons**: Each of the circles in *Figure 6.8* is called a neuron. A neuron could be in the input layer, output layer, and hidden layers. We will cover three tree types of layers in the following section.

- **Input layer**: A layer of neurons from which values are inputted to the network. In a prediction task, for as many as the number of independent attributes, we will have neurons in the input layer. In *Figure 6.8*, you can see we have two neurons in the input layer, one for each of our independent attributes.

- **Output layer**: A layer of neurons out of which the processed values of the network come. In a prediction task, for as many as the number of dependent attributes, we will have neurons in the output layer. More often than not, we only have one dependent attribute. This holds true for *Figure 6.8*, as our prediction task only has one dependent attribute and the network has only one neuron in the output layer.

- **Hidden layers**: One or more layers of neurons that come between the input and output layers. The number of hidden layers and the number of neurons in each hidden layer can be—and should be—adjusted for the desired level of model complexity and computational cost. For example, *Figure 6.8* only has one hidden layer and six neurons in that hidden layer.

- **Connections**: The lines that connect the neurons of one layer to the next level are called connections. These connections must exist exhaustively from one level to the next; *exhaustively* means that all the neurons in a left layer are connected to all the neurons to its right layer.

Now that you understand each part of the preceding MLP network, we will turn our attention to how MLP goes about finding the relationship between the independent attributes and the dependent attribute.

How does MLP work?

MLP works both similarly to and differently from linear regression. Let's first go over their similarities, and then we will cover their differences. Their similarities are listed here:

- Linear regression relies on its structured equation to capture the relationships between the independent attributes and the dependent attribute. MLP, too, relies on its network structure to capture the same relationships.

- Linear regression estimates the βs as a way to use its structured equation to fit itself to the data and hence find the relationship between the independent attributes and the dependent attribute. MLP, too, estimates a value for each of the connections on its structure to fit itself to the data; these values are called the connection's weight. So, both linear regression and MLP use the data to update themselves so that they can explain the data using their predefined structures.

- Once the βs for linear regression and the connections' weight for MLP are properly estimated using the data, both algorithms are ready to be used to predict new cases.

We can see that both algorithms are very similar; however, they also have many differences. Let's go over those now, as follows:

- While the linear regression algorithm's structured equation is fixed and simple, MLP's structure is adjustable and can be set to be very complex. In essence, the more hidden layers and neurons an MLP structure has, the more the algorithm is capable of capturing more complex relationships.

- While linear regression relies on proven mathematical formulas to estimate the βs, MLP has to resort to heuristics and computations to estimate the best connections' weights for the data.

The most famous heuristic that is used to estimate the connections' weights for MLP is called **backpropagation**. The heuristic is very simple in essence; however, coding it and getting it to work can be tricky. The good news for us is that we do not have to worry about coding it, as there are stable modules we can use. However, let's go through its simple idea once before seeing how we can use the aforementioned modules.

Backpropagation

For backpropagation, each connection's weight is first assigned a random number between -1 and 1. Yes—this is done completely randomly and it is called MLP's **random initialization**.

After MLP's random initialization, the algorithm will be capable of predicting a value for any inputted data object. Of course, these predictions will be erroneous. Backpropagation uses these errors and the extent of these errors to **learn**.

Every time a data object is exposed to the MLP network, MLP expects its dependent attribute. As mentioned, this expectation is wrong, at least in the beginning. So, backpropagation calculates the error of the network for each exposure, moves backward on the network, and updates the connection's weight in such a way that if the same data object is exposed again, the amount of error will be a little less.

The network will be exposed to all data objects in the dataset more than once. Every time all the data objects are exposed to the network, we call that one **epoch of learning**. Backpropagation makes the network undergo enough epochs of learning so that the collective amount of error for the network will be acceptable.

Now that we have this general understanding of MLP and its major heuristic to estimate the connections' weights, let's together see an example of using the `scikit-learn` module to perform a prediction task using MLP.

Example of applying MLP to perform regression analysis

To implement MLP using the `scikit-learn` module, we need to take the same four steps that we took for linear regression. In short, these four steps are listed as follows.

1. Specifying our independent and dependent attributes
2. Creating two separate datasets: `data_X` and `data_y`
3. Creating a model and introducing the data
4. Predicting

The following code snippet shows these four steps being applied to the number of MSU applications problem. It shows the MLPRegressor class being imported from the sklearn.neural_network module first:

```
from sklearn.neural_network import MLPRegressor
X = ['P_Football_Performance','SMAn2']
y = 'N_Applications'
data_X = msu_df[X]
data_y = msu_df[y]
mlp = MLPRegressor(hidden_layer_sizes=6, max_iter=10000)
mlp.fit(data_X, data_y)
mlp.predict(newData)
```

The code is almost the same as the code that we used for linear regression, with some minor changes. Let's go over those, as follows:

- Instead of creating lm using LinearRegression(), we created mlp using MLPRegressor().

- The LinearRegression() function did not need any input, as linear regression is a simple algorithm with no hyperparameters. But MLPRegressor() needed at least two inputs, hidden_layer_sizes=6 and max_iter=10000. The first input (hidden_layer_sizes=6) specifies the network structure. By inputting only one number, we are indicating we only have one hidden layer, and by using the number 6, we are indicating that the hidden layer has six neurons. This is in line with the network design we saw in *Figure 6.8*. The second input (max_iter=10000) specifies that you want at least 10,000 epochs of learning before the module should give up on converging.

If you successfully run the preceding code a few times, you will observe the following two general trends:

- The code will output a somewhat different prediction for newData every time, but the values are all around 18,000.

- On some runs, the code will also create a warning. The warning is that the MLP algorithm was not able to converge even after 10,000 epochs of learning.

Now, let's discuss these two trends.

MLP reaching different predictions on every run

Let's discuss the first observation: *The code will output a somewhat different prediction for newData every time, but the values are all around 18,000.*

MLP is a random-based algorithm. If you remember from our backpropagation learning, every time the network is initialized, a random number between -1 and 1 is assigned to each of the connections. These values are then updated so that the network fits the data better; however, the beginning is random, and therefore the results are going to be different.

However, if you pay attention to these different conclusions the random-based model reached, you will see that even though they are different, they are somewhat consistent. They are all around 18,000. This shows that the random-based procedure is capable of finding similar and meaningful patterns in the data.

MLP needing significant epochs of learning

Let's now discuss the second observation: *On some runs, the code will also create a warning. The warning is that the MLP algorithm was not able to converge even after 10,000 epochs of learning.*

As we will never know when the random-based algorithm will converge, we will have to put a cap on the number of epochs of learning. In fact, having 10,000 epochs of learning is extravagantly high, and we can afford it only because the data has only 16 data objects. The default value of `max_iter` for `MLPRegressor()` is `200`. That means if we had not specified `max_iter=10000`, the function would have assumed `max_iter=200`. In this case, that would mean the algorithm would not converge more often, and its conclusions would be less consistent. Give this a try and observe the aforementioned patterns.

Pay Attention!

MLP is a very complex and flexible algorithm; here, we only discussed two of its hyperparameters (`hidden_layer_sizes` and `max_iter`), but it has many more, and to successfully use MLP, you will need to tune it first. To tune an algorithm is to find the hyperparameters that work best for a dataset. We will not cover how MLP is tuned here, as we only need a basic understanding of the algorithm so that it will support our data preprocessing journey.

Furthermore, just as with linear regression, MLP should be rigorously evaluated for validity and reliability before implementation. We will not use those concepts and techniques in this book either for the same reason.

Summary

Congratulations! You made really good progress in this chapter. Together, we learned the fundamental concepts and techniques for using data to perform predictions. We separated the predictions into predicting numerical values and predicting events and labels. In data mining, the term **prediction** is used for predicting numerical values, and we use **classification** for predicting events and labels. In this chapter, we covered data mining task prediction, and in the next chapter, we will cover data mining task classification.

Before moving forward and starting your journey to learn about classification and how it can be done in the next chapter, spend some time on the following exercises and solidify your learnings.

Exercises

1. *MLP has the potential to create prediction models that are more accurate than prediction models that are created by linear regression.* This statement is generally correct. In this exercise, we want to explore one of the reasons why the statement is correct. Answer the following questions:

   a) The following formula shows the linear equation that we used to connect the dependent and independent attributes of the number of MSU applications problem. Count and report the number of coefficients that linear regression can play with to fit the equation to the data.

   $$N\_Applications = \beta_0 + \beta_1 \times P\_Football\_Performance + \beta_2 \times SMA2$$

   b) *Figure 6.8* shows the MLP network structure we used to connect the dependent and independent attributes of the number of MSU applications problem. Count and report the number of connections' weights MLP can play with to fit the network to the data.

   c) Use your answers from a) and b) to state why MLP has more potential in terms of creating prediction models with higher accuracy.

2. In this exercise, we will be using `ToyotaCorolla_preprocessed.csv`.
    This dataset has the following columns: `Age`, `Mileage_KM`, `Quarterly_Tax`,
    `Weight`, `Fuel_Type_CNG`, `Fuel_Type_Diesel`, `Fuel_Type_Petrol`, and
    `Price`. Each data object in this dataset is a used Toyota Corolla car. We would like
    to use this dataset to predict the price of used Toyota Corolla cars.

    a) Read the data into the `car_df` pandas DataFrame.

    b) Use the skills you picked up in the previous chapter to come up with data
       visualizations that show the relationship between the attribute price and the rest
       of the attributes.

    c) Use the visuals in b) to describe the relationship each of the attributes has with
       the attribute price.

    d) Create a correlation matrix for all the attributes, and report the correlation values
       for the relationship that you investigated in b) and c).

    e) Were the visual investigations you performed in b) and c) confirmed in d)? For
       which types of attributes were the conclusions for c) not confirmed in d)?

    f) Perform linear regression to predict the attribute price. Use all the attributes that
       you detect had a meaningful relationship with the attribute price as independent
       attributes. Predict the price of a car with the following specifications: `Age`: 74
       months, `Mileage_KM`: 124,057, `Quarterly_Tax`: 69, and `Weight`: 1,050. The
       car fuel type is petrol.

    g) Implement an MLP algorithm to predict the attribute price. Use all the attributes
       that you used in f) and predict the price of the same new car presented in f).
       Use 15 neurons in one hidden layer (`hidden_layer_sizes`), and set the
       `max_iter` attribute as `100`.

    h) The actual price of the new car presented under f) is 7,950. Report which
       algorithm performed a better prediction.

7
Classification

As you learned how to go about predicting numerical values in the previous chapter, in this chapter, we will turn our attention to predicting categorical ones. Essentially, that is what classification is: *predicting future categorical values*. While prediction focuses on estimating what some numerical values will be in the future, classification predicts the occurrence or non-occurrence of events in the future. For instance, in this chapter, we will see how classification can predict whether an individual will default on their loan or not.

In this chapter, we will also discuss the procedural similarities and differences between prediction and classification and will cover two of the most famous classification algorithms: **Decision Trees** and **K-Nearest Neighbors** (**KNN**). While this chapter provides a fundamental understanding of classification algorithms and also shows how they are done using Python, this chapter cannot be looked at as a comprehensive reference for classification. Rather, you want to focus on the fundamental concepts so that you will be ready for your data preprocessing journey, which you will start in *Chapter 9, Data Cleaning Level I – Cleaning Up the Table*.

These are the main topics that this chapter will cover:

- Classification models
- KNN
- Decision Trees

Technical requirements

You will be able to find all of the code and the dataset that is used in this book in a GitHub repository exclusively created for this book. To find the repository, click on this link: `https://github.com/PacktPublishing/Hands-On-Data-Preprocessing-in-Python`. In this repository, you will find a folder titled `Chapter07`, from which you can download the code and the data for better learning.

Classification models

In the previous chapter, we covered predictive modeling. Classification is a type of predictive modeling; specifically, classification is a regression analysis where the dependent attribute or the target is categorical instead of numerical.

Even though classification is a subset of predictive modeling, it is the area of data mining that has received the most attention due to its usefulness. At the core of many **machine learning** (**ML**) solutions in the real world today is a classification algorithm. Despite its prevalent applications and complicated algorithms, the fundamental concepts of classification are simple.

Just as with prediction, for classification, we need to specify our independent attributes (*predictors*) and the dependent attribute (*target*). Once we are clear about these and we have a dataset that includes these attributes, we are set to employ classification algorithms.

Classification algorithms, just as with prediction algorithms, seek to find the relationship between independent attributes and the dependent attribute, so by knowing the values of the independent attributes of the new data object, we can guess the class of (classify) the new data object.

Let's now look at an example together so that these rather abstract concepts start making more sense to you.

Example of designing a classification model

When you apply for a cash loan these days, make no mistake that a classification algorithm is going to have a major role in deciding if you are going to get the loan or not. The classification models that are used in real cases tend to be very complex with many independent attributes. However, the two most important pieces of information these algorithms rely on are your income and credit score.

Here, we will present a simple version of these complex classifications. The classification design shown in the following diagram uses **Income** and **Credit Score** as independent attributes to classify if an applicant will default on an accepted loan or not. The **Default?** binary attribute is the dependent attribute of the classification design:

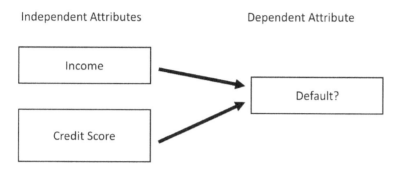

Figure 7.1 – Classification design of loan application problem

If you compare *Figure 6.4* from the previous chapter with the preceding diagram, you might assert that there is no difference between prediction and classification; you would not be completely wrong. Prediction and classification are almost identical but for one simple distinction: a classification's dependent attribute is categorical, but a prediction's dependent attribute is numerical. That small distinction amounts to lots of algorithmic and analytic changes for these two data mining tasks.

Classification algorithms

There are many well-researched, -designed, and -developed classification algorithms. In fact, there are more classification algorithms than there are prediction algorithms. To name a few, we have **KNN**, **Decision Trees**, **Multi-Layer Perceptron (MLP)**, **Support Vector Machine (SVM)**, and **Random Forest**. Some of these algorithms are listed for both prediction and classification. For instance, MLP will always be listed for both; however, MLP is inherently designed for the prediction task, but it can be modified so that it can also successfully tackle classification. On the other hand, we have the Decision Trees algorithm, which is inherently designed for classification, but it can also be modified to address prediction.

In this chapter, we are going to be briefly introduced to two of these algorithms: KNN and Decision Trees.

KNN

KNN is one of the simplest classification algorithms, and almost everything you need to know about its mechanism is presented in its name. In simple terms, to classify a new data object, KNN finds the *K-nearest neighbors* to the new data object from the training dataset and uses the label of those data objects to assign the likely label of the new data object.

It might be the case that KNN is too simple, and because of that, you do not fully understand its mechanism. Let's continue our learning, using the following example.

Example of using KNN for classification

We are going to continue working on the loan application problem that was introduced earlier. After completing the classification design, we specified **Income** and **Credit Score** as independent attributes and **Default?** as the dependent attribute. The following screenshot shows a dataset that can support this classification design. The dataset is from the `CustomerLoan.csv` file:

	income	score	default
0	78479	800	NO
1	95483	801	NO
2	101641	815	NO
3	104234	790	NO
4	108726	795	NO
5	112845	750	NO
6	114114	799	NO
7	114799	801	NO
8	119147	805	NO
9	119976	790	NO
10	84519	740	Yes
11	86504	753	Yes
12	89292	750	Yes
13	93941	706	Yes
14	97262	777	Yes
15	102658	680	Yes
16	103760	740	Yes
17	104451	730	Yes
18	107388	789	Yes
19	107400	690	Yes

Figure 7.2 – CustomerLoan.csv file

Now, let's assume that we want to use the preceding data to classify whether a customer with a yearly income of **US Dollars (USD)** $98,487 and a credit score of 785 will default on a loan or not.

As this example only includes three dimensions, we can use visualizations to perform and understand the KNN algorithm. The following screenshot shows the classification problem we would like to solve at one glance:

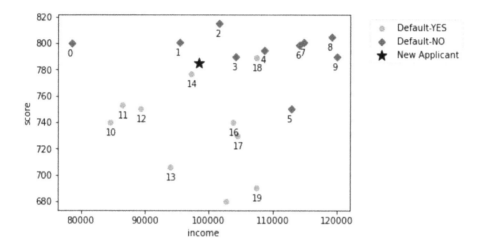

Figure 7.3 – Visualization of the loan application problem

The first step in performing KNN is to decide on *K*. Basically, we need to decide the number of nearest neighbors we would like to base our classification on. Let's assume we would like to use *K=4*.

Tuning KNN

Similar to many other data mining algorithms, to successfully use KNN for classification, you will need to tune the algorithm. Tuning KNN would mean finding the best number of *K* that would allow KNN to reach its best performance for every case study. In this book, we will not cover tuning as we are learning about algorithms, mainly to help us perform more successful data preprocessing.

So, when *K=4*, we can easily eyeball the preceding screenshot and see that the four nearest neighbors of the new applicant are data objects 1, 2, 3, and 14. As three out of four nearest data objects have a label of **Default-NO**, we will classify the new applicant as **Default-NO**. That is it—it's as simple as that.

While KNN is that simple in terms of its mechanism, creating a computer program that implements this algorithm is more difficult. Why is that? A few reasons are presented as follows:

- Here, we learned the mechanism of KNN, using an example that only had three dimensions. So, using a scatterplot and colors, we were able to display the problem and summarize all the data that we need to work with. Real-world problems will likely have more than just three dimensions.

- While we were able to eyeball the visual and detect the nearest neighbors, computers do not have the capability to just "*see*" which are the nearest neighbors. A computer program would need to calculate the distance between the new data object with all the data objects in the dataset so that it would find the K-nearest neighbors.

- What will happen if there is a tie? Let's say we have selected *K=4*, and two of the nearest neighbors are of one class and two others are from another.

   The great news for us is that we don't need to worry about any of these challenges because we can simply use a stable module that includes this algorithm. Let's import `KNeighborsClassifier` from the `sklearn.neighbors` module and apply it to our example here.

Before we can apply the algorithm, we need to take action about the following two matters:

1. First, if you have never used the `sklearn` module on **Anaconda Navigator**, you have to install it. Running the following code will install the module:

   ```
   conda install scikit-learn
   ```

2. Next, we will need to normalize our data. This is a data preprocessing concept, and we will cover it in depth when we get to it. However, let's briefly discuss its necessity here.

The reason that we need normalization of the data before applying KNN is that normally, the scale of the independent attributes are different from one another, and if the data is not normalized, the attribute with the larger scale will end up being more important in the distant calculation of the KNN algorithm, effectively canceling the role of other independent attributes. In this example, **income** ranges from 78,479 to 119,976, while **score** (for credit score) ranges from 680 to 815. If we were to calculate the distance between the data objects using these scales, all that would matter is *income* and not *credit score*.

So, to avoid letting the scale of the attributes meddle with the mechanism of the algorithm, we will normalize the data before using KNN. When an attribute is normalized, its values are transformed so that the updated attribute ranges from 0 to 1 without influencing the attribute's relative differentiation between the data objects.

The following code reads the `CustomerLoan.csv` file into the `applicant_df` DataFrame and creates two new columns in `applicant_df` that are the normalization transformation of the two columns in the original data:

```
applicant_df = pd.read_csv('CustomerLoan.csv')
applicant_df['income_Normalized'] = (applicant_df.income
- applicant_df.income.min())/(applicant_df.income.max() -
applicant_df.income.min())
applicant_df['score_Normalized'] = (applicant_df.score
- applicant_df.score.min())/(applicant_df.score.max() -
applicant_df.score.min())
```

The preceding code has created two new columns by using the following formula:

$$Normalized\ Value = \frac{Original\ Value - min}{max - min}$$

The preceding code has used the formula to transform the **income** column to **income_Normalized**, and **score** to **score_Normalized**. The following screenshot shows the result of this data transformation:

	income	score	default	income_Normalized	score_Normalized
0	78479	800	NO	0.000000	0.888889
1	95483	801	NO	0.409765	0.896296
2	101641	815	NO	0.558161	1.000000
3	104234	790	NO	0.620647	0.814815
4	108726	795	NO	0.728896	0.851852
5	112845	750	NO	0.828156	0.518519
6	114114	799	NO	0.858737	0.881481
7	114799	801	NO	0.875244	0.896296
8	119147	805	NO	0.980023	0.925926
9	119976	790	NO	1.000000	0.814815
10	84519	740	Yes	0.145553	0.444444
11	86504	753	Yes	0.193387	0.540741
12	89292	750	Yes	0.260573	0.518519
13	93941	706	Yes	0.372605	0.192593
14	97262	777	Yes	0.452635	0.718519
15	102658	680	Yes	0.582669	0.000000
16	103760	740	Yes	0.609225	0.444444
17	104451	730	Yes	0.625877	0.370370
18	107388	789	Yes	0.696653	0.807407
19	107400	690	Yes	0.696942	0.074074
20	98487	785	NaN	0.482155	0.777778

Figure 7.4 – Transformed applicant_df DataFrame

Take a moment to study the preceding screenshot; specifically, see the relationship between the columns and their normalized version. You will notice that the relevant distance and order between the values under the original attribute and its normalized version do not change. To see this, find the minimum and maximum under both the original attribute and its normalized version, and study those.

Pay attention to the fact that the last row of the data in the preceding screenshot is the new applicant that we would like to classify.

Now that the data is ready, we can apply the `KneighborsClassifier` module from `sklearn.neighbors` to do this. You can carry this out in four steps, as follows:

1. First, the `KneighborsClassifier` module needs to be imported. The following code does the import:

    ```
    from sklearn.neighbors import KNeighborsClassifier
    ```

2. Next, we need to specify our independent attributes and the dependent attribute. The following code keeps the independent attributes in `Xs` and the dependent attribute in `y`.

    Pay attention to the fact that we are dropping the last row of the data, as this is the row of the data we want to perform the prediction for. The `.drop(index=[20])` part will take care of this dropping:

    ```
    predictors = ['income_Normalized','score_Normalized']
    target = 'default'
    Xs = applicant_df[predictors].drop(index=[20])
    y= applicant_df[target].drop(index=[20])
    ```

3. Next, we will create a KNN model and then fit the data into it. The following code shows how this is done:

    ```
    knn = KNeighborsClassifier(n_neighbors=4)
    knn.fit(Xs, y)
    ```

4. Now, knn is ready to classify the new data objects. The following code shows how we can separate the last row of the dataset and make a prediction for it using knn:

    ```
    newApplicant = pd.DataFrame({'income_Normalized':
    applicant_df.iloc[20].income_Normalized,'score_
    Normalized': applicant_df.iloc[20].score_
    Normalized},index = [20])
    ```

```
predict_y = knn.predict(newApplicant)
print(predict_y)
```

If you put all the preceding four code snippets together, you will get the following output, which also reports the prediction for newApplicant:

In [7]: ▶
```
from sklearn.neighbors import KNeighborsClassifier

predictors = ['income_Normalized','score_Normalized']
target = 'default'

Xs = applicant_df[predictors].drop(index=[20])
y= applicant_df[target].drop(index=[20])

knn = KNeighborsClassifier(n_neighbors=4)
knn.fit(Xs, y)

newApplicant = pd.DataFrame({'income_Normalized':
                                applicant_df.iloc[20].income_Normalized,
                                'score_Normalized':
                                applicant_df.iloc[20].score_Normalized},
                                index = [20])
predict_y = knn.predict(newApplicant)
print(predict_y)

['NO']
```

Figure 7.5 – Classification using sklearn.neighbors

The output in the preceding screenshot, which is the class for newApplicant, confirms the conclusion we had already decided that KNN should arrive at.

So far in this chapter, you have learned about classification analysis, and you have also learned how the KNN algorithm works and how to get KneighborsClassifier from the sklearn.neighbors module to apply KNN to a dataset. Next, you will be introduced to another classification algorithm: **Decision Trees**.

Decision Trees

While you can use the Decision Trees algorithm for classification, just like KNN, it goes about the task of classification very differently. While KNN finds the most similar data objects for classification, Decision Trees first summarizes the data using a tree-like structure and then uses the structure to perform the classification.

Let's learn about Decision Trees using an example.

Example of using Decision Trees for classification

We will use `DecisionTreeClassifier` from `sklearn.tree` to apply the **Decision Trees algorithm** to `applicant_df`. The code needed to use Decision Trees is almost identical to that of KNN. Let's see the code first, and then I will draw your attention to their similarities and differences. Here it is:

```
from sklearn.tree import DecisionTreeClassifier
predictors = ['income','score']
target = 'default'
Xs = applicant_df[predictors].drop(index=[20])
y= applicant_df[target].drop(index=[20])
classTree = DecisionTreeClassifier()
classTree.fit(Xs, y)
predict_y = classTree.predict(newApplicant)
print(predict_y)
```

There are two differences between the preceding code and the KNN code. Here, we list these differences:

- First, the decision tree, due to the way it works, does not need the data to be normalized, so that is why the `predictors = ['income','score']` line of code uses the original attributes. We used the normalized version for KNN.

- Second, and obviously, we have used `DecisionTreeClassifier()` instead of `KneighborsClassifier()`. We also named our classification model `classTree` here, as opposed to `knn`, which we used for KNN.

Pay Attention!

As you probably have noticed, the code to use any predictive model (prediction and classification) in Python is very similar. Here are the steps we take for every single one of the models. First, we import the module that has the algorithm we would like to use. Next, we separate the data into independent and dependent attributes. After that, we create a model using the module we imported. Then, we use the `.fit()` function of the model we created to fit the data into the model. Lastly, we use the `.predict()` function to predict the dependent attribute for the new data objects.

If you successfully run the preceding code, you will see that the decision tree, unlike KNN, classifies newApplicant as **YES**. Let's look at the tree-like structure that DecisionTreeClassifier() created to come to this conclusion. To do this, we will use the plot_tree() function from the sklearn.tree module. Try running the following code to draw the tree-like structure:

```
from sklearn.tree import plot_tree
plot_tree(classTree,
          feature_names=predictors,
          class_names=y.unique(),
          filled=True,
          impurity=False)
```

The preceding code will output the following:

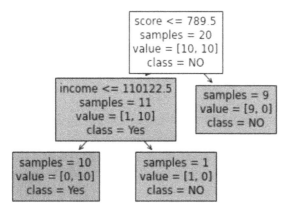

Figure 7.6 – Classification using sklearn.neighbors

The output in the preceding screenshot will intuitively tell you why Decision Trees arrived at a different conclusion from that of KNN. Starting from the top node, the dataset is separated into two groups: data objects whose scores are greater than **789.5** and data objects whose scores are lower than the cutoff value. All of the data objects with scores higher than **789.5** are labeled **NO-default**; therefore, the decision tree has come to the conclusion that if an applicant's score is higher than **789.5**, they should be classified as **NO**.

Since the score of newApplicant is 785, this rule does not apply to this data object. To find the class of the data object based on this tree-like structure. we need to go deeper. From the tree-like structure, we see that the data object that has scores lower than **789.5** and an income lower than **110,122.5** has defaulted on the loan. So, again, Decision Trees has reached the rule that when applicant scores are lower than **789.5** and **110,122.5**, they should be classified as **YES**. As the score and income of newApplicant are both lower than these cutoff values, the decision tree has concluded **YES** for it.

> **Tuning Decision Trees**
>
> Just as with KNN, Decision Trees also needs tuning to reach its fullest potential. In fact, Decision Trees requires even more tuning than what KNN needs, as Decision Trees has more hyperparameters that could be adjusted. However, for the same reasons mentioned for KNN, we will not cover the how-to of the tunings in this book.

The way Decision Trees works is also simple—Decision Trees splits the dataset into two segments again and again, at different stages, using one of the independent attributes until all segments of the data are *pure*. Purity means that all of the data in the segment is of the same class.

Before making our way to the end of this chapter, let's take a moment to discuss why the two algorithms have reached a different conclusion. First, we need to understand that when two distinct algorithms arrive at different conclusions about the same data object, this is a sign that classification of that data object is difficult, meaning that there are different patterns in the data that show the data object could be either of the classes. Second, as these algorithms have various ways of pattern recognition and decision-making, the algorithms that conclude differently may have prioritized the patterns in dissimilar ways.

Summary

Congratulations on your excellent progress in this chapter! Together, we learned the fundamental concepts and techniques of classification analysis. Specifically, we understood the distinction between classification and prediction, and we also learned about two famous classification algorithms and used them on a sample dataset to understand them even deeper.

In the next chapter, we will cover another important analytics task: clustering analysis. We will use the famous **K-Means** algorithm to learn more about clustering and also run a few experiments.

Before moving forward and starting your journey to learn about clustering, spend some time on the following exercises and solidify your learning.

Exercises

1. The chapter asserts that before using KNN, you will need to have your independent attributes normalized. This is certainly true, but how come we were able to get away with no normalization when we performed KNN using visualization? (See *Figure 7.3*.)

2. We did not normalize the data when applying Decision Trees to the loan application problem. For practice and a deeper understanding, apply Decision Trees to the normalized data, and answer the following questions:

   a) Did the conclusion of Decision Trees change? Why do you think that is? Use the mechanism of the algorithm to explain.

   b) Did the Decision Trees tree-like structure change? In what ways? Did the change make a meaningful difference in the way that the tree-like structure could be used?

3. For this exercise, we are going to use the `Customer Churn.csv` dataset. This dataset is randomly collected from an Iranian telecom company's database over a period of 12 months. A total of 3,150 rows of data, each representing a customer, bear information for 9 columns. The attributes that are in this dataset are listed here:

   Call Failures: Number of call failures

   Complaints: Binary (0: No complaint; 1: complaint)

   Subscription Length: Total months of subscription

   Seconds of Use: Total seconds of calls

   Frequency of Use: Total number of calls

   Frequency of SMS: Total number of text messages

   Distinct Called Numbers: Total number of distinct phone calls

   Status: Binary (1: active; 0: non-active)

   Churn: Binary (1: churn; 0: non-churn)—class label

   All of the attributes except for attribute churn are the aggregated data of the first 9 months. The churn labels are the state of the customers at the end of 12 months. 3 months is the designated planning gap.

   Using the preceding data, we would like to use this dataset to predict if the following customer will churn in 3 months:

   Call Failures: 8; Complaints: 1; Subscription Length: 40; Seconds of Use: 4,472; Frequency of Use: 70; Frequency of SMS: 100; Distinct Called Numbers: 25; Status: 1.

To do this, perform the following steps:

a) Read the data into the pandas `customer_df` DataFrame.

b) Use the skills you picked up in *Chapter 5*, *Data Visualization*, to come up with data visualizations that show the relationship between the churn attribute and the rest of the attributes.

c) Use the visuals in *Step 2* to describe the relationship each of the attributes has with the attribute Churn.

d) Perform KNN to predict if the aforementioned customer will be churned using all of the attributes that had a meaningful relationship with churn. Do you need to normalize the data first? Use *K=5*.

e) Repeat *Step 4*, but this time use *K=10*. Are the conclusions different?

f) Now, use the Decision Trees algorithm for classification. Do you need to normalize the data? Use `max_depth=4`. Is the conclusion of the Decision Trees algorithm different from that of the KNN algorithm?

   `max_depth` is a hyperparameter of the Decision Trees algorithm that controls how deep the learning can be. The number that is assigned is the maximum number of splits from the root of the tree.

g) Draw the tree-like structure of the decision tree and explain how the decision tree came to the conclusion it did.

8
Clustering Analysis

Finally, you have made your way to the last chapter of the second part of this book. **Clustering analysis** is another useful and popular algorithmic pattern recognition tool. When performing classification or prediction, the algorithms find the patterns that help create a relationship between the independent attributes and the dependent attribute. However, clustering does not have a dependent attribute, so it does not have an agenda in pattern recognition. Clustering is an algorithmic pattern recognition tool with no prior goals. With clustering, you can investigate and extract the inherent patterns that exist in a dataset. Due to these differences, classification and prediction are called **supervised learning**, while clustering is known as **unsupervised learning**.

In this chapter, we will use examples to fundamentally understand clustering analysis. Then, we will learn about the most popular clustering algorithm: **K-Means**. We will also perform some K-Means clustering analysis and examine the clustering output using centroid analysis.

In this chapter, we will cover the following topics:

- Clustering model
- K-Means algorithm

Technical requirements

You can find all the code and the dataset for this book in this book's GitHub repository. To find the repository, go to https://github.com/PacktPublishing/Hands-On-Data-Preprocessing-in-Python. You can find Chapter08 in this repository and download the code and the data for ease of learning.

Clustering model

Since you've already learned how to perform prediction and classification tasks in data analytics, in this chapter, you will learn about clustering analysis. In clustering, we strive to meaningfully group the data objects in a dataset. We will learn about clustering analysis through an example.

Clustering example using a two-dimensional dataset

In this example, we will use WH Report_preprocessed.csv to cluster the countries based on two scores called Life_Ladder and Perceptions_of_corruption in 2019.

The following code reads the data into report_df and uses Boolean masking to preprocess the dataset into report2019_df, which only includes the data of 2019:

```
report_df = pd.read_csv('WH Report_preprocessed.csv')
BM = report_df.year == 2019
report2019_df = report_df[BM]
```

The result of the preceding code is that we have a DataFrame, reprot1019_df, that only includes the data of 2019, as requested by the prompt.

Since we only have two dimensions to perform the clustering, we can take advantage of a scatterplot to visualize all the countries in relation to one another based on the two attributes in question: Life_Ladder and Perceptions_of_corruption.

The following code creates the scatterplot in two steps:

1. Create the scatterplot as we learned about in *Chapter 5, Data Visualization*.
2. Loop over all the data objects in report2019_df and annotate each point in the scatterplot using plt.annotate():

    ```
    plt.figure(figsize=(12,12))
    plt.scatter(report2019_df.Life_Ladder,
    report2019_df.Perceptions_of_corruption)
    ```

```
for _, row in report2019_df.iterrows():
    plt.annotate(row.Name, (row.Life_Ladder,
    row.Perceptions_of_corruption))
plt.xlabel('Life_Ladder')
plt.ylabel('Perceptions_of_corruption')
plt.show()
```

The output of the preceding code is as follows:

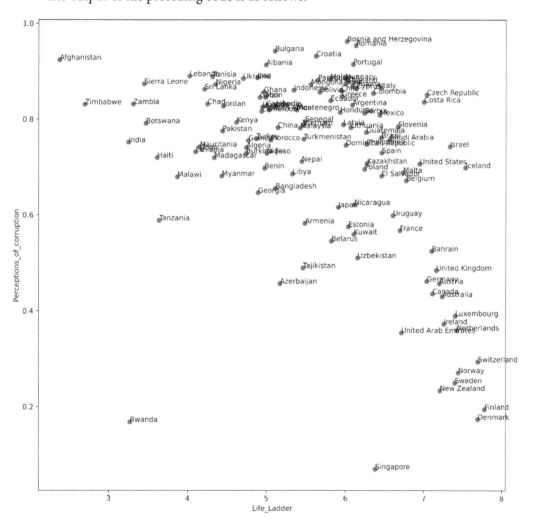

Figure 8.1 – Scatterplot of countries based on two happiness indices called Life_Ladder and Perception_of_corruption in 2019

As the data only has two dimensions, we can just look at the preceding figure and see the groups of countries that have more similarities to one another based on `Life_Ladder` and `Perceptions_of_corruption`. For instance, the following figure depicts the groups of countries based on the preceding scatterplot. The countries that are within the boundaries of more than one cluster should be assigned to one of the clusters.

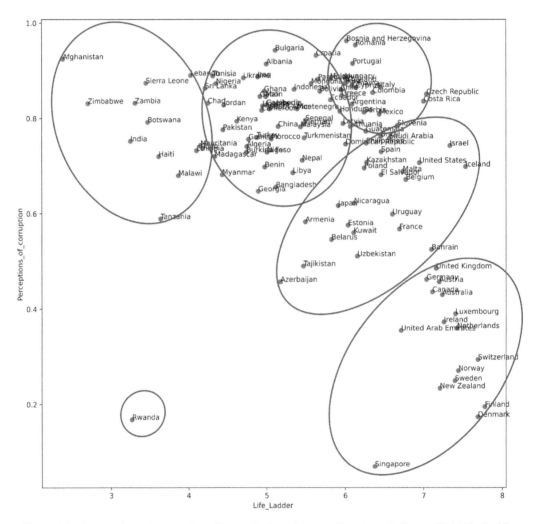

Figure 8.2 – Scatterplot and clustering of countries based on two happiness indices called Life_Ladder and Perceptions_of_corruption in 2019

Here, we see that we can meaningfully group all of the countries in the dataset into six clusters. One of the clusters only has one data object, indicating that the data object is an outlier based on the `Life_Ladder` and `Perceptions_of_corruption` attributes.

The key term here is *meaningful clusters*. So, let's use this example to understand what we mean by meaningful clusters. The six clusters shown in the preceding figure are meaningful for the following reasons:

- The data objects that are in the same clusters have similar values under `Life_Ladder` and `Perceptions_of_corruption`.

- The data objects that are in different clusters have different values under `Life_Ladder` and `Perceptions_of_corruption`.

In summary, meaningful clustering means that the clusters are grouped in such a way that the members of the same clusters are similar, while the members of different clusters are different.

When we cluster in two dimensions, meaning that we only have two attributes, the task of clustering is simple, as shown in the preceding example. However, when the number of dimensions increases, our ability to see patterns among the data using visualization either decreases or becomes impossible.

For instance, in the following example, we will learn about the difficulty of visual clustering when we have more than two attributes.

Clustering example using a three-dimensional dataset

In this example, we will use `WH Report_preprocessed.csv`. Try to cluster the countries based on the three happiness indexes, called `Life_Ladder`, `Perceptions_of_corruption`, and `Generosity`, in 2019.

The following code creates a scatterplot that uses color to add a third dimension:

```
plt.figure(figsize=(12,12))
plt.scatter(report2019_df.Life_Ladder,
            report2019_df.Perceptions_of_corruption,
            c=report2019_df.Generosity,cmap='binary')
plt.xlabel('Life_Ladder')
plt.ylabel('Perceptions_of_corruption')
plt.show()
```

Running the preceding code will create the following figure. The following figure visualizes `Life_Ladder` as the x dimension, `Perceptions_of_corruption` as the y dimension, and `Generosity` as `color`. The lighter the markers, the lower the `Generosity` score, while the darker the markers the higher the `Generosity` score:

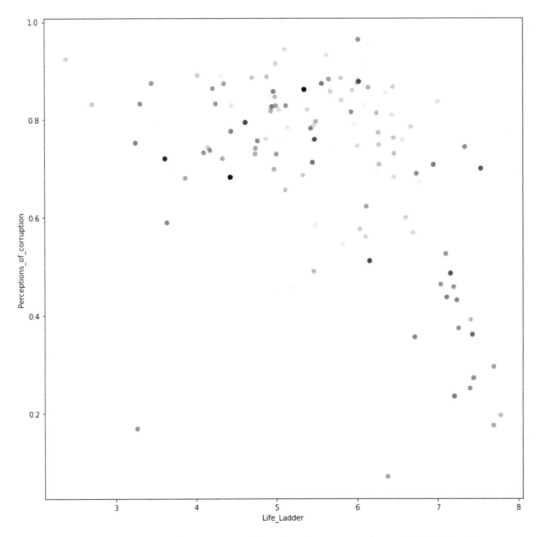

Figure 8.3 – Scatterplot of countries based on three happiness indices called Life_Ladder, Perceptions_of_corruption, and Generosity in 2019

Try to use the preceding visualizations to find the meaningful clusters of data objects based on the three attributes all at once. This task will be overwhelming for us as our brains aren't good at performing tasks where we need to process more than two dimensions at once.

The preceding figure does not include the names of the countries because even without them, we have difficulty using this figure for clustering. Adding the country label would only overwhelm us further.

The purpose of this example was not to complete it, but the conclusion we arrived at is very important: we need to rely on tools other than data visualization and our brains to perform meaningful clustering when the data has more than two dimensions.

The tools that we use for higher-dimensional clustering are algorithms and computers. There are many different types of clustering algorithms with various working mechanisms. In this chapter, we will learn about the most popular clustering algorithm: **K-Means**. This algorithm is simple, scalable, and effective for clustering.

K-Means algorithm

K-Means is a random-based heuristic clustering algorithm. Random-based means that the output of the algorithm on the same data may be different on every run, while heuristic means that the algorithm does not reach the optimal solution. However, from experience, we know that it reaches a good solution.

K-Means clusters the data objects using a simple loop. The following diagram shows the steps that the algorithm performs, as well as the loop that heuristically finds the clusters in the data:

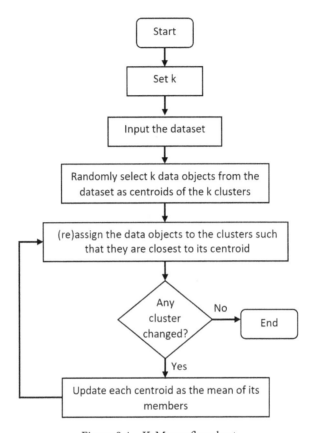

Figure 8.4 – K-Means flowchart

As we can see, the algorithm starts by randomly selecting k data objects as the cluster centroids. Then, the data objects are assigned to the cluster that is closest to its centroid. Next, the centroids are updated via the mean of all the data objects in the clusters. As the centroids are updated, the data objects are reassigned to the cluster that is closest to its centroid. Now, as the clusters are updated, the centroids will be updated as the mean of all the new data objects in the clusters. These last two steps keep occurring until there is no change in the cluster after updating the centroids. Once this stability has been reached, the algorithm terminates.

From a coding perspective, applying K-means is very similar to applying any of the other algorithms that we have learned about so far. The following example shows how we could have reached a similar result we reached using visualization. See *Figure 8.2* for more information.

Using K-Means to cluster a two-dimensional dataset

Earlier in this chapter, we grouped the countries into six clusters using `Life_Ladder` and `Perception_of_corruption`. Here, we would like to confirm the same clustering using K-Means.

The following code uses the `KMeans` function from the `sklearn.cluster` module to perform this clustering:

```
from sklearn.cluster import KMeans
dimensions = ['Life_Ladder','Perceptions_of_corruption']
Xs = report2019_df[dimensions]
kmeans = KMeans(n_clusters=6)
kmeans.fit(Xs)
```

The preceding code performs `KMeans` clustering in four lines:

1. `dimensions = ['Life_Ladder','Perceptions_of_corruption']`: This line of code specifies the attributes of the data we want to use for clustering.

2. `Xs = report2019_df[dimensions]`: This line of code separates the data we want to use for clustering.

3. `kmeans = KMeans(n_clusters=6)`: This line of code creates a K-Means model that is ready to cluster input data into six clusters.

4. `kmeans.fit(Xs)`: This line of code introduces the dataset we want to be clustered to the model we created in the previous step.

When we run the preceding code successfully, almost nothing happens. However, clustering has been performed, and the cluster membership of every row can be accessed using `kmeans.labels_`. The following code uses a loop, `kmeans.labels_`, and Boolean masking to print the members of each cluster:

```
for i in range(6):
    BM = kmeans.labels_==i
    print('Cluster {}: {}'.format(
          i,report2019_df[BM].Name.values))
```

The following screenshot puts the two preceding codes together and shows the output of the code as well. After running the code, you will probably get a different output from the one shown in the following screenshot. If you run the same code a few times, you will get a different output every time.

The reason for this inconsistency is that K-Means is a random-based algorithm. Please refer to the K-Means flowchart shown in *Figure 8.4*: K-Means starts by randomly selecting *k* data objects as the initial centroids. As this initialization is random, the outputs are different from one another.

Even though the outputs are different, the same countries are grouped under the same cluster each time. For instance, notice that the United Kingdom and Canada are in the same cluster every time. This is reassuring; it means that K-Means finds the same pattern in the data, even though it follows a random procedure:

```
In [10]:    from sklearn.cluster import KMeans
            dimensions = ['Life_Ladder','Perceptions_of_corruption']
            Xs = report2019_df[dimensions]
            kmeans = KMeans(n_clusters=6)
            kmeans.fit(Xs)

            for i in range(6):
                BM = kmeans.labels_==i
                print('Cluster {}: {}'.format(i,report2019_df[BM].Name.values))

            Cluster 0: ['Australia' 'Austria' 'Bahrain' 'Canada' 'Denmark' 'Finland' 'G
            ermany'
             'Iceland' 'Ireland' 'Israel' 'Luxembourg' 'Netherlands' 'New Zealand'
             'Norway' 'Sweden' 'Switzerland' 'United Kingdom']
            Cluster 1: ['Albania' 'Algeria' 'Armenia' 'Azerbaijan' 'Bangladesh' 'Benin'
             'Bulgaria' 'Burkina Faso' 'Cambodia' 'Cameroon' 'China' 'Gabon' 'Georgia'
             'Ghana' 'Guinea' 'Indonesia' 'Iraq' 'Liberia' 'Libya' 'Malaysia' 'Mali'
             'Mongolia' 'Montenegro' 'Morocco' 'Nepal' 'Niger' 'Senegal'
             'South Africa' 'Tajikistan' 'Turkey' 'Turkmenistan' 'Uganda' 'Vietnam']
            Cluster 2: ['Argentina' 'Belarus' 'Bolivia' 'Bosnia and Herzegovina' 'Chil
            e'
             'Colombia' 'Croatia' 'Cyprus' 'Dominican Republic' 'Ecuador' 'Estonia'
             'Greece' 'Guatemala' 'Honduras' 'Hungary' 'Japan' 'Kazakhstan' 'Kuwait'
             'Latvia' 'Lithuania' 'Moldova' 'Nicaragua' 'Panama' 'Paraguay' 'Peru'
             'Philippines' 'Poland' 'Portugal' 'Romania' 'Serbia' 'Thailand'
             'Uzbekistan']
            Cluster 3: ['Afghanistan' 'Botswana' 'Haiti' 'India' 'Rwanda' 'Sierra Leon
            e'
             'Tanzania' 'Zambia' 'Zimbabwe']
            Cluster 4: ['Belgium' 'Brazil' 'Costa Rica' 'Czech Republic' 'El Salvador'
             'France'
             'Italy' 'Malta' 'Mexico' 'Saudi Arabia' 'Singapore' 'Slovenia' 'Spain'
             'United Arab Emirates' 'United States' 'Uruguay']
            Cluster 5: ['Chad' 'Ethiopia' 'Jordan' 'Kenya' 'Lebanon' 'Madagascar' 'Mala
            wi'
             'Mauritania' 'Myanmar' 'Nigeria' 'Pakistan' 'Sri Lanka' 'Togo' 'Tunisia'
             'Ukraine']
```

Figure 8.5 – K-Means clustering based on two happiness indices called Life_Ladder and Perception_of_corruption in 2019 – Original data

Now, let's compare the clusters we found using K-Means (*Figure 8.5*) and the clusters we found using visualization (*Figure 8.2*). These clusters are different, even though the data that was used for clustering was the same. For instance, while **Rwanda** was an outlier in *Figure 8.2*, it is the member of a cluster in *Figure 8.5*. Why is this happening? Give this question some thought before reading on.

The following code will output a visual that can help you answer this question:

```
plt.figure(figsize=(21,4))
plt.scatter(report2019_df.Life_Ladder, report2019_
df.Perceptions_of_corruption)
for _, row in report2019_df.iterrows():
    plt.annotate(row.Name, (row.Life_Ladder,
                 row.Perceptions_of_corruption),
                 rotation=90)
plt.xlim([2.3,7.8])
plt.xlabel('Life_Ladder')
plt.ylabel('Perceptions_of_corruption')
plt.show()
```

This code will produce the following output:

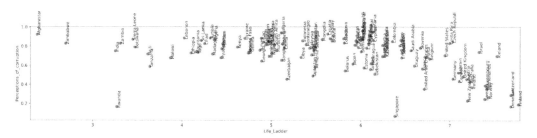

Figure 8.6 – The resized version of *Figure 8.1* and *Figure 8.2*

The only difference between the preceding output and *Figure 8.1* and *Figure 8.2* is that in the preceding output, the numerical scale of `Life_Ladder` and `Perceptions_of_corruption` has been adjusted to be the same.

`Matplotlib` automatically scaled both dimensions of *Figure 8.1* and *Figure 8.2* – `Life_Ladder` and `Perceptions_of_corruptions` – so that they appear to have a similar visual range. This can be seen if you pay attention to the amount of visual space between 3 and 4 on the `Life_Ladder` dimension, and then compare that to the amount of visual space between `0.2` and `0.4` on the `Perceptions_of_corruption` dimension. So, we can see that while the amounts of visual space are equal, the numerical values that represent them are very different. This realization answers the question that was raised earlier: why is the clustering outcome of *Figure 8.5* entirely different from the one we detected visually in *Figure 8.2*? The answer is that the two clusterings are not using the same data. The clustering represented in *Figure 8.2* uses a scaled version of the data, while the clustering represented in *Figure 8.5* (K-Means clustering) uses the original data.

Now, a second question we need to answer is, which clustering output should we use? Let me help you come to the right answer. When we want to cluster our data objects using two dimensions, `Life_Ladder` and `Perceptions_of_corruption`, how much weight do we want each dimension to play in the result of the clustering? Don't we want both attributes to play an equal role? Yes, that is the case. So, we want to choose the clustering that has given both dimensions equal importance. Since K-Means clustering used the original data without scaling it, the fact that `Life_Ladder` happened to have larger numbers influenced K-Means to prioritize `Life_Ladder` over `Perceptions_of_corruption`.

To overcome this challenge, before applying K-Means or any other algorithm that uses the distance between data objects as an important deciding factor, we need to normalize the data. Normalizing the data means the attributes are rescaled in such a way that all of them are represented in the same range. For instance, as you may recall, we normalized our datasets before applying KNN in the previous chapter for the same reason.

The following screenshot shows the code and the clustering output when the dataset is normalized before using K-Means. In this code, `Xs = (Xs - Xs.min())/(Xs.min()-Xs.max())` is used to rescale all the attributes in `Xs` to be between zero and one. The rest of the algorithm code is the same as the code we tried earlier in this chapter. Now, you can compare the clustering outcome in the following screenshot and the one shown in *Figure 8.2* to detect that the two ways of clustering are achieving almost the same results:

```
In [12]:  ▶  dimensions = ['Life_Ladder','Perceptions_of_corruption']
             Xs = report2019_df[dimensions]
             Xs = (Xs - Xs.min())/(Xs.max()-Xs.min())
             kmeans = KMeans(n_clusters=6)
             kmeans.fit(Xs)

             for i in range(6):
                 BM = kmeans.labels_==i
                 print('Cluster {}: {}'.format(i,report2019_df[BM].Name.values))

          Cluster 0: ['Australia' 'Austria' 'Canada' 'Denmark' 'Finland' 'Germany' 'I
          reland'
           'Luxembourg' 'Netherlands' 'New Zealand' 'Norway' 'Singapore' 'Sweden'
           'Switzerland' 'United Arab Emirates' 'United Kingdom']
          Cluster 1: ['Argentina' 'Bolivia' 'Bosnia and Herzegovina' 'Brazil' 'Chile'
           'Colombia' 'Costa Rica' 'Croatia' 'Cyprus' 'Czech Republic'
           'Dominican Republic' 'Ecuador' 'Greece' 'Guatemala' 'Honduras' 'Hungary'
           'Italy' 'Latvia' 'Lithuania' 'Mexico' 'Moldova' 'Mongolia' 'Panama'
           'Paraguay' 'Peru' 'Philippines' 'Portugal' 'Romania' 'Saudi Arabia'
           'Serbia' 'Slovenia' 'Thailand']
          Cluster 2: ['Albania' 'Algeria' 'Bangladesh' 'Benin' 'Bulgaria' 'Burkina Fa
          so'
           'Cambodia' 'Cameroon' 'China' 'Gabon' 'Georgia' 'Ghana' 'Guinea'
           'Indonesia' 'Iraq' 'Jordan' 'Kenya' 'Liberia' 'Libya' 'Malaysia' 'Mali'
           'Montenegro' 'Morocco' 'Myanmar' 'Nepal' 'Niger' 'Pakistan' 'Senegal'
           'South Africa' 'Turkey' 'Turkmenistan' 'Uganda' 'Ukraine' 'Vietnam']
          Cluster 3: ['Afghanistan' 'Botswana' 'Chad' 'Ethiopia' 'Haiti' 'India' 'Leb
          anon'
           'Madagascar' 'Malawi' 'Mauritania' 'Nigeria' 'Sierra Leone' 'Sri Lanka'
           'Tanzania' 'Togo' 'Tunisia' 'Zambia' 'Zimbabwe']
          Cluster 4: ['Armenia' 'Azerbaijan' 'Bahrain' 'Belarus' 'Belgium' 'El Salvad
          or'
           'Estonia' 'France' 'Iceland' 'Israel' 'Japan' 'Kazakhstan' 'Kuwait'
           'Malta' 'Nicaragua' 'Poland' 'Spain' 'Tajikistan' 'United States'
           'Uruguay' 'Uzbekistan']
          Cluster 5: ['Rwanda']
```

Figure 8.7 – K-Means clustering based on two happiness indices called Life_Ladder and Perceptions_of_corruption in 2019 – Normalized data

In this example, we saw how K-Means, when applied correctly, can produce a meaningful clustering compared to what we had reached using data visualization. However, the K-Means clustering in this example was applied to a two-dimensional dataset. In the next example, we will see that, from a coding perspective, there is almost no difference between applying K-Means to a two-dimensional dataset and applying the algorithm to a dataset with more dimensions.

Using K-Means to cluster a dataset with more than two dimensions

In this section, we will use K-Means and form three meaningful clusters of countries in report2019_df based on all the Life_Ladder, Log_GDP_per_capita, Social_support, Healthy_life_expectancy_at_birth, Freedom_to_make_life_choices, Generosity, Perceptions_of_corruption, Positive_affect, and Negative_affect happiness indices.

Go ahead and run the following code; you will see that it will form three meaningful clusters and print out the members of each cluster:

```
dimensions = [ 'Life_Ladder', 'Log_GDP_per_capita', 'Social_
support', 'Healthy_life_expectancy_at_birth', 'Freedom_to_
make_life_choices', 'Generosity', 'Perceptions_of_corruption',
'Positive_affect', 'Negative_affect']
Xs = report2019_df[dimensions]
Xs = (Xs - Xs.min())/(Xs.max()-Xs.min())
kmeans = KMeans(n_clusters=3)
kmeans.fit(Xs)
for i in range(3):
    BM = kmeans.labels_==i
    print('Cluster {}: {}'.format(i,report2019_df[BM].Name.
    values))
```

Here, the only difference between the preceding code and the code presented in *Figure 8.7* is the first line, where the dimensions of the data are selected. After this, the code is the same. The reason for this is that K-Means can handle as many dimensions as inputted.

How Many Clusters?

Choosing the number of clusters is the most challenging part of performing a successful K-Means clustering analysis. The algorithm itself does not accommodate finding out how many meaningful clusters are in the data. Finding the meaningful number of clusters in the data is a difficult task when the dimensions of the data increase.

While there is no one perfect solution to go about finding the meaningful number of clusters in a dataset, there are a few different approaches you can adopt. In this book, we will not cover this aspect of clustering analysis as we know enough about clustering analysis to perform effective data preprocessing.

So far, we have learned how to use K-Means to form meaningful clusters. Next, we are going to learn how to profile these clusters using centroid analysis.

Centroid analysis

Centroid analysis, in essence, is a canonical data analytics task that is done once meaningful clusters have been found. We perform centroid analysis to understand what formed each cluster and gain insight into the patterns in the data that led to the cluster's formation.

This analysis essentially finds the centroids of each cluster and compares them with one another. A color-coded table or a heatmap can be very useful for comparing centroids.

The following code finds the centroids using a loop and **Boolean masking** and then uses the `sns.heatmap()` function from the `seaborn` module to draw the color-coded table.

The following code must be run once you've run the preceding code snippet:

```
import seaborn as sns
clusters = ['Cluster {}'.format(i) for i in range(3)]
Centroids = pd.DataFrame(0.0, index =  clusters, columns =
Xs.columns)
for i,clst in enumerate(clusters):
    BM = kmeans.labels_==i
    Centroids.loc[clst] = Xs[BM].median(axis=0)
sns.heatmap(Centroids, linewidths=.5, annot=True,
cmap='binary')
plt.show()
```

The preceding code will output the following heatmap:

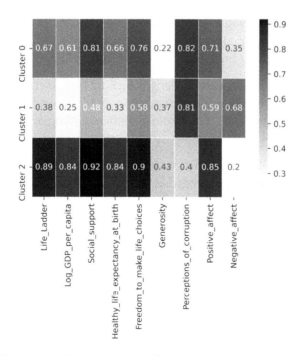

Figure 8.8 – Using sns.heatmap() to perform centroid analysis

Before we analyze the preceding heatmap, allow me to give you a heads up. As K-Means is a random-based algorithm, your output may be different to the one printed here. We would expect to see the same patterns emerge from the data, but the cluster names might be different.

In the preceding heatmap, we can see that `Cluster 0` has the best happiness scores among all the clusters, so we may label this cluster as *Very Happy*. On the other hand, `Cluster 2` is second best in every index except for `Generosity` and `Perception_ of_corruption`, so we will label this cluster *Happy but Crime-ridden*. Finally, `Cluster 1` has the lowest value for almost all of the happiness indices, but `Geneoristy` has a close second rank among all the centroids; we will call this cluster *Unhappy but Generous*.

Summary

Congratulations on your excellent progress in this chapter and this book! By finishing this chapter, you have also finished the second part of this book. In this chapter, we learned about clustering analysis and some techniques we can use to perform it. In this part of this book, we learned about the four most in-demand data analytics goals: data visualization, prediction, classification, and clustering.

In the first part of this book, you learned about data and databases, as well as programming skills that allow you to effectively manipulate data for data analytics. In the second part, which is the one you just finished, you learned about the four most important data analytics goals and learned how they can be met using programming.

Now, you are ready to take on the next challenge: learning how to effectively preprocess data for the data analytics goals you just learned about in the second part of this book using your programming skills, your fundamental understanding of data, and your appreciation of data analytics goals.

In the next part of this book, we will start our journey of data preprocessing. The next part of this book is comprised of data cleaning, data fusion and integration, data reduction, and data massaging and transformation. These processes are the pieces of a puzzle that, when put together appropriately and effectively, improve data preprocessing and improve the quality of data analytics.

Before you move on and start your journey on data cleaning, spend some time on the following exercises and solidify what you've learned.

Exercises

1. In your own words, answer the following two questions. Use 200 words (at most) to answer each question:

    a) What is the difference between classification and prediction?

    b) What is the difference between classification and clustering?

2. Consider *Figure 8.6* regarding the necessity of normalization before performing clustering analysis. With your new appreciation for this process, would you like to change your answer to the first exercise question from the previous chapter?

3. In this chapter, we used `WH Report_preprocessed.csv` to form meaningful clusters of countries using 2019 data. In this exercise, we want to use the data from 2010-2019. Perform the following steps to do this:

    a) Use the `.pivot()` function to restructure the data so that each combination of the year and happiness index has a column. In other words, the data of the year is recorded in long format, and we would like to change that into wide format. Name the resulting data `pvt_df`. We will not need the `Population` and `Continent` columns in `pvt_df`.

    b) Normalize `pvt_df` and assign it to `Xs`.

    c) Use K-Means and `Xs` to find three clusters among the data objects. Report the members of each cluster.

    d) Use a heatmap to perform centroid analysis. As there are many columns for this clustering, you may have to resize the heatmap so that you can use it for analysis. Make sure you've named each cluster.

4. For this exercise, we will be using the `Mall_Customers.xlsx` dataset to form four meaningful clusters of customers. The following steps will help you do this correctly:

    a) Use `pd.read_excel()` to load the data into `customer_df`.

    b) Set `CustomerID` as the index of `customer_df` and binary code the `Gender` column. This means replacing `Male` values with `0` and `Female` values with `1`.

    c) Clean the names of the columns by using the following names: `Gender`, `Age`, `Annual_income`, and `Spending_score`.

    d) Normalize `customer_df` and load it into the `Xs` variable.

e) Use K-Means and Xs to find four clusters among the data objects. Report the members of each cluster.

f) Use a heatmap to perform centroid analysis. Make sure you've named each cluster.

g) Why did we binary code the Gender attribute in *Step b*?

Part 3: The Preprocessing

In this part, you will learn how to use Python to perform data cleaning, data integration, data reduction, and data transformation to prepare data for successful analytic purposes.

This part comprises the following chapters:

- Chapter 9, Data Cleaning Level I – Cleaning Up the Table
- Chapter 10, Data Cleaning Level II – Unpacking, Restructuring, and Reformulating the Table
- Chapter 11, Data Cleaning Level III – Missing Values, Outliers, and Errors
- Chapter 12, Data Fusion and Data Integration
- Chapter 13, Data Reduction
- Chapter 14, Data Transformation and Massaging

9
Data Cleaning Level I – Cleaning Up the Table

We are finally here! After making sure that we have the required technical skills (part 1 of this book) and analytics skills (part 2 of this book), we can start discussing effective data preprocessing. We will start this journey by looking at data cleaning. This chapter divides data cleaning into three levels: levels I, II, and III. As you move up these levels, learning about the concept of data cleaning will become deeper and more complex. We will talk about what they are, how they are different, and what types of situations require us to perform each level of data cleaning. Furthermore, for each level of data cleaning, we will see examples of data sources that will require different levels of data cleaning.

In this chapter, we will focus on data cleaning level I – cleaning up the table. The next two chapters are also dedicated to data cleaning but at levels II and III.

In this chapter, we're going to cover the following main topics:

- The levels, tools, and purposes of data cleaning – a roadmap to *Chapter 9, Data Cleaning Level I – Cleaning Up the Table, Chapter 10, Data Cleaning Level* II – *Unpacking, Restructuring, and Reformulating the Table,* and *Chapter 11, Data Cleaning Level* III *– Missing Values, Outliers, and Errors*

- Data cleaning level I – cleaning up the table

Technical requirements

You can find all of the code and the dataset for this book in this book's GitHub repository. To find the repository, go to `https://github.com/PacktPublishing/Hands-On-Data-Preprocessing-in-Python`. You can find *Chapter09* in this repository and download the code and the data to aid with your learning.

The levels, tools, and purposes of data cleaning – a roadmap to chapters 9, 10, and 11

One of the most exciting moments in any data analytics project is when you have one dataset that you believe contains all the data you need to effectively meet the goals of the project. This moment comes normally in one of the following situations:

- You are done collecting data for the analysis you have in mind.

- You have done extensive data integration from different data sources. Data integration is a very important skillset and we will cover it in *Chapter 12, Data Fusion and Data Integration.*

- The dataset is just shared with you and it contains everything that you need.

Regardless of how you got your hands on the dataset, this is an exciting moment. But beware that more often than not, you still have many steps to take before you can analyze the data. First, you need to clean the dataset.

To learn about and perform data cleaning, we need to fully understand the following three aspects:

- **Purpose of data analytics**: Why are we cleaning the dataset? In other words, how are we going to use the dataset once it has been cleaned?

- **Tools for data analytics**: What will be used to perform **data analytics**? **Python (Matplotlib/sklearn)**? **Excel**? **MATLAB**? **Tableau**?

- **Levels of data cleaning**: What aspects of the dataset need cleaning? Is our cleaning at the surface level, in that we are only cleaning up the name of the columns, or is our cleaning deeper, in that we are making sure that the recorded values are correct?

In the next three subsections, we will look at each of these aspects in more detail.

Purpose of data analytics

While it might sound like data cleaning can be done separately without us paying too much attention to the purpose of the analysis, in this chapter, we will see that more often than not, this is not the case. In other words, you will need to know what analytics you will be performing on the dataset when you are cleaning your data. Not only that, but you also need to know exactly how the analytics and perhaps the algorithms that you have in mind will be using and manipulating the data.

So far in this book, we have learned about four different data analytic goals: **data visualization**, **prediction**, **classification**, and **clustering**. We learned about these analytics goals and how data is manipulated to meet them. We needed a more profound level of understanding and appreciation for these goals so that they can support our data cleaning. By knowing how the data will be used after we have cleaned it, we are in a position to make better decisions regarding how the data should be cleaned. In this chapter, we will see that our deeper understanding of the analytic goals will guide us to perform more effective data cleaning.

Tools for data analytics

The software tools you intend to use will also have a major role in how you will go about data cleaning. For instance, if you intend to use **MATLAB** to perform clustering analysis and you've completed data cleaning in Python and have the completed data in Pandas DataFrame format, you will need to transform the data into a structure that MATLAB can read. Perhaps you could use `.to_csv()` to save the DataFrame as a `.csv` file and open the file in MATLAB since `.csv` files are compatible with almost any software.

Levels of data cleaning

The data cleaning process has both high-level goals and many nitty-gritty details. Not only that but what needs to be done for data cleaning from one project to another can be completely different. So, it is impossible to give clear-cut, step-by-step instructions on how you should go about data cleaning. However, we can loosely place the data cleaning procedure at three levels, as follows:

1. **Level** I: Clean up the table.

2. **Level** II: Unpack, restructure, and reformulate the table.

3. **Level** III: Evaluate and correct the values.

In this chapter and the next two, we will learn about various data cleaning situations that fall under one of the preceding levels. While each of these levels will have a specific section in this book, we will briefly go over *what they are* and *how they differ* from one another here.

Level I– cleaning up the table

This level of cleaning is all about how the table looks. A level I cleaned dataset has three characteristics: it is in a standard data structure, it has codable and intuitive column titles, and each row has a unique identifier.

Level II– restructuring and reformulating the table

This level of cleaning has to do with the type of data structure and format you need your dataset to be in so that the analytics you have in mind can be done. Most of the time, the tools you use for analytics dictate the structure and the format of the data. For instance, if you need to create multiple box plots using `plt.boxplot()`, you need to separate the data for each box plot. For instance, see the *Comparing populations using box plots* example in the *Comparing populations* section of *Chapter 5, Data Visualization*, where we restructured the data before using the function to draw multiple box plots.

Level III– evaluating and correcting the values

This level of cleaning is about the correctness and existence of the recorded values in the dataset. At this level of cleaning, you want to make certain that the recorded values are correct and are presented in a way that best supports the analytics goals. This level of data cleaning is the most technical and theoretical part of the data cleaning process. Not only do we need to know how the tools we will be using need the data to be, but we also need to understand how the data should be corrected, combined, or removed, as informed by the goals of the analytics process. Dealing with missing values and handling outliers are also major parts of this level of data cleaning.

So far, we have looked at the three most important dimensions of data cleaning: the purpose of data analytics, the tools for data analytics, and the three data cleaning levels. Next, we will understand the roles these three dimensions – analytics purposes, analytic tools, and the levels of data cleaning – play when it comes to effective data cleaning.

Mapping the purposes and tools of analytics to the levels of data cleaning

The following diagram shows the map of these three dimensions. Having a dataset that has been cleaned at level I is the very first step, and taking the time to make sure this level of data cleaning has been performed will make the next data cleaning levels and the data analytics process easier. While we can perform data cleaning level I without knowing the analytics we have for the dataset, it would be unwise to do any level II or level III data cleaning without knowing the software tools or the analytics you intend to employ. The following diagram shows that level II data cleaning needs to be done while you're informed about the tools and the analytic goals, while level III data cleaning needs to be executed once you know about the data analytics goals:

Figure 9.1 – Relevant amount of general and specific steps for three different levels of data cleaning

In the remainder of this chapter, we will cover data cleaning level I in more detail by providing data cleaning examples that tend to occur frequently. In the next few chapters, we will do the same thing for data cleaning levels II and III.

Data cleaning level I – cleaning up the table

Data cleaning level I has the least deep data preprocessing steps. Most of the time, you can get away with not having your data cleaned at level I. However, having a dataset that is level I cleaned would be very rewarding as it would make the rest of the data cleaning process and data analytics much easier.

We will consider a level I dataset clean where the dataset has the following characteristics:

- It is in a standard and preferred data structure.

- It has codable and intuitive column titles.

- Each row has a unique identifier.

The following three examples feature at least one or a combination of the preceding characteristics for ease of learning.

Example 1 – unwise data collection

From time to time, you might come across sources of data that are not collected and recorded in the best possible way. These situations occur when the data collection process has been done by someone or a group of people who don't have the appropriate skills regarding database management. Regardless of why this situation might have occurred, you are given access to a data source that requires significant preprocessing before it can be put in one standard data structure.

For instance, imagine that you have been hired by an election campaign to use the power of data to help move the needle. Omid was hired just before you, and he knows a lot about the political aspects of the election but not much about data and data analytics. You have been assigned to join Omid and help process what he has been tasked with. In your first meeting, you realize that the task is to analyze the speeches that have been made by the 45th President of the United States, Donald Trump. To bring you up to speed, he smiles and tells you that he has completed the data collection process and that all that needs to be done is the analysis now; he shows you a folder on his computer that contains text files (.txt) for every one of Donald Trump's speeches made in 2019 and 2020. The following screenshot shows this folder on Omid's computer:

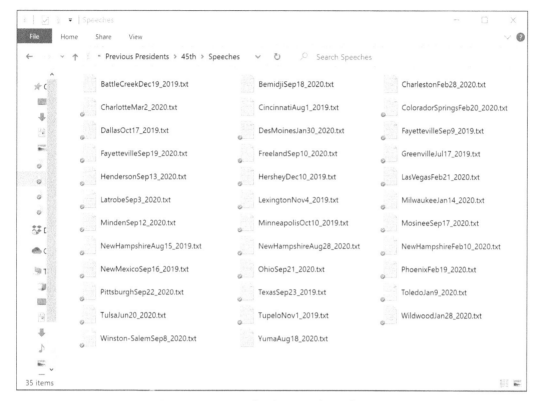

Figure 9.2 – Example of unwise data collection

After viewing the folder, you instantly realize that data preprocessing must be done before any analytics can be considered. In the interest of building a good working relationship with Omid, you don't tell him directly that a huge data preprocessing task needs to be done; instead, you comment on the aspects of his data collection that are great and can be used as a cornerstone for data preprocessing. You mention that it is great that the naming of these files follows a predictable order. The order is that city names come first, comes the name of the month as three letters, then the day as one or two digits, and finally the year as four digits.

As you are well-versed with Pandas DataFrame, you suggest that the data should be processed into a DataFrame and Omid, eager to learn, accepts.

You can perform the following steps to process the data into a DataFrame:

1. First, we need to access the filenames so that we can use them to open and read each file. Pay attention: we can type the names of the files ourselves as there are only 35 of them. However, we must do this using programing as we are trying to learn scalable skills; imagine that we have one million files instead of 35. The following code shows how using the `listdir()` function from the `os` module can do that for us very easily:

    ```
    from os import listdir
    FileNames = listdir('Speeches')
    print(FileNames)
    ```

2. Next, we need to create a placeholder for our data. In this step, we need to imagine what our dataset would look like after this data cleaning process has been completed. We want to have a DataFrame that contains the names of each file and its content. The following code uses the `pandas` module to create this placeholder:

    ```
    import pandas as pd
    speech_df = pd.DataFrame(index=range(len(FileNames)),
    columns=['File Name','The Content'])
    print(speech_df)
    ```

3. Lastly, we need to open each file and insert its content into `speech_df`, which we created in the previous step. The following code loops through the elements of `FineNames`. As each element is the name of one of the files that can be used to open and read the file, we can use the `open()` and `.readlines()` functions here:

    ```
    for i,f_name in enumerate(FileNames):
        f = open('Speeches/' + f_name, "r", encoding='utf-8')
        f_content = f.readlines()
        f.close()
        speech_df.at[i,'File Name'] = f_name
        speech_df.at[i,'The Content'] = f_content[0]
    ```

Once you have completed these three steps, run `Print(speech_df)` and study it before moving on. Here, you can see that `speech_df` has two of the three characteristics of level I cleaned data. The dataset has the first characteristics as it is now one standard data structure, which is also your preferred one.

The dataset, after being processed into `speech_df`, also has the third characteristic as each row has a unique index. You can run `speech_df.index` to investigate this. You might be pleasantly surprised that we didn't do anything to acquire this cleaning characteristic. This is automatically done for us by Pandas.

However, we could have done better regarding the second characteristic. The `File Name` and `The Content` column names are intuitive enough, but they are not as codable as they can be. We can access them using the `df['ColumnName']` method but not `df.ColumnName`, as shown here:

1. First, run `speech_df['File Name']` and `speech_df['The Content']`; you will see that you can easily access each column using this method.

2. Second, run `speech_df.File Name` and `speech_df.The Content`; you will get errors. Why? To jog your memory, please go back to *Chapter 1*, *Reviewing the Core Modules of NumPy and Pandas*, find the *DataFrame access columns* section, and study the error shown in *Figure 1.16*. The cause of the error is very similar here.

So, to make the column titles codable when using a Pandas DataFrame, we only have to follow a few guidelines, as follows:

- Try to shorten the column's titles as much as possible without them becoming unintuitive. For instance, `The Content` can simply be `Content`.

- Avoid using spaces and possible programming operators such as -, +, =, %, and & in the names of the columns. If you have to have more than one word as the column's name, either use camel case naming (`FileName`) or use an underscore (`File_Name`).

You may have noticed in the second to last piece of code that I could have used more codable column titles; I could have used `columns=['FileName','Content']` instead of `columns=['File Name','The Content']`. You are right. I should have done this there; I only did this so I was able to make this point afterward. So, go ahead and improve the code before moving on. Alternatively, you can use the following code to change the column names to their codable versions:

```
speech_df.columns = ['FileName','Content']
```

Now that we have completed this example, let's review the characteristics of Level I data cleaning that the sources of data in this example needed. This source of data needed all three characteristics of Level I data cleaning to be improved. We had to take action explicitly to make sure that the data is in standard data structure and also has intuitive and codable column names. Also, the tool we used, Pandas, automatically gave each row a unique identifier.

Example 2 – reindexing (multi-level indexing)

In this example, we want to perform Level 1 data Cleaning on `TempData.csv`. The following screenshot shows how to use Pandas to read the data into a DataFrame:

```
In [7]:  ▶| air_df = pd.read_csv('TempData.csv')
            air_df
```

Out[7]:

	Temp	Year	Month	Day	Time
0	79.0	2016	1	1	00:00:00
1	79.0	2016	1	1	00:30:00
2	79.0	2016	1	1	01:00:00
3	77.0	2016	1	1	01:30:00
4	78.0	2016	1	1	02:00:00
...	...	...	...	...	...
20448	77.0	2016	12	31	22:00:00
20449	77.0	2016	12	31	22:30:00
20450	77.0	2016	12	31	23:00:00
20451	77.0	2016	12	31	23:00:00
20452	77.0	2016	12	31	23:30:00

20453 rows × 5 columns

Figure 9.3 – Reading TempData.CSV into a Pandas DataFrame

Our first evaluation of the dataset reveals that the data is in one standard data structure, the column titles are intuitive and codable, and each row has a unique identifier. However, upon looking at this more closely, the default indices assigned by Pandas are unique but not helpful for identifying the rows. The `Year`, `Month`, `Day`, and `Time` columns would be better off as the indexes of the rows. So, in this example, we would like to reindex the DataFrame using more than one column. We will use Pandas's special capability known as **multi-level indexing**. We covered this in the *Pandas multi-level indexing* section *Chapter 1, Reviewing the Core Modules of NumPy and Pandas*.

This can be done easily by using the `.set_index()` function of a Pandas DataFrame. However, before we do that, let's remove the `Year` column as its value is only 2016. To check this, run `air_df.Year.unique()`. In the following line of code, so that we don't lose the information stating that this dataset is for 2016, we will change the DataFrame's name to `air2016_df`:

```
air2016_df = air_df.drop(columns=['Year'])
```

Now that the unnecessary column has been removed, we can use the .set_index() function to reindex the DataFrame:

```
air2016_df.set_index(['Month','Day','Time'],inplace=True)
```

If you print air2016_df after running the preceding code, you will get the DataFrame with a multi-level index, as shown in the following screenshot:

Month	Day	Time	Temp
1	1	00:00:00	79.0
		00:30:00	79.0
		01:00:00	79.0
		01:30:00	77.0
		02:00:00	78.0
...	...	...	...
12	31	22:00:00	77.0
		22:30:00	77.0
		23:00:00	77.0
		23:00:00	77.0
		23:30:00	77.0

20453 rows × 1 columns

Figure 9.4 – air2016_df with a multi-level index

Our achievement here is that not only does each row have a unique index but the indices can be used to meaningfully identify each row. For instance, you can run air2016_df.loc[2,24,'00:30:00'] to get the temperature value of February 24 at 30 minutes after midnight.

In this example, we focused on the third characteristic of level I data cleaning: each row has a unique identifier. In the following example, we will focus on the second characteristic: having a codable and intuitive column name.

Example 3 – intuitive but long column titles

In this example, we will be using `OSMI Mental Health in Tech Survey 2019.csv` from `https://osmihelp.org/research`. The following screenshot shows the code that reads the dataset into `response_df`, and then uses the `.head()` function to show the first row of the data:

```
In [12]:  ▶  response_df = pd.read_csv('OSMI Mental Health in Tech Survey 2019.csv')
              response_df.head(1)
```

Out[12]:

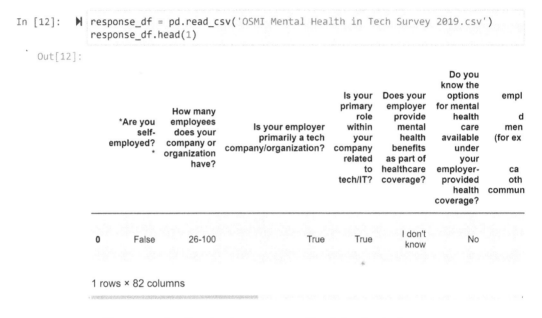

	Are you self-employed?	How many employees does your company or organization have?	Is your employer primarily a tech company/organization?	Is your primary role within your company related to tech/IT?	Does your employer provide mental health benefits as part of healthcare coverage?	Do you know the options for mental health care available under your employer-provided health coverage?	empl d men (for ex ca oth commun
0	False	26-100		True	True	I don't know	No

1 rows × 82 columns

Figure 9.5 – Reading data into response_df and showing its first row

Working with a dataset that has very long column titles can be hard from a programing and visualization perspective. For instance, if you would like to access the sixth column of the dataset, you would have to type out the following line of code:

```
response_df['Do you know the options for mental health care
available under your employer-provided health coverage?']
```

For cases where we cannot have short and intuitive titles for the columns, we need to use a column dictionary. The idea is to use a key instead of each full title of columns, which is somewhat intuitive but significantly shorter. The dictionary will also provide access to the full title if need be through the relevant key.

The following code creates a column dictionary using a Pandas Series:

```
keys = ['Q{}'.format(i) for i in range(1,83)]
columns_dic = pd.Series(response_df.columns,index=keys)
```

The preceding code breaks the process of creating the `dictionary` column into two steps:

1. First, the code creates the `keys` variable, which is the list of shorter substitutes for column titles. This is done using a list comprehension technique.

2. Second, the code creates a Pandas Series called `columns_dic`, whose indices are `keys` and whose values are `response_df.columns`.

Once the preceding code has been run successfully, the `columns_dic` Panda Series can act as a dictionary. For instance, if you run `columns_dic['Q4']`, it will give you the full title of the fourth column (the fourth question).

Next, we need to update the columns of `response_df`, which can be done with a simple line of code: `response_df.columns = keys`. Once you've done this, `response_df` will have short and somewhat intuitive column titles whose full descriptions can easily be accessed. The following screenshot shows the transformed version of `response_df` once the preceding steps have been performed:

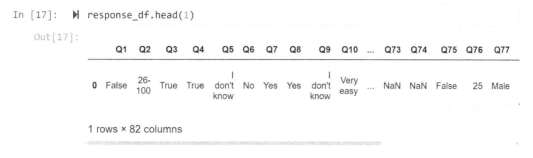

Figure 9.6 – Showing the first row of the cleaned response_df

In this example, we took steps to ensure that the second characteristic of level I data cleaning has been met since the dataset was in good shape in terms of the first and third characteristics.

So far, you've learned and practiced, by example, some examples of data cleaning. In the next chapter, we will learn about and see examples of level II data cleaning.

Summary

Congratulations on your excellent progress. In this chapter, we introduced you to three different levels of data cleaning and their relevance, along with the goals and tools of analytics. Moreover, we covered level I of data cleaning in more detail and practiced dealing with situations where this type of data cleaning is needed. Finally, by looking at three examples, we used the programming and analytics skills that we had developed in the previous chapters to effectively preprocess example datasets and meet the examples' analytical goals.

In the next chapter, we will focus on level II of data cleaning. Before moving forward and starting your journey on data cleaning level II, spend some time on the following exercises and solidify what you've learned.

Exercises

1. In your own words, describe the relationship between the analytics goals and data cleaning. Your response should answer the following questions:

    a) Is data cleaning a separate step of data analytics and can be done in isolation? In other words, can data cleaning be performed without you knowing about the analytics process?

    b) If the answer to the previous question is no, are there any types of data cleaning that can be done in isolation?

    c) What is the role of analytic tools in the relationship between analytic goals and data cleaning?

2. A local airport that analyzes the usage of its parking has employed a **Single-Beam Infrared Detector** (**SBID**) technology to count the number of people who pass the gate from the parking area to the airport.

    As shown in the following diagram, an SBDI records every time the infrared connection is blocked, signaling a passenger entering or exiting:

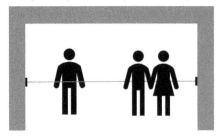

Figure 9.7 – An example of a Single-Beam Infrared Detector (SBID)

Unfortunately, the person who installed the SBID was not up to date with the latest and greatest database technology, so they have set up the system in a way that the recorded date of each day is stored in an Excel file. The Excel files are named after the days the records were created. You have been hired to help and analyze the data. Your manager has given you access to a zipped file called SBID_Data. zip. This zipped file contains 14 files, each containing the data of one day between October 12, 2020, and October 25, 2020. Your manager has informed you that due to security reasons, she cannot share all 3,000 files with you. She has asked you to do the following for the 14 files she has shared with you:

a) Write some code that can automatically consolidate all the files into one Pandas DataFrame.

b) Create a bar chart that shows the average airport passenger traffic per hour.

c) Label and describe the data cleaning steps you did in this exercise.

10
Data Cleaning Level II – Unpacking, Restructuring, and Reformulating the Table

In level I data cleaning, we were only concerned about the neat and codable organization of our dataset. As we mentioned previously, level I data cleaning can be done in isolation, without having to keep an eye on what data will be needed next. However, level II data cleaning is deeper. It is more about preparing the dataset for analysis and the tools for this process. In other words, in level II data cleaning, we have a dataset that is reasonably clean and is in a standard data structure, but the analysis we have in mind cannot be done because the data needs to be in a specific structure due to the analysis itself, or the tool we plan to use for the analysis.

In this chapter, we will look at three examples of level II data cleaning that tend to happen frequently. Pay attention to the fact that, unlike level I data cleaning, where the examples were merely a source of data, the examples for level II date cleaning must be coupled with an analytical task.

In this chapter, we're going to cover the following main topics:

- Example 1 – unpacking columns and reformulating the table

- Example 2 – restructuring the table

- Example 3 – level I and II data cleaning

Technical requirements

You can find all the code and the dataset for this book in this book's GitHub repository: `https://github.com/PacktPublishing/Hands-On-Data-Preprocessing-in-Python`. You can find the `Chapter10` directory in this repository and download the code and the data for a better learning experience.

Example 1 – unpacking columns and reformulating the table

In this example, we will use the level I cleaned `speech_df` dataset to create the following bar chart. We cleaned this DataFrame in the *Example 1 – unwise data collection* section of *Chapter 9, Data Cleaning Level I – Cleaning Up the Table*. The level I cleaned `speech_df` database only has two columns: `FileName` and `Content`. To be able to create the following visual, we need columns such as the month of the speech and the number of times the four words (**vote**, **tax**, **campaign**, and **economy**) have been repeated in each speech. While the level I cleaned `speech_df` dataset contains all this information, it is somewhat buried inside the two columns.

The following is a list of the information we need and the column of `speech_df` that this information is stored in:

- **The month of the speech**: This information is in the `FileName` column.

- **The number of times the words vote, tax, campaign, and economy have been repeated in each speech**: This information is in the `Content` column:

Example 1 – unpacking columns and reformulating the table   229

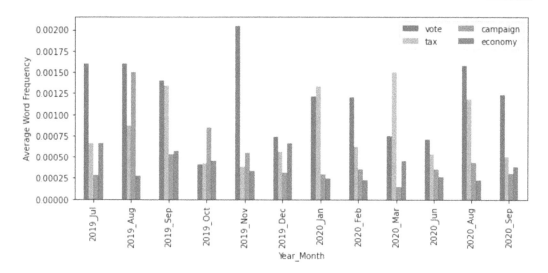

Figure 10.1 – Average frequency of the words vote, tax, campaign, and economy per month
in speech_df

So, for us to be able to meet our analytic goal, which is to create the previous visualization, we need to unpack the two columns and then reformulate the table for visualization. Let's do this one step at a time. First, we will unpack `FileName` and then we bring our attention to unpacking `Content`. After that, we will reformulate the table for the requested visualization.

Unpacking FileName

Let's take a look at the values of the `FileName` column. To do this, you can run `speech_df.FileName` and study the values under this column. You will notice that the values follow a predictable pattern. The pattern is *CitynameMonthDD_YYYY.txt*; *Cityname* is the name of the city where the speech was given, *Month* is the three-letter version of the month when the speech was given, *DD* is the one- or two-digit number that represents the day of the month, *YYYY* is the four digits that represent the year during which the speech was given, and *.txt* is the file extension, which is the same for all the values.

You can see that the `FileName` column contains the following information about the speeches in the dataset:

- *City*: The city where the speech was given
- *Date*: The date when the speech was given
- *Year*: The year when the speech was given
- *Month*: The month when the speech was given
- *Day*: The day when the speech was given

In the following code, we will use our programming skills to unpack the `FileName` column and include the preceding information as separate columns. Let's plan our unpacking first and then put it into code. The following are the steps we need to take for the unpacking process:

1. Extract `City`: Use `Month` from the *CitynameMonthDD_YYYY.txt* pattern to extract the city. Based on this pattern, everything that comes before *Month* is *Cityname*.

2. Extract `Date`: Use the extracted *Cityname* to extract *Date*.

3. Extract `Year`, *Month*, and `Day` from *Date*.

Now, let's put these steps into code:

1. Extract `City`: The following code creates the `SeparateCity()` function and applies it to the `speech_df.FileName` Series. The `SeparateCity()` function loops through the previously created `Months` list to find the three-letter word that represents a month, which is used for each filename. Then, we can use the `.find()` function and the slicing capability of the Python strings to return the city's name:

    ```
    Months = ['Jan','Feb','Mar','Apr','May','Jun','Jul','Aug'
    ,'Oct','Sep','Nov','Dec']
    def SeperateCity(v):
        for mon in Months:
            if (mon in v):
                return v[:v.find(mon)]
    speech_df['City'] = speech_df.FileName.apply(
    SeperateCity)
    ```

Example 1 – unpacking columns and reformulating the table   231

> **Pay Attention!**
>
> Here, we had to use *Month* as the separator between *Cityname* and the date. If the naming convention of the files was a bit more organized, we could have done this a bit easier; in the `speech_df.FileName` column, some days are presented by one digit, such as `LatrobeSep3_2020.txt`, while some days are presented by two digits, such as `BattleCreekDec19_2019.txt`. If all the days were presented with two digits, in that they used `LatrobeSep03_2020.txt` instead of *LatrobeSep3_2020.txt*, the task of unpacking the column, from a programming perspective, would have been much simpler. For an example, see *Exercise 2*, later in this chapter.

2. Extract `Date`: The following code creates the `SeparateDate()` function and applies it to `speech_df`. This function uses the extracted city as the starting point, and the `.find()` function to separate the date from the city:

```
def SeperateDate(r):
    return r.FileName[len(r.City):r.FileName.find(
    '.txt')]
speech_df['Date'] = speech_df.apply(SeparateDate,axis=1)
```

Every time we work with date information, it is better to make sure that Pandas knows the recording is a *datetime* programming object so that we can use its properties, such as sorting by date or accessing the day, month, and year values. The following code uses the `pd.to_datetime()` function to transform the strings that represent the dates to *datetime* programming objects. To effectively use the `pd.to_datetime()` function, you need to be able to write the format pattern that the strings that represent dates follow. Here, the format pattern is `'%b%d_%Y'`, which means the string starts with a three-letter month representation (`%b`), then a digit representation for the day (`%d`), followed by an underscore (`_`), and then a four-digit year representation (`%Y`). To be able to come up with a correct format pattern, you need to know the meaning of each of the directives, such as `%b`, `%d`, and so on. Go to `https://docs.python.org/3/library/datetime.html#strftime-and-strptime-behavior` to find a comprehensive list of these directives:

```
speech_df.Date = pd.to_datetime(speech_df.Date,
    format='%b%d_%Y')
```

3. Extract `Year`, `Month`, and `Day` from `Date`: The following code creates the `extractDMY()` function and applies it to `speech_df` to add three new columns to each row. Note that the code is taking advantage of the fact that the `speech_df` column is a datetime programming object that has properties such as `.day` and `.month` to access the day and the month for each date:

```
def extractDMY(r):
    r['Day'] = r.Date.day
    r['Month'] = r.Date.month
    r['Year'] = r.Date.year
    return r
speech_df = speech_df.apply(extractDMY, axis=1)
```

After running the preceding code snippets successfully, you will have managed to unpack the `FileName` column of `speech_df`. Since all of the information that was packed in `FileName` is not presented under other columns, we can go ahead and remove this column by running the following command:

```
speech_df.drop(columns=['FileName'], inplace=True)
```

Before unpacking the other column, `Content`, let's take a look at the state of the data and enjoy looking at the progress we've made. The following screenshot shows the first five rows of the data:

```
In [25]:  ▶ speech_df.head()
```

Out[25]:

	Content	City	Date	Day	Month	Year
0	Thank you. Thank you. Thank you to Vice Presid...	BattleCreek	2019-12-19	19	12	2019
1	There's a lot of people. That's great. Thank y...	Bemidji	2020-09-18	18	9	2020
2	Thank you. Thank you. Thank you. All I can say...	Charleston	2020-02-28	28	2	2020
3	I want to thank you very much. North Carolina,...	Charlotte	2020-03-02	2	3	2020
4	Thank you all. Thank you very much. Thank you ...	Cincinnati	2019-08-01	1	8	2019

Figure 10.2 – speech_df after unpacking FileName

Example 1 – unpacking columns and reformulating the table   233

Now that we have unpacked `FileName` into five new columns called `City`, `Date`, `Day`, `Month`, and `Year`, we have taken one step toward the end goal: we've got access to create the *x axis* shown in *Figure 10.1*. Now, we need to pay attention to unpacking the column `Content`.

Unpacking Content

Unpacking the column `Content` differs somewhat from unpacking `FileName`. As the column `FileName` only had a limited amount of information, we were able to unpack everything this column had to offer. However, the column `Content` has a lot of information and it could be unpacked in many different ways. However, we only need to unpack a small portion of what is under the column `Content`; we need to know about the ratio of the usage of four words: `vote`, `tax`, `campaign`, and `economy`.

We can unpack what we need from the column `Content` in one step. The following code creates the `FindWordRatio()` function and applies it to `speech_df`. The function uses a `for` loop to add four new columns to the DataFrame, one column for each of the four words. The calculation for each word is simple: the returning value for each word is the total occurrence of the word in the speech (`row.Content.count(w)`), divided by the total number of words in the speech (`total_n_words`):

```
Words = ['vote','tax','campaign','economy']
def FindWordRatio(row):
    total_n_words = len(row.Content.split(' '))
    for w in Words:
        row['r_{}'.format(w)] = row.Content.count(w)/total_n_
        words
    return row
speech_df = speech_df.apply(FindWordRatio,axis=1)
```

The resulting `speech_df` after running the previous code will have 10 columns, as shown in the following screenshot:

```
In [27]:  ▶ speech_df.head()
```

Out[27]:

	Content	City	Date	Day	Month	Year	r_vote	r_tax	r_campaign	r_econon
0	Thank you. Thank you. Thank you to Vice Presid...	BattleCreek	2019-12-19	19	12	2019	0.000561	0.000505	0.000224	0.0006
1	There's a lot of people. That's great. Thank y...	Bemidji	2020-09-18	18	9	2020	0.000710	0.000237	0.000533	0.0000
2	Thank you. Thank you. Thank you. All I can say...	Charleston	2020-02-28	28	2	2020	0.000950	0.000317	0.000106	0.0000
3	I want to thank you very much. North Carolina,...	Charlotte	2020-03-02	2	3	2020	0.000750	0.001500	0.000150	0.0004
4	Thank you all. Thank you very much. Thank you ...	Cincinnati	2019-08-01	1	8	2019	0.001713	0.000857	0.001224	0.0002

Figure 10.3 – speech_df after extracting the needed information from Content

Example 1 – unpacking columns and reformulating the table   235

So far, we have restructured the table, so we are inching closer to drawing *Figure 10.1*; we've got the information for both the *x axis* and *y axis*. However, the dataset needs to be modified further before we can visualize *Figure 10.1*.

Reformulating a new table for visualization

So far, we have cleaned `speech_df` for our analytic goals. However, the table we need for *Figure 10.1* needs each row to be Donald Trump's speeches in a month while each of the rows in `speech_df` is one of Donald Trump's speeches. In other words, to be able to draw the visualization, we need to reformulate a new table so that the definition of our data object is *Donald Trump's speeches in a month* instead of *one Donald Trump speech*.

The new definition of the *Donald Trump's speeches in a month* data object is an aggregation of some of the data objects that are defined as *Donald Trump's speeches*. When we need to reformulate a dataset so that its new definition of data objects is an aggregation of the current definition of data objects, we need to perform two steps:

1. Create a column that can be the unique identifier for the reformulated dataset.

2. Use a function that can reformulate the dataset while applying the aggregate functions. The pandas functions that can do this are `.groupby()` and `.pivot_table()`.

So, let's perform these two steps on `speech_df` to create the new DataFrame called `vis_df`, which is the reformulated table we need for our analytics goal:

1. The following code applies a lambda function that attaches the `Year` and `Month` properties of each row to create a new column called `Y_M`. This new column will be the unique identifier of the reformulated dataset we are trying to create:

    ```
    Months = ['Jan','Feb','Mar','Apr','May','Jun','Jul','Aug'
    ,'Oct','Sep','Nov','Dec']
    lambda_func = lambda r: '{}_{}'.format(r.Year,Months[r.
    Month-1])
    speech_df['Y_M'] = speech_df.apply(lambda_func,axis=1)
    ```

    The preceding code created the lambda function (`lambda_func`) in a separate line in the interest of making the code more readable. This step could have been skipped and the lambda function could have been created "on the fly."

2. The following code uses the `.pivot_table()` function to reformulate `speech_df` into `vis_df`. If you've forgotten how the `.pivot_table()` function works, please revisit the *pandas pivot and melt functions* section of *Chapter 1, Review of the Core Modules of NumPy and Pandas*:

```
Words = ['vote','tax','campaign','economy']
vis_df = speech_df.pivot_table( index= ['Y_M'],
values= ['r_{}'.format(w) for w in Words],
aggfunc= np.mean)
```

The preceding code uses the `aggfunc` property of the `.pivot_table()` function, which was not mentioned in *Chapter 1, Review of the Core Modules of NumPy and Pandas*. Understanding `aggfunc` is simple; when `index` and `values` of `.pivot_table()` are specified in a way that more than one value needs to be moved into one cell in the reformulated table, the `.pivot_table()` uses the function that is passed for `aggfunc` to aggregate the values into one value.

The preceding code also uses a list comprehension to specify the values. The list comprehension is `['r_{}'.format(w) for w in Words]`, which is essentially the list of four columns from `speech_df`. Run the list comprehension separately and study its output.

3. We could have also reformulated the data into `vis_df` using `.groupby()`. The following is the alternative code:

```
vis_df = pd.DataFrame({
    'r_vote': speech_df.groupby('Y_M').r_vote.mean(),
    'r_tax': speech_df.groupby('Y_M').r_tax.mean(),
    'r_campaign': speech_df.groupby('Y_M').r_campaign.
    mean(),
    'r_economy': speech_df.groupby('Y_M').r_economy.
    mean() })
```

While the preceding code might feel more intuitive since working with `.groupby()` function might be easier than using `.pivot_table()`, the first piece of code is more scalable.

Example 1 – unpacking columns and reformulating the table   237

More Scalable Code

When coding, if possible, you want to avoid repeating the same line of code for a collection of items. For example, in the second alternative in the two preceding codee blocks, we had to use the .groupby() function four times, one for each of the four words. What if, instead of 4 words, we needed to do this analysis for 100,000 words? The first alternative is certainly more scalable as the words are passed as a list and the code will be the same, regardless of the number of words in the list.

At this point, you have created the reformulated vis_df, which we created to draw *Figure 10.1*. The following screenshot shows vis_df:

Y_M	r_campaign	r_economy	r_tax	r_vote
2019_Aug	0.001499	0.000270	0.000872	0.001596
2019_Dec	0.000316	0.000665	0.000558	0.000739
2019_Jul	0.000283	0.000660	0.000660	0.001603
2019_Nov	0.000551	0.000333	0.000385	0.002048
2019_Oct	0.000533	0.000572	0.001340	0.001398
2019_Sep	0.000843	0.000448	0.000419	0.000409
2020_Aug	0.000428	0.000222	0.001189	0.001577
2020_Feb	0.000353	0.000224	0.000625	0.001206
2020_Jan	0.000299	0.000240	0.001331	0.001215
2020_Jun	0.000356	0.000267	0.000535	0.000713
2020_Mar	0.000150	0.000450	0.001500	0.000750
2020_Oct	0.000306	0.000386	0.000504	0.001235

Figure 10.4 – vis_df

Now that we have vis_df, all that remains is to represent the information in vis_df in the form of a bar chart. The following subsection shows how this is done.

The last step – drawing the visualization

Figure 10.4 and *Figure 10.1* are essentially presenting the same information. While *Figure 10.4* (`vis_df`) uses a table to present the information, *Figure 10.1* used a bar chart. In other words, we have almost made it and we need to perform one more step to create the requested visualization.

The following code block shows the code that creates the visualization shown in *Figure 10.1*. Pay attention before running the following code as you must import the `matplotlib.pyplot` module first. You can use `import matplotlib.pyplot as plt` to do this:

```
column_order = vis_df.sum().sort_values(ascending=False).index
row_order = speech_df.sort_values('Date').Y_M.unique()
vis_df[column_order].loc[row_order].plot.bar(figsize=(10,4))
plt.legend(['vote','tax','campaign','economy'],ncol=2)
plt.xlabel('Year_Month')
plt.ylabel('Average Word Frequency')
plt.show()
```

The preceding code creates two lists: `column_order` and `row_order`. As their names suggest, these lists are the order in which the columns and rows will be shown on the visual. The `column_order` is the list of words based on the summation of their occurrence ratio, while `row_order` is the list of `Y_M` based on their natural order in the calendar.

In this example, we learned about different techniques for level II data cleaning; we learned how to unpack columns and reformulate the data for the analytics tools and goals. The next example will cover data preprocessing to restructure the dataset.

What's the difference between restructuring and reformulating a dataset? We tend to use reformulate when the definition of data objects needs to change for the new dataset. In contrast, we use restructure when the table structure does not support our analytic goals or tools, and we have to use alternative structures such as a dictionary. In this example, we change the definition of a data object from one *Donald Trump speech* to *Donald Trump's speeches in a month* so we called this a dataset reformulation.

Here, we are being introduced to the new materials while immersing ourselves in examples. In this example, we learned about *unpacking columns* and *reformulating the table*. In the next example, we will be exposed to a situation that requires *restructuring the table*.

Example 2 – restructuring the table   239

Example 2 – restructuring the table

In this example, we will use the `Customer Churn.csv` dataset. This dataset contains the records of 3,150 customers of a telecommunication company. The rows are described by demographic columns such as gender and age, and activity columns such as the distinct number of calls in 9 months. The dataset also specifies whether each customer was churned or not 3 months after the 9 months of collecting the activity data of the customers. Customer churning, from a telecommunication company's point of view, means the customer stops using the company's services and receives the services from the company's competition.

We would like to use box plots to compare the two populations of churning customers and non-churning customers for the following activity columns: **Call Failure**, **Subscription Length**, **Seconds of Use**, **Frequency of use**, **Frequency of SMS**, and **Distinct Called Numbers**.

Let's start by reading the `Customer Churn.csv` file into the `customer_df` DataFrame. The following screenshot shows this step:

```
In [34]:  ▶ customer_df = pd.read_csv('Customer Churn.csv')
             customer_df.head(1)

   Out[34]:
```

	Call Failure	Complains	Subscription Length	Seconds of Use	Frequency of use	Frequency of SMS	Distinct Called Numbers	Status	Churn
0	8	0	38	4370	71	5	17	1	

Figure 10.5 – customer_df before level I cleaning

At first glance, we can see that this dataset needs some level I data cleaning. While the column titles are intuitive, they can become more codable. The following line of code makes sure that the columns are also codable:

```
customer_df.columns = ['Call_Failure', 'Complains',
'Subscription_Length', 'Seconds_of_Use', 'Frequency_of_use',
'Frequency_of_SMS', 'Distinct_Called_Numbers', 'Status',
'Churn']
```

Before you move on, make sure that you study the new state of `customer_df` after running the preceding code.

Now that the dataset has been level I cleaned, we can pay attention to level II data cleaning.

This example needs us to draw six box plots. Let's focus on the first box plot; the rest will follow the same data cleaning process.

Let's focus on creating multiple box plots that compare the Call_Failure attribute of churning customers with that of non-churning customers. A box plot is an analytic tool that needs a simpler data structure than a dataset. A box plot only needs a dictionary.

What is the difference between a dataset and a dictionary? A dataset is a table that contains rows that are described by columns. As described in *Chapter 3, Data – What is it Really?*, in the *The most universal data structure – a table* section, we specified that the glue of a table is the definition of the data objects that each row represents. Each column also describes the rows. On the other hand, a dictionary is a simpler data structure where values are associated with a unique key.

For the box plot we want to draw, the dictionary we need has two keys – churn and non-churn – one for each population that will be presented. The value for each key is the collection of Call_Failure records for each population. Pay attention to the fact that, unlike a table data structure that has two dimensions (rows and columns), a dictionary only has one dimension.

The following code shows the usage of a pandas Series as a dictionary to prepare the data for the box plot. In this code, box_sr is a pandas Series that has two keys called 0 and 1, with 0 being non-churn and 1 being churn. The code uses a loop and Boolean masking to filter the churning and non-churning data objects and record them in box_sr:

```
churn_possibilities = customer_df.Churn.unique()
box_sr = pd.Series('',index = churn_possibilities)
for poss in churn_possibilities:
    BM = customer_df.Churn == poss
    box_sr[poss] = customer_df[BM].Call_Failure.values
```

Before moving on, execute print(box_sr) and study its output. Pay attention to the simplicity of the data structure compared to the data's initial structure.

Now that we have restructured the data for the analytic tool we want to use, the data is ready to be used for visualization. The following code uses plt.boxplot() to visualize the data we have prepared in box_sr. Don't forget to import matplotlib.pyplot as plt before running the following code:

```
plt.boxplot(box_sr,vert=False)
plt.yticks([1,2],['Not Churn','Churn'])
plt.show()
```

Example 2 – restructuring the table   241

If the preceding code runs successfully, your computer will show multiple box plots that compare the two populations.

So far, we have drawn a box plot that compares `Call_Failure` for churning and non-churning populations. Now, let's create some code that can do the same process and visualizations for all of the requested columns to compare the populations. As we mentioned previously, these columns are `Call_Failure`, `Subscription_Length`, `Seconds_of_Use`, `Frequency_of_use`, `Frequency_of_SMS`, and `Distinct_Called_Numbers`.

The following code uses a loop and `plt.subplot()` to organize the six required visuals for this analytic so that they're next to one another. *Figure 10.6* shows the output of the code. The data restructuring that's required to draw the box plot happens for each box plot shown in *Figure 10.6*. As practice, try to spot them in the following code and study them. I recommend that you review *Chapter 1, Review of the Core Modules – NumPy and pandas*, and *Chapter 2, Review of Another Core Module – Matplotlib*, if you don't know what the `enumerate()`, `plt.subplot()`, and `plt.tight_layout()` functions are:

```python
select_columns = ['Call_Failure', 'Subscription_Length',
'Seconds_of_Use', 'Frequency_of_use', 'Frequency_of_SMS',
'Distinct_Called_Numbers']
churn_possibilities = customer_df.Churn.unique()
plt.figure(figsize=(15,5))
for i,sc in enumerate(select_columns):
    for poss in churn_possibilities:
        BM = customer_df.Churn == poss
        box_sr[poss] = customer_df[BM][sc].values
    plt.subplot(2,3,i+1)
    plt.boxplot(box_sr,vert=False)
    plt.yticks([1,2],['Not Churn','Churn'])
    plt.title(sc)
plt.tight_layout()
plt.show()
```

The following diagram is what you will get once the preceding code has been successfully executed:

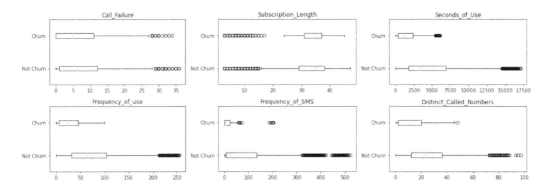

Figure 10.6 – End solution for Example 2 – restructuring the table

In this example, we looked at a situation where we needed to restructure the data so that it was ready for the analytic tool of our choice, the box plot. In the next example, we will look at a more complicated situation where we will need to perform both dataset reformulation and restructuring to make predictions.

Example 3 – level I and II data cleaning

In this example, we want to use `Electric_Production.csv` to make predictions. We are specifically interested in being able to predict what the monthly electricity demand will be 1 month from now. This 1-month gap is designed in the prediction model so that the predictions that come from the model will have decision-making values; that is, the decision-makers will have time to react to the predicted value.

We would like to use **linear regression** to perform this prediction. The independent and dependent attributes for this prediction are shown in the following diagram:

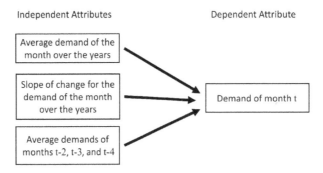

Figure 10.7 – The independent and dependent attributes needed for the prediction task

Example 3 – level I and II data cleaning   243

Let's go through the independent attributes shown in the preceding diagram:

- **Average demand of the month over the years**: For instance, if the month we want to predict demands for is March 2022, we want to use the average of the demands for every March in the previous years. So, we will collate the historical demands of March from the beginning of the data collection process (1985) to 2021 and calculate its average. This is shown in the following diagram.

- **Slope of change for the demand of the month over the years**: For instance, if the month we want to predict demands for is March 2022, we want to use the slope of change in the demand in March over the years. As shown in the following diagram, we can fit a line on the **Demand in March** data points across the years. The slope of that fitted line will be used for prediction.

- **Average demands of months t-2, t-3, and t-4**: In the preceding diagram, the **t, t-2, t-3**, and **t-4** notations are used to create a time reference. This time reference is that if we want to predict the demand of a month, we want to use the average demand of the following data points: the monthly demand of 2 months ago, the monthly demand of 3 months ago, and the monthly demand of 4 months ago. For instance, if we want to predict the monthly demand of March 2021, we'd want to calculate the average of January 2021, December 2020, and November 2020. Note that we skipped February 2021 as it was our planned decision-making gap.

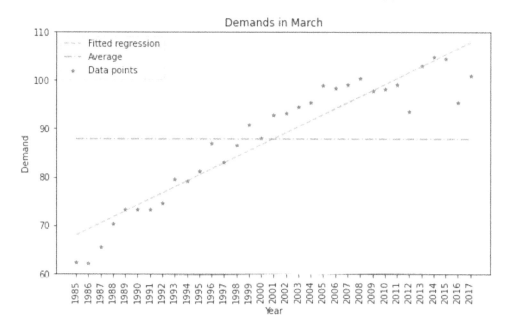

Figure 10.8 – Example of extracting the first two independent attributes for March

Now that we have a clear understanding of the data analytic goal, we will focus on preprocessing the data. Let's start by reading the data and covering its level I data cleaning process. The following screenshot shows the code that reads the `Electric_Production.csv` file into `month_df` and shows its first five and last five rows:

```
In [39]:    ▶  month_df = pd.read_csv('Electric_Production.csv')
               month_df
```

Out[39]:

	DATE	IPG2211A2N
0	1/1/1985	72.5052
1	2/1/1985	70.6720
2	3/1/1985	62.4502
3	4/1/1985	57.4714
4	5/1/1985	55.3151
...	...	...
392	9/1/2017	98.6154
393	10/1/2017	93.6137
394	11/1/2017	97.3359
395	12/1/2017	114.7212
396	1/1/2018	129.4048

397 rows × 2 columns

Figure 10.9 – month_df before level I data cleaning

At first glance, you can see that `month_df` can use some level I data cleaning. Let's get started.

Level I cleaning

The `month_df` dataset could do with the following level I data cleaning steps:

- The title of the second column can be more intuitive.
- The data type of the DATE column can be switched to datetime so that we can take advantage of datetime programming properties.
- The default index that's been assigned to the data by pandas can be improved as the DATE column would provide a better and more unique identification.

Example 3 – level I and II data cleaning   245

The following code takes care of the aforementioned level I data cleaning properties:

```
month_df.columns = ['Date','Demand']
month_df.set_index(pd.to_datetime(month_df.Date,
format='%m/%d/%Y'),inplace=True)
month_df.drop(columns=['Date'],inplace=True)
```

Print `month_df` and study its new state.

Next, we will learn what level II data cleaning we need to perform.

Level II cleaning

Looking at *Figure 10.7* and *Figure 10.9* may give you the impression that the prescribed prediction model in *Figure 10.7* is not possible as the dataset that's shown in *Figure 10.9* only has one column, while the prediction model needs four attributes. This is both a correct and incorrect observation. While it is a correct observation that the data has only one value column, the suggested independent attributes in *Figure 10.7* can be driven from `month_df` by some column unpacking and restructuring. That is the level II data cleaning that we need to do.

We will start by structuring a DataFrame that we want to restructure the current table into. The following code creates `predict_df`, which is the table structure that we will need for the prescribed prediction task:

```
attributes_dic={'IA1':'Average demand of the month',
'IA2':'Slope of change for the demand of the month', 'IA3':
'Average demands of months t-2, t-3 and t-4', 'DA': 'Demand of
month t'}
predict_df = pd.DataFrame(index=month_df.iloc[24:].index,
columns= attributes_dic.keys())
```

When creating the new table structure, `predict_dt`, the code is drafted while taking the following into consideration:

- The preceding code uses the `attributes_dic` dictionary to create intuitive and concise columns that are also codable. As `predict_df` needs to include rather long attribute titles, as shown in *Figure 10.7*, the dictionary allows the title columns to be concise, intuitive, and codable, and at the same time, you will have access to the title's longer versions through `attributes_dic`. This is a form of level I data cleaning, as shown in *Chapter 9, Data Cleaning Level I – Cleaning Up the Table*, in the *Example 3 – intuitive but long column titles* section. However, since we are the ones creating this new table, why not start with a level I cleaned table structure?

- The table structure we have created, `predict_df`, uses the indices of `month_df`, but not all of them. It uses all of them except for the first 24 rows, as specified in the code by `month_df.iloc[24:].index`. Why are the first 24 indices not included? This is due to the second independent attribute: *Slope of change for the demand of the month over the years*. As the slope of demand change for each month will be needed for the described prediction model, we cannot have a meaningful slope value for the first 24 rows of `month_df` in `predict_df`. This is because we at least need two historical data points for each month to be able to calculate a slope for the second independent attribute.

The following diagram summarizes what we want to accomplish by level II data cleaning `month_df`. The DataFrame on the left shows the first and last five rows of `month_df`, while the DataFrame on the right shows the first and last five rows of `predict_df`. As you already know, `predict_df` is empty as we just created an empty table structure that supports the prediction task. The following diagram, in a nutshell, shows that we need to fill `predict_df` using the data of `month_df`:

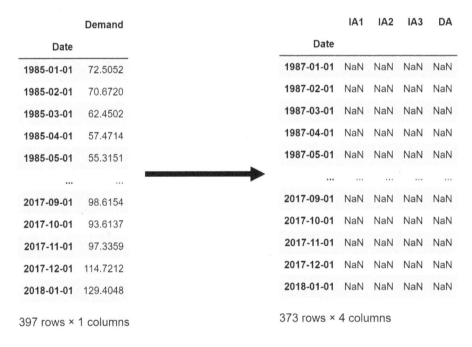

Figure 10.10 – Summary of data cleaning level II for Example 3

We will complete the depicted data processing and fill out the columns in `predict_df` in the following order: DA, IA1, IA2, and IA3.

Example 3 – level I and II data cleaning   247

Filling out DA

This is the simplest column filling process. We just need to specify the correct portion of month_df.Demand to be placed under predict_df.DA. The following screenshot shows the code and its impact on predict_df:

```
In [44]:    ▶  predict_df.DA = month_df.loc['1987-01-01':].Demand
               predict_df
```

Out[44]:

	IA1	IA2	IA3	DA
Date				
1987-01-01	NaN	NaN	NaN	73.8152
1987-02-01	NaN	NaN	NaN	70.0620
1987-03-01	NaN	NaN	NaN	65.6100
1987-04-01	NaN	NaN	NaN	60.1586
1987-05-01	NaN	NaN	NaN	58.8734
...	...	...	...	...
2017-09-01	NaN	NaN	NaN	98.6154
2017-10-01	NaN	NaN	NaN	93.6137
2017-11-01	NaN	NaN	NaN	97.3359
2017-12-01	NaN	NaN	NaN	114.7212
2018-01-01	NaN	NaN	NaN	129.4048

373 rows × 4 columns

Figure 10.11 – Code for filling out predict_df.DA and its result

As we can see, predict_df.DA was filled out properly. Next, we will fill out predict_df.IA1.

Filling out IA1

To compute IA1, which is the *Average demand of the month over the years*, we need to be able to filter month_df using the value of the month. To create such a capability, the following code maps a lambda function to month_df and extracts the month of each row:

```
month_df['Month'] = list(map(lambda v:v.month, month_df.index))
```

Before you move on, print out month_df and study its new state.

The following code creates the `ComputeIA1()` function, which uses `month_df` to filter out the data points needed for the correct value of each cell under `predict_df.IA1`. Once it's been created, the `ComputeIA1()` function is applied to `predict_df`:

```
def ComputeIA1(r):
    row_date = r.name
    wdf = month_df.loc[:row_date].iloc[:-1]
    BM = wdf.Month == row_date.month
    return wdf[BM].Demand.mean()
predict_df.IA1 = predict_df.apply(ComputeIA1,axis=1)
```

The function `ComputeIA1()` that is written to be applied to the rows of `predict_df`, performs the following steps:

1. First, it filters out `month_df` using the calculated `row_date` to remove the data points whose dates are after `row_date`.

2. Second, the function uses a Boolean mask to keep the data points with the same month as the row's month (`row_date.month`).

3. Next, the function calculates the average demand of the filtered data points and then returns it.

> **Note**
>
> Let me share a side note before moving on. The `wdf` variable that was created in the preceding code is short for Working DataFrame. The abbreviation `wdf` is what I use every time I need a DataFrame inside a loop or a function but where I won't need it afterward.

After successfully running the preceding code, make sure that you print out `predict_df` and study its new state before moving on.

So far, we have filled out DA and IA1. Next, we will fill out IA2.

Filling out IA2

To fill out IA2, we will follow the same general steps that we did for filling out IA1. The difference is that the function we will create and apply to `predict_df` to calculate the IA2 values is more complex; for IA1, we created and applied `ComputeIA1()`, while for IA2, we will create and apply `ComputeIA2()`. The difference is that `ComputeIA2()` is more complex.

Example 3 – level I and II data cleaning   249

The code that creates and applies the ComputeIA2() function is shown here. Try to study the code and figure out how it works before moving on:

```
from sklearn.linear_model import LinearRegression
def ComputeIA2(r):
    row_date = r.name
    wdf = month_df.loc[:row_date].iloc[:-1]
    BM = wdf.Month == row_date.month
    wdf = wdf[BM]
    wdf.reset_index(drop=True,inplace=True)
    wdf.drop(columns = ['Month'],inplace=True)
    wdf['integer'] = range(len(wdf))
    wdf['ones'] = 1
    lm = LinearRegression()
    lm.fit(wdf.drop(columns=['Demand']), wdf.Demand)
    return lm.coef_[0]
predict_df.IA2 = predict_df.apply(ComputeIA2,axis=1)
```

The preceding code is both similar and different to the code we used to fill out IA1. It is similar since both ComputeIA1() and ComputeIA2() start by filtering out month_df to get to a DataFrame that only includes the data objects that are needed to compute the value. You may notice that the three lines of code under def ComputeIA1(r): and def ComputeIA2(r): are the same. The difference between the two starts from there. As computing IA1 was a simple matter of calculating the mean of a list of values, the rest of ComputeIA1() was very simple. However, for ComputeIA2(), the code needs to fit a linear regression to the filtered data points so that it can calculate the slope of the change over the years. The ComputeIA2() function uses LinearRegression from sklearn.linear_model to find the fitted regression equation and then return the calculated coefficient of the model.

After successfully running the preceding code, make sure that you print out predict_df and study its new state before moving on.

To understand the way `ComputeIA2()` finds the slope of change for each cell under `predict_df.IA2`, see the following screenshot, which shows the code and its output for calculating the slope for one cell under `predict_df.IA2`. The following screenshot calculates the IA2 value for the row with an index of `2017-10-01`:

```
In [51]:    row_date = '2017-10-01'
            wdf = month_df.loc[:row_date].iloc[:-1]
            BM = wdf.Month == 10
            wdf = wdf[BM]
            wdf.reset_index(drop=True,inplace=True)
            wdf.drop(columns = ['Month'],inplace=True)
            wdf['integer'] = range(len(wdf))
            wdf['ones'] = 1

            lm = LinearRegression()
            lm.fit(wdf.drop(columns=['Demand']), wdf.Demand)
            print('Slope = {}'.format(lm.coef_[0]))

            wdf.plot.scatter(x='integer',y='Demand',marker='*',
                            label='Data points',c='C0')

            b = lm.intercept_
            a = lm.coef_[0]

            X = wdf.integer
            y = b + a*X

            plt.plot(X,y,label = 'Fitted regression',linestyle='--',c='C1')
            plt.show()

Slope = 1.1857728189149566
```

Figure 10.12 – A sample calculation of the slope (IA2) for one row of predict_df

So far, we have filled out DA, IA1, and IA2. Next, we will fill out IA3.

Example 3 – level I and II data cleaning   251

Filling out IA3

Among all the independent attributes, IA3 is the easiest one to process. IA3 is the *Average demands of months t-2, t-3, and t-4*. The following code creates the ComputeIA3() function and applies it to predict_df. This function uses the index of predict_df to find the demand values from 2 months ago, 3 months ago, and 4 months ago. It does this by filtering out all the data that is after row_date using .loc[:row_date], and then by only keeping the fourth, third, and second rows of the remaining data from the bottom using .iloc[-5:-2]. Once the data filtering process is complete, the average of three demand values is returned:

```
def ComputeIA3(r):
    row_date = r.name
    wdf = month_df.loc[:row_date].iloc[-5:-2]
    return wdf.Demand.mean()
predict_df.IA3 = predict_df.apply(ComputeIA3,axis=1)
```

Once the preceding code has been run successfully, we will be done performing level II data cleaning on month_df. The following screenshot shows the state of predict_df after the steps we took to create and clean it:

Date	IA1	IA2	IA3	DA
1987-01-01	72.905450	0.800500	59.291467	73.8152
1987-02-01	69.329450	-2.685100	61.669767	70.0620
1987-03-01	62.336150	-0.228100	67.097433	65.6100
1987-04-01	57.252150	-0.438500	70.670867	60.1586
1987-05-01	55.564400	0.498600	69.829067	58.8734
...	...	...	...	...
2017-09-01	86.105297	1.378406	102.129167	98.6154
2017-10-01	79.790228	1.185773	107.746067	93.6137
2017-11-01	82.692128	1.190510	106.566800	97.3359
2017-12-01	95.164994	1.421533	100.386767	114.7212
2018-01-01	101.272830	1.537419	96.521667	129.4048

373 rows × 4 columns

Figure 10.13 – Level II cleaned predict_df

Now that the dataset is level II cleaned and has been prepared for the prediction, we can use any prediction algorithm to predict the future monthly demands. In the next section, we'll apply linear regression to create a prediction tool.

Doing the analytics – using linear regression to create a predictive model

First, we will import `LinearRegression` from `sklearn.linear_model` to fit the data to a regression equation. As we learned in *Chapter 6, Prediction* to apply prediction algorithms to our data, we need to separate the data into independent and dependent attributes. Customarily, we use X to denote independent attributes and y to denote the dependent attribute. The following code performs these steps and feeds the data into the model:

```
from sklearn.linear_model import LinearRegression
X = predict_df.drop(columns=['DA'])
y = predict_df.DA
lm = LinearRegression()
lm.fit(X,y)
```

As we learned in *Chapter 6, Prediction*, once the preceding code has been executed, almost nothing happens, but the analysis has been performed. We can use `lm` to access the estimated βs and also perform prediction.

The following code extracts the βs from `lm`:

```
print('intercept (b0) ', lm.intercept_)
coef_names = ['b1','b2','b3']
print(pd.DataFrame({'Predictor': X.columns,
                    'coefficient Name':coef_names,
                    'coefficient Value': lm.coef_}))
```

Using the output of the preceding code, we can figure out the following regression equation:

$$DA = -25.75 + 1.29 * IA1 + 1.43 * IA2 + 0.15 * IA3$$

To find out the quality of the prediction model, we can see how well the model has been able to find the patterns in the dependent attribute, DA. The following screenshot shows the code that draws the actual and fitted data of the linear regression model:

```
In [269]:   ▶  plt.figure(figsize=(10,4))
                plt.plot(X.index,y, label='Actual')
                plt.plot(X.index,lm.predict(X),
                        label = 'Fitted',linestyle='--')
                plt.legend()
                plt.show()
```

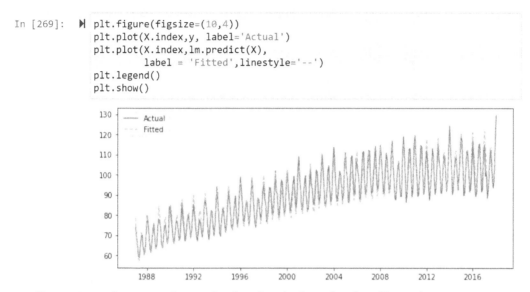

Figure 10.14 – Comparing the actual and predicted values of predict_df using linear regression

From the preceding diagram, we can see that the model has been able to capture the trends in the data very well and that it is a great model to be used to predict future data points.

Before moving on, take a moment to consider all we did to design and implement an effective predictive model. Most of the steps we took were data preprocessing steps rather than analytics ones. As you can see, being able to perform effective data preprocessing will take you a long way in becoming more successful at data analytics.

Summary

Congratulations on your excellent progress. In this chapter and through three examples, we were able to use the programming and analytics skills that we have developed throughout this book to effectively preprocess example datasets and meet the example's analytics goals.

In the next chapter, we will focus on level III data cleaning. This level of data cleaning is the toughest data cleaning level as it requires an even deeper understanding of the analytic goals of data preprocessing.

Before moving on and starting your journey regarding level III data cleaning, spend some time on the following exercises and solidify what you've learned.

Exercises

1. This question is about the difference between dataset reformulation and dataset restructuring. Answer the following questions:

   a) In your own words, describe the difference between dataset reformulation and dataset restructuring.

   b) In *Example 3* of this chapter, we moved the data from `month_df` to `predict_df`. The text described the level II data cleaning for both table reformulation and table restructuring. Which of the two occurred? Is it possible that the distinction we provided for the difference between table restructuring and reformulation cannot specify which one happened? Would that matter?

2. For this exercise, we will be using `LaqnData.csv`, which can be found on the London Air website (`https://www.londonair.org.uk/LondonAir/Default.aspx`) and includes the hourly readings of five air particles (NO, NO2, NOX, PM2.5, and PM10) from a specific site. Perform the following steps for this dataset:

   a) Read the dataset into `air_df` using pandas.

   b) Use the `.unique()` function to identify the columns that only have one possible value and then remove them from `air_df`.

   c) Unpack the `readingDateTime` column into two new columns called `Date` and `time`. This can be done in different ways. The following are some clues about the three approaches you must take to perform this unpacking:

   - Use `air_df.apply()`.
   - Use `air_df.readingDateTime.str.split(' ',expand=true)`.
   - Use `pd.to_datetime()`.

   d) Use what you learned in this chapter to create the following visual. Each line in each of the five line plots represents 1 day's reading for the plot's relevant air particle:

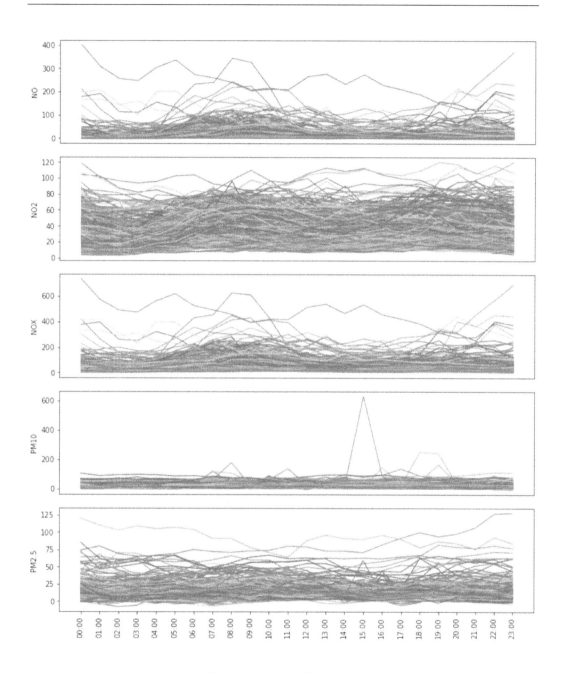

Figure 10.15 – air_df summary

e) Label and describe the data cleaning steps you performed in this exercise. For example, did you have to reformulate a new dataset to draw the visualization? Specify which level of data cleaning each of the steps performed.

3. In this exercise, we will be using `stock_index.csv`. This file contains hourly data for the *Nasdaq*, *S&P*, and *Dow Jones* stock indices from November 7, 2019, until June 10th, 2021. Each row of data represents an hour of the trading day, and each row is described by the opening value, the closing value, and the volume for each of the three stock indices. The opening value is the value of the index at the beginning of the hour, the closing value is the value of the index at the end of the hour, and the volume is the amount of trading that happened in that hour.

    In this exercise, we would like to perform a clustering analysis to understand how many different types of trading days we experienced during 2020. Using the following attributes, which can be found in `stock_df.csv`, we'd like to use K-Means to cluster the stock trading days of 2020 into four clusters:

    a) `nasdaqChPe`: Nasdaq change percentage over the trading day.

    b) `nasdaqToVo`: Total Nasdaq trading volume over the trading day.

    c) `dowChPe`: Dow Jones change percentage over the trading day.

    d) `dowToVo`: Total Dow Jones trading volume over the trading day.

    e) `sNpChPe`: S&P change percentage over the trading day.

    f) `sNpToVo`: Total S&P trading volume over the trading day.

    g) `N_daysMarketClose`: The number of days before the market closes for the weekend; for Mondays, it is 5, for Tuesdays, it is 4, for Wednesdays, it is 3, for Thursdays, it is 2, and for Fridays, it is 0.

    Make sure that you finish the clustering analysis by performing a centroid analysis via a heatmap and give each cluster a name. Once the clustering analysis is complete, label and describe the data cleaning steps you performed in this exercise.

11
Data Cleaning Level III – Missing Values, Outliers, and Errors

In level I, we cleaned up the table without paying attention to the data structure or the recorded values. In level II, our attention was to have a data structure that would support our analytic goal, but we still didn't pay much attention to the correctness or appropriateness of the recorded values. That is the objective of data cleaning level III. In data cleaning level III, we will focus on the recorded values and will take measures to make sure that three matters regarding the values recorded in the data are addressed. First, we will make sure missing values in the data have been detected, that we know why this has happened, and that appropriate measures have been taken to address them. Second, we will ensure that we have taken appropriate measures so that the recorded values are correct. Third, we will ascertain that the extreme points in the data have been detected and appropriate measures have been taken to address them.

Level III data cleaning is similar to level II in its relationship to data analytic goals and tools. While level I data cleaning can be done in isolation without having an eye on data analytics goals and tools, levels II and III data cleaning must be done while we are informed by the analytic goals and tools. In examples 1, 2, and 3 in the previous chapter, we experienced how level II data cleaning was performed for analytic tools. The examples in this chapter are also going to be very well connected to analytical situations.

In this chapter, we're going to cover the following main topics:

- Missing values
- Outliers
- Errors

Technical requirements

You will be able to find all of the code and the datasets that are used in this book in a GitHub repository exclusively created for this book. To find the repository, click on this link: `https://github.com/PacktPublishing/Hands-On-Data-Preprocessing-in-Python`. In this repository, you will find a folder titled `Chapter11`, from where you can download the code and the data for better learning.

Missing values

Missing values, as the name suggests, are values we expect to have but we don't. In the simplest terms, missing values are empty cells in a dataset that we want to use for analytic goals. For example, the following screenshot shows an example of a dataset with missing values—the first and third students' **grade point average** (**GPA**) is missing, the fifth student's height is missing, and the sixth student's personality type is missing:

	Gender	Height	Year	GPA	Personality Type
1	1	190	Sophomore		ISTJ
2	1	189	Freshman	3.81	ESNJ
3	0	160	Freshman		ISTJ
4	1	181	Sophomore	3.95	INTP
5	1		Freshman	3.62	ISTJ
6	0	184	Freshman	3.87	
7	0	172	Junior	3.31	ISTP

Figure 11.1 – A dataset example with missing values

In Python, missing values are not presented with emptiness—they are presented via NaN, which is short for **Not a Number**. While the literal meaning of **Not a Number** does not completely capture all the possible situations for which we have missing values, NaN is used in Python whenever we have missing values.

The following screenshot shows a pandas DataFrame that has read and presented the table represented in *Figure 11.1*. After comparing the two screenshots, you will see that every cell that is empty in *Figure 11.1* has NaN in *Figure 11.2*.

	Gender	Height	Year	GPA	Personality Type
0	1	190.0	Sophomore	NaN	ISTJ
1	1	189.0	Freshman	3.81	ESNJ
2	0	160.0	Freshman	NaN	ISTJ
3	1	181.0	Sophomore	3.95	INTP
4	1	NaN	Freshman	3.62	ISTJ
5	0	184.0	Freshman	3.87	NaN
6	0	172.0	Junior	3.31	ISTP

Figure 11.2 – A dataset example with missing values presented in pandas

We now know what missing values are and how they are presented in our analytic environment of choice, Python. Unfortunately, missing values are not always presented in a standard way; for example, having NaN on a pandas DataFrame is a standard way of presenting missing values. However, someone who did not know any better may have used some internal agreements to present missing values with an alternative such as MV, None, 99999, and N/A. If missing values are not presented in a standard way, the first step of dealing with them is to rectify that. In such cases, we detect the values that the author of the dataset meant as missing values and replace them with np.nan.

Even if missing values are presented in the standard way, detecting them might sometimes be as easy as just eyeballing the dataset. When the dataset is large, we cannot rely on eyeballing the data to detect and understand missing values. Next, we will turn our attention to how we can detect missing values, especially for larger datasets.

Detecting missing values

Every Pandas DataFrame comes with two functions that are very useful in detecting which attributes have missing values and how many there are: .info() and .isna(). The following example shows how these functions can be used to detect whether a dataset has missing values and how many values are missing.

Example of detecting missing values

The `Airdata.csv` air quality dataset comprises hourly recordings of the year 2020 from three locations. The dataset—apart from `NO2` readings for three locations A, B, and C—has `DateTime`, `Temperature`, `Humidity`, `Wind_Speed`, and `Wind_Direction` readings. The following screenshot shows the code that reads the file into the `air_df` DataFrame and shows the first and last few rows of the dataset:

```
In [3]:  ▶ air_df = pd.read_csv('Airdata.csv')
           air_df
```

Out[3]:

	DateTime	Temperature	Humidity	Wind_Speed	Wind_Direction	NO2_Location_A	NO2_
0	1/1/2020 0:00	2.180529	87	1.484318	75.963760	39.23	
1	1/1/2020 1:00	1.490529	89	2.741678	113.198590	38.30	
2	1/1/2020 2:00	1.690529	85	3.563818	135.000000	NaN	
3	1/1/2020 3:00	1.430529	84	2.811690	129.805570	37.28	
4	1/1/2020 4:00	0.840529	86	1.800000	126.869896	29.97	
...	...	...	...	...	...	...	
8779	12/31/2020 19:00	4.920528	72	4.553679	251.565060	53.44	
8780	12/31/2020 20:00	4.990529	74	3.259938	186.340200	49.80	
8781	12/31/2020 21:00	4.360529	84	10.587917	252.181120	43.32	
8782	12/31/2020 22:00	3.820529	88	8.435069	219.805570	39.88	
8783	12/31/2020 23:00	3.170529	89	6.792466	212.005390	39.04	

8784 rows × 8 columns

Figure 11.3 – Reading Airdata.csv into air_df

The first method we can use to detect whether any columns of the data have any missing values is to use the `.info()` function. The following screenshot showcases the application of this function on `air_df`:

```
In [4]:  ▶ air_df.info()

            <class 'pandas.core.frame.DataFrame'>
            RangeIndex: 8784 entries, 0 to 8783
            Data columns (total 8 columns):
             #   Column          Non-Null Count   Dtype
            ---  ------          --------------   -----
             0   DateTime        8784 non-null    object
             1   Temperature     8784 non-null    float64
             2   Humidity        8784 non-null    int64
             3   Wind_Speed      8784 non-null    float64
             4   Wind_Direction  8784 non-null    float64
             5   NO2_Location_A  8664 non-null    float64
             6   NO2_Location_B  8204 non-null    float64
             7   NO2_Location_C  8652 non-null    float64
            dtypes: float64(6), int64(1), object(1)
            memory usage: 549.1+ KB
```

Figure 11.4 – Using .info() to detect missing values in air_df

As you can see in the preceding screenshot, air_df has 8784 rows (*entries*) of data, but the NO2_Location_A, NO2_Location_B, and NO2_Location_C columns have fewer non-null values, and that means these attributes have missing values.

A second method to figure out which attributes have missing values is to use the .isnan() function of Pandas Series. Both Pandas DataFrames and Pandas Series have the .isnan() function, and it outputs the same data structure with all the cells filled with Booleans indicating whether the cell is NaN. The following screenshot uses the .isnan() function to count the number of NaN entries in each attribute of air_df:

```
In [5]:  ▶ print('Number of missing values:')
            for col in air_df.columns:
                n_MV = sum(air_df[col].isna())
                print('{}:{}'.format(col,n_MV))

            Number of missing values:
            DateTime:0
            Temperature:0
            Humidity:0
            Wind_Speed:0
            Wind_Direction:0
            NO2_Location_A:120
            NO2_Location_B:580
            NO2_Location_C:132
```

Figure 11.5 – Detecting missing values in air_df

In the preceding screenshot, we see that the NO2 readings in all three locations have missing values. This only confirms the detection of missing values we performed in *Figure 11.4* using the `.info()` function.

Now that we know how to detect missing values, let's turn our attention to understanding what could have caused these values to be missing. In our quest to deal with missing values, we first and foremost need to know why this has happened. In the next subchapter, we will focus on which situations cause missing values.

Causes of missing values

There can be a wide range of reasons as to why missing values may occur. As we will see in this chapter, knowing why a value is missing is the most important piece of information that enables us to handle missing values effectively. The following list provides the most common reasons why values may be missing:

- Human error.
- Respondents may refuse to answer a survey question.
- The person taking the survey does not understand the question.
- The provided value is an obvious error, so it was deleted.
- Not enough time to respond to questions.
- Lost records due to lack of effective database management.
- Intentional deletion and skipping of data collection (probably with fraudulent intent).
- Participant exiting in the middle of the study.
- Third-party tampering with or blocking data collection.
- Missed observations.
- Sensor malfunctions.
- Programing bugs.

When working with data as a data analyst, sometimes all you have is the data and you do not have anyone to whom you can ask questions about the data. So, the important thing here would be to be inquisitive about the data and imagine what could be the reasons behind the missing values. Committing the preceding list to memory and understanding these reasons will be beneficial to you when you have to guess what could have caused missing values.

It goes without saying that if you have access to someone who knows about the data, the best course of action on finding out the causes of missing values is to ask the informant.

Regardless of what caused missing values, from a data analytic perspective, we can categorize all the missing values into three types. Understanding these types will be very important in deciding how missing values should be addressed.

Types of missing values

One missing value or a group of missing values in one attribute could fall under one of the following three types: **missing completely at random (MCAR)**, **missing at random (MAR)**, and **missing not at random (MNAR)**. There is an ordinal relationship between these types of missing values. Moving from MCAR to MNAR, the missing values become more problematic and harder to deal with.

MCAR is used when we do not have any reason to believe the values are missing due to any systematic reasons. When a missing value is classed as MCAR, the data object that has a missing value could be any of the data objects. For instance, if an air quality sensor fails to communicate with its server to save records due to random fluctuations in the internet connection, the missing values are of the MCAR type. This is because internet connection issues could have happened for any of the data objects, but it just happened to occur for the ones it did.

On the other hand, we have MAR when some data objects in the data are more likely to have missing values. For instance, if a high wind speed sometimes causes a sensor to malfunction and renders it unable to give a reading, the missing values that have happened in the high wind are classed as MAR. The key to understanding MAR is that the systematic reason that leads to having missing values does not always cause missing values but increases the tendency of the data objects to have missing values.

Lastly, MNAR happens when we know exactly which data object will have missing values. For instance, if a power plant that tends to emit too much air pollutant tampers with the sensor to avoid paying a penalty to the government, the data objects that are not collected due to this situation would be classed as MNAR. MNAR missing values are the most problematic ones, and figuring out why they happen and stopping them from happening is often the priority of a data analytic project.

Next, we will learn how we can use data analytic tools to diagnose the types of missing values. In the following section, we will see an example that showcases the three types of missing values.

Diagnosis of missing values

An attribute with missing values has, in fact, the information of two variables: itself, and a hidden attribute. The hidden attribute is a binary attribute whose value is one when there is a missing value, and zero otherwise. To figure out the types of missing values (MCAR, MAR, and MNAR), all we need to do is to investigate whether there is a relationship between the hidden binary variable of the attribute with missing values and the other attributes in the dataset. The following list shows the kinds of relationships we would expect to see based on each of the missing value types:

- **MCAR**: We don't expect the hidden binary variable to have a meaningful relationship with the other attributes.

- **MAR**: We expect a meaningful relationship between the hidden binary variable and at least one of the other attributes.

- **MNAR**: We expect a strong relationship between the hidden binary variable and at least one of the other attributes.

The following subsections showcase three situations with different types of missing values, and we will use our data analytic toolkit to help us diagnose them.

We will continue using the `air_df` dataset that we saw earlier. We saw that `NO2_Location_A`, `NO2_Location_B`, and `NO2_Location_C` have `120`, `560`, and `176` missing values, respectively. We will tackle diagnosing missing values under each column one at a time.

Diagnosing missing values in NO2_Location_A

To diagnose the types of missing values, there are two methods at our disposal: *visual* and *statistical* methods. These diagnosis methods must be run for all of the attributes in the dataset. There are four numerical attributes in the data: `Temperature`, `Humidity`, `Wind_Direction`, and `Wind_Speed`. There is also one `DateTime` attribute in the data that can be unpacked into four categorical attributes: `month`, `day`, `hour`, and `weekday`. The way we need to run the analysis is different for numerical attributes than for categorical attributes. So, first, we will learn about numerical attributes, and then we will turn our attention to categorical attributes.

Let's start with the `Temperature` numerical attribute. Also, we'll first do the diagnosis visually and then we will do it statistically.

Diagnosing missing values based on temperature

The visual diagnosis is done by comparing the temperature values for the two populations: first, data objects with missing values for NO2_Location_A, and second, data objects with no missing values for NO2_Location_A. In *Chapter 5, Data Visualization*, under *Comparing populations*, we learned how we use data visualizations to compare populations. Here, we will use those techniques. We can either use a boxplot or histogram to do this. Let's use both—first, a boxplot, and then a histogram.

The following screenshot shows the code and the boxplot that compares the two populations. The code is very similar to what we learned in *Chapter 5, Data Visualization*, so we will just discuss the implications of the visualizations.

```
In [6]:  ▶ BM_MV = air_df.NO2_Location_A.isna()
           MV_labels = ['With Missing Values','Without Missing Values']

           box_sr = pd.Series('',index = BM_MV.unique())

           for poss in BM_MV.unique():
               BM = BM_MV == poss
               box_sr[poss] = air_df[BM].Temperature

           plt.boxplot(box_sr,vert=False)
           plt.yticks([1,2],MV_labels)
           plt.show()
```

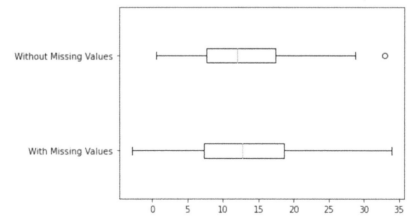

Figure 11.6 – Code for the diagnosis of missing values in NO2_Location_A using the boxplots of temperature

Looking at the boxplot in the preceding screenshot, we can see that the value of
Temperature does not meaningfully change between the two populations. That shows
that a change in Temperature could not have caused or influenced the occurrence of
missing values under NO2_Location_A.

We could also have done this analysis using a histogram. This was also shown in *Chapter
5*, *Data Visualization*, under *Comparing populations*. The following screenshot shows the
code to create a histogram and compare the two populations:

```
In [7]:  ▶  BM_MV = air_df.NO2_Location_A.isna()
            temp_range = (air_df.Temperature.min(),air_df.Temperature.max())
            MV_labels = ['With Missing Values','Without Missing Values']

            plt.figure(figsize=(10,4))

            for i,poss in enumerate(BM_MV.unique()):
                plt.subplot(1,2,i+1)
                BM = BM_MV == poss
                air_df[BM].Temperature.hist()
                plt.xlim = temp_range
                plt.title(MV_labels[i])

            plt.show()
```

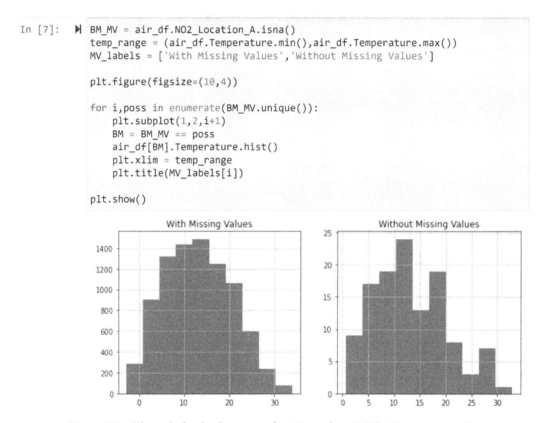

Figure 11.7 – The code for the diagnosis of missing values in NO2_Location_A using
the histogram of temperature

The preceding screenshot confirms the same conclusion we arrived at when using
boxplots. As we do not see a significant difference between the two populations, we
conclude that the value of Temperature could not have influenced or caused the
occurrence of missing values.

Lastly, we would also like to confirm this using a statistical method: a *two-sample t-test*. The two-sample t-test evaluates whether the value of a numerical attribute is significantly different among the two groups. The two groups here are the data objects having missing values under NO2_Location_A and the data objects without missing values under NO2_Location_A.

In short, the two-sample t-test hypothesizes that there is no significant difference between the attributes' value among the two groups and then calculates the probability of the data turning out the way it has if the hypothesis is correct. This probability is called the *p-value*. So, if the p-value is very small, we have meaningful evidence to suspect the hypothesis of the two-sample t-test could have been wrong.

We can easily do any hypothesis testing using Python. The following screenshot uses the ttest_ind function from the scipy.stats module to do a two-sample t-test:

```
In [8]:   ▶  from scipy.stats import ttest_ind
              BM_MV = air_df.NO2_Location_A.isna()
              ttest_ind(air_df[BM_MV].Temperature, air_df[~BM_MV].Temperature)

  Out[8]:  Ttest_indResult(statistic=0.05646499065315542, pvalue=0.9549726689684548)
```

Figure 11.8 – Using t-test to evaluate whether the value of temperature is different in NO2_Location_A between data objects with missing values and without missing values

As you can see in the previous screenshot, to use the ttest_ind() function, all we need to do is to pass the two groups of numbers.

The p-value of the t-test is very large—0.95 out of 1, which means we do not have any reason to suspect the value of Temperature can be meaningfully different between the two groups. This conclusion confirms the one that we arrived at using boxplots and histograms.

Here, we showcased the code for diagnosing missing values based on only one numerical attribute. The code and analysis for the rest of the numerical attributes are similar. Now that you know how to do this for one numerical attribute, we will next create a code that outputs all we need for missing value diagnosis using numerical attributes.

Diagnosing missing values based on all the numerical attributes

To do a complete diagnosis of missing values, a similar analysis to what we did for the Temperature attribute needs to be done for all of the attributes. While each part of the analysis is simple to understand and interpret, the fact that the diagnosis analysis has many parts begs a very organized way of coding and analysis.

To do this in an organized way, we will first create a function that performs all of the three analyses that we showed can be done for `Temperature`. Apart from the dataset, the function takes the name of the numerical attribute we want to perform the analysis and the Boolean mask that is `True` for the data objects with missing values and `False` for the data object without missing values. The function outputs boxplots, a histogram, and the p-value of the t-test for the inputted attribute. The code in the following screenshot shows how this function is created. The code is rather long; if you'd like to copy it, please find it in the `Ch 11 Data Cleaning Level III - missing values, outliers, and errors` folder in the dedicated GitHub repository for this book.

```python
In [10]:   from scipy.stats import ttest_ind
           def Diagnose_MV_Numerical(df,str_att_name,BM_MV):
               MV_labels = {True:'With Missing Values',False:'Without Missing Values'}

               labels=[]
               box_sr = pd.Series('',index = BM_MV.unique())
               for poss in BM_MV.unique():
                   BM = BM_MV == poss
                   box_sr[poss] = df[BM][str_att_name].dropna()
                   labels.append(MV_labels[poss])

               plt.boxplot(box_sr,vert=False)
               plt.yticks([1,2],labels)
               plt.xlabel(str_att_name)
               plt.show()

               plt.figure(figsize=(10,4))

               att_range = (df[str_att_name].min(),df[str_att_name].max())

               for i,poss in enumerate(BM_MV.unique()):
                   plt.subplot(1,2,i+1)
                   BM = BM_MV == poss
                   df[BM][str_att_name].hist()
                   plt.xlim = att_range
                   plt.xlabel(str_att_name)
                   plt.title(MV_labels[poss])

               plt.show()

               group_1_data = df[BM_MV][str_att_name].dropna()
               group_2_data = df[~BM_MV][str_att_name].dropna()

               p_value = ttest_ind(group_1_data,group_2_data).pvalue

               print('p-value of t-test: {}'.format(p_value))
```

Figure 11.9 – Creating a Diagnose_MV_Numerical() function for diagnosing missing values based on numerical attributes

Simply put, the previous code is a parameterized and combined version of the code presented in *Figure 11.6*, *Figure 11.7*, and *Figure 11.8*. After running the preceding code, which creates a `Diagnose_MV_Numerical()` function, running the following code will run this function for all of the numerical attributes in the data, and it allows you to investigate whether the missing values of `NO2_Location_A` happen due to any systematic reasons that are linked to numerical attributes in the dataset.

```
numerical_attributes = ['Temperature', 'Humidity', 'Wind
Speed', 'Wind Direction']
BM_MV = air_df.NO2_Location_C.isna()
for att in numerical_attributes:
    print('Diagnosis Analysis of Missing Values for {}:'.
    format(att))
    Diagnose_MV_Numerical(air_df,att,BM_MV)
    print('- - - - - - - - - - divider - - - - - - - - - - ')
```

Running the preceding code will produce four diagnosis reports, one for each of the numerical attributes. Each report has three parts: diagnosis using boxplots, diagnosis using a histogram, and diagnosis using a t-test.

Studying the ensuing reports from the preceding code snippet shows that the tendency of the missing value under `NO2_Location_A` does not change based on values of either numerical attribute in the data.

Next, we will do a similar coding and analysis for categorical attributes. Like what we did for numerical attributes, let's do a diagnosis for one attribute first, and then we will create code that can output all the analysis we need all at once. The first attribute that we will do the diagnosis for is `weekday`.

Diagnosing missing values based on weekday

You may be confused that the `air_df` dataset does not have a categorical attribute named `weekday`, and you would be right, but unpacking the `air_df.DataTime` attribute can give us the following attributes: `weekday`, `day`, `month`, and `hour`.

If you are thinking that sounds like level II data cleaning, you are absolutely right. To be able to do level III data cleaning more effectively, we need to do some level II data cleaning first. The following code performs the described level II data cleaning:

```
air_df.DateTime = pd.to_datetime(air_df.DateTime)
air_df['month'] = air_df.DateTime.dt.month
air_df['day'] = air_df.DateTime.dt.day
air_df['hour'] = air_df.DateTime.dt.hour
air_df['weekday'] = air_df.DateTime.dt.day_name()
```

After running the preceding code and before reading on, check the new state of `air_df` and study the new columns that are added to it. You will see that the `month`, `day`, `hour`, and `weekday` categorical attributes are unpacked into their own attributes.

Now that this data cleaning level II is done, we can perform a diagnosis of missing values in the `air_df.NO2_Location_A` column based on the `weekday` categorical attribute. As we saw in *Chapter 5, Data Visualization*, a bar chart is a data visualization technique to compare populations based on a categorical attribute. The following screenshot shows a modification of what we learned in *Chapter 5, Data Visualization*, under the heading *Example of comparing populations using bar charts, the first way*, for this situation:

```
In [14]:    ▶|  BM_MV = air_df.NO2_Location_A.isna()
                MV_labels = ['Without Missing Values','With Missing Values']

                plt.figure(figsize=(10,4))
                for i,poss in enumerate(BM_MV.unique()):
                    plt.subplot(1,2,i+1)
                    BM = BM_MV == poss
                    air_df[BM].weekday.value_counts().plot.bar()
                    plt.title(MV_labels[i])
                plt.show()
```

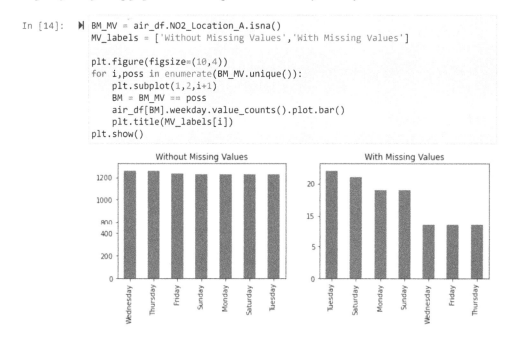

Figure 11.10 – Using a bar chart to evaluate whether the value of weekday is different between data objects in NO2_Location_A with missing values and without missing values

Looking at the preceding screenshot, we can see that the missing values could have happened randomly and we don't have a meaningful trend to believe there is a systematic reason for the missing values happening due to a change of the value of `airt_df.weekday`.

We can also do a similar diagnosis using a **chi-square test of independence** statistical test. In short and for this situation, this test hypothesizes that there is no relationship between the occurrence of missing values and the `weekday` attribute. Based on this hypothesis, the test calculates a p-value that is the probability of the data we have happening if the hypothesis is true. Using that p-value, we can decide whether we have any evidence to suspect a systematic reason for missing values.

What Is a P-Value?

This is the second time we are seeing the concept of a p-value in this chapter. A p-value is the same concept across all statistical tests and it has the same meaning. Every statistical test hypothesizes something (which is called a null hypothesis), and the p-value is calculated based on this hypothesis and the observations (data). The p-value is the probability that the data that has already happened is happening if the null hypothesis is true.

A popular rule of thumb for using p-value is to employ the famous 5% significance level. A 0.05 significance level denotes that if the p-value turns out to be larger than 0.05, then we don't have any evidence to suspect the null hypothesis is not correct. While this is a fairly good rule of thumb, it is best to understand the p-value and then complement the statistical test with data visualization.

The following screenshot shows a chi-square test of independence being performed using `chi2_contingency()` from `scipy.stats`. The code first uses `pd.crosstab()` to create a contingency table that is a visualization tool, to investigate the relationship between two categorical attributes (this was covered in the *Visualizing the relationship between two categorical attributes* section in *Chapter 5, Data Visualization*). Then, the code passes `contigency_table` to the `chi2_contingency()` function to perform the test. The test outputs some values, but not all of them are useful for us. The p-value is the second value, which is 0.4127.

```
In [15]:    from scipy.stats import chi2_contingency
            BM_MV = air_df.NO2_Location_A.isna()
            contigency_table = pd.crosstab(BM_MV,air_df.weekday)
            contigency_table
```

Out[15]:

weekday	Friday	Monday	Saturday	Sunday	Thursday	Tuesday	Wednesday
NO2_Location_A							
False	1235	1229	1227	1229	1259	1226	1259
True	13	19	21	19	13	22	13

```
In [16]:    chi2_contingency(contigency_table)
```

```
Out[16]:   (6.048964133655503,
            0.41772751510388023,
            6,
            array([[1230.95081967, 1230.95081967, 1230.95081967, 1230.95081967,
                    1254.62295082, 1230.95081967, 1254.62295082],
                   [  17.04918033,   17.04918033,   17.04918033,   17.04918033,
                      17.37704918,   17.04918033,   17.37704918]]))
```

Figure 11.11 – Using the chi-square test of independence to evaluate whether the value of weekday is different between data objects in NO2_Location_A with missing values and without missing values

Having a p-value of 0.4127 confirms the observation we made under *Figure 11.10*, which is that there is no relationship between the occurrence of missing values in `air_df.NO2_Location_A` and the value of `weekday`, and the fact that the missing values happened the way they did could have just been a random chance.

Here, we showcased the code for diagnosing missing values based on only one categorical attribute. The code and analysis for the rest of the categorical attributes are similar. Now that you know how to do this for one numerical attribute, we will next create a code that outputs all we need for missing value diagnosis using categorical attributes.

Diagnosing missing values based on all the categorical attributes

To do a complete diagnosis of missing values, a similar analysis to what we did for the `Weekday` attribute needs to be done for all of the other categorical attributes. To do this in an organized way, we will first create a function that performs the two analyses that we showed can be done for `Weekday`. Along with the dataset, the function takes the name of the categorical attribute we want to perform the analysis and the Boolean mask, which is `True` for the data objects with missing values and `False` for the data objects without missing values. The function outputs bar charts, and the p-value of the chi-squared test of independence for the inputted attribute. The following code snippet shows how this function is created:

```python
from scipy.stats import chi2_contingency
def Diagnose_MV_Categorical(df,str_att_name,BM_MV):
    MV_labels = {True:'With Missing Values', False:'Without
    Missing Values'}
    plt.figure(figsize=(10,4))
    for i,poss in enumerate(BM_MV.unique()):
        plt.subplot(1,2,i+1)
        BM = BM_MV == poss
        df[BM][str_att_name].value_counts().plot.bar()
        plt.title(MV_labels[poss])
    plt.show()
    contigency_table = pd.crosstab(BM_MV,df[str_att_name])
    p_value = chi2_contingency(contigency_table)[1]
    print('p-value of Chi_squared test: {}'.format(p_value))
```

The preceding code snippet is a parameterized and combined version of the code presented in *Figure 11.10* and *Figure 11.11*. After running the preceding code, which creates a `Diagnose_MV_Categorical()` function, running the following code will run this function for all of the categorical attributes in the data, and it allows you to investigate whether the missing values of `NO2_Location_A` happen due to any systematic reasons that are linked to the categorical attributes in the dataset:

```
categorical_attributes = ['month', 'day','hour', 'weekday']
BM_MV = air_df.NO2_Location_A.isna()
for att in categorical_attributes:
    print('Diagnosis Analysis for {}:'.format(att))
    Diagnose_MV_Categorical(air_df,att,BM_MV)
    print('- - - - - - - - - - divider - - - - - - - - - - ')
```

When you run the preceding code, it will produce four diagnosis reports, one for each of the categorical attributes. Each report has two parts, as follows:

- Diagnosis using a bar chart
- Diagnosis using a chi-squared test of independence

Studying the reports shows that the tendency of the missing value under `NO2_Location_A` does not change based on values of either categorical attribute in the data.

Combined with what we learned for numerical attributes earlier in this subchapter and what we just learned about categorical attributes, we do see that none of the attributes in the data—namely, `Temperature`, `Humidity`, `Wind_Speed`, `Wind_Direction`, `weekday`, `day`, `month`, and `hour`—may have influenced the tendency of missing values. Based on all the diagnoses that we ran for the missing values, we conclude that missing values in `NO2_Location_A` are of the MCAR type.

Now that we have been able to determine the missing values of `NO2_Location_A`, let's also run the diagnosis that we learned so far for the missing values of `NO2_Location_B` and `NO2_Location_C`. We will do so in the following two subsections.

Diagnosing missing values in NO2_Location_B

To diagnose missing values in `NO2_Location_B`, we need to do exactly the same analysis we did for `NO2_Location_A`. The coding part is very easy as we have already done this, for the most part. The following code uses the `Diagnose_MV_Numerical()` and `Diagnose_MV_Categorical()` functions that we already created to run all needed diagnoses in order to figure out which types of missing values happen under `NO2_Location_B`:

```
categorical_attributes = ['month', 'day','hour', 'weekday']
numerical_attributes = ['Temperature', 'Humidity',
'Wind_Speed', 'Wind_Direction']
BM_MV = air_df.NO2_Location_B.isna()
for att in numerical_attributes:
    print('Diagnosis Analysis for {}:'.format(att))
    Diagnose_MV_Numerical(air_df,att,BM_MV)
    print('- - - - - - - - - divider - - - - - - - - - ')
for att in categorical_attributes:
    print('Diagnosis Analysis for {}:'.format(att))
    Diagnose_MV_Categorical(air_df,att,BM_MV)
    print('- - - - - - - - - divider - - - - - - - - - ')
```

When you run the preceding code, this produces a long report that investigates whether the tendency of missing values happening may have been influenced by the values of any of the categorical or numerical attributes.

After studying the report, you can see that there are a couple of attributes that seem to have a meaningful relationship with the occurrence of missing values. These attributes are `Temperature`, `Wind_Speed`, `Wind_Direction`, and `month`. The following screenshot shows a diagnosis analysis for `Wind_Speed` that has the strongest relationship with the missing values:

Diagnosis Analysis of Missing Values for Wind_Speed:

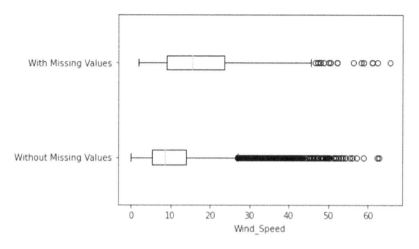

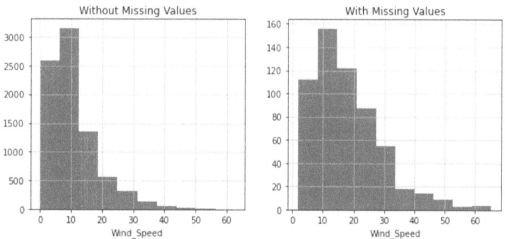

p-value of t-test: 1.3126894108159327e-85

Figure 11.12 – Diagnosis of missing values in NO2_Location_B based on the Wind_Speed attribute

In the preceding screenshot, you can see all three analytic tools are showing that there is a significant difference in the value of Wind_Speed between data objects that have missing values under NO2_Location_B and data objects that don't have missing values. In short, a higher Wind_Speed value tends to increase the chance of NO2 Location_B having missing values.

After this diagnosis, the results were shared with the company that sold us the air quality sensor. Here is the email that was sent to the company:

Dear Sir/Madam,

I am writing this email to share with you what seems to be a pattern of malfunction with the electrochemical sensors with serial number 231703612 that we purchased from you. The sensor seems to skip recording when the temperature is lower, and the wind speed is higher. We thought to let you know and we would appreciate it if you could tell us what you make of this pattern.

Sincerely,

Iman Ahmadian

After a few days, we received the following email:

Dear Analytic Team,

Thanks for sharing your concern and the information regarding the issues with the electrochemical sensors.

What you shared with us is consistent with our recent findings. We have understood that the model of the sensor that you have listed tends to malfunction in high wind conditions.

For future cases, you would expect to experience similar issues with the sensors whose serial numbers start with 2317.

We sincerely apologize for this inconvenience and would be more than happy to accommodate you with a 50% discount on our brand-new sensors that do not suffer from this malfunction. If you wish to use this discount, please follow up with our sales department citing this email.

Best wishes

Nima Ghaderi

There we have it—now we know why some of the missing values under NO2_Location_B occurred. As we know, the value of Temperature can cause an increase in the occurrence of missing values, so we can conclude that the missing values under NO2_Location_B are of the MAR type.

A good question to ask here is that if a high Wind_Speed value is a culprit for the missing values, how come the missing values also showed meaningful patterns with Temperature, Wind_Direction, and month? The reason is that Wind_Speed has a strong relationship with Temperature, Wind_Direction, and month. Use what you learned in *Chapter 5*, *Data Visualization*, in the *Investigating the relationship between two attributes* section, to put this into an analysis. Due to those strong relationships, it may look as though the other attributes also influence the tendency of missing values. We know that is not the case from our communication with the manufacturer of the sensor.

So far, we have been able to diagnose missing values under NO2_Location_A and NO2_Location_B. Next, we will perform a diagnosis for NO2_Location_C.

Diagnosing missing values in NO2_Location_C

We only need to change one line in the code for the diagnosis of missing values in NO2_Location_B so that we can diagnose missing values in NO2_Location_C. You need to change the third line of code from BM_MV = air_df.NO2_Location_B.isna() to BM_MV = air_df.NO2_Location_C.isna(). Once that change is applied and the code is run, you will get a diagnosis report based on all the categorical and numerical attributes in the data. Try to go through and interpret the diagnosis report before reading on.

The diagnosis report shows a relationship between the tendency of missing values and most of the attributes—namely, `Temperature`, `Humidity`, `Wind_Speed`, `day`, `month`, `hour`, and `weekday`. However, the relationship with the `weekday` attribute is the strongest. The following screenshot shows a missing value diagnosis based on `weekday`. The bar chart in the screenshot shows that the missing values happen exclusively on Saturdays. The p-value of the chi-square test is very small.

`Diagnosis Analysis for weekday:`

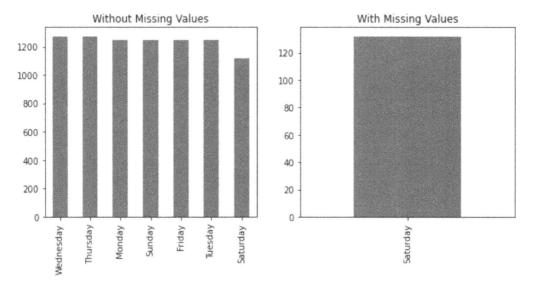

`p-value of Chi_squared test: 1.554165460861991e-171`

Figure 11.13 – Diagnosis of missing values in NO2_Location_C based on the weekday attribute

The diagnosis based on `hour` and `day` also shows meaningful patterns (the diagnosis report for the `hour` and `day` attributes is not printed here, but please look at the report you just created). The missing values happen equally only when the value of the `hour` attribute is 10, 11, 12, 13, 14, 15, 16, 17, 18, 19, and 20, or when the value of the `day` attribute is 25, 26, 27, 28, and 29. From these reports, we can deduce that the missing values happen predictably on the last Saturday of every month from 10 A.M. to 8 P.M. That is the pattern we see in the data, but why?

After letting the local authority of location C know, it turned out that a group of employees at the power plant in location C had been taking advantage of the resources of the power plant to engage in the mining of various cryptocurrencies. This abuse of resources had happened only on the last Saturday of the month as the power plant in question had a complete day off for regular and preventive maintenance. As this group of employees had been under a lot of stress to cover their tracks and avoid getting caught, they had decided to tamper with the sensor that had been put in place to regulate the air pollution from the power plant. Little did they know that tampering with data collection leaves a mark on the dataset that is not easily hidden from the eyes of a high-quality data analyst such as yourself.

This last piece of information and the diagnosis brings us to the conclusion that the missing value in NO2_Location_C is an MNAR value. Such values are missed due to a direct reason as to why the data was being collected in the first place. A lot of times when a dataset has a significant number of MNAR missing values, the dataset becomes worthless and cannot be of value in meaningful analytics. A very first step in dealing with MNAR missing values is to prevent them from happening ever again.

After learning how to detect and diagnose missing values, now is the perfect time to discuss dealing with missing values. Let's get straight to it.

Dealing with missing values

As shown in the following list, there are four different approaches to dealing with missing values:

- Keep them as is.
- Remove the data objects (rows) with missing values.
- Remove the attributes (columns) with missing values.
- Estimate and impute a value.

Each of the previous strategies could be the best strategy in different circumstances. Regardless, when dealing with missing values, we have the following two goals:

- Keeping as much data and information as possible
- Introducing the least possible amount of bias in our analysis

Simultaneously achieving these two goals is not always possible, and a balance often needs to be struck. To effectively find that balance in dealing with missing values, we need to understand and consider the following items:

- Our analytic goals
- Our analytic tools
- The cause of the missing values
- The type of the missing values (MCAR, MAR, MNAR)

In most situations when there is sufficient understanding of the preceding items, the best course of action in dealing with missing values shows itself to you. In the following subsection, we will first describe each of the four approaches in dealing with missing values, and then we will put what we learn into practice, with some examples.

First approach – Keep the missing value as is

As the heading suggests, this approach keeps the missing value as a missing value and enters the next stage of data preprocessing. This approach is the best way to deal with missing values in the following two situations.

First, you would use this strategy in cases where you will be sharing this data with others and you are not necessarily the one who is going to be using it for analytics. In this way, you will allow them to decide how they should deal with missing values based on their analytics needs.

Second, if both data analytic goals and data analytic tools you will be using can seamlessly handle missing values, *keep as is* is the best approach. For instance, the **K-Nearest Neighbors (KNN)** algorithm that we learned about in *Chapter 7, Classification*, can be adjusted to deal with missing values without having to remove any data objects. As you remember, KNN calculates the distance between data objects to find the nearest neighbors. So, every time the distance between a data object with missing values and other data objects is being calculated, a value will be assumed for the missing values. The assumed values will be selected in such a way that the assumed values will not help, so the data object with the missing value will be selected. In other words, a data object with missing values will be selected as one of the nearest neighbors only if its non-missing values show a very high level of similarity that cancels out the negative effect of the assumed values for the missing values.

You can see that if the KNN is adjusted in this way, then it would be best if we kept the missing values as is so as to meet both of the listed goals in dealing with missing values: keeping as much information as possible and avoiding the introduction of bias in the analysis.

While the described modification to the KNN algorithm is an accepted approach in the literature, it is not guaranteed that every analytic tool that features KNN has incorporated the described modification so that the algorithm can deal with missing values. For instance, KNeighborsClassifier that we used from the sklearn.neighbors module will give you an error if the dataset has missing values. If you are planning to use this analytics tool, then you cannot use a *keep as is* approach and have to use one of the other approaches.

Second approach – Remove data objects with missing values

This approach must be selected with great care because it can work against the two goals of successfully dealing with missing values: not introducing bias into the dataset, and not removing valuable information from the data. For instance, when the missing values in a dataset are of the type MNAR or MAR, we should refrain from removing data objects with missing values. That is because doing so means that you are removing a meaningfully distinct part of the population in the dataset.

Even if the missing values are of type MCAR, we should first try to find other ways of dealing with missing values before turning toward removing data objects. Removing data objects from a dataset should be considered as a last resort when there are no other ways to deal with missing values.

Third approach – Remove the attributes with missing values

When most of the missing values in a dataset come from one or two attributes, we might consider removing the attributes as a way of dealing with missing values. Of course, if the attribute is a key attribute without which you cannot proceed with the project, facing too many missing values in the key attribute means the project is not doable. However, if the attributes are not absolutely essential to the project, removing the attributes with too many missing values might be the right approach.

When the number of missing values in one attribute is large enough (roughly more than 25%), estimating and inputting missing values becomes meaningless, and letting go of the attribute is better than estimating missing values.

Fourth approach – Estimate and impute missing values

In this approach, we would use our knowledge, understanding, and analytic tools to fill missing values. The term *imputing* captures the essence of what this does to a dataset—we put *value* instead of *missing value* while knowing that this could cause bias in our analysis. If the missing values are of the MCAR or MAR type and the analytic we have chosen cannot process the dataset with missing values, imputing the missing values might be the best approach.

There are four general methods to estimate a replacement for missing values. The following list outlines these methods:

- Impute with the general central tendency (mean, median, or mode). This is better for MCAR missing values.

- Impute with the central tendency of a more relevant group of data to the missing values. This is better for MAR missing values.

- **Regression analysis**. Not ideal, but if we have to proceed with a dataset that has MNAR missing values, this method is better for such a dataset.

- **Interpolation**. When the dataset is a time series dataset and the missing values are of the MCAR type.

A common misconception about the process of estimation and imputation is that we want to impute missing values with the most accurate replacements. That is not correct at all. When imputing, we do not aim to best predict the value of missing values but to impute with values that would create the least amount of bias for our analysis. For instance, for clustering analysis, if a dataset has MCAR missing values, imputing with the whole-population central tendency is the best way to go. The reason is that the central tendency value will act as a neutral vote in the process of grouping the data objects, and if the data objects with missing values are pushed to be a part of one cluster, this is not due to the imputed value.

Now that we have had a chance to understand the different approaches to dealing with missing values, let's put things together and see a step-by-step decision-making process in selecting the right strategy.

Choosing the right approach in dealing with missing values

The following diagram summarizes what we have discussed in dealing with missing values so far. The diagram shows that the selection of the right approach in dealing with missing values must be informed from four items: analytic goals, analytic tools, the cause of missing values, and the type of missing values (MCAR, MAR, MNAR).

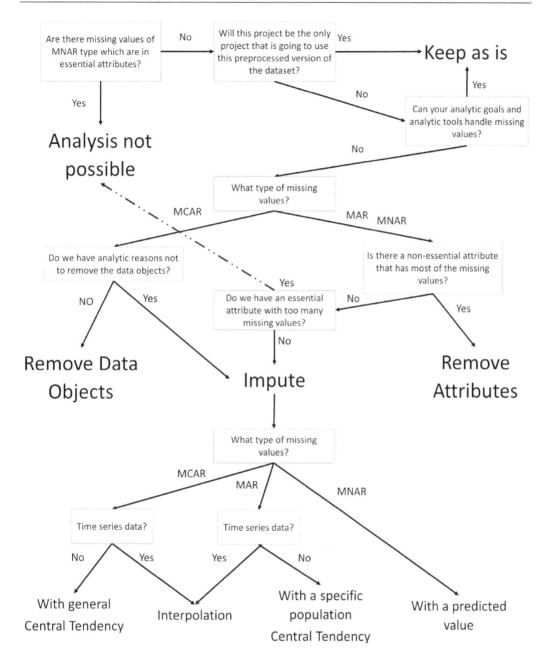

Figure 11.14 – Diagram for choosing approaches and methods for dealing with missing values

Now, let's put what we have learned so far into practice and see some examples.

Example 1

Using air_df, whose missing values we detected and diagnosed earlier in this chapter, we would like to draw a bar chart that shows the average NO2 per hour value in Location A.

If you remember, the missing values in `air_df.NO2_Location_A` are of the MCAR missing value type. Since the missing values are not of the MNAR type and a bar chart can easily handle missing values, the strategy we chose to deal with the missing values will be to keep them as it is. The following screenshot shows the code and the bar chart that it creates:

```
In [22]:  ▶  air_df.groupby('hour').NO2_Location_A.mean().plot.bar()
             plt.show()
```

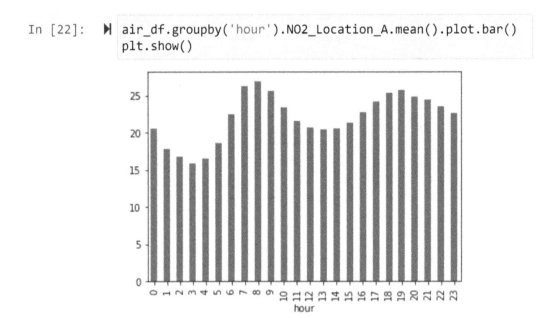

Figure 11.15 – Dealing with missing values of NO2_Location_A to draw an hourly bar chart

In the preceding screenshot, you observed that the `.groupby()` and `.mean()` functions were able to handle missing values. When the data is aggregated and the number of missing values is not significant, the aggregation of the data handles the missing values without imputation. In fact, the `.mean()` function ignores the existence of attributes with missing values and calculates the mean based on data objects that have a value.

Example 2

Using air_df, whose missing values we detected and diagnosed earlier in this chapter, we would like to draw a line chart that compares the NO2 variation of the first day of each month in Location A.

We know that the missing values in air_df.NO2_Location_A are of the MCAR type; however, assume that we don't know if a line plot can handle the missing values or not. So, let's give it a try and see if the *keep as is* strategy will work. The following screenshot shows the line plot we need without dealing with the missing values:

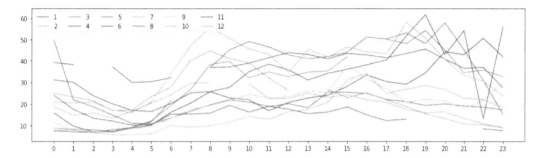

Figure 11.16 – Daily line plot of NO2_Location_A for the first day of every month

In the preceding screenshot, we see that the line plots are cut in between due to the existence of missing values. If the figure meets our analytic need, then we are done and there is no need to do anything further. However, if we would like to deal with the missing values and remove the empty spots in the line plots, we would need to use interpolation as the missing values are of the MCAR type and the data is time series data. The following code snippet shows how to deal with the missing values and then draw complete line plots:

```
NO2_Location_A_noMV = air_df.NO2_Location_A.interpolate(
method='linear')
month_poss = air_df.month.unique()
hour_poss = air_df.hour.unique()
plt.figure(figsize=(15,4))
for mn in month_poss:
    BM = (air_df.month == mn) & (air_df.day ==1)
    plt.plot(NO2_Location_A_noMV[BM].values, label=mn)
plt.legend(ncol=6)
plt.xticks(hour_poss)
plt.show()
```

The preceding code snippet uses the .interploate() function to impute the missing values. When method='linear' is used, the function imputes with the average of the data points before and after it. In our eyes, it will appear as though the empty spots are connected with a ruler. Run the preceding code and compare its output with *Figure 11.16*.

Example 3

Using air_df, we would like to draw a bar chart that compares the average NO2 per hour value in Location A and Location B.

We remember that the missing values in `air_df.NO2_Location_A` are of the MCAR type and that those in `air_df.NO2_Location_B` are of the MAR type. As neither of the attributes has MNAR missing values and the bar chart can handle missing values, we can use a *keep as is* strategy. The following screenshot shows the code needed to create a bar chart for this situation:

```
In [25]:   ▶ air_df.groupby('hour')[
               ['NO2_Location_A','NO2_Location_B']].mean().plot.bar()
             plt.show()
```

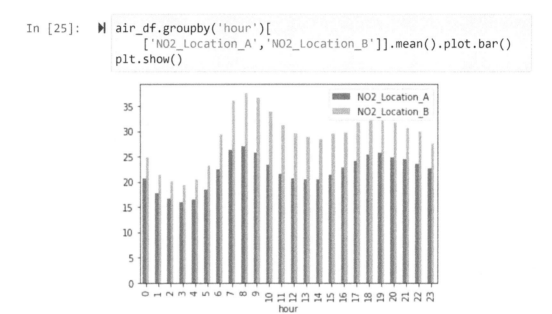

Figure 11.17 – Dealing with missing values of NO2_Location_A and NO2_Location_B to draw an hourly bar chart

Example 4

Using air_df, we would like to draw a bar chart that compares the average NO2 per hour value in Location A, Location B, and Location C.

We remember that the missing values are of types MCAR, MAR, and MNAR, respectively, in `NO2_Location_A`, `NO2_Location_B`, and `NO2_Location_C`. As we mentioned, dealing with MCAR and MAR missing values is much easier than dealing with MNAR missing values. For MCAR and MAR, we already saw that we can use a *keep as is* strategy.

For MNAR, we need to answer the question: *Are the MNAR missing values essential attributes?* Answering this question requires a deep understanding of the analytic goals. In two different analytic situations, we may have to deal with the missing values differently.

In one analytic situation, a bar chart is requested from an air pollution regulatory government body. In this situation, we cannot move past the MNAR missing values in NO2_Location_C, and instead of sending them what they have requested, we need to reject their request and instead inform the regulatory body about the existence of missing values. This is because a bar chart would be misleading, as the missing values are due to data tampering, with the intention of downplaying air pollution data.

In another situation, a bar chart is requested from a researcher who would like to investigate general air pollution in different regions. In this situation, even though the missing values are of the MNAR type, the systematic reason behind them is not essential to our analytic goals. Therefore, we can use a *keep as is* strategy for all three columns. Creating a bar chart is very similar to what we did in *Figure 11.17*. Running air_df.groupby('hour') [['NO2_Location_A', 'NO2_Location_B', 'NO2_Location_C']].mean(). plot.bar() will create the requested visual.

Example 5

We would like to use the kidney_disease.csv dataset to classify between the cases of **chronic kidney disease (CKD)** and those cases that are not CKD. The dataset shows the data of 400 patients and has 5 independent attributes—namely, **red blood cells** (rc), **serum creatinine** (sc), **packed cell volume** (pcv), **specific gravity** (sg), and **hemoglobin** (hemo). Of course, the dataset also has a dependent attribute named diagnosis whereby the patients are labeled with either CKD or not CKD. **Decision Tree** is the classification algorithm we would like to use.

In our initial look at the dataset, we notice that the dataset has missing values, and after using the code we learned under *Detecting missing values*, we conclude that the number of missing values for rc, sc, pcv, sg, and hemo are 131, 17, 71, 47, and 52, respectively. This means the percentage of missing values under rc, sc, pcv, sg, and hemo is 32.75%, 4.25%, 17.75%, 11.75%, and 13%, respectively.

Use what you've learned in this chapter to confirm the information in the previous paragraph before reading on.

When the number of missing values are across different attributes and are high (more than 15%), it might be the case that most of the missing values happen for the same data objects, and that could be very problematic for our analysis. So, before moving to the diagnosis of missing values for each attribute, let's use the `heatmap()` function from the `seaborn` module to visualize missing values across the dataset. The following screenshot shows the code and the heatmap it produces:

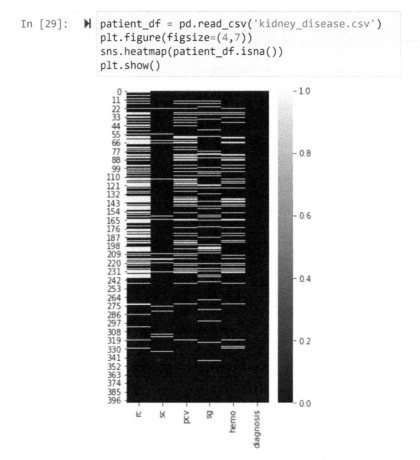

Figure 11.18 – Using seaborn to visualize missing values in kidney_disease.csv

The heatmap in the preceding screenshot shows that the missing values are somewhat scattered across the data objects, and it is certainly not the case that the missing values under different attributes are only from specific data objects.

Next, we turn our attention to the missing value diagnosis per attribute. After performing what we've learned in this chapter, we can conclude that the missing values of the `sc` attribute are of the type MCAR, and the missing values of `rc`, `pcv`, `sg`, and `hemo` are of the type MAR. The tendency of all of the MAR missing values is highly linked to the `diagnosis` dependent attribute.

Use what you've learned in this chapter to confirm the information in the previous paragraph before reading on.

Now that we have a better idea of the types of missing values, we need to turn our focus to the essence of analytic goals and tools. We want to perform classification using the Decision Tree algorithm. When we want to deal with missing values, before using the dataset in an algorithm, we need to first consider how the algorithm uses the data and then try to choose a strategy that simultaneously optimizes the two goals of dealing with missing values. Let's remind ourselves of the two goals of dealing with missing values, as follows:

- Keeping as much data and information as possible
- Introducing the least possible amount of bias in our analysis

We know that Decision Tree is not inherently designed to deal with missing values, and the tool we know for the Decision Tree algorithm—the `DecisionTreeClassifier()` function from the `sklearn.tree` module—will give an error if the input data has missing values. Knowing that will tell us that a *keep as is* strategy is not an option.

We also just realized that the tendency of some of the missing values can be a predictor of the dependent attribute. This is important because if we were to impute the missing values, that would remove this valuable information from the dataset; the valuable information is that the missing values of some of the attributes (the MAR ones) predict the dependent attribute. Therefore, regardless of the imputation method that we will use, we will add a binary attribute to the dataset for every attribute with MAR missing values that describes whether the attribute had a missing value. These new binary attributes will be added to the independent attributes of the classification task to predict the `diagnosis` dependent attribute.

The following code snippet shows these binary attributes being added to the `patient_df` dataset:

```
patient_df['rc_BMV'] = patient_df.rc.isna().astype(int)
patient_df['pcv_BMV'] = patient_df.pcv.isna().astype(int)
patient_df['sg_BMV'] = patient_df.sg.isna().astype(int)
patient_df['hemo_BMV'] = patient_df.hemo.isna().astype(int)
```

Run the preceding lines of code first and study the state of `patient_df` before reading on.

Let's now turn our attention to imputing missing values. If you do not remember how the **Decision Tree** algorithm goes about the task of classification, please go back to *Chapter 7, Classification*, to jog your memory before reading on. The Decision Tree algorithm consecutively splits data objects into groups based on the value of the attributes, and when the data objects have values that are larger than or smaller than the central tendencies of the attribute, they are more likely to be classified with a specific label. Therefore, by imputing with the central tendency of the attributes, we will not introduce a bias into the dataset, so the imputed value will not cause the classifier to predict one label over the other more often.

Thus, we have concluded that imputing with the central tendency of attributes is a reasonable way to address missing values. The question that we now need to answer is: *Which central tendency should we use—median or mean?* The answer to that question is that the mean is better if the attribute does not have many outliers.

After investigating the boxplots of the attributes with missing values, you will see that `sc` has too many outliers, and the rest of the attributes are not highly skewed. Therefore, the following code snippet shows the missing values of `patient_df.sc` being imputed with `patient_df.sc.median()`, and the rest of the attributes with missing values with their means:

```
patient_df.sc.fillna(patient_df.sc.median(),inplace=True)
patient_df.fillna(patient_df.mean(),inplace=True)
```

The preceding code snippet uses the `.fillna()` function, which is very useful when imputing missing values. After running the preceding code, recreate the heatmap shown in *Figure 11.18* to see the state of missing values in your data.

Phew! The detection of, diagnosis of, and dealing with missing values have now been completed. The dataset is now preprocessed for the classification task. All we need to do is use the code we learned from *Chapter 7, Classification*, to run the Decision Tree algorithm. The following code snippet shows the modified code from *Chapter 7, Classification*, for this analytic situation:

```
from sklearn.tree import DecisionTreeClassifier, plot_tree
predictors = ['rc', 'sc', 'pcv', 'sg', 'hemo', 'rc_BMV', 'pcv_
BMV', 'sg_BMV', 'hemo_BMV']
target = 'diagnosis'
Xs = patient_df[predictors]
y= patient_df[target]
```

```
classTree = DecisionTreeClassifier(min_impurity_decrease= 0.01,
min_samples_split= 15)
classTree.fit(Xs, y)
```

The preceding code snippet creates a Decision Tree model and trains it using the data we've preprocessed. Pay attention to the fact that `min_impurity_decrease= 0.01` and `min_samples_split= 15` are hyperparameters of the Decision Tree algorithm that are adjusted using a process of tuning.

The following code snippet uses the `classTree` trained decision tree model to visually draw its tree for analysis and use:

```
from sklearn.tree import plot_tree
plt.figure(figsize=(15,15))
plot_tree(classTree,
          feature_names=predictors,
          class_names=y.unique(),
          filled=True,
          impurity=False)
plt.show()
```

Successfully running the preceding code will create the following output:

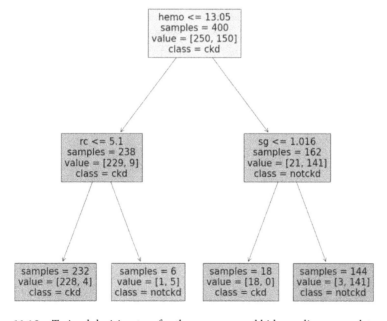

Figure 11.19 – Trained decision tree for the preprocessed kidney_disease.csv data source

We can now use the preceding decision tree to make decisions regarding incoming patients.

You've made excellent progress so far in this chapter. You are now capable of detecting, diagnosing, and dealing with missing values from both a technical and an analytic standpoint. Next in this chapter, we will discuss the issue of extreme points and outliers.

Outliers

Outliers, a.k.a. extreme points, are data objects whose values are too different than the rest of the population. Being able to recognize and deal with them is important from the following three perspectives:

- Outliers may be data errors in data and should be detected and removed.

- Outliers that are not errors can skew the results of analytic tools that are sensitive to the existence of outliers.

- Outliers may be fraudulent entries.

We will first go over the tools we can use to detect outliers, and then we will cover dealing with them based on the analytic situation.

Detecting outliers

The tools we use for detecting outliers depend on the number of attributes involved. If we are interested in detecting outliers only based on one attribute, we call that **univariate outlier detection**; if we want to detect them based on two attributes, we call that **bivariate outlier detection**; and finally, if we want to detect outliers based on more than two attributes, we call that **multivariate outlier detection**. We will cover the tools we can use for outlier detection for each of these mentioned categories. We will also cover detecting outliers for time series data as there are better tools for this.

Univariate outlier detection

The tools we will use for univariate outlier detection depend on the attribute's type. For numerical attributes, we can use a boxplot or the *[Q1-1.5*IQR, Q3+1.5*IQR]* statistical range. The concept of outliers does not have much meaning for a single categorical attribute, but we can use tools such as a frequency table or a bar chart.

The following two examples feature univariate outlier detection. In these examples, we will use responses.csv and columns.csv files. The two files are used to record the date of a survey conducted in Slovakia. To access the data on Kaggle, use this link: https://www.kaggle.com/miroslavsabo/young-people-survey.

The dataset uses two files to keep the records due to a level I data cleaning reason— intuitive and codable attribute names. The columns.csv file keeps the codable attribute titles and their complete titles, and the file responses.csv has a table of data objects (survey responses) whose attributes are named using the codable titles.

The following screenshot shows the reading of these two files into Pandas DataFrames and the first two rows of both DataFrames:

```
In [42]:  ▶ column_df = pd.read_csv('columns.csv')
            column_df.head(2)
```

Out[42]:

	original	short
0	I enjoy listening to music.	Music
1	I prefer. Slow songs or fast songs	

```
In [43]:  ▶ response_df = pd.read_csv('responses.csv')
            response_df.head(2)
```

Out[43]:

	Music	Slow songs or fast songs	Dance	Folk	Country	Classical music	Musical	Pop	Rock	Metal or Hardrock	...	Age	H
0	5.0	3.0	2.0	1.0	2.0	2.0	1.0	5.0	5.0	1.0	...	20.0	˙
1	4.0	4.0	2.0	1.0	1.0	1.0	2.0	3.0	5.0	4.0	...	19.0	˙

2 rows × 150 columns

Figure 11.20 – Reading responses.csv and columns.csv into response_df and column_df and showing them

Now, let's look at the first example of univariate outlier detection across one numerical attribute.

Example of detecting outliers across one numerical attribute

In this example, we would like to detect outliers in the `response_df.Weight` numerical attribute. There are two ways we can go about this; both ways will lead to the same conclusion. The first way is visual; we will use a boxplot. The following screenshot shows the code for creating a boxplot for `response_df.Weight`:

```
In [44]:    ▶   fig = plt.boxplot(response_df.Weight.dropna(),vert=False)
```

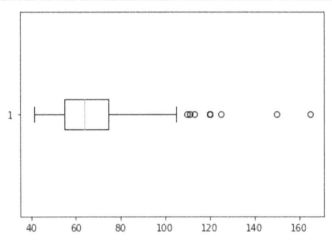

Figure 11.21 – Creating a boxplot for response_df.Weight

The circles that come before the lower cap and and after the upper cap represent data objects in the data that are statistically too different from the rest of the numbers. These circles are called fliers in the context of boxplot analysis.

There are different ways we can access the data objects that are fliers in a boxplot. First, we can do this visually. We can see that the fliers have a `Weight` value larger than 105, so we can use a Boolean mask to filter out these data objects. Running `response_df[response_df.Weight>105]` will list the outliers presented in the preceding screenshot.

Second, we can access the fliers directly from the boxplot itself. If you pay attention to the preceding screenshot, you will notice that for the first time in this book, the output of a plot function—in this case, `plt.boxplot()`—is assigned to a new variable—in this case, `fig`. The reason for this is that up until now, the end goal of data visualization was the visualization itself, and we did not need to access the details of the visualization. However, here, we would like to access the fliers and find out their values to avoid possible visual mistakes.

We can access all aspects of every Matplotlib visualization similarly. If you run print(fig) and study its results, you will see that fig is a dictionary whose keys are different elements of the visualization. As the visualization in this case is a boxplot, the elements are caps, whiskers, fliers, boxes, and median. Each key is associated with a list of one or multiple matplotlib.lines.Line2D programming objects. This is a programing object that Matplotlib uses in its internal processes, but here we want to use this to give us the values of the fliers. Each matplotlib.lines.Line2D object has the .get_data() function that gives you values that are shown on the plot. For instance, running fig['fliers'][0].get_data() gives you the weight values that are shown as fliers in *Figure 11.21*.

We didn't need to use a boxplot to find outliers. A boxplot itself uses the following formulas to calculate the upper cap and lower cap of the boxplot. *Q1* and *Q3* are the first and third quarters of the data:

Upper cap $=$ $Q3 + 1.5 * IQR$

Lower cap $=$ $Q1 - 1.5 * IQR$

$IQR =$ $Q3 - Q1$

Anything that is not between the upper cap and the lower cap will be marked as outliers. The following code uses the .quantile() function and the preceding formulas to output the outliers:

```
Q1 = response_df.Weight.quantile(0.25)
Q3 = response_df.Weight.quantile(0.75)
IQR = Q3-Q1
BM = (response_df.Weight > (Q3+1.5 *IQR)) | (response_df.Weight
< (Q1-1.5 *IQR))
response_df[BM]
```

Using any of the two methods we covered in this example, you will realize that there are nine data objects whose Weight values are statistically too different from the rest of the data objects. The Weight values for these outliers are 120, 110, 111, 120, 113, 125, 165, 120, and 150. Make sure to confirm this using both methods before reading on.

Next, we will see an example that showcases detecting outliers based on one categorical attribute.

Example of detecting outliers across one categorical attribute

In this example, we would like to detect the outliers in the `response_df.Education` categorical attribute. For detecting outliers across one categorical attribute, we can use a frequency table or a bar chart. As we learned in *Chapter 5, Data Visualization*, you may run `response_df.Education.value_counts()` to get a frequency table, and running `response_df.Education.value_counts().plot.bar()` will create a bar chart. Run both lines of code to confirm that the data object whose `Education` value is `doctorate degree` is an outlier across this one categorical attribute.

We are now equipped with the tools for univariate outlier detection. Let's turn our attention to bivariate outlier detection.

Bivariate outlier detection

As univariate outlier detection was across only one attribute, bivariate outlier detection is across two attributes. In bivariate outlier detection, outliers are data objects whose combination of values across the two attributes is too different from the rest. Similar to univariate outlier detection, the tools we will use for bivariate outlier detection depend on the attributes' type. For numerical-numerical attributes, it is best to use a scatterplot; for numerical-categorical attributes, it is best to use multiple boxplots; and for categorical-categorical attributes, the tool we use is a color-coded contingency table.

Each of the following three examples features one of the three possible paired combinations of categorical and numerical attributes.

Example of detecting outliers across two numerical attributes

In this example, we would like to detect outliers when they are described by two numerical attributes, `response_df.Height` and `response_df.Weight`. When detecting outliers across two numerical attributes, it is best to use a scatterplot. Running `response_df.plot.scatter(x='Weight', y='Height')` will result in the following output:

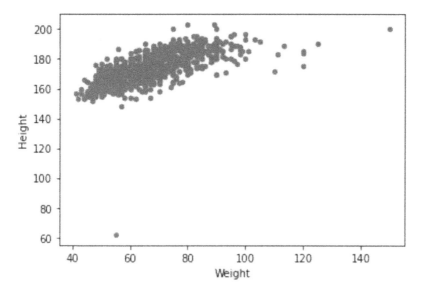

Figure 11.22 – Scatterplot to detect outliers across response_df.Weight and response_df.Height

Based on the preceding screenshot, we can clearly see two outliers, one with a Weight value larger than 120, and one with a Height value smaller than 70. To filter out these two outliers, we can use a Boolean mask. The following code snippet shows how this can be done:

```
BM = (response_df.Weight>130) | (response_df.Height<70)
response_df[BM]
```

When the preceding code is run, you will see three data objects. If you check the Height and Weight values of these data objects, you will see one of them has a missing value for Height and therefore is not shown on the scatterplot.

This example featured a bivariate outlier detection when two attributes are numerical. The next example will be a bivariate outlier detection when two attributes are categorical.

Example of detecting outliers across two categorical attributes

In this example, we want to detect outliers across two categorical attributes, `response_df.God` and `response_df.Education`. As the two attributes are categorical, it is best to use a contingency table to detect outliers. Running `pd.crosstab(response_df['Education'],response_df['God'])` will create a contingency table. To help see the outliers, you can turn the table into a heatmap by using `.heatmap()` from the `seaborn` module. The code shown in the following snippet will create a heatmap from the contingency table:

```
cont_table = pd.crosstab(response_df['Education'],
response_df['God'])
sns.heatmap(cont_table,annot=True, center=0.5 ,cmap="Greys")
```

The following screenshot shows the heatmap that the preceding code will produce:

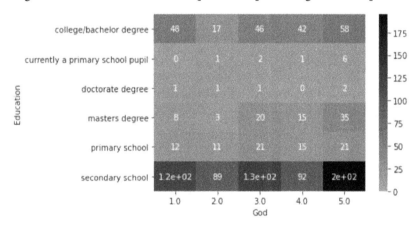

Figure 11.23 – Color-coded contingency table to detect outliers across response_df.God and
response_df.Education

From the preceding screenshot, we can see that there are cases of one data object that have some combinations of values across `response_df.God` and `response_df.Education`. To filter out these outliers, we can also use a Boolean mask, but as there will be a lot of typing due to the values of the categorical attributes, we might be better off using another Pandas DataFrame function. The `.query()` function, as its name suggests, can also help us perform filtering of a DataFrame based on the values of the attributes. Run the following lines of code one at a time to filter out each of the data objects we spotted as outliers:

- `response_df.query('Education== "currently a primary school pupil" & God==2')`

- `response_df.query('Education== "currently a primary school pupil" & God==4')`

- `response_df.query('Education== "doctorate degree" & God==1')`

- `response_df.query('Education== "doctorate degree" & God==2')`

- `response_df.query('Education== "doctorate degree" & God==3')`

In this example, we covered categorical-categorical bivariate outlier detection. In the example preceding this, we covered numerical-numerical bivariate outlier detection. Next, we will feature numerical-categorical bivariate outlier detection.

Example of detecting outliers across two attributes – one categorical and the other numerical

In this example, we want to detect outliers across two attributes, `response_df.Education` and `response_df.Age`. Pay attention to the fact that `response_df.Education` is categorical and `response_df.Age` is numerical. When performing bivariate outlier detection across one numerical and one categorical attribute, we use multiple boxplots. In essence, we will create one boxplot across the numerical attribute for each of the categories of the categorical attribute. Running `sns.boxplot(x=response_df.Age,y=response_df.Education)` will create the following boxplot that can be used for outlier detection:

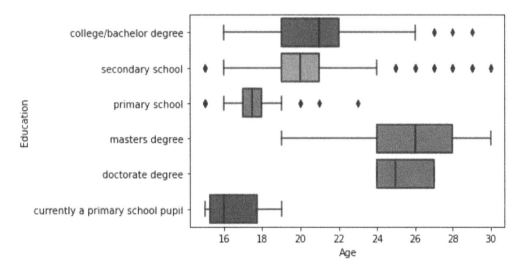

Figure 11.24 – Multiple boxplots to detect outliers across response_df.Age and response_df.Education

This is the first time we are using `sns.boxplot()` in this book. We did learn how we would be able to do this using Matplotlib in *Chapter 5, Data Visualization*. Try to recreate the boxplot using Matplotlib before reading on. You will see that using the `seaborn` function is significantly easier.

Looking at the multiple boxplots, we can see that we have some fliers for `Education` categories: `college/bachelor degree`, `secondary school`, and `primary school`. To filter out the outliers, we can use Boolean masks or the `query()` function. The following code shows how we can create one Boolean mask to include all the fliers:

```
BM1 = (response_df.Education=='college/bachelor degree') &
(response_df.Age>26)
BM2 = (response_df.Education == 'secondary school') &
((response_df.Age>24) | (response_df.Age<16))
BM3 = (response_df.Education == 'primary school') & ((response_
df.Age>19) | (response_df.Age<16))
BM = BM1 | BM2 | BM3
response_df[BM]
```

So far, we have managed to learn how to perform univariate and bivariate outlier detection. Next, we will cover multivariate outlier detection.

Multivariate outlier detection

Detecting outliers across more than two attributes is called multivariate outlier detection. The best way to go about multivariate outlier detection is through clustering analysis. The following example features a case of multivariate outlier detection.

Example of detecting outliers across four attributes using clustering analysis

In this example, we would like to see whether we have outliers based on the following four attributes: `Country`, `Musical`, `Metal or Hardrock`, and `Folk`. If you check the complete description of these attributes on `columns_df`, you will realize these attributes describe the liking level of data objects for each of four kinds of music. As mentioned, the best way to perform multivariate outlier detection is through cluster analysis. In *Chapter 8, Clustering Analysis,* we learn about the K-Means algorithm, and here, we will use it to see whether we have outliers.

If K-Means groups one data object or only a handful of data objects in one cluster, that will be our clue that there are multivariate outliers in our data. If you remember, the one big weakness of the K-Means algorithm is that the number of clusters, *k*, must be specified. To ensure the K-Means algorithm's weakness will not stand in the way of effective outlier detection and to give the analysis the best chance of success, we will use different *k* values: 2, 3, 4, 5, 6, and 7. We need to do this in multiple steps, as follows:

1. First, we will create an `Xs` attribute, which includes the attributes we want to be used for clustering analysis. The following code snippet shows how this is done:

    ```
    dimensions = ['Country', 'Metal or Hardrock', 'Folk',
    'Musical']
    Xs = response_df[dimensions]
    ```

2. Second, we need to check whether there are any missing values. You may use `Xs.info()` for the quick detection of missing values.

3. If there are missing values, we need to do a similar analysis to what we did in *Figure 11.18* to check whether all the missing values are from one of the data objects. If that is the case, the fact that one data object has more than two missing values could be a reason for concern. However, if the missing values seem to be happening randomly across Xs, we may impute them with *Q3+1.5*IQR*.

    Why not impute them with a central tendency? The reason we don't is that we would decrease the likelihood of a data object with a missing value being detected as outliers if we imputed with a central tendency. We don't want to help a data object that has the potential to be an outlier with our missing value imputation.

    In this case, the missing values are spread across the data objects and the dimensions of Xs. So, we can use the following line of code to impute the missing values with `Q3+IQR*1.5`:

    ```
    Q3 = Xs.quantile(0.75)
    Q1 = Xs.quantile(0.25)
    IQR = Q3 - Q1
    Xs = Xs.fillna(Q3+IQR*1.5)
    ```

4. Next, of course, we will not forget to standardize the dataset using `Xs = (Xs - Xs.min())/(Xs.max()-Xs.min())`.

5. Lastly, we can use a loop to perform clustering analysis for different Ks and report its results. The following line of code shows how this can be done:

```
from sklearn.cluster import KMeans
for k in range(2,8):
    kmeans = KMeans(n_clusters=k)
    kmeans.fit(Xs)
    print('k={}'.format(k))
    for i in range(k):
        BM = kmeans.labels_==i
        print('Cluster {}: {}'.format(i,Xs[BM].index.
        values))
    print('--------- Divider ----------')
```

Once the preceding code is successfully run, you can scroll through its prints to see that under none of the Ks, has K-Means grouped one data object or a handful of data objects in one cluster. This will allow us to conclude that there is no multivariate outlier in Xs.

Time series outlier detection

Outliers in time series data are best detected using line plots, the reason being that between consecutive records of a time series there is a close relationship, and using the close relationship is the best way to check the correctness of a record. All you need is to evaluate the value of the record against its closest consecutive records, and that is easily done using line plots. We will see an example of time series outlier detection in this chapter—please see the example under *Detecting systematic errors* toward the end of this chapter.

Now that we have covered all the three possible outlier detections—univariate, bivariate, and multivariate—we can turn our attention to dealing with outliers.

Dealing with outliers

When we have detected outliers in a dataset we want to analyze, we also need to effectively deal with outliers. The following list highlights the four approaches we can use to deal with outliers:

- Do nothing
- Replace with the upper cap or lower cap
- Perform a log transformation
- Remove data objects with outliers

Next, we will talk more about each of the preceding approaches.

First approach – Do nothing

Although it may not feel like this, especially after going through so many hoops to detect outliers, *do nothing* is the best strategy in most analytic situations. The reason for this is that most analytic tools we use can easily handle outliers. In fact, if you know the analytic tools you want to use can handle outliers, you might not perform outlier detection in the first place. However, outlier detection itself may be the analytic you need, or the analytic tool you need to use is prone to outliers.

The table shown in the following screenshot lists all the analytic tools/goals we have covered in this book and specifies the best approach for dealing with outliers:

Analytic goals/tools	Prone to outliers	How best to deal with outliers?
Visualization: Summarizing a population/histogram	Yes	- Do nothing. - Remove data objects with outliers.
Visualization: Summarizing a population/boxplot	No	- Do nothing.
Visualization: Summarizing a population/bar chart	No	- Do nothing.
Visualization: Comparing populations	No	- Do nothing.
Visualization: The relationship between two attributes/scatterplot	Could be	- Do nothing. - Remove data objects with outliers. - Perform log transformation.
Visualization: The relationship between two attributes/contingency table	No	- Do nothing.
Visualization: Adding visual dimensions/adding size and color	Yes	- Replace with the upper cap or lower cap.
Visualization: Visualizing and comparing trends/line plots	No	- Do nothing.
Prediction: Regression	Yes	- Remove data objects with outliers. - Replace with the upper cap or lower cap.
Prediction: MLP	No	- Do nothing.
Classification: Decision Tree	No	- Do nothing.
Classification: KNN	Yes	- Replace with the upper cap or lower cap.
Clustering: K-Means	Could be	- Do nothing. - Replace with the upper cap or lower cap.

Figure 11.25 – Summary table of analytic goals and tools and the best way to deal with outliers if they exist

As you can see in *Figure 11.25*, in most analytic situations, it will be better to adopt the first approach: *do nothing*. Now, let's continue and learn about the next approaches.

Second approach – Replace with the upper cap or the lower cap

Applying this approach may be wise when the following criteria are met:

- The outlier is univariate.

- The analytic goals and/or tools are sensitive to outliers.

- We do not want to lose information by removing data objects.

- An abrupt change of value will not lead to a significant change in the analytic conclusions.

If the criteria are met, in this approach the outliers are replaced with the correct upper or lower cap. The upper and lower caps are statistical concepts we discussed earlier in this chapter in the *Univariate outlier detection* section. They are also an essential part of any boxplot. We replace the univariate outliers that are too much smaller than the rest of the data object with the lower cap of the $Q1-1.5*IQR$ attribute, and replace the univariate outliers that are too much larger than the rest of the data objects with the upper cap of the $Q3+1.5*IQR$ attribute.

Third approach – Perform a log transformation

This approach is not just a method to deal with outliers but is also an effective data transformation technique that we will cover in the relevant chapter. As a method to deal with outlier detection, it is only applicable in certain situations. When an attribute follows an exponential distribution, it is only typical for some of the data objects to be very different from the rest of the population. In those situations, applying a log transformation will be the best approach.

Fourth approach – Remove data objects with outliers

When the other methods are not helpful or possible, we may be reduced to removing the data objects with the outliers. This is our least favorite approach and should only be used when absolutely necessary. The reason that we would like to avoid this approach is that the data is not incorrect; the values of the outliers are correct but happen to be too different from the rest of the population. It is our analytic tool that is incapable of dealing with the actual population.

> **Pay Attention!**
>
> As to when and whether you should adopt the approach of removing data objects due to being outliers, I would like to share with you an important word of advice. First, only apply this approach to the preprocessed version of the dataset that you've created for the specific analysis and not to the source data. The fact that this analysis needed the data objects with outliers to be removed does not mean all the analysis will need that. Second, make it a priority to inform the audience of the resulting analytic as they will be aware of this invasive approach in dealing with outliers.

Now that we know all four approaches in dealing with outliers, let's spend some time going over a summary of how best we should go about selecting the best one.

Choosing the right approach in dealing with outliers

The selection of the right approach in dealing with outliers must be informed from analytic goals and analytic tools. As shown in *Figure 11.25*, in most situations, the best way to deal with outliers is using a *do nothing* approach. When and if the other approaches are necessary, make sure to only apply them to the preprocessed version of the data you are creating for your analytics and refrain from changing the source dataset.

We now know everything we need to know about dealing with outliers, so let's see a couple of examples to put what we learned into practice.

Example 1

We earlier saw that the `response_df.Weight` attribute has some outliers. We would like to use a histogram to draw the distribution of the population across this attribute.

As our analytic end goal is to visualize the population distribution, the existence of outliers might consume some visualization space, and therefore removing them can open the visualization space.

The following code snippet and its output show how to create both histogram versions for `response_df.Weight`, one with outliers and the other without them:

```
response_df.Weight.plot.hist(histtype='step')
plt.show()
BM = response_df.Weight<105
response_df.Weight[BM].plot.hist(histtype='step')
plt.show()
```

The preceding code will produce the following output:

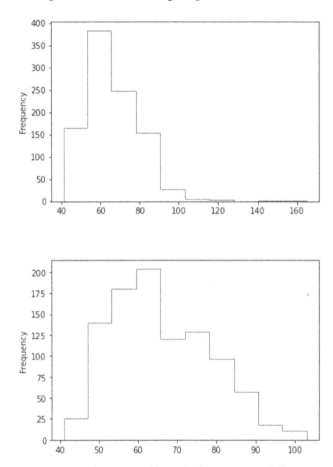

Figure 11.26 – Histogram of response_df.Weight featuring two different approaches in dealing with outliers

In the previous screenshot, from an analytic perspective, you may imagine situations where either visual would be more appropriate. For instance, if we are interested in seeing the frequency changes where most of the population is between 40 and 100, then a histogram without outliers would be better. On the other hand, if a true representation of the population is our end goal, then a histogram with outliers would be ideal.

In the previous screenshot, from a data preprocessing perspective, pay attention to the fact that to create a histogram without outliers, we did not edit response_df but created a DataFrame *on the fly* just for the purpose of creating a histogram without outliers.

Now, let's consider another example.

Example 2

We would like to visualize the relationship between two attributes, `response_df.Height` and `response_df. Weight`. As the two attributes are both numerical, we do know the best way to visualize this relationship is a scatterplot. We also would like to include a **linear regression** (**LR**) line in the visualization so as to augment its analytic values.

We have been told that LR is prone to outliers. Let's use this opportunity to learn why. We will first adopt a *do nothing* approach and create a visualization to see what would happen if there were outliers in the data for regression analysis.

The following screenshot shows the application of the `.regplot()` function from the `seaborn` module to create a scatterplot visualization:

```
In [70]:   ▶   sns.regplot(x='Height',
                       y='Weight',data=response_df)
               plt.show()
```

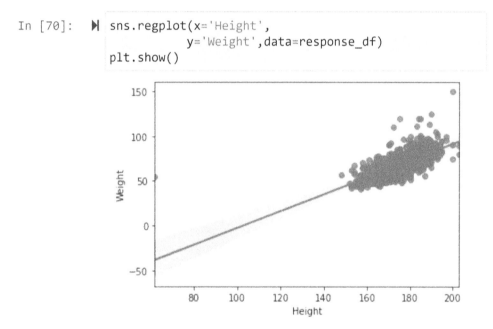

Figure 11.27 – Scatterplot to visualize the relationship between response_df.Height and
response_df.Weight without dealing with outliers

You can see in the preceding screenshot that the outliers we detected in *Figure 11.22* are consuming the visualization space and do not allow the relationship to show itself fully.

However, the following screenshot shows the code that removes the outliers at the last step of the visualization:

```
In [71]:    ▶ BM = (response_df.Weight>130) | (response_df.Height<70)
              sns.regplot(x='Height',
                          y='Weight',data=response_df[~BM])
              plt.show()
```

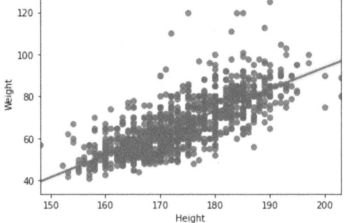

Figure 11.28 – Scatterplot to visualize the relationship between response_df.Height and
response_df.Weight after dealing with outliers

Comparing the last two screenshots, we can see how removing the two outliers allows the visualization to show the relationship between the two variables much better. You can see in the preceding screenshot how higher Height values can lead to higher Weight values.

Example 3

In this example, we would like to use regression to capture the linear relationship between Weight, Height, and Gender to predict Weight, which we saw in the previous example. In other words, we would like to find the *β0* and *β1* values in the following equation:

$$Weight = \beta_0 + \beta_1 \times Height + \beta_2 \times Gender$$

As we saw in *Figure 11.25*, regression analysis is sensitive to outliers. We also observed in *Figure 11.28* that both Weight and Height have outliers. We also need to check whether Gender has any outliers.

This is going to be a long example, so please bear with me throughout. In this example, we will go over the following steps, one by one:

1. Dealing with missing values
2. Detecting univariate outliers and dealing with them
3. Detecting bivariate outliers and dealing with them
4. Detecting multivariate outliers and dealing with them
5. Applying LR

Let's start with the first step.

Dealing with missing values

However, before doing that, we will first need to deal with the missing values in these three attributes, as `LinearRegression` from `sklearn.linear_model` gives an error when the input data has missing values. The following code snippet shows how we would start preprocessing the data for this example:

```
select_attributes = ['Weight','Height','Gender']
pre_process_df = pd.DataFrame(response_df[select_attributes])
pre_process_df.info()
```

After running the previous code, you will be able to see that `Weight` and `Height` have 20 missing values, and `Gender` has 6 missing values. Assume that we know that the missing values are of the MCAR type.

To deal with missing values for regression analysis, we cannot use a *keep as is* strategy, as the tool we plan to use cannot handle outliers. Imputing values will not be a good option either as this will create bias in the data. Therefore, the only doable option that remains is dropping the data objects. The following line of code uses the `.dropna()` function to remove the data objects with missing values:

```
pre_process_df.dropna(inplace=True)
```

After running this code, rerun `pre_process_df.info()` to confirm that `pre_process_df` does not have missing values anymore.

Now that we are certain there are no missing values in `pre_process_df`, we can turn our attention to detecting and dealing with outliers, as LR is prone to outliers. We need to detect whether the data has univariate, bivariate, or multivariate outliers. In the following subsections, we will do this one step at a time.

Detecting univariate outliers and dealing with them

The following screenshot shows the code that has created boxplots for the numerical attributes and a bar chart for the categorical attribute in this example:

```
In [75]:    num_attributes = ['Weight','Height']
            for i,att in enumerate(num_attributes):
                plt.subplot(1,3,i+1)
                pre_process_df[att].plot.box()

            plt.subplot(1,3,3)
            pre_process_df.Gender.value_counts().plot.bar()
            plt.tight_layout()
            plt.show()
```

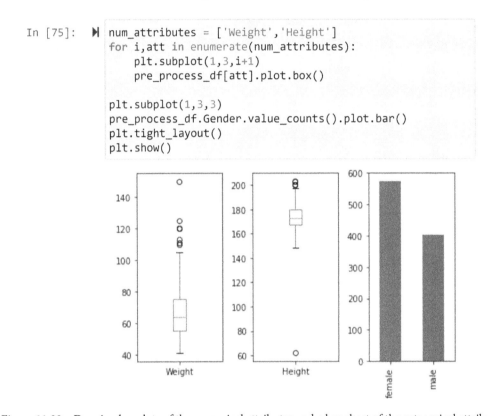

Figure 11.29 – Drawing boxplots of the numerical attributes and a bar chart of the categorical attribute in the example

In the preceding screenshot, we can see that both Height and Weight have outliers, but Gender does not. So, before moving on to the LR analysis, we need to deal with the outliers. As suggested by *Figure 11.25*, we can use one of the following two approaches in dealing with outliers:

- Remove these data objects
- Replace them with their statistical upper cap or lower cap

But which approach is better? When the data objects are univariate outliers, it is better to use the second approach, as replacing the statistical upper or the lower cap will help to keep the data objects and at the same time mitigate the negative effect of the data object with the outliers.

On the other hand—and this also applies generally—when the data objects are bivariate or multivariate outliers, it would be better to remove them. This is because these outliers will not allow the regression model to capture the patterns among the non-outlier data objects. In the special case of bivariate outliers whereby the pair of attributes is categorical-numerical, it might also be sensible to replace the outlier values with the upper or lower caps of the specific population.

So, let's first deal with the univariate outliers by replacing them with the statistical lower and upper caps. The following code replaces the fliers of pre_process_df.Weight with the statistical upper cap of the attribute:

```
Q3 = pre_process_df.Weight.quantile(0.75)
Q1 = pre_process_df.Weight.quantile(0.25)
IQR = Q3 - Q1
upper_cap = Q3+IQR*1.5
BM = pre_process_df.Weight > upper_cap
pre_process_df.loc[pre_process_df[BM].index,'Weight'] = upper_
cap
```

After running the previous code, run pre_process_df.Weight.plot.box() to see that the outliers are taken care of. Also, pay attention to two matters before moving on to replace the flier in pre_process_df.Height, as follows:

- First, by looking at *Figure 11.29*, you will realize that pre_process_df.Weight only has fliers that are larger than the statistical upper cap of the attribute. That is why in the previous code, we don't have any replacement with the statistical lower cap of the attribute. This will change when we do the same procedure for pre_process_df.Height.

- Second, we could have the boxplot itself extract the statistical upper caps and lower caps of the attribute, but instead, we use the formulas *Q1-1.5*IQR* and *Q3+1.5*IQR*, respectively, to calculate the statistical lower and upper caps. This is because we don't want to waste computational resources by having the computer draw unnecessarily when we have the formula to calculate it ourselves.

Next, we will do the same procedure for `pre_process_df.Height` to deal with the univariate outliers. The following code shows how this is done:

```
Q3 = pre_process_df.Height.quantile(0.75)
Q1 = pre_process_df.Height.quantile(0.25)
IQR = Q3 - Q1
lower_cap = Q1-IQR*1.5
upper_cap = Q3+IQR*1.5
BM = pre_process_df.Height < lower_cap
pre_process_df.loc[pre_process_df[BM].index,'Height'] = lower_
cap
BM = pre_process_df.Height > upper_cap
pre_process_df.loc[pre_process_df[BM].index,'Height'] = upper_
cap
```

After running the previous code successfully, run `pre_process_df.Weight.plot.box()` to check the state of the outliers.

Now that the univariate outliers are taken care of, let's see whether we have bi- or multivariate outliers.

Detecting bivariate outliers and dealing with them

Running `pre_process_df.plot.scatter(x='Height', y='Weight')` will show that we don't have bivariate outliers based on the `Height` and `Weight` numerical attributes. However, running the following code will tell us that we do have bivariate outliers under `Height` and `Gender`, and under `Weight` and `Gender`:

```
plt.subplot(1,2,1)
sns.boxplot(y=pre_process_df.Height, x=pre_process_df.Gender)
plt.subplot(1,2,2)
sns.boxplot(y=pre_process_df.Weight, x=pre_process_df.Gender)
plt.tight_layout()
```

Running the preceding code successfully will create the following output:

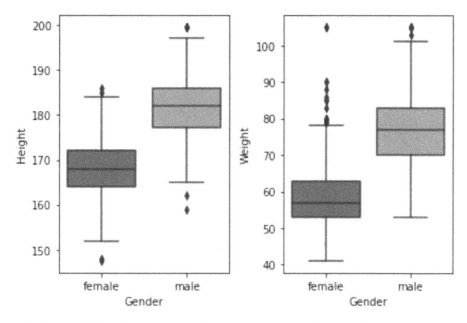

Figure 11.30 – Multiple boxplots to investigate bivariate outliers under numerical-categorical attributes for Height-Gender and Weight-Gender

Given the recognized bivariate outliers in the preceding screenshot, we will need to deal with them. As these outliers are bivariate in a pair of categorical-numerical attributes, we may be replacing them with the specific population's upper or lower caps.

The following code replaces the outliers for the attribute pairs of `Height-Gender`:

```
for poss in pre_process_df.Gender.unique():
    BM = pre_process_df.Gender == poss
    wdf = pre_process_df[BM]
    Q3 = wdf.Height.quantile(0.75)
    Q1 = wdf.Height.quantile(0.25)
    IQR = Q3 - Q1
    lower_cap = Q1-IQR*1.5
    upper_cap = Q3+IQR*1.5


    BM = wdf.Height > upper_cap
```

```
pre_process_df.loc[wdf[BM].index,'Height'] = upper_cap


BM = wdf.Height < lower_cap
pre_process_df.loc[wdf[BM].index,'Height'] = lower_cap
```

Very similar code will replace the outliers for the attribute pairs of Weight-Gender, as illustrated here:

```
for poss in pre_process_df.Gender.unique():
    BM = pre_process_df.Gender == poss
    wdf = pre_process_df[BM]
    Q3 = wdf.Weight.quantile(0.75)
    Q1 = wdf.Weight.quantile(0.25)
    IQR = Q3 - Q1
    lower_cap = Q1-IQR*1.5
    upper_cap = Q3+IQR*1.5


    BM = wdf.Weight > upper_cap
    pre_process_df.loc[wdf[BM].index,'Weight'] = upper_cap


    BM = wdf.Weight < lower_cap
    pre_process_df.loc[wdf[BM].index,'Weight'] = lower_cap
```

After running the preceding codes successfully, running the code shown in the following screenshot, which is the same code as under *Detecting bivariate outliers and dealing with them*, will show us that the bivariate outliers are taken care of:

```
In [84]:  ▶  plt.subplot(1,2,1)
             sns.boxplot(y=pre_process_df.Height,x=pre_process_df.Gender)
             plt.subplot(1,2,2)
             sns.boxplot(y=pre_process_df.Weight, x=pre_process_df.Gender)
             plt.tight_layout()
```

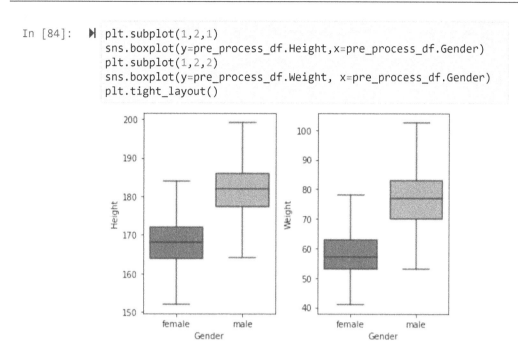

Figure 11.31 – Checking the state of bivariate outliers under numerical-categorical attributes for Height-Gender and Weight-Gender

Next, we will need to see whether there are any multivariate outliers, and if there are, we will see how we can deal with them.

Detecting multivariate outliers and dealing with them

To detect multivariate outliers, the standard method is to use clustering analysis; however, when two of the three attributes are numerical and the other is categorical, we can do outlier detection using a specific visualization technique.

The following code creates a scatterplot of Height and Weight for each possibility of the Gender categorical attribute:

```
Cat_attribute_poss = pre_process_df.Gender.unique()
for i,poss in enumerate(cat_attribute_poss):
    BM = pre_process_df.Gender == poss
    pre_process_df[BM].plot.scatter(x='Height',y='Weight')
    plt.title(poss)
    plt.show()
```

Running the preceding code will create the following visualization:

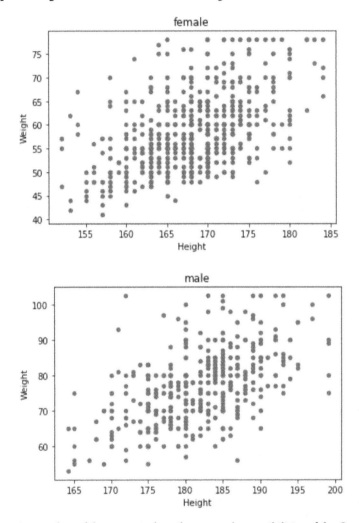

Figure 11.32 – Scatterplots of the numerical attributes per the possibilities of the Gender attribute

Based on the preceding screenshot, we can conclude that there are no multivariate outliers in the data. If there were any, the only choice we would have would be to remove them, as outliers can negatively impact LR performance. Also, as mentioned before, replacing the outliers with upper and lower caps is not an option for multivariate outliers.

After dealing with the outliers and the missing values, we are finally ready to use LR to estimate the relationship between Height, Gender, and Weight to predict Weight.

Applying LR

Before applying LR to `pre_process_df`, we need to take another preprocessing step. Pay attention to the fact that the `Gender` attribute is categorical and not numerical, and LR can only work with numbers. So, the following code performs the data transformation so that the attribute is binary coded:

```
pre_process_df.Gender.
replace({'male':0,'female':1},inplace=True)
```

The following code prepares the independent and dependent attributes, respectively, in `data_X` and `data_Y`, and then uses `LinearRegression()` from `sklearn.linear_model` to fit the preprocessed data into the model:

```
from sklearn.linear_model import LinearRegression
X = ['Height','Gender']
y = 'Weight'
data_X = pre_process_df[X]
data_y = pre_process_df[y]
lm = LinearRegression()
lm.fit(data_X, data_y)
```

If the preceding code runs successfully, then we can run the code in the following screenshot to access the estimated β values from the fitted `lm` value:

```
In [88]:  ▶  print('intercept (b0) ', lm.intercept_)
             coef_names = ['b1','b2']
             print(pd.DataFrame({'Predictor': data_X.columns,
                                 'coefficient Name':coef_names,
                                 'coefficient Value': lm.coef_}))

             intercept (b0)  -51.10382582783839
               Predictor coefficient Name  coefficient Value
             0    Height               b1           0.704025
             1    Gender               b2          -8.602017
```

Figure 11.33 – Extracted β values from the train lm value

Therefore, the following equation can be driven from the output in the preceding screenshot. The equation can now predict the individual `Weight` value based on their `Height` and `Gender` values:

$$Weight = -51.1038 + 0.7040 \times Height - 8.6020 \times Gender$$

For instance, my height is 189 **centimeters** (**cm**) and my gender is male (0). Using the following equation, my weight can be predicted to be 82.895:

$$My\ Weight = -51.1038 + 0.7040 \times 189.5 - 8.6020 \times 0 = 82.3042$$

That's pretty good, but my current weight is 86 **kilograms** (**kg**), so there is an error of around 4 kg.

Example 4

In this example, we would like to repeat the previous example, but this time, we would like to use a **multilayer perceptron** (**MLP**) to predict weight based on gender and height.

The data preprocessing difference between this example and the previous one is that MLP is resilient toward outliers, and we don't need to worry about the dataset having outliers. However, we do need to take care of missing values and also binary code for the Gender attribute. The following code recreates pre_process_df, deals with missing values, and performs the binary coding transformation of the Gender attribute:

```
select_attributes = ['Weight','Height','Gender']
pre_process_df = pd.DataFrame(response_df[select_attributes])
pre_process_df.dropna(inplace=True)
pre_process_df.Gender.replace(
{'male':0,'female':1},inplace=True)
```

After running the preceding code, pre_process_df is ready to be used for MLP. The following code prepares the independent and dependent attributes, respectively, in data_X and data_Y, and then uses MLPRegressor() from sklearn.linear_model to fit the preprocessed data into the model:

```
from sklearn.neural_network import MLPRegressor
X = ['Height','Gender']
y = 'Weight'
data_X = pre_process_df[X]
data_y = pre_process_df[y]
mlp = MLPRegressor(hidden_layer_sizes=5, max_iter=2000)
mlp.fit(data_X, data_y)
```

Once the preceding code is run successfully, we can use the trained mlp attribute to perform predictions. The following code snippet shows how to extract the prediction of my Weight value based on my Height and Gender values using mlp:

```
newData = pd.DataFrame({'Height':189.5,'Gender':0}, index=[0])
mlp.predict(newData)
```

The prediction I received the last time I ran the preceding code was *80.0890*. You will remember that MLP is a random variable and that every time it is run, we expect a new result. Anyhow, as my weight is 86, mlp is about 6 kg out. Does this mean that lm (previous example) is a predictor compared to mlp? Not necessarily—after all, I am only one data point. More test data is needed to make that determination.

Let's look at another example that features dealing with outliers for the purpose of applying clustering analysis, before moving on to the next item.

Example 5

In this example, we would like to use chicago_population.csv. The data objects in this dataset are communities in Chicago. These data objects are described by the following attributes:

- population: The population of the community
- income: The median income of the community
- latino: The percentage of Latinos in the population
- black: The percentage of blacks in the population
- white: The percentage of whites in the population
- asian: The percentage of Asians in the population
- other: The percentage of other races in the population

The mayor of Chicago would like to assign 5 communication liaisons for these 77 communities. The data analyst in the office suggests employing K-Means clustering to group the communities into five groups and assigning the appropriate liaisons based on the characteristics of clustered groups.

First, we will read the file into the `community_df` pandas DataFrame and check whether there are missing values in the dataset. The following code shows how this is done:

```
community_df = pd.read_csv('chicago_population.csv')
community_df.info()
```

Reading the output of the previous code will show us that there are no missing values in `community_df`. Next, we will need to detect outliers and deal with them.

Detecting univariate outliers and dealing with them

The following code uses `sns.boxplot()` to create boxplots of all the numerical attributes:

```
numerical_atts = ['population', 'income', 'latino', 'black',
'white', 'asian','other']
plt.figure(figsize=(12,3))
for i,att in enumerate(numerical_atts):
    plt.subplot(1,len(numerical_atts),i+1)
    sns.boxplot(y=community_df[att])
plt.tight_layout()
plt.show()
```

Running the preceding code will create the following output:

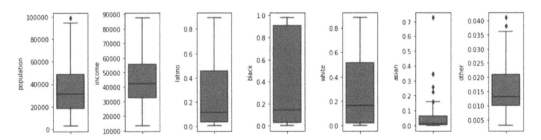

Figure 11.34 – Boxplots of all the numerical attributes in community_df

In the preceding screenshot, we can see we have some univariate outliers in the `population`, `asian`, and `other` attributes.

As we are using K-Means to cluster the communities into five homogenous groups to assign communication liaisons, the best way to deal with the outliers is to replace them with statistical lower or upper caps. We don't want the extreme values of the outliers to impact the results of the clusters.

Please pay attention to the fact this is not the only or the best way to deal with outliers before applying cluster analysis. If we use clustering analysis to find out the inherent pattern in the data, then the best way to deal with the outliers is to do nothing.

The following code uses similar code to what we used under *Example 3* to filter the outliers and then replace them with the appropriate cap. Notice that this code is a bit smarter than what we saw in *Example 3*, as the process of dealing with the outliers is parameterized in one loop:

```
pre_process_df = community_df.set_index('name')
candidate_atts = ['population','asian','other']
for att in candidate_atts:
    Q3 = pre_process_df[att].quantile(0.75)
    Q1 = pre_process_df[att].quantile(0.25)
    IQR = Q3 - Q1
    lower_cap = Q1-IQR*1.5
    upper_cap = Q3+IQR*1.5
    BM = pre_process_df[att] < lower_cap
    candidate_index = pre_process_df[BM].index
    pre_process_df.loc[candidate_index,att] = lower_cap
    BM = pre_process_df[att] > upper_cap
    candidate_index = pre_process_df[BM].index
    pre_process_df.loc[candidate_index,att] = upper_cap
```

After running the preceding code, the univariate outliers will have been replaced with the appropriate statistical cap.

Detecting bivariate and multivariate outliers and dealing with them

It adds no value to detect bivariate and multivariate outliers as the only strategy we can use for them at this stage is to do nothing—we cannot replace them with the upper or lower caps as there is more than one numerical attribute; neither can we remove the data objects as we need all the data objects to be in at least one of the clusters. Therefore, the current state of pre_process_df is the best possible it can be for the clustering analysis.

As the data preprocessing is complete, the only remaining step in this example is to perform clustering. That is what we will do next.

Applying K-Means

The following code snippet shows the adjusted version of the code for K-Means clustering from *Chapter 8, Clustering Analysis*:

```
From sklearn.cluster import Kmeans
dimensions = ['population', 'income', 'latino', 'black',
'white', 'asian','other']
Xs = pre_process_df[dimensions]
Xs = (Xs - Xs.min())/(Xs.max()-Xs.min())
kmeans = Kmeans(n_clusters=5)
kmeans.fit(Xs)
```

Once the preceding code is run successfully, clusters are formed. The following screenshot shows the code we can use to extract the clusters and the code's output:

```
In [97]:    ▶  for i in range(5):
                   BM = kmeans.labels_==i
                   print('Cluster {}: {}'.format(i,pre_process_df[BM].index.values))

               Cluster 0: ['Armour Square' 'Douglas' 'McKinley Park' 'Bridgeport']
               Cluster 1: ['Montclare' 'Belmont Cragin' 'Hermosa' 'Avondale' 'Logan Squar
               e'
                'Humboldt Park' 'South Lawndale' 'Lower West Side' 'East Side'
                'Hegewisch' 'Archer Heights' 'Brighton Park' 'New City' 'West Elsdon'
                'Gage Park' 'Clearing' 'West Lawn' 'Chicago Lawn' 'Ashburn']
               Cluster 2: ['Rogers Park' 'West Ridge' 'Uptown' 'Lincoln Square' 'North Par
               k'
                'Albany Park' 'Irving Park' 'Near West Side' 'Loop' 'Near South Side'
                'Hyde Park' 'Edgewater']
               Cluster 3: ['Austin' 'West Garfield Park' 'East Garfield Park' 'North Lawnd
               ale'
                'Oakland' 'Fuller Park' 'Grand Boulevard' 'Kenwood' 'Washington Park'
                'Woodlawn' 'South Shore' 'Chatham' 'Avalon Park' 'South Chicago'
                'Burnside' 'Calumet Heights' 'Roseland' 'Pullman' 'South Deering'
                'West Pullman' 'Riverdale' 'West Englewood' 'Englewood'
                'Greater Grand Crossing' 'Auburn Gresham' 'Washington Heights'
                'Morgan Park']
               Cluster 4: ['North Center' 'Lake View' 'Lincoln Park' 'Near North Side' 'Ed
               ison Park'
                'Norwood Park' 'Jefferson Park' 'Forest Glen' 'Portage Park' 'Dunning'
                'West Town' 'Garfield Ridge' 'Beverly' 'Mount Greenwood' "O'Hare"]
```

Figure 11.35 – Extracting the clusters of data objects in community_df

We can also perform centroid analysis for the clusters that were just formed. The code for centroid analysis was presented in *Chapter 8*, *Clustering Analysis,* in the *Using K-Means to cluster a dataset with more than two dimensions* section. Find the code and adjust it to confirm the following heatmap as a result of centroid analysis. Note that as K-Means is a random algorithm, we do expect the heatmap to be different. At the same time, we expect the patterns that emerge from the data to be similar:

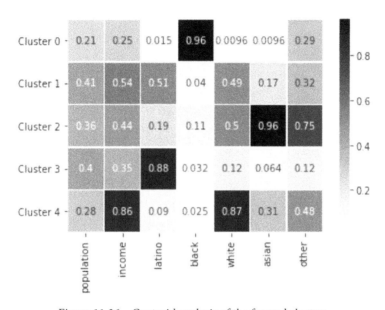

Figure 11.36 – Centroid analysis of the formed clusters

We can see in the preceding screenshot that the communities in each cluster are distinctively different, and this result will be tremendously helpful in assigning communication liaisons.

So far in this chapter, we have covered and seen examples of how to detect and deal with missing values and outliers. Next, we will turn our attention to detecting errors and dealing with them in the dataset.

Errors

Errors are an inevitable part of any data collection and measurement. The following formula best captures this fact:

$Data = True\ Signal + Error$

The *True Signal* is the reality we are trying to measure and present in the form of *Data*, but due to the incapability of our measurement system or data presentation, we cannot capture the *True Signal*. Therefore, *Error* is the difference between the *True Signal* and the recorded *Data*.

For instance, let's say we have purchased seven thermometers and we would like to accurately calculate the room temperature using these seven thermometers. At a given point in time, we take the following readings from them:

Thermometer 1	70.16
Thermometer 2	69.94
Thermometer 3	70.35
Thermometer 4	69.83
Thermometer 5	70.01
Thermometer 6	70.38
Thermometer 7	70.12

Figure 11.37 – Seven thermometers' readings

Looking at the preceding screenshot, what would you say the temperature of the room—the *True Signal*—is? The answer is that we cannot measure or capture the *True Signal*—in this case, the exact temperature of the room. With seven thermometers, we may have been able to come to a more accurate reading, but we cannot eliminate error.

Types of errors

There are two types of errors: **random errors** and **systematic errors**. The biggest distinction between these two types of errors is that random errors are not avoidable, but systematic errors are.

Random errors happen due to unavoidable inconsistencies and the limitations of our measurement equipment. What we saw in the seven thermometers example was a case of random errors. Another example is random errors that happen when measuring people's opinions using surveys due to unavoidable miscommunications and misunderstandings.

On the other hand, systematic errors are avoidable inconsistencies that happen because of a problem that persists throughout the entire data collection. Systematic errors happen on top of random errors, meaning random errors are always present. For example, if an uncalibrated thermometer is used for measuring a room temperature, we have random errors due to the incapability of the device in capturing the true signal, and we also have a systematic error due to failing to calibrate the thermometer before the act of measuring.

Dealing with errors

We will deal with errors differently based on their types. Random errors are unavoidable and, at best, we may be able to mitigate them using smoothing or aggregation. These are techniques that we will cover in one of the future chapters: *Data Massaging and Transformation*.

However, systematic errors are avoidable, and once recognized, we should always take the following steps in dealing with them:

1. Adjust and improve the data collection so that systematic errors will not happen in the future.

2. Try to use other data resources if available to find the correct value, and if there are none, we will regard the systematic error as a missing value.

From the second step onward, you would deal with systematic errors as missing values. That is great, as we have already covered values and have got many powerful tools and techniques in dealing with missing values.

Detecting systematic errors

Detecting systematic errors is not very easy, and it is likely that they go unnoticed and negatively influence our analysis. The best chance we have in detecting systematic errors is the techniques we learned in the *Detecting outliers* section. When outliers are detected and there is no explanation why the value of the outliers are correct, then we can conclude that outliers are systematic errors. The following example will help to shed light on this distinction.

Example of systematic errors and correct outliers

In this example, we would like to analyze `CustomerEntries.xlsx`. The dataset contains about 2 months of customer-visiting data from a local coffee shop between October 1, 2020, and November 24, 2020. The goal of the analysis is to profile the hours of the day to see at which times and days peak customer visits happen.

The following screenshot shows the code to read the file into the hour_df pandas DataFrame and the use of the .info() function to evaluate the state of the dataset in terms of the missing values:

```
In [99]:  ▶  hour_df = pd.read_excel('CustomerEnteries.xlsx')
             hour_df.info()

             <class 'pandas.core.frame.DataFrame'>
             RangeIndex: 495 entries, 0 to 494
             Data columns (total 3 columns):
              #   Column      Non-Null Count  Dtype
             ---  ------      --------------  -----
              0   Date        495 non-null    datetime64[ns]
              1   Time        495 non-null    int64
              2   N_Cusotmers 495 non-null    int64
             dtypes: datetime64[ns](1), int64(2)
             memory usage: 11.7 KB
```

Figure 11.38 – Reading CustomerEntries.xlsx into hour_df and using .info() function to check outliers

We can see in the preceding screenshot that the dataset does not have missing values. Next, we will turn our attention to checking for outliers. As the dataset is essentially a time series, it is best to use a line plot to see whether there are any outliers. The following screenshot shows the output of running hour_df.N_Customers.plot() to create a line plot:

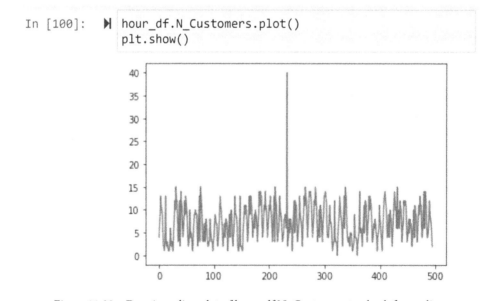

```
In [100]:  ▶  hour_df.N_Customers.plot()
              plt.show()
```

Figure 11.39 – Drawing a line plot of hour_df.N_Customers to check for outliers

In the preceding screenshot, we can see we have a clear case of an outlier between the 200 and 300 indexes. Running `hour_df[hour_df.N_Customers>20]` will reveal that the outlier happens in index 232, which is timestamped `2020-10-26` at 16.

To check whether this outlier is a case of a systematic error or not, we investigate using our other sources and we realize that nothing out of the ordinary had happened during that day, and this record could simply be a manual data entry error. This shows us that this is a systematic error, and therefore we need to take the following two steps in dealing with systematic errors:

1. *Step 1*: We inform the entity who is in charge of data collection about this mistake and ask them to take appropriate measures to prevent such a mistake from happening in the future.

2. *Step 2*: If we do not have ways to find the correct value using other resources within a reasonable time and effort, we regard the data entry as a missing value and replace it with `np.nan`. The following code can take care of that:

```
err_index = hour_df[hour_df.N_Cusotmers>20].index
hour_df.at[err_index, 'N_Customers']=np.nan
```

After successfully running the previous code, you should rerun `hour_df.N_Customers.plot()` to check the status of `day_df` regarding outliers. The following screenshot shows the new line plot:

```
In [103]:  ▶  hour_df.N_Customers.plot()
               plt.show()
```

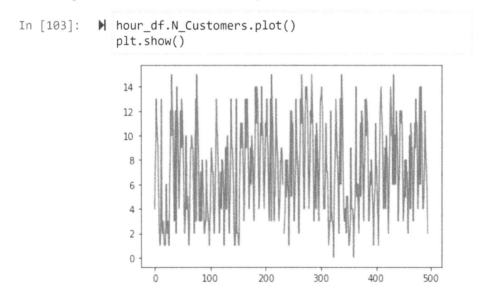

Figure 11.40 – Drawing a line plot of hour_df.N_Customers to check for outliers after dealing with the systematic error

You can see in the preceding screenshot that we do not see a univariate outlier anymore.

Although the time series looks like a univariate dataset, it is not univariate and we can always perform level II data cleaning to unpack new columns such as month, day, weekday, hour, and minute. In this dataset, time and data have already been separated, so we can perform the following bivariate outlier detection.

As you remember, the best way to perform bivariate outlier detection for a pair of numerical-categorical attributes is to use multiple boxplots. The following screenshot shows the output of sns.boxplot(y=hour_df.N_Customers, x=hour_df.Time), which are multiple boxplots we need to see whether there are bivariate outliers for the N_Customers and Time attributes:

```
In [104]:   ▶| sns.boxplot(y=hour_df.N_Customers,x=hour_df.Time)
               plt.show()
```

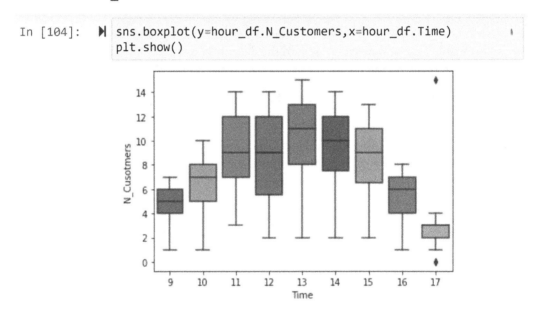

Figure 11.41 – Drawing multiple boxplots for the N_Customers and Time attributes to check for bivariate outliers

Looking at the preceding screenshot, we do see that we have two other outliers that could be systematic errors. The first one is the smallest value of N_Customers, which is zero, under the Time value of 17. The value is consistent with the rest of the data. The Time value of 17 (or 5 P.M.) seems to be getting the least number of customers, and we can imagine occasionally having no customers at that hour.

However, the second flier at the same hour (5 P.M.) seems more troubling. After running `hour_df.query("Time==17 and N_Customers>12")`, which filters the flier, we can see the outlier has happened on November 17, 2020. After investigation, it turns out that on November 17, 2020 at 4:25, a biking club made a half hour stop for refreshment, which was out of the ordinary for the store. Therefore the data entry was not erroneous and just a correct outlier.

After preprocessing `hour_df`, it now has a missing value (the systematic error that was replaced with `np.nan`) and two bivariate outliers. Knowing this, we allow ourselves to enter that last step: the analysis.

Drawing a bar chart that shows and compares the central tendency of `N_Customers` per working hour of the coffee shop (`Time`) will be the visualization we need for this analysis. The prescribed bar chart can easily deal with missing values as per the aggregation of the data to calculate the central tendencies. As we have outliers in the dataset, we chose to use median over mean as the central tendency for this analysis. Running the following line of code will create the described bar chart:

```
hour_df.groupby('Time').N_Customers.median().plot.bar()
```

As you experienced during this example, the techniques that we use for detecting and dealing with systematic errors are already covered under the subsection on missing values and outliers. In a nutshell, when we don't find any support to believe an outlier is a correct value, we regard this as a systematic error and consequently a missing value.

Summary

Congratulations on your learning in this chapter. This chapter covered data cleaning level III. Together, we learned how to detect and deal with missing values, outliers, and errors. This may sound like too short of a summary for such a long chapter, but as we saw, detection, diagnosis, and dealing with each of the three issues (missing values, outliers, and errors) can have many details and delicacies. Finishing this chapter was a significant achievement, and now you know how to detect, diagnose, and deal with all of these three possible issues you may encounter when working with a dataset.

This chapter concludes our three-chapter-long data cleaning journey. In the next chapter, we move to another important data preprocessing area, and that is data fusion and integration. Before moving on to the next chapter, spend some time working on the following exercises to solidify your learnings.

Exercises

1. In this exercise, we will be using `Temperature_data.csv`. This dataset has some missing values. Do the following:

    a) After reading the file into a pandas DataFrame, check whether the dataset is level I clean, and if not, clean it. Also, describe the cleanings (if any).

    b) Check whether the dataset is level II clean, and if not, clean it. Also, describe the cleanings (if any).

    c) The dataset has missing values. See how many, and run a diagnosis to see which types of missing values they are.

    d) Are there any outliers in the dataset?

    e) How should we best deal with missing values if our goal is to draw multiple boxplots that show the central tendency and variation of temperature across the months? Draw the described visualization after dealing with the missing values.

2. In this exercise, we are going to use the `Iris_wMV.csv` file. The Iris dataset includes 50 samples of 3 types of iris flowers, totaling 150 rows of data. Each flower is described by its sepal and petal length or width. The `PetalLengthCm` column has some missing values.

    a) Confirm that `PetalLengthCm` has five missing values.

    b) Figure out the types of missing values (MCAR, MAR, MNAR).

    c) How would you best deal with missing values if your end goal was to draw the following visualization? Comment on all four different approaches of dealing with missing values in this chapter, citing why the approach would or wouldn't be appropriate:

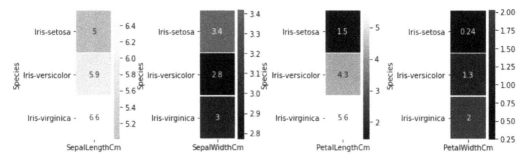

Figure 11.42 – Exercise 2

d) Draw the preceding screenshot twice, once after adopting a *keep as is* approach, and once after adopting an *imputing with the central tendency of the appropriate iris species* approach. Compare the two outputs and comment on their differences.

3. In this exercise, we will be using imdb_top_1000.csv. More information about this dataset may be found at this link: https://www.kaggle.com/harshitshankhdhar/imdb-dataset-of-top-1000-movies-and-tv-shows. Perform the following steps for this dataset:

a) Read the file into movie_df, and list the level I data cleaning steps that the dataset needs. Implement the listed items, if any.

b) We want to employ a Decision Tree Classification algorithm using the following columns to predict IMDB_rating values: Certificate, Runtime, Genre, and Gross. For this analytic goal, list the level II data cleanings that need to be done, and then implement them.

c) Does the dataset have issues regarding missing values? If yes, which types are they, and how best should we deal with them given the listed data analytic goals in b)?

d) Use the following function from sklearn.tree to create RegressTree, which will be a prediction model that can predict IMDB_rating values using Certificate, Runtime, Genre, and Gross attributes: DecisionTreeRegressor(max_depth=5, min_impurity_decrease=0, min_samples_split=20, splitter='random'). The tuning parameters have been set for you so that the DecisionTreeRegressor algorithm can perform better. Once the model is trained; draw the trained tree and check whether the Gross attribute is used for the prediction of IMDB_rating values.

e) Run the following code and then explain what summary_df is:

```
dt_predicted_IMDB_rating = RegressTree.predict(Xs)
mean_predicted_IMDB_rating = np.ones(len(y))*y.mean()
summary_df = pd.DataFrame({'Prediction by Decision Tree':
dt_predicted_IMDB_rating, 'Prediction by mean': mean_
predicted_IMDB_rating, 'Actual IMDB_rating': y})
```

f) Run the following code and explain the visualization it creates. What can you learn from the visualization?

```
summary_df['Decision Tree Error'] = abs(summary_
df['Prediction by Decision Tree']- summary_df['Actual
IMDB_rating'])
summary_df['Mean Error'] = abs(summary_df['Prediction by
mean'] - summary_df['Actual IMDB_rating'])
plt.figure(figsize=(2,10))
table = summary_df[['Decision Tree Error','Mean Error']]
sns.heatmap(table, cmap='Greys')
```

4. In this exercise, we will be using two CSV files: `responses.csv` and `columns.csv`. The two files are used to record the data of a survey conducted in Slovakia. To access the data on Kaggle, use this link: `https://www.kaggle.com/miroslavsabo/young-people-survey`. Perform the following exercises for this data source:

a) Are there respondents in this survey that are suspected to be outliers based on their age? How many? List them in a separate DataFrame.

b) Are there respondents in this survey that are suspected to be outliers based on their level of liking for country and hard rock music? How many? List them in a separate DataFrame.

c) Are there respondents in this survey that are suspected to be outliers based on their **body mass index** (**BMI**) or education level? How many? List them in a separate DataFrame. BMI can be calculated using the following formula:

$$BMI = \frac{Weight}{Height^2}$$

The weight has to be in kg and height in **meters** (**m**) for the preceding formula. In the dataset, weight is recorded in kg but height is recorded in cm and has to be transformed to m.

d) Are there respondents in this survey that are suspected to be outliers based on their BMI and age? How many? List them in a separate DataFrame.

e) Are there respondents in this survey that are suspected to be outliers based on their BMI and gender? How many? List them in a separate DataFrame.

5. One of the most common approaches for fraud detection is using outlier detection. In this exercise, you will use `creditcard.csv` from `https://www.kaggle.com/mlg-ulb/creditcardfraud` to evaluate the effectiveness of outlier detection for credit card fraud detection. Note that most of the columns in this data source are processed values to uphold data anonymity. Perform the following steps:

a) Check the state of the dataset for missing values and address them, if any.

b) Using the `Class` column, which shows whether a transaction has been fraudulent or not, find out what percentage of the transactions in the dataset are fraudulent.

c) Using data visualization or the appropriate statistical set (and, if necessary, both), specify which univariate outliers have a relationship with the `Class` column— in other words, if the values of this column are outliers, then we may suspect fraudulent activity. Which statistical test is appropriate here?

d) First, use the K-Means algorithm to group the transactions into 200 clusters by the attributes that were found to have a relationship with the `Class` column in part c). Then, filter out the members of the clusters with fewer than 50 transactions. Do any of them contain significantly fraudulent transactions?

e) If there are any clusters with significant fraudulent transactions, perform centroid analysis for them.

6. In *Chapter 5*, *Data Visualization*, and *Chapter 8*, *Clustering Analysis*, we used `WH Report_preprocessed.csv`, which is the preprocessed version of `WH Report.csv`. Now that you have learned numerous data preprocessing skills, you will be preprocessing the dataset yourself. Proceed as follows:

a) Check the status of the dataset for missing values.

b) Check the status of the dataset for outliers.

c) We would like to cluster the countries based on their happiness indices over the years. Based on these analytic goals, address the missing values.

d) Based on the listed goal in part c), address the outliers.

e) Does the data need any level I or level II data cleaning before clustering is possible? If any, prepare the dataset for K-Means clustering.

f) Perform K-Means clustering to separate the countries into three groups, and do all the possible analytics that we do when clustering.

7. Specify whether the following items describe random errors or systematic errors:

    a) The data has these types of errors as the thermometer that the lab has purchased can give precise readings to one-thousandth of a degree.

    b) The data has these types of errors as the survey records were gathered by five different surveyors who attended five rigorous training sessions.

    c) The data has these types of errors because when asking for salary questions in a survey, there were no options such as *I would not like to share.*

    d) The data has these types of errors because the cameras were tampered with so that the robbery would not be recorded.

8. Study *Figure 11.14* one more time and run the first three exercises by this diagram, noting down the path that led to your decisions regarding the missing values. Did you take steps in dealing with missing values that were not listed in this diagram or this chapter? Would it be better to have a more complex diagram so every possibility would be included, or not? Why or why not?

9. Explain why the following statement is incorrect: a row may have a significant number of MCAR missing values.

12
Data Fusion and Data Integration

The popular understanding of data pre-processing goes hand in hand with data cleaning. Although data cleaning is a major and important part of data preprocessing, there are other important areas regarding this subject. In this chapter, we will learn about two of those important areas: data fusion and data integration. In short, data fusion and integration have a lot to do with mixing two or more sources of data for analytic goals.

First, we will learn about the similarities and differences between data fusion and data integration. After that, we will learn about six frequent challenges regarding data fusion and data integration. Then, by looking at three complete analytic examples, we will get to encounter these challenges and deal with them.

In this chapter, we are going to cover the following main topics:

- What are data fusion and data integration?
- Frequent challenges regarding data fusion and integration
- Example 1 (Challenges 3 and 4)
- Example 2 (Challenges 2 and 3)
- Example 3 (Challenges 1, 2, 3, 5, and 6)

Technical requirements

You can find the code and dataset for this chapter in this book's GitHub repository, which can be found at `https://github.com/PacktPublishing/Hands-On-Data-Preprocessing-in-Python`. You can find `chapter12` in this repository and download the code and the data for a better learning experience.

What are data fusion and data integration?

In most cases, data fusion and data integration are terms that are used interchangeably, but there are conceptual and technical distinctions between them. We will get to those shortly. Let's start with what both have in common and what they mean. Whenever the data we need for our analytic goals are from different sources, before we can perform the data analytics, we need to integrate the data sources into one dataset that we need for our analytic goals. The following diagram summarizes this integration visually:

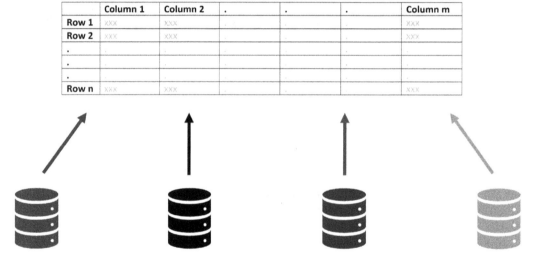

Figure 12.1 – Data integration from different sources

In the real world, data integration is much more difficult than what's shown in the preceding figure. There are many challenges that you need to overcome before integration is possible. These challenges could be due to organizational privacy and security challenges that restrict our data accessibility. But even assuming that these challenges are not in the way when different data sources need to be integrated, they arise because each data source is collected and structured based on the needs, standards, technology, and opinions of the people who have collected them. Regardless of correctness, there are always differences in the ways that the data is structured and because of that, data integration becomes challenging.

In this chapter, we will cover the most frequently faced data integration challenges and learn how to deal with them. These challenges will be discussed in the next subchapter. First, let's understand the difference between data fusion and data integration.

Data fusion versus data integration

As we implied previously, both data integration and data fusion are all about mixing more than one source of data. With data integration, the act of mixing is easier as all the data sources have the same definition of data objects, or with simple data restructuring or transformation, the definitions of the data objects can become the same. When the definitions of the data objects are the same and the data objects are indexed similarly across the data sources, mixing the data sources becomes easy; it will be one line of code. This is what data integration does; it matches the definitions of the data objects across the data sources and then mixes the data objects.

On the other hand, data fusion is needed when the data sources do not have the same definitions as the data objects. With restructuring and simple data transformation, we cannot create the same definitions of data objects across the data sources. For data fusion, we often need to imagine a definition of data objects that is possible for all the data sources and then make assumptions about the data. Based on those assumptions, we must restructure the data sources. So, again, the data sources are in states that have the same definitions of data objects. At that point, the act of mixing the data sources becomes very easy and can be done in one line of code.

Let's try and understand the differences between the two by using two examples: one that needs data integration and one that needs data fusion.

Data integration example

Imagine that a company would like to analyze its effectiveness in how it advertises. The company needs to come up with two columns of data – the *total sales per customer* and the *total amount of advertisement expenditure per customer*. As the sales department and marketing department keep and manage their databases, each department will be tasked with creating a list of customers with the relevant information. Once they've done that, they need to connect the data of each customer from the two sources. This connection can be made by relying on the existence of real customers, so no assumptions need to be made. No changes need to be made to connect this data. This is a clear example of data integration. The definition of data objects for both sources is customers.

Data fusion example

Imagine a technology-empowered farmer who would like to see the influence of irrigation (water dispersion) on yield. The farmer has data regarding both the amount of water its revolving water stations have dispensed and the amount of harvest from each point in the farm. Each stationary water station has a sensor and calculates and records the amount of water that is dispensed. Also, each time the blade in the combine harvester moves, the machine calculates and record the amount of harvest and the location.

In this example, there is no clear connection between the sources of data. In the previous example, the clear connection was the definition of data objects - customers. However, we don't have that here, so we need to make assumptions and change the data so that a connection is possible. The situation in this example could look like something like the following figure. The blue dots represent the water stations, while the gray ones represent harvest points:

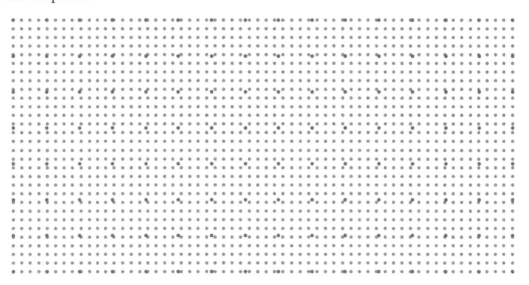

Figure 12.2 – Water points and harvest points

To perform data fusion, we need different sets of assumptions and sets of preprocessing that combine or fuse these data sources. Next, let us see how these assumptions to make the fusion possible may look like.

How about if we defined our data objects as the pieces of land that are harvested? In other words, we define our data objects as harvest points. Then, based on the proximity of the revolving water station to each harvest point, we calculate a number that represents the amount of water the point received. Each water point could be attributed a radius of reach. The closer a harvest point is to the water point within this radius of reach, the more the harvest point got from the amount of water that was dispensed from the water station. We don't know how much water arrives at the harvest points, but we make assumptions about it. These assumptions could be completely naïve or based on some careful experimentation or research.

In this example, we had to come up with a definition of data objects that did not exist within both data sources. Then, we had to make many assumptions about the collected data so that the data sources could be fused.

Good news! You will get to do this data fusion yourself in *Exercise 8* at the end of this chapter.

You will see the term **data integration** for both **data integration** and **data fusion** throughout this chapter. When you need to be aware of the distinction between them, the text will inform you of that.

You are almost ready to start seeing the frequent challenges that occur in these areas, as well as some examples, but first, let's discuss one more thing. In the next section, we will introduce two directions of data integration.

Directions of data integration

Data integration may happen in two different directions. The first is by adding attributes; we might want to supplement a dataset with more describing attributes. In this direction, we have all the data objects that we need, but other sources might be able to enrich our dataset. The second is by adding data objects; we might have multiple sources of data with distinct data objects, and integrating them will lead to a population with more data objects that represent the population we want to analyze.

Let's look at two examples to understand the two directions of data integration better.

Examples of data integration by adding attributes

The examples we saw earlier in the *Data integration example* and *Data fusion example* sections were both data integration by adding attributes. In these examples, our aim was to supplement the dataset by including more attributes that would be beneficial or necessary for the analytic goals. In both examples, we looked at situations where we would need to perform data integration by adding attributes. Next, we will examine situations that needs data integration by adding data objects.

Examples of data integration by adding data objects

In the first example (*Data integration example*), we wanted to integrate customer data from the sales and marketing departments. The data objects and customers were the same, but different databases included the data we needed for the analytic goals. Now, imagine that the company has five regional managing bodies and that each managing body is in charge of keeping the data of their customers. In this scenario, data integration will happen after each managing body has come up with a dataset that includes the *total sales per customer* and the *total amount of advertisement expenditure per customer*. This type of integration, where we're using five sources of data that include the data of distinct customers, is known as performing data integration by adding data objects.

In the second example (*Data fusion example*), our goal was to fuse the irrigation and yield data for one piece of land. Regardless of how we would define the data objects to serve the purpose of our analysis, at the end of the day, we will have analyzed only one piece of land. So, different sets of assumptions that would allow the data sources to be fused may have led to different numbers of data objects, but the piece of land stays the same. However, let's imagine that we had more than one piece of land whose data we wanted to integrate. That would become data integration by adding data objects.

So far, we have learned about different aspects of data integration. We have learned what it is and its goals. We've also covered the two directions of data integration. Next, we will learn about the six challenges of data integration and data fusion. After that, we will look at examples that will feature those frequent challenges.

Frequent challenges regarding data fusion and integration

While every data integration task is unique, there are a few challenges that you will face frequently. In this chapter, you will learn about those challenges and, through examples, you will pick up the skills to handle them. First, let's learn about each. Then, through examples that feature one or more of them, we will pick up valuable skills to handle them.

Challenge 1 – entity identification

The entity identification challenge – or as it is known in the literature, the entity identification problem – may occur when the data sources are being integrated by adding attributes. The challenge is that the data objects in all the data sources are the same real-world entities with the same definitions of data objects, but they are not easy to connect due to the unique identifiers in the data sources. For instance, in the *data integration example* section, the sales department and the marketing department did not use a *central customer unique identifier* for all their customers. Due to this lack of data management, when they want to integrate the data, they will have to figure out which customer is which in the data sources.

Challenge 2 – unwise data collection

This data integration challenge happens, as its name suggests, due to unwise data collection. For instance, instead of using a centralized database, the data of different data objects is stored in multiple files. We covered this challenge in *Chapter 9*, *Data Cleaning Level I – Cleaning Up the Table*, as well. Please go back and review *Example 1 – Unwise data collection*, before reading on. This challenge could be seen as both level I data cleaning or a data integration challenge. Regardless, in these situations, our goal is to make sure that the data is integrated into one standard data structure. This type of data integration challenge happens when data objects are being added.

Challenge 3 – index mismatched formatting

When we start integrating data sources by adding attributes, we will use the pandas DataFrame .join() function to connect the rows of two DataFrames that have the same indices. To use this valuable function, the integrating DataFrames needs to have the same index formatting; otherwise, the function will not connect the rows. For example, the following figure shows three attempts of combining two DataFrames: temp_df and electric_df. temp_df contains the hourly temperature (**temp**) of 2016, while electric_df carries the hourly electricity consumption (**consumption**) for the same year. The first two attempts (the top one and the middle one) are unsuccessful due to the index mismatched formatting challenge. For instance, consider the attempt at the top; while both DataFrames are indexed with **Date** and **Time** and both show the same **Date** and **Time**, attempting the .join() function will produce a "*cannot join with no overlapping index names*" error. What is happening? The attempt to integrate was unsuccessful because the index formatting from the two DataFrames is not the same:

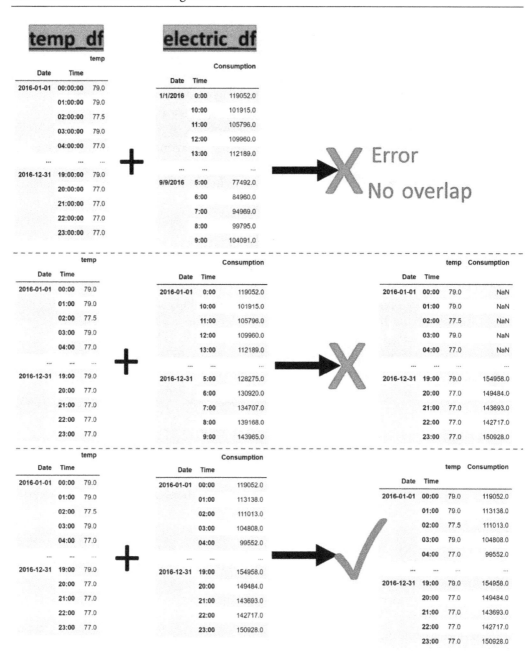

Figure 12.3 – Examples of index mismatched formatting when combining two data sources

In the preceding diagram, while the attempt in the middle is better than the one at the top, it is still unsuccessful. Pay close attention and see if you can figure out why there are so many **NaN**s in the output of the integration.

Challenge 4 – aggregation mismatch

This challenge occurs when integrating data sources by adding attributes. When integrating time series data sources whose time intervals are not identical, this challenge arises. For example, if the two DataFrames presented in the following figure are to be integrated, not only do we have to address the challenge of *index mismatch formatting*, but we will also need to face the aggregation mismatch challenge. This is because **temp_df** carries the hourly temperature data but **electric_df** carries the electricity consumption of every half an hour:

	temp_df				electric_df		
	Timestamp	temp			Date	Time	Consumption
0	2016-01-01T00:00:00	79.0		0	12/1/2017	0:00:00	72650.0
1	2016-01-01T01:00:00	79.0		1	12/1/2017	0:30:00	70553.0
2	2016-01-01T02:00:00	77.5		2	12/1/2017	1:00:00	68277.0
3	2016-01-01T03:00:00	79.0		3	12/1/2017	1:30:00	67611.0
4	2016-01-01T04:00:00	77.0		4	12/1/2017	2:00:00	67388.0
...	...	...		...	...	...	...
8726	2016-12-31T19:00:00	79.0		19051	1/1/2016	21:30	56059.0
8727	2016-12-31T20:00:00	77.0		19052	1/1/2016	22:00	55107.0
8728	2016-12-31T21:00:00	77.0		19053	1/1/2016	22:30	55609.0
8729	2016-12-31T22:00:00	77.0		19054	1/1/2016	23:00	58199.0
8730	2016-12-31T23:00:00	77.0		19055	1/1/2016	23:30	57539.0

Figure 12.4 – Example of an aggregation mismatch when combining two data sources

To deal with this challenge, we will have to restructure one source or both sources to get them to have the same level of data aggregation. We will see this shortly, so now, let's cover another challenge.

Challenge 5 – duplicate data objects

This challenge occurs when we're integrating data sources by adding data objects. When the sources contain data objects that are also in the other sources, when the data sources are integrated, there will be duplicates of the same data objects in the integrated dataset. For example, imagine a hospital that provides different kinds of healthcare services. For a project, we need to gather the socioeconomic data of all of the patients in the hospital. The imaginary hospital does not have a centralized database, so all of the departments are tasked with returning a dataset containing all the patients they have provided services for. After integrating all of the datasets from different departments, you should expect that there are multiple rows for the patients that had to receive care from different departments in the hospital.

Challenge 6 – data redundancy

This challenge's name seems to be appropriate for the previous challenge as well, but in the literature, the term data redundancy is used for a unique situation. Unlike the previous challenge, this challenge may be faced when you're integrating data sources by adding attributes. As the name suggests, after data integration, some of the attributes may be redundant. This redundancy could be shallow as there are two attributes with different titles but the same data. Or, it could be deeper. In deeper data redundancy cases, the redundant attribute does not have the same title, nor is its data the same as one of the other attributes, but the values of the redundant attribute can be derived from the other attributes.

For example, after integrating data sources into a dataset of customers, we have the following seven attributes: *age, average order $, days from the last visit, weekly visit frequency, weekly $ purchase*, and *satisfaction score*. If we use all seven attributes to cluster customers, we have made a mistake regarding data redundancy. Here, the *weekly visit frequency, weekly $ purchase,* and *average order $* attributes are distinct but the value of *weekly $ purchase* can be derived from *weekly visit frequency* and *average order $*. By doing so, inadvertently, we will have given the information regarding the customer's visit and their purchase amount more weight in the clustering analysis.

We should deal with data redundancy challenges that are informed by the analytic goals and data analysis tools. For instance, if we were employing the **decision tree** algorithm to predict the satisfaction score of the customers, we needn't have worried about data redundancy. This is because the decision tree algorithm only uses the attributes that help its performance.

Example 1 (challenges 3 and 4)   345

However, if the same task were to be done using linear regression, you would have a problem if you didn't remove *weekly $ purchase*. This is because the same information being in more than one attribute would confuse the linear regression. There are two reasons for this:

- First, the linear regression algorithm will have to use all the independent attributes as they are inputted.

- Second, the algorithm needs to come up with a set of weights that works for all the data objects for all the independent attributes, all at the same time. In regression analysis, this situation is referred to as **collinearity** and it should be avoided.

Now that we've learned about these six common challenges of data integration, let's look at some examples that feature one or some of these challenges.

Example 1 (challenges 3 and 4)

In this example, we have two sources of data. The first was retrieved from the local electricity provider that holds the electricity consumption (*Electricity Data 2016_2017. csv*), while the other was retrieved from the local weather station and includes temperature data (*Temperature 2016.csv*). We want to see if we can come up with a visualization that can answer if and how the amount of electricity consumption is affected by the weather.

First, we will use `pd.read_csv()` to read these CSV files into two pandas DataFrames called `electric_df` and `temp_df`. After reading the datasets into these DataFrames, we will look at them to understand their data structure. You will notice the following issues:

- The data object definition of `electric_df` is the electric consumption in 15 minutes, but the data object definition of `temp_df` is the temperature every 1 hour. This shows that we have to face the aggregation mismatch challenge of data integration (*Challenge 4*).

- `temp_df` only contains the data for 2016, while `electric_df` contains the data for 2016 and some parts of 2017.

- Neither `temp_df` nor `electric_df` has indexes that can be used to connect the data objects across the two DataFrames. This shows that we will also have to face the challenge of index mismatched formatting (*challenge 3*).

To overcome these issues, we will perform the following steps:

1. Remove the 2017 data objects from `electric_df`. The following code uses Boolean masking and the `.drop()` function to do so:

    ```
    BM = electric_df.Date.str.contains('2017')
    dropping_index = electric_df[BM].index
    electric_df.drop(index = dropping_index, inplace=True)
    ```

    Check the state of `electric_df` after successfully running the preceding code. You will see that `electric_df` in 2016 is recorded every half an hour.

2. Add a new column titled `Hour` to `electric_df` from the `Time` attribute. The following code manages to do this in one line of code using the `.apply()` function:

    ```
    electric_df['Hour'] = electric_df.Time.apply(lambda v:
    '{}:00'.format(v.split(':')[0]))
    ```

3. Create a new data structure whose definition of the data object is hourly electricity consumption. The following code uses the `.groupby()` function to create `integrate_sr`. The Pandas `integrate_sr` series is a stopgap data structure that will be used for integration in the later steps:

    ```
    integrate_sr = electric_df.groupby(['Date','Hour']).
    Consumption.sum()
    ```

    One good question to ask here is this, why are we using the `.sum()` aggregate function instead of `.mean()`? The reason is the nature of the data. The electricity consumption of an hour is the summation of the electricity consumption of its half-hour pieces.

4. In this step, we will turn our attention to `temp_df`. We will add the `Date` and `Hour` columns to `temp_df` from `Timestamp`. The following code does this by applying an explicit function:

    First, we will create the function:

    ```
    def unpackTimestamp(r):
        ts = r.Timestamp
        date,time = ts.split('T')
        hour = time.split(':')[0]
        year,month,day = date.split('-')
        r['Hour'] = '{}:00'.format(int(hour))
        r['Date'] = '{}/{}/{}'.
        format(int(month),int(day),year)
        return(r)
    ```

Example 1 (challenges 3 and 4)   347

Then, we will apply the function to the `temp_df` DataFrame:

```
temp_df = temp_df.apply(unpackTimestamp,axis=1)
```

Check the status of `temp_df` after successfully running the preceding code block before moving to the next step.

5. For `temp_df`, set the `Date` and `Hour` attributes as the index and then drop the `Timestamp` column. The following code does this in one line:

```
temp_df = temp_df.set_index(['Date', 'Hour']).drop(
columns = ['Timestamp'])
```

Again, check the status of `temp_df` after successfully running the preceding code before moving on to the next step.

6. After all this reformatting and restructuring, we are ready to use `.join()` to integrate the two sources. The hard part is what comes before using `.join()`. Applying this function is just as easy as applying it. See for yourself:

```
integrate_df =temp_df.join(integrate_sr)
```

Note that we came to `integrate_sr` as a stopgap data structure from *Step 3*. As always, take a moment to investigate what `integrate_df` looks like before reading on.

7. Reset the index of `integrate_df` as we no longer need the index for integration purposes, nor do we need those values for visualization purposes. Running the following code will take care of this:

```
integrate_df.reset_index(inplace=True)
```

8. Create a line plot of the whole year's electricity consumption, where the dimension of temperature is added to the line plot using color. This visualization is shown in *Figure 12.5* and was created using the tools we have learned about in this book. The following code creates this visualization:

```
days = integrate_df.Date.unique()
max_temp, min_temp = integrate_df.temp.max(), integrate_
df.temp.min()
green =0.1
plt.figure(figsize=(20,5))
for d in days:
    BM = integrate_df.Date == d
    wdf = integrate_df[BM]
```

```
        average_temp = wdf.temp.mean()
        red = (average_temp - min_temp)/ (max_temp - min_
        temp)
        blue = 1-red
        clr = [red,green,blue]
        plt.plot(wdf.index,wdf.Consumption,c = clr)
    BM = (integrate_df.Hour =='0:00') & (integrate_df.Date.
    str.contains('/28/'))
    plt.xticks(integrate_df[BM].index,integrate_df[BM].
    Date,rotation=90)
    plt.grid()
    plt.margins(y=0,x=0)
    plt.show()
```

The preceding code brings many parts together to make the following visualization happen. The most important aspects of the code are as follows:

- The code created the days list, which contains all the unique dates from integrate_df. By and large, the preceding code is a loop through the days list, and for each unique day, the line plot of electricity consumption is drawn and added to the days before and after. The color of each day's line plot is determined by that day's temperature average, that is, temp.mean().

- The colors in the visualization are created based on the **RGB color codes**. **RGB** stands for Red, Green, and Blue. All colors can be created by using a combination of these three colors. You can specify the amount of each color you'd like and **Matplotlib** will produce that color for you. These colors can take values from 0 to 1 for Matplotlib. Here, we know that when green is set to 0.1, and the red and blue have a blue = 1 - red relationship with one another, we can create a red-blue spectrum of color that can nicely represent hot and cold colors. The spectrum can be used to show hotter and colder temperatures. This has been done by calculating the maximum and minimum of the temperature (using max_temp and min_temp) and calculating the three red, green, and blue elements of clr at the right time to pass as the color value to the plt.plot() function.

Example 2 (challenges 2 and 3)   349

- A **Boolean Mask** (**BM**) and `plt.xticks()` are used to include the 28th of each month on the *x* axis so that we don't have a cluttered *x* axis:

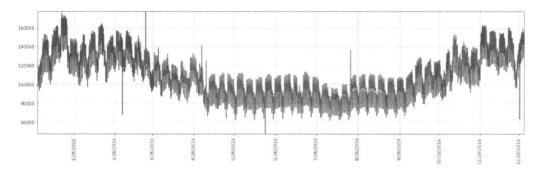

Figure 12.5 – Line plot of electricity consumption color-coded by temperature

Now, let's bring our attention to the analytic values shown in the preceding diagram. We can see a clear relationship between `temp` and `Consumption`; as the weather becomes colder, the electricity consumption also increases.

We would not be able to draw this visualization without integrating these two data sources. By experiencing the added analytic values of this visualization, you can also appreciate the value of data integration and see the point of having to deal with both *Challenge 3 – index mismatched formatting* and *Challenge 4 – aggregation mismatch*.

Example 2 (challenges 2 and 3)

In this example, we will be using the *Taekwondo_Technique_Classification_Stats. csv* and *table1.csv* datasets from `https://www.kaggle.com/ali2020armor/ taekwondo-techniques-classification`. The datasets were collected by *2020 Armor* (`https://2020armor.com/`), the first ever provider of e-scoring vests and applications. The data includes the sensor performance readings of six taekwondo athletes, who have varying levels of experience and expertise. We would like to see if the athlete's gender, age, weight, and experience influence the level of impact they can create when they perform the following techniques:

- **Roundhouse/Round Kick (R)**
- **Back Kick (B)**
- **Cut Kick (C)**
- **Punch (P)**

The data is stored in two separate files. We will use `pd.read_csv()` to read `table1.csv` into `athlete_df` and `Taekwondo_Technique_Classification_Stats.csv` into `unknown_df`. Before reading on, take a moment to study `athlete_df` and `unknown_df` and evaluate their state to perform the analysis.

After analysis, it will be obvious that the data structure that's been chosen for `athlete_df` is simple to understand. The data object's definition of `athlete_df` is athletes, which means that each row represents a taekwondo `athelete_df`. However, the `unknown_df` data structure is not readily understandable and is somewhat confusing. The reason for this is that even though a very common data structure – a table – is being used, it is not appropriate. As we discussed in *Chapter 3, Data – What Is It Really?*, *The most universal data structure – a table*, we know that the glue that holds a table together is an understandable definition of data objects. Therefore, the major data integration challenge we will face in this example is *Challenge 2 – unwise data collection*.

To integrate the data when we face *unwise data collection challenges*, similar to what we did in *Chapter 9, Data Cleaning Level I – Cleaning Up the Table*, in *Example 1 – unwise data collection*, we need the data structure and its design to support the following two matters:

- The data structure can include the data of all the files.

- The data structure can be used for the mentioned analysis.

As we've discussed, the `athlete_df` dataset is simple and easy to understand, but what does the information in `unknown_df` include? After putting two and two together, we will realize that the sensor readings from the performance of six taekwondo athletes are in `athlete_df`. From studying `unknown_df`, we also realize that each athlete has performed each of the four aforementioned techniques five times. These techniques are coded in `unknown_df` using the letters R, B, C, and P; R stands for roundhouse, B stands for back kick, C stands for cut kick, and P stands for punch. Furthermore, we can see that each technique is performed five times by each athlete.

Running the following code will create an empty pandas DataFrame called `performance_df`. This dataset has been designed so that both `athlete_df` and `unknown_df` can be integrated into it.

The number of rows (n_rows) we have designed for `performance_df` is one minus the number of columns in `unknown_df`: `len(unknown_df.columns)-1`. We will see why that is the case when we are about to fill up `performance_df`:

```
designed_columns = ['Participant_id', 'Gender', 'Age',
 'Weight', 'Experience', 'Technique_id', 'Trial_number',
 'Average_read']
```

Example 2 (challenges 2 and 3)   351

```
n_rows = len(unknown_df.columns)-1
performance_df = pd.DataFrame(index=range(n_rows),columns
=designed_columns)
```

The following table shows `performance_df`, which the preceding code creates:

	Participant_id	Gender	Age	Weight	Experience	Technique_id	Trial_number	Average_read
0	NaN	NaN	NaN	NaN	NaN	NaN	NaN	NaN
1	NaN	NaN	NaN	NaN	NaN	NaN	NaN	NaN
2	NaN	NaN	NaN	NaN	NaN	NaN	NaN	NaN
3	NaN	NaN	NaN	NaN	NaN	NaN	NaN	NaN
4	NaN	NaN	NaN	NaN	NaN	NaN	NaN	NaN
...	...	...	...	...	...	...	...	...
115	NaN	NaN	NaN	NaN	NaN	NaN	NaN	NaN
116	NaN	NaN	NaN	NaN	NaN	NaN	NaN	NaN
117	NaN	NaN	NaN	NaN	NaN	NaN	NaN	NaN
118	NaN	NaN	NaN	NaN	NaN	NaN	NaN	NaN
119	NaN	NaN	NaN	NaN	NaN	NaN	NaN	NaN

Figure 12.6 – The empty performance_df DataFrame before being filled in

Because the dataset has been collected unwisely, we cannot use simple functions such as `.join()` for data integration here. Instead, we need to use a loop to go through the many records of `unknown_df` and `athlete_df` and fill out `performance_df` row by row and, at times, cell by cell.

The following pieces of code will use both `athlete_df` and `unknown_df` to fill `performance_df`. Let's get started:

1. First, we need to perform some level I data cleaning for `athlete_df` so that accessing this DataFrame within the loop becomes easier. The following code takes care of these cleaning steps for `athlete_df`:

    ```
    athlete_df.set_index('Participant ID',inplace=True)
    athlete_df.columns = ['Sex', 'Age', 'Weight',
    'Experience', 'Belt']
    ```

    Study the state of `athlete_df` after running the preceding code and make sure that you understand what each line of code does before reading on.

2. Now that `athlete_df` is cleaner, we can create and run the loop that will fill up `performance_df`. As shown in the following screenshot, the loop goes through all of the columns in `unknown_df`. Except for the first column in `unknown_df`, each column contains information for one of the rows in `performance_df`. So, in each iteration of looping through the columns of `unknown_df`, one of the rows of `performance_df` will be filled. To fill up each row in `performance_df`, the data must come from both `athlete_df` and `unknown_df`. We will use the structures we know about from `athlete_df` and `unknown_df`:

```
In [23]:  ▶  techniques = ['R','B','C','P']
             index = 0
             for col in unknown_df.columns:
                 if(col[0] in techniques):
                     performance_df.loc[index,'Technique_id'] = col[0]
                     performance_df.loc[index,'Trial_number'] = unknown_df[col][1]

                     P_id = unknown_df[col][0]
                     performance_df.loc[index,'Participant_id'] = P_id
                     performance_df.loc[index,'Gender'] = athlete_df.loc[P_id].Sex
                     performance_df.loc[index,'Age'] = athlete_df.loc[P_id].Age
                     performance_df.loc[index,'Weight'] = athlete_df.loc[P_id].Weight
                     performance_df.loc[
                         index,'Experience'] = athlete_df.loc[P_id].Experience
                     BM = unknown_df[col][2:].isna()
                     performance_df.loc[
                         index,'Average_read'] = unknown_df[
                         col][2:][~BM].astype(int).mean()
                     index +=1
```

Figure 12.7 – The code that fills performance_df

Attention!

In this chapter, there are going to be a few instances of very large code, such as that shown in the preceding screenshot. Because of the size of this code, we had to include a screenshot instead of a copiable code block. To copy this code, please see the `chapter12` folder in this book's GitHub repository.

---

3. After successfully running the code in the preceding screenshot, `performance_df` will be filled up. Print `performance_df` to check its status before reading on.

4. Now that data integration has been performed, we can bring our attention to the data analytic goals. The following code creates a box plot of `Average_read` based on `Gender`, `Age`, `Weight`, and `Experience`:

```
select_attributes = ['Gender', 'Age', 'Experience',
'Weight']
```

Example 2 (challenges 2 and 3)   353

```
for i,att in enumerate(select_attributes):
    plt.subplot(2,2,i+1)
    sns.boxplot(data = performance_df,
                y='Average_read', x=att)
plt.tight_layout()
plt.show()
```

After running the preceding code, the following visualization will be created:

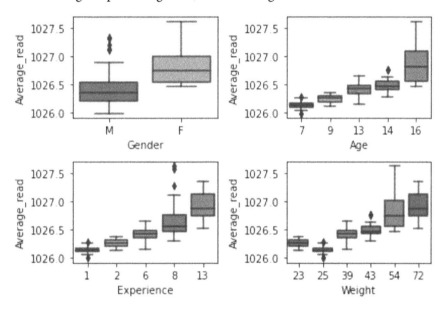

Figure 12.8 – A box plot of Average_read based on Gender, Age, Experience, and Weight

In the preceding diagram, we can see meaningful relationships between **Average_read** and **Gender**, **Age**, **Experience**, and **Weight**. In a nutshell, these attributes can change the impact of the techniques that are performed by the athletes. For example, we can see that as the experience of an athlete increases, the impact of the techniques that are performed by the athlete increases.

We can also see a surprising trend: the impact of the techniques that are performed by female athletes is significantly higher than the impact of male athletes. After seeing this surprising trend, let's look back at `athlete_df`. We will realize that there is only one female athlete in the data, so we cannot count on this visualized trend.

Before we move on to the next data integration example, let's have some fun and create visualizations with higher dimensions. The following code creates multiple box plots that include the `Average_read`, `Experience`, and `Technique_id` dimensions:

```
sns.boxplot(data = performance_df, y= 'Average_read', x=
'Experience', hue='Technique_id')
```

The following diagram will be created after running the preceding code:

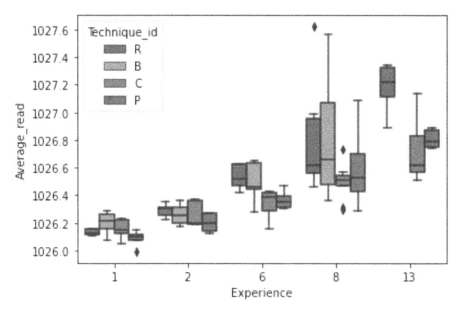

Figure 12.9 – A three-dimensional box plot of Average_read, Experience, and Technique_id

Before reading on, look at the preceding diagram and see if you can detect more relationships and patterns.

Now, let's bring our attention to the next example. Buckle up – the next example is going to be a complex one with many different aspects.

Example 3 (challenges 1, 3, 5, and 6)   355

Example 3 (challenges 1, 3, 5, and 6)

In this example, we would like to figure out what makes a song rise to the top 10 songs on Billboard (`https://www.billboard.com/charts/hot-100`) and stay there for at least 5 weeks. Billboard magazine publishes a weekly chart that ranks popular songs based on sales, radio play, and online streaming in the United States. We will integrate three CSV files – `billboardHot100_1999-2019.csv`, `songAttributes_1999-2019.csv`, and `artistDf.csv` from `https://www.kaggle.com/danield2255/data-on-songs-from-billboard-19992019` to do this.

This is going to be a long example with many pieces that come together. How you organize your thoughts and work in such data integration challenges is very important. So, before reading on, spend some time getting to know these three data sources and form a plan. This will be a very valuable practice.

Now that you've had a chance to think about how you would go about this, let's do this together. These datasets seem to have been collected from different sources, so there may be duplicate data objects among any or all of the three data files. After reading the files into `billboard_df`, `songAttributes_df`, and `artist_df`, respectively, we will check if there are duplicate data objects in them. This is dealing with *Challenge 5 – duplicate data objects*.

Checking for duplicate data objects

We will have to do this for every file. We will start with `billboard_df` before doing the same for `songAttributes_df` and `artist_df`.

Checking for duplicates in billboard_df

The following code reads the `billboardHot100_1999-2019.csv` file into `Billboard_df` and then creates a pandas series called `wsr`. The name `wsr` is short for **Working SeRies**. As I've mentioned previously, I tend to create a `wdf` (Working DataFrame) or `wsr` when I need a temporary DataFrame or series to do some analysis. In this case, `wsr` is used to create a new column that is a combination of the `Artists`, `Name`, and `Week` columns, so we can use it to check if the data objects are unique.

The reason for this multi-column checking is obvious, right? There might be different unique songs with the same name from different artists; every artist may have more than one song; or, the same song may have a different weekly report. So, to check for the uniqueness of the data objects across `billboard_df`, we need this column:

```
billboard_df = pd.read_csv('billboardHot100_1999-2019.csv')
wsr = billboard_df.apply(lambda r: '{}-{}-{}'.format(r.
Artists,r.Name,r.Week),axis=1)
wsr.value_counts()
```

After running the preceding code, the output shows that all the data objects appear once except for the song `Outta Control` by `50 Cent` in week `2005-09-14`. Running `billboard_df.query("Artists == '50 Cent' and Name=='Outta Control' and Week== '2005-09-14'")` will filter out these two data objects. The following screenshot displays the outcome of running this code:

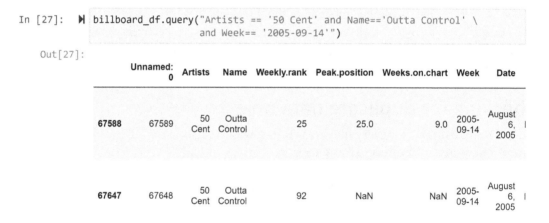

Figure 12.10 – Filtering the duplicates in bilboard_df

Here, we can see that the two rows are almost identical and that there is no need to have both of them. We can use the `.drop()` function to delete one of these two rows. This is shown in the following line of code:

```
billboard_df.drop(index = 67647,inplace=True)
```

After running the preceding line of code successfully, it seems that nothing has happened. This is due to `inplace=True`, which makes Python update the DataFrame in place instead of outputting a new DataFrame.

Example 3 (challenges 1, 3, 5, and 6)   357

Now that we are certain about the uniqueness of each row in `bilboard_df`, let's move on and do the same thing for `songAttributes_df`.

Checking for duplicates in songAttributes_df

We will use a very similar code and approach to see if there are any duplicates in `songAttributes_df`. The following code has been altered for the new DataFrame.

First, the code reads the `songAttributes_1999-2019.csv` file into `songAttributes_df`, then creates the new column and checks for the duplicates using `.value_counts()`, which is a function of every pandas Series:

```
songAttribute_df = pd.read_csv('songAttributes_1999-2019.csv')
wsr = songAttribute_df.apply(lambda r: '{}---{}'.format(r.
Artist,r.Name),axis=1)
wsr.value_counts()
```

After running the preceding code, we will see that many songs have duplicate rows in `songAttributes_df`.

We need to find out the causes of these duplicates. We can filter out the duplicates of a few songs and study them. For instance, from the top, we can run the following lines of codes separately to study their output:

- `songAttribute_df.query("Artist == 'Jose Feliciano' and Name == 'Light My Fire'")`

- `songAttribute_df.query("Artist == 'Dave Matthews Band' and Name == 'Ants Marching - Live'")`

After studying the output of these codes, we will realize that there are two possible reasons for the existence of duplicates:

- First, there might be different versions of the same song.

- Second, the data collection process may have been done from different resources.

Our study also shows that the attributes' value of these duplicates, while not identical, are very similar.

To be able to do this analysis, we need to have only one row for each song. Therefore, we need to either remove all but one row for the songs with duplicates or aggregate them. Either might be the right course of action, depending on the circumstances. Here, we will drop all the duplicates except for the first one. The following code loops through the songs with duplicate data objects in `songAttributes_df` and uses `.drop()` to delete all the duplicate data objects, except for the first one. First, the code creates `doFrequencies` (do is short for data object), which is a pandas series that shows the frequencies of each song in `songAttributes_df`, and loops through the elements of `doFrequencies` whose frequency is higher than 1:

```
songAttribute_df = pd.read_csv('songAttributes_1999-2019.csv')
wsr = songAttribute_df.apply(lambda r: '{}---{}'.format(r.
Name,r.Artist),axis=1)
doFrequencies = wsr.value_counts()
BM = doFrequencies>1
for i,v in doFrequencies[BM].iteritems():
    [name,artist] = i.split('---')
    BM = ((songAttribute_df.Name == name) & (songAttribute_
df.Artist == artist))
    wdf = songAttribute_df[BM]


    dropping_index = wdf.index[1:]
    songAttribute_df.drop(index = dropping_index, inplace=True)
```

If you try running the preceding code, you will see that it will take a long time. It took around 30 minutes on my computer. In these situations, it is nice to add some elements to the code that give users some idea of how much the code has run and how much more time will be needed. The following code is the same as the preceding one, but some more elements have been added to create a mechanism for reporting the progress of the runtime. I would suggest running the following code instead. But before doing so, compare the two options and study how the reporting mechanism is added. Do not forget that you will need to import the `time` module before you can run the following code. The `time` module is an excellent module that allows us to work with time and time differences:

Example 3 (challenges 1, 3, 5, and 6)   359

```
In [34]:  ▶  songAttribute_df = pd.read_csv('songAttributes_1999-2019.csv')
             wsr = songAttribute_df.apply(lambda r: '{}---{}'
                                          .format(r.Name,r.Artist),axis=1)
             doFrequencies = wsr.value_counts()

             BM = doFrequencies>1
             n_totalSongs = sum(BM)
             print('Total processings: ' + str(n_totalSongs))

             t = time.time()
             i_progress = 0
             for i,v in doFrequencies[BM].iteritems():
                 [name,artist] = i.split('---')
                 BM = ((songAttribute_df.Name == name) &
                       (songAttribute_df.Artist == artist))

                 wdf = songAttribute_df[BM]
                 dropping_index = wdf.index[1:]
                 songAttribute_df.drop(index = dropping_index, inplace=True)

                 i_progress +=1
                 if(i_progress%500==0):
                     print('Processed: ' + str(i_progress))
                     process_time = time.time() - t
                     print('Elapsed: ' + str(round(process_time,1)) + ' s')
                     estimate_finish = round((n_totalSongs-i_progress) *
                                             (process_time/500)/60,1)

                     print('To finish: ' + str(estimate_finish)+ 'mins')
                     t = time.time()
                     print('------------------------------------')
```

Figure 12.11 – Dropping the duplicates that were added with code to report progress

Once you've successfully run the preceding code, which will take a while, songAttributes_df will not suffer from duplicate data object problems.

Next, we will check if artist_df contains duplicates and address them if it does.

Checking for duplicates in artist_df

Checking the uniqueness of the data objects in artisit_df is easier than it was for the two DataFrames we looked at previously. The reason for this is that there is only one identifying column in artist_df. There were two and three identifying columns for songAttribute_df and billboard_df.

The following code reads `artistDf.csv` into `artisit_df` and uses the
`.value_counts()` function to check if all the rows in `artisit_df` are unique:

```
artist_df = pd.read_csv('artistDf.csv')
artist_df.Artist.value_counts()
```

After running the preceding code and studying its results, you will see that two rows
represent the artist *Reba McEntire*. Running `artist_df.query("Artist == 'Reba
McEntire'")` will filter out these two rows. The following screenshot displays the
outcome of running this code:

In [37]:   ▶ artist_df.query("Artist == 'Reba McEntire'")

Out[37]:

	X	Artist	Followers	Genres	NumAlbums	YearFirstAlbum	Gender	Gr
398	398	Reba McEntire	974392	contemporary country,country,country dawn	40	1977	F	
716	716	Reba McEntire	974392	contemporary country,country,country dawn	40	1977	F	

Figure 12.12 – Filtering the duplicates in artist_df

Here, we can see that the two rows are the same and that there is no need to have both
of them. The following line of code uses the `.drop()` function to delete one of these
two rows:

```
artist_df.drop(index = 716, inplace=True)
```

After running the preceding line of code successfully, it seems that nothing has happened.
This is due to `inplace=True`, which makes Python update the DataFrame in place
instead of outputting a new DataFrame.

Well done! Now, we know that all of our DataFrames only contain unique data objects. We
can use this knowledge to tackle the challenging task of data integration.

We are better off if we start with the end in sight. In the next section, we will envision
and create the structure of the DataFrame we would like to have at the end of the data
integration process.

Example 3 (challenges 1, 3, 5, and 6)   361

Designing the structure for the result of data integration

As there are more than two data sources involved, it is paramount that we have a vision in sight for the result of our data integration. The best way to do this is to envision and create a dataset whose definition of data objects and its attribute have the potential to answer our analytic questions and, at the same time, can be filled by the data sources that we have.

The following screenshot shows the code that can create a dataset that contains the listed characteristics. The definition of the data objects is songs, while the attributes can be filled in using one of three DataFrames. Once `songIntegrate_df` has been filled, it can help us answer the question of what makes a song go all the way up to the top 10 on Billboard and stay there for at least 5 weeks:

```
In [39]:    songIntegrate_df = pd.DataFrame(
                columns = ['Name', 'Artists', 'Top_song', 'First_date_on_Billboard',
                           'Acousticness', 'Danceability', 'Duration', 'Energy',
                           'Explicit', 'Instrumentalness', 'Liveness', 'Loudness',
                           'Mode', 'Speechiness', 'Tempo', 'TimeSignature', 'Valence',
                           'Artists_n_followers', 'n_male_artists', 'n_female_artists',
                           'n_bands', 'artist_average_years_after_first_album',
                           'artist_average_number_albums'])
            songIntegrate_df

Out[39]:
```

Name	Artists	Top_song	First_date_on_Billboard	Acousticness	Danceability	Duration	Ene

0 rows × 23 columns

Figure 12.13 – Designing and creating the result of data integration for songIntegrate_df

Most of the envisioned attributes in `songIntegrate_df` are intuitive. Let's go over the ones that might not be as obvious:

- `Top_song`: A binary attribute that describes if the song has been in the top 10 songs of Billboard for at least 5 weeks.

- `First_date_on_Billboard`: The first date that the song was on Billboard.

- `Acousticness`, `Danceability`, `Duration`, `Energy`, `Explicit`, `Instrumentalness`, `Liveness`, `Loudness`, `Mode`, `Speechiness`, `Tempo`, `TimeSignature`, and `Valence` are the artistic properties of songs. These attributes will be integrated into `songIntegrate_df` from `songAttribute_df`.

- `Artists_n_followers`: The artist's or artists' number of followers on social media. If there is more than one artist, the summation of their number of followers will be used.

- `n_male_artists` and `n_female_artists` are the attributes that show the gender of the artists. If one female artist has produced the song, their values will be 0 and 1, respectively. If two male artists have produced the song, their values will be 2 and 0, respectively.

- `n_bands`: The number of bands that have been involved in producing the song.

- `artist_average_years_after_first_album` tries to capture the experience of the artists in the business. If one artist has created the song, then a single value will be used, and when more than one artist is involved, an average value is used. These values will be calculated based on `First_date_on_Billboard`.

- `artist_average_number_albums` also attempts to capture the experience of the artists in the business. Similar to the previous attribute, if one artist has created the song, then a single value will be used, while when more than one artist is involved, an average value will be used.

The first four attributes will be filled using `billboard_df`, the last six attributes will be filled using `artist_df`, and the rest will be filled using `songAttribute_df`.

Note that the `First_date_on_Billboard` attribute will be created temporarily. It will be filled from `billboard_df` so that when we get around to filling from `artist_df`, we can use `First_date_on_Billboard` to calculate `artist_average_years_after_first_album`.

Before we start filling up `songIntegrate_df` from the three sources, let's go over the possibility of having to remove some songs from `songIntegrate_df`. This might become inevitable because the information we may need for every song on file may not exist in the other resource. Therefore, the rest of the subsections in this example will be as follows:

- *Filling* `songIntegrate_df` *from* `billboard_df`
- *Filling* `songIntegrate_df` *from* `songAttribute_df`
- *Removing data objects with incomplete data*
- *Filling* `songIntegrate_df` *from* `artist_df`
- *Checking the status of* `songIntegrate_df`
- *Performing the analysis*

It seems that we've got a lot of ground to cover, so let's get to it. We will start by using `billboard_df` to fill `songIntegrate_df`.

Example 3 (challenges 1, 3, 5, and 6)   363

Filling songIntegrate_df from billboard_df

In this part of filling `songIntegrate_df`, we will be filling the first four attributes: `Name`, `Artists`, `Top_song`, and `First_date_on_Billboard`. Filling the first two attributes is simpler; the latter two need some of the rows in `billboard_df` to be calculated and aggregated.

The challenge of filling data from `billboard_df` into `songIntegrate_df` is two-fold. First, the definitions of the data objects in the two DataFrames are different. We have designed the definition of the data objects in `songIntegrate_df` to be songs, while the definition of the data objects in `billboard_df` is the weekly reports of songs' billboard standings. Second, as `billboard_df` has a more complex definition of data objects, it will also need more identifying attributes to distinguish between unique data objects. For `billboard_df`, the three identifying attributes are `Name`, `Artists`, and `Week`, but for `songIntegrate_df`, we only have `Name` and `Artists`.

The `songIntegrate_df` DataFrame is empty and contains no data objects. Since the definition of data objects we have considered for this DataFrame is songs, it is best to allocate a new row in `songIntegrate_df` for all the unique songs in `billboard_df`.

The following code loops through all the unique songs in `billboard_df` using nested loops to fill `songIntegrate_df`. The first loop goes over all the unique song names, so each iteration will be processing one unique song name. As there might be different songs with the same song name, the code does the following within the first loop:

1. First, it will filter all the rows with the song name of the iteration.

2. Second, it will figure out all `Artists` who have had a song with the song name of the iteration.

3. Third, it will go over all `Artists` we recognized in the second step and as per each iteration of this second loop, we will add a row to `songIntegrate_df`.

To add a row to `songIntegrate_df`, the following code has used the `.append()` function. This function either takes a pandas Series or a Dictionary to add it to a DataFrame. Here, we are using a dictionary; this dictionary will have four keys, which are the four attributes – `Name`, `Artists`, `Top_song`, `First_date_on_Billboard` – of `songIntegrate_df` that we intend to fill from `billboard_df`. Filling `Name` and `Artists` is easy as all we need to do is insert the values from `billboard_df`. However, we need to make some calculations to figure out the values of `Top_song` and `First_date_on_Billboard`.

Study the following code and try to understand the logic behind the parts of the code that try to calculate these two attributes. For `Top_song`, try to see if you can connect the logic to what we are trying to do. Go back to the very first paragraph in this example. For `First_date_on_Billboard`, the code has assumed something about `billboard_df`. See if you can detect what that assumption is and then investigate if that assumption is reliable.

Now, it is time for you to give the code a try. Just a heads-up before you hit run: it might take a while to finish. It will not be as lengthy as the preceding code to run, but it won't be instantaneous either:

```
SongNames = billboard_df.Name.unique()
for i, song in enumerate(SongNames):
    BM = billboard_df.Name == song
    wdf = billboard_df[BM]
    Artists = wdf.Artists.unique()
    for artist in Artists:
        BM = wdf.Artists == artist
        wdf2 = wdf[BM]
        topsong = False
        BM = wdf2['Weekly.rank'] <=10
        if(len(wdf2[BM])>=5):
            topsong = True
        first_date_on_billboard = wdf2.Week.iloc[-1]
        dic_append = {'Name':song,'Artists':artist, 'Top_
        song':topsong, 'First_date_on_Billboard': first_date_
        on_billboard}

        songIntegrate_df = songIntegrate_df.append(dic_append,
        ignore_index=True)
```

After successfully running the preceding code, print `songIntegrate_df` to study the state of the DataFrame.

Example 3 (challenges 1, 3, 5, and 6)   365

The challenge we just faced and addressed here can be categorized as *Challenge 3 – index mismatched formatting*. This particular challenge is more difficult as not only do we have different index formatting but also we have different definitions of data objects. To be able to perform data integration, we had to refrain from declaring the identifying attributes as indexes. Why? Because that would not help our data integration goal. However, having to do that also forced us to take things into our hands and use loops instead of simpler functions such as `.join()`, as we saw in *Example 1 (challenges 3 and 4)* and *Example 2 (challenges 2 and 3)*.

Next, we will fill in some of the remaining attributes of `songIntegrate_df` from `songAttribute_df`. Doing this will challenge us somewhat differently; we will have to deal with *Challenge 1 – entity identification*.

Filling songIntegrate_df from songAttribute_df

The challenge we have to reckon with in this part of data integration is *entity identification*. While the definitions of the data objects for both `songIntegrate_df` and `songAttribute_df` are the same – that is, songs – the way the unique data objects are distinguished in the two DataFrames is different. The crux of the difference goes back to the `songIntegrate_df.Artists` and `songAttribute_df.Artist` attributes; pay attention to the plural of `Artists` and the singular of `Artist`. You will see that the songs that have more than one artist are recorded differently in these two DataFrames. However, in `songIntegrate_df`, all of the artists of a song are included in the `songIntegrate_df.Artists` attribute, separated by commas (`,`); in `songAttribute_df`, only the main artist is recorded in `songAttribute_df.Artist` and if other artists are involved in a song, they are added to `songAttribute_df.Name`. This makes identifying the same songs from the two DataFrames very difficult. So, we need to have a plan before we approach data integration here.

The following table shows the five different situations where the same songs entered our two sources. Let's answer two questions about these five situations.

First, how did we come up with these five situations? That is an excellent question. When dealing with the *entity identification challenge*, you will need to study the sources of the data and figure out how to work with the identifying attributes in the sources. Then, you can use a computer to connect the rows that are for the same entity but not coded the same way. So, the answer to this question is that we just studied the two sources enough to realize that these five situations exist.

Second, what do we do with these situations? Answering this question is simple. We will use them to draft some code that will connect the identifiable songs from both sources to connect and integrate the datasets:

Situations	Description	Example

Situation 1	- Songs with only one artist
	- Songs with unique song names
		`songIntegrate_df`
		
		Artists **Name**
		16 Taylor Swift You Need To Calm Down
		
		`songAttribute_df`
		
		Artist **Name**
		154047 Taylor Swift You Need To Calm Down

Situation 2	- Songs with only one artist
	- Songs with non-unique song names
	To see the difference between situations 1 and 2, run and compare the following code:
	- `songAttribute_df.query("Name == 'Sucker'")`
	- `songAttribute_df.query("Name == 'You Need To Calm Down'")`
		`songIntegrate_df`
		
		Artists **Name**
		9 Jonas Brothers Sucker
		
		`songAttribute_df`
		
		Artist **Name**
		21644 New Found Glory Sucker
		154557 Jonas Brothers Sucker

Situation 3	- Songs with more than one artist
	- Both artists are recognized in both sources but in different ways
		`songIntegrate_df`
		
		Artists **Name**
		6 Ed Sheeran, Justin Bieber I Don't Care
		
		`songAttribute_df`
		
		Artist **Name**
		154921 Ed Sheeran I Don't Care (with Justin Bieber)

Situation 4	- Songs with more than one artist but only `songAttribute_df` recognizes the second artist	`songIntegrate_df`
		
		Artists **Name**
		12 Chris Brown No Guidance
		
		`songAttribute_df`
		
		Artist **Name**
		154214 Chris Brown No Guidance (feat. Drake)

Situation 5	Songs with more than one artist but only `songIntegrate_df` recognizes the second artist	`songIntegrate_df`
		
		Artists **Name**
		137 DJ Sammy, Yanou Heaven
		
		`songAttribute_df`
		
		Artist **Name**
		22487 DJ Sammy Heaven

Figure 12.14 – Five situations in the integration of songIntegrate_df with songAttribute_df due to the entity identification challenge

The following code, which is rather long, uses the five extracted situations from the preceding diagram and all the other coding capabilities we've picked up in this book to perform the integration task. The code loops through the rows of `songIntegrate_df` and searches for any rows in `songAttribute_df` that have listed the song. The code employs the five situations we've extracted to create the preceding diagram as a guideline to search for `songAttribute_df`.

Before you look at the following code, allow me to bring your attention to a quick matter. Since the code is lengthy, it's been commented to help you decipher it. Python line comments can be created using #, so, for example, when you see # `Situation 1`, that means what's coming has been created by our understanding of `situation 1`.

Example 3 (challenges 1, 3, 5, and 6)   367

Now, spend some time using the preceding diagram and the code in the following screenshot to understand how the connection between `songIntegrate_df` and `songAttribute_df` has been made:

```
In [42]:  ▶  adding_columns = ['Acousticness','Danceability','Duration','Energy','Explicit','Instrumentalness',
                               'Liveness','Loudness','Mode','Speechiness','Tempo','TimeSignature', 'Valence']
             template = 'Index= {} - The song {} by {} was integrated using sitution {}.'
             for i, row in songIntegrate_df.iterrows():
                 filled = False
                 Artists = row.Artists.split(',')
                 Artists = list(map(str.strip,Artists))
                 # Situation 1
                 BM = songAttribute_df.Name == row.Name
                 if(sum(BM) == 1):
                     for col in adding_columns:
                         songIntegrate_df.loc[i,col]= songAttribute_df[BM][col].values[0]
                     filled = True
                     print(template.format(i,row.Name,row.Artists,1))
                 # Situation 2
                 elif(sum(BM) > 1):
                     wdf = songAttribute_df[BM]
                     if(len(Artists)==1):
                         BM2 = wdf.Artist.str.contains(Artists[0])
                         if(sum(BM2)==1):
                             for col in adding_columns:
                                 songIntegrate_df.loc[i,col]= wdf[BM2][col].values[0]
                             filled = True
                             print(template.format(i,row.Name,row.Artists,2))
                 # Situation 3
                 if((not filled) and len(Artists)>1):
                     BM2= (songAttribute_df.Name.str.contains(row.Name)&songAttribute_df.Artist.isin(Artists))
                     if(sum(BM2)==1):
                         for col in adding_columns:
                             songIntegrate_df.loc[i,col]= songAttribute_df[BM2][col].values[0]
                         filled = True
                         print(template.format(i,row.Name,row.Artists,3))
                 if(not filled):
                     # Situation 4
                     BM2 = songAttribute_df.Name.str.contains(row.Name)
                     if(sum(BM2)==1):
                         for artist in Artists:
                             if(artist == songAttribute_df[BM2].Artist.iloc[0]):
                                 for col in adding_columns:
                                     songIntegrate_df.loc[i,col]= songAttribute_df[BM2][col].values[0]
                                 filled = True
                                 print(template.format(i,row.Name,row.Artists,4))
                     # Situation 5
                     if(sum(BM2)>1):
                         wdf2 = songAttribute_df[BM2]
                         BM3 = wdf2.Artist.isin(Artists)
                         if(sum(BM3)>0):
                             wdf3 = wdf2[BM3]
                             for i3, row3 in wdf3.iterrows():
                                 if(row3.Name == row.Name):
                                     for col in adding_columns:
                                         songIntegrate_df.loc[i,col]= row3[col]
                                     filled = True
                                     print(template.format(i,row.Name,row.Artists,5))
```

Figure 12.15 – Creating the connection between songIntegrate_df and songAttribute_df

After successfully running the preceding code, which might take a while, spend some time studying the report it provided. If you have paid attention, then you'll know that the code is printed out every time a connection between songs is found. This also happens if the connection was possible. Study the printout to see the frequencies of the situations. Answer the following questions:

- Which situation was the most frequent?

- Which situation was the least frequent?

- Were all of the rows in `songIntegrate_df` filled in with the values found in `songAttribute_df`?

The answer to the last question is no – running `songIntegrate_df.info()` will only show you that 4,045 out of 7,213 rows were filled from `songAttribute_df`. A critical question to answer regarding this data not being filled completely is to see if there is meaningful discrimination between the top songs and not the top song. If there is any meaningful discrimination, then the values listed in `songAttribute_df` become much less valuable. This is because our goal is to study the impact that the song attributes have on the song becoming a top song. So, let's study this before moving on to the next filling.

The following screenshot shows the contingency table for the two binary variables, `songIntegrate_df.Top_song`, and the missing values. It also shows the p-value of the chi-square test of association:

```
In [45]:   ▶  B_MV = songIntegrate_df.Acousticness.isna()
              B_MV.rename('Missing Values',inplace=True)
              contigency_table = pd.crosstab(songIntegrate_df.Top_song,B_MV)
              contigency_table
```

Out[45]:

Missing Values	False	True
Top_song		
False	3618	2874
True	427	294

```
In [46]:   ▶  from scipy.stats import chi2_contingency
              p_value = chi2_contingency(contigency_table)[1]
              p_value
```

Out[46]:   0.07952275342130063

Figure 12.16 – The code and their output for studying if missing values in songIntegrate_df after integrating with songAttribute_df are meaningfully connected to songIntegrate_df.Top_song

Example 3 (challenges 1, 3, 5, and 6)   369

After studying the preceding screenshot, we can conclude that there is not enough evidence for us to reject the hypothesis that the missing values don't have a relationship with the songs being a top song or not.

This makes our job easier as we won't need to do anything but remove the rows that don't contain values before we start using `artist_df` to fill `songIntegrate_df`. The following code uses the `.drop()` function to delete the rows in `songIntegrate_df` that `songAttribute_df` failed to fill. Note that the `B_MV` variable comes from the code in the preceding screenshot:

```
dropping_index = songIntegrate_df[B_MV].index
songIntegrate_df.drop(index = dropping_index, inplace=True)
```

Successfully running the preceding code and before moving on to the next step, which is using `artist_df` to fill the rest of `songIntegrate_df`, run `songIntegrate_df.info()` to evaluate the state of the DataFrame and ensure that the drops went as planned.

Filling songIntegrate_df from artist_df

The last six attributes of `songIntegrate_df`, which are `Artists_n_followers`, `n_male_artsits`, `n_female_artsits`, `n_bands`, `artist_average_years_after_first_album`, and `artist_average_number_albums`, will be filled from `artist_df`. The entity identification challenge that we face here is much simpler than what we did when integrating `songIntegrate_df` and `songAttribute_df`. The definitions of the data objects in `artist_df` are artists, and that is only one part of the definition of the data objects in `songIntegrate_df`. All we need to do is find the unique artist or artists of each song of `songIntegrate_df` in `artist_df` and then fill in `songIntegrate_df`.

All of the attributes we need to fill in here need information from `artist_df`, but there will be no direct filling. All of the aforementioned attributes will need to be calculated using the information from `artist_df`.

Before data integration is possible, we will need to perform one pre-processing task on `artist_df`. We need to make `artist_df` searchable by the name of the artist; that is, we must set the index of `artist_df` as `Artist`. The following line of code makes sure that happens. The following code also drops the `X` column, which will not serve any purpose at this point:

```
artist_df = artist_df.set_index('Artist').drop(columns=['X'])
```

Now, before moving on to the data integration part, give the searchable `artist_df` a chance to show you how easy it can gather the information of each artist. For example, try `artist_df.loc['Drake']` or any other artist you may know of.

The code in the following screenshot loops through all the rows of `songIntegrate_df` to find the needed information about the songs' artists and fill up the last six attributes of `songIntegrate_df`. In each iteration, the code separates the artists of the songs in `songIntegrate_df` and checks if `artists_df` contains the information of all of the song's artists. If not, the code terminates as there is not enough information in `artist_df` to fill out the six attributes. If this information exists, the code assigns zero to all six new attributes and then, within some conditional and logical calculations, updates the zero values.

Before you get your teeth into this rather large piece of code, a few words of caution. First, the lines of code are rather long, so they may have been cut into more than one line. There are two different ways to cut a line of code into more lines. The better method is called **implicit line continuation**; whenever the line breaks after a parenthesis, (, a curly brace, {, or square bracket, [, Python assumes there is more to come and automatically goes to the next line while looking for it. The other method – the one we try to avoid if we can – is known as explicit line continuation and is where Python will not go looking for more in the next line unless we explicitly request this by using a backslash, \, at the end of the line.

The second word of caution is that the code uses what is called **augmented arithmetic assignment** to save space when writing code. These types of assignments are used to avoid writing the same variable twice when the calculation of the new value of the variable involves the old value of the variable. For instance, you can write $x+=1$ instead of $x = x +1$, or you can write $y/=5$ instead of $y = y/5$. Augmented arithmetic assignment has been used in multiple places throughout the following code:

Example 3 (challenges 1, 3, 5, and 6)   371

```
In [52]:  ▶  for i,row in songIntegrate_df.iterrows():
                Artists = row.Artists.split(',')
                Artists = list(map(str.strip,Artists))
                ArtistsIn_artist_df = True
                for artist in Artists:
                    if(artist not in artist_df.index.values):
                        ArtistsIn_artist_df= False
                        break
                if(not ArtistsIn_artist_df):
                    continue

                songIntegrate_df.loc[i,'Artists_n_followers'] = 0
                songIntegrate_df.loc[i,'n_male_artists'] = 0
                songIntegrate_df.loc[i,'n_female_artists'] = 0
                songIntegrate_df.loc[i, 'artist_average_years_after_first_album'] = 0
                songIntegrate_df.loc[i, 'artist_average_number_albums'] = 0
                songIntegrate_df.loc[i,'n_bands'] = 0

                for artist in Artists:
                    songIntegrate_df.loc[i,'Artists_n_followers'] += artist_df.loc[artist].Followers
                    if(artist_df.loc[artist]['Group.Solo']=='Solo'):
                        if(artist_df.loc[artist].Gender == 'M'):
                            songIntegrate_df.loc[i,'n_male_artists'] += 1
                        if(artist_df.loc[artist].Gender == 'F'):
                            songIntegrate_df.loc[i,'n_female_artists'] += 1

                    if(artist_df.loc[artist]['Group.Solo']=='Group'):
                        if(artist_df.loc[artist].Gender == 'M'):
                            songIntegrate_df.loc[i,'n_male_artists'] += 2
                        if(artist_df.loc[artist].Gender == 'F'):
                            songIntegrate_df.loc[i,'n_female_artists'] += 2
                        songIntegrate_df.loc[i,'n_bands'] += 1
                    First_date_on_Billboard = int(row.First_date_on_Billboard[:4])
                    songIntegrate_df.loc[i, 'artist_average_years_after_first_album'] += \
                        (First_date_on_Billboard - int(artist_df.loc[artist].YearFirstAlbum))

                    songIntegrate_df.loc[i,
                        'artist_average_number_albums'] += int(artist_df.loc[artist].NumAlbums)

                songIntegrate_df.loc[i,'artist_average_years_after_first_album'] /= len(Artists)
                songIntegrate_df.loc[i, 'artist_average_number_albums'] /= len(Artists)
```

Figure 12.17 – Filling up the last six attributes of songIntegrate_df

You may have noticed that the code adds 2 to n_male_artists when the song's artist is a group and the gender is listed as male, while it adds 2 to n_female_artists when the song's artist is a group and the gender is listed as female. This includes the assumption that all the groups have only two artists. As we don't have other sources so that we can be more accurate about these situations, this is a reasonable assumption that lets us continue while avoiding the infliction of too much bias in the data. However, this assumption must be communicated if the results are going to be presented to any interested decision-maker.

After successfully running the preceding code, run `songIntegrate_df.info()` to investigate how many of the rows in `songIntegrate_df` were completed using the information from `artist_df`. You will see that 3,672 out of 4,045 songs were completed. While this is the major portion of `songIntegrate_df`, we still need to make sure that there are no missing values due to reasons connected to the songs being top songs or not. So, we will do a similar analysis to what we did for *Figure 12.16*. The following screenshot shows the result of the same analysis with the updated `songIntegrate_df`:

```
In [54]:  ▶  B_MV = songIntegrate_df.Artists_n_followers.isna()
             B_MV.rename('Missing Values',inplace=True)
             contigency_table = pd.crosstab(songIntegrate_df.Top_song,B_MV)
             contigency_table
```

Out[54]:

Missing Values	False	True
Top_song		
False	3280	338
True	392	35

```
In [55]:  ▶  from scipy.stats import chi2_contingency
             p_value = chi2_contingency(contigency_table)[1]
             p_value
```

Out[55]: 0.4931640410927335

Figure 12.18 – The code and their output for studying if missing values in songIntegrate_df after integrating with artist_df are meaningfully connected to songIntegrate_df.Top_song

After studying the preceding screenshot, we can see that there is no meaningful pattern that points to the possible connection between a song being a top song and its tendency to have missing values at this juncture. So, we can comfortably remove the rows with missing values and proceed. The following line of code does the prescribed removal:

```
droping_indices = songIntegrate_df[B_MV].index.values
songIntegrate_df.drop(index = droping_indices, inplace=True)
```

The preceding code uses the `.drop()` function to delete the rows in `songIntegrate_df` that `artist_df` failed to fill. Note that the `B_MV` variable comes from the code in the preceding screenshot.

Example 3 (challenges 1, 3, 5, and 6)   373

Congratulations – you have integrated these three data sources! This was due to your excellent understanding of data structures and your capability to see the definitions of data objects in each of these sources. Furthermore, you were able to envision a dataset that could house the information from all the sources and, at the same time, be useful for your analytic goals.

Before we proceed to the analysis, we need to tackle another challenge. Whenever we bring data together from different sources, we may have inadvertently created a case that we called data redundancy earlier (*Challenge 6 – data redundancy*). As we mentioned previously, data redundancy is where you repeat the same attribute but where you repeat the same information.

Checking for data redundancy

As we mentioned previously, this part deals with *Challenge 6 – data redundancy*. Even though we've never dealt with this challenge before in this book, we've seen many examples of investigating the relationships between attributes. If there are attributes in `songIntegrate_df` that have a strong relationship with each other, that can be our red flag for data redundancy. It's as simple as that!

So, let's get to it. First, we will use correlation analysis to investigate the relationship between the numerical attributes. Then, we will use box plots and t-tests to investigate the relationship between numerical attributes and categorical ones.

We would have investigated the relationships between categorical attributes as well if we didn't only have one categorical attribute. If you do have more than one categorical attribute, to evaluate data redundancy, you would need to use contingency tables and the chi-squared test of independence.

Checking for data redundancy among numerical attributes

As we mentioned previously, to evaluate the existence of data redundancy, we will use correlation analysis. If the correlation coefficient between two attributes is two high (we will use the rule thumb of 0.7), then this means that the information presented in the two attributes is too similar and there might be a case of data redundancy.

The following code uses the `.corr()` function to calculate the correlation between the numerical attributes that are explicitly listed in `num_atts`. The code also uses a **Boolean mask (BM)** to help our eyes find the correlation coefficient that is either greater than 0.7 or smaller than -0.7. Pay attention to the reason why the code had to include `.astype(float)`: during the data integration process, some of the attributes may have been carried over as strings instead of numbers:

```
num_atts = ['Acousticness', 'Danceability', 'Duration',
'Energy', 'Instrumentalness', 'Liveness', 'Loudness', 'Mode',
'Speechiness', 'Tempo', 'TimeSignature', 'Valence', 'Artists_n_
followers', 'n_male_artists', 'n_female_artists', 'n_bands',
'artist_average_years_after_first_album',  'artist_average_
number_albums']
corr_Table = songIntegrate_df[num_atts].astype(float).corr()
BM = (corr_Table > 0.7) | (corr_Table<-0.7)
corr_Table[BM]
```

After running the preceding code successfully, a correlation matrix will appear that has *NaN* for most of the cells, but only for the ones that have had a correlation coefficient that's either greater than `0.7` or smaller than `-0.7`. You will notice that the only flagged correlation coefficient is between `Energy` and `Loudness`.

It makes sense that these two attributes have a relationship with one another. As these attributes come from the same source, we will put our confidence in the creators of these attributes that they do show different values and that around 30% of the information that is different between the two is worth keeping.

Here, we can conclude that there are no issues regarding data redundancy between the numerical attributes. Next, we will investigate whether the relationships between the categorical attributes and the numerical attributes are too strong.

Checking for data redundancy between numerical and categorical attributes

To evaluate if there is data redundancy, similar to what we did for the numerical attributes, we need to examine the relationship between the attributes. As the attributes are of different natures – that is, numerical and categorical – we need to use boxplots and t-tests.

Example 3 (challenges 1, 3, 5, and 6)   375

The only categorical attribute that has been integrated and has analytic values at this point is the Explicit attribute. Why not the top_song attribute? The top song does have an analytic value for us – in fact, it is the hinge of our analysis – but it was not integrated from different sources. Instead, was calculated for our analysis. Once we get to the analysis part of this example, we will look at the relationship between this attribute and all the other ones. Why not Name or Artists? These are merely identifying columns. Why not First_date_on_Billboard? This was a temporary attribute to allow us to perform calculations where we needed information from more than one source of data. This attribute will be dropped before the analysis.

The following code creates the box plots that show the relationship between the numerical attribute and the categorical attribute; that is, Explicit. Furthermore, the code uses the ttest_ind() function from scipy.stats to run the t-test:

```
from scipy.stats import ttest_ind
for n_att in num_atts:
    sns.boxplot(data=songIntegrate_df, y=n_att,x='Explicit')
    plt.show()
    BM = songIntegrate_df.Explicit == True
    print(ttest_ind(songIntegrate_df[BM][n_att],
                    songIntegrate_df[~BM][n_att]))
    print('-----------------divide-------------------')
```

After running the preceding code, per each numerical attribute, a box plot and the result of the t-test that evaluates the relationship between the Explicit attribute and the numerical attribute will appear. After studying the output, you will realize that the Explicit attribute has a relationship with all the numerical attributes except for Loudness, Mode, and Valence. As it is very unlikely that the Explicit attribute will contain any new information that has not already been included in the data, we will flag Explicit for possible data redundancy.

Note that we will not necessarily need to remove Explicit at the data preprocessing stage. How we will deal with data redundancy will depend on the analytic goals and the tools. For instance, if we intend to use a decision tree to see the multivariate patterns that lead to a song being a top song or not, then we won't need to do anything about the data redundancy. This is because the decision tree has a mechanism for selecting the features (attributes) that help with the success of the algorithm. On the other hand, if we are using K-means to group the songs, then we would need to remove Explicit as the information has already been introduced in the other attributes. If we include it twice, then it will create bias in our results.

The analysis

Finally, the data sources are appropriately integrated into `songIntegrate_df` and the dataset is ready for analysis. Our goal is to answer the question of what makes a song become a top song. There is more than one approach we can adopt here to answer this question, now that the data has been preprocessed. Here, we will use two of them. We will use data visualization to recognize the univariate patterns of top songs, and we will use a decision tree to extract the multi-variate patterns.

We will start with the data visualization process.

Before we start, there is no need to remove the `Explicit` attribute for any of the aforementioned analytic tools due to the attribute being flagged as redundant. As we mentioned previously, the decision tree has a smart mechanism for feature selection, so for data visualization, keeping `Explicit` will only mean one more simple visualization that does not interfere with the other visualizations.

The data visualization approach to finding patterns in top songs

To investigate what makes a song become a top song, we can investigate the relationship that all the other attributes in `songIntegrate_df` have with the `Top_song` attribute and see if any meaningful pattern emerges.

The following code creates a box plot for each of the numerical attributes in `songIntegrate_df` to investigate if the value of the numerical attribute changes in two populations: top songs and not top songs. The code also outputs the result of a t-test that answers the same question statistically. Furthermore, the code outputs the median of the two populations in case it is hard to recognize the minute comparisons between the values of the two populations in the box plots:

```
from scipy.stats import ttest_ind
for n_att in num_atts:
    sns.boxplot(data=songIntegrate_df, y=n_att,x='Top_song')
    plt.show()
    BM = songIntegrate_df.Top_song == True
    print(ttest_ind(songIntegrate_df[BM][n_att], songIntegrate_
    df[~BM][n_att]))
    dic = {'not Top Song Median': songIntegrate_df[~BM][n_att].
    median(), 'Top Song Median': songIntegrate_df[BM][n_att].
    median()}
    print(dic)
    print('---------------divide-------------------')
```

Example 3 (challenges 1, 3, 5, and 6)   377

Moreover, the following code outputs a contingency table that shows the relationship betweenn the two categorical attributes; that is, `songIntegrate_df.Top_song` and `songIntegrate_df.Explicit`. It also prints out the p-value of the chi-squared test of independence for these two categorical attributes:

```
from scipy.stats import chi2_contingency
contingency_table = pd.crosstab(songIntegrate_df.Top_song,
songIntegrate_df.Explicit)
print(contingency_table)
print('p-value = {}'.format(chi2_contingency(contingency_table)
[1]))
```

After studying the outputs of the two preceding pieces of code, we may come to the following conclusions:

- There is no evidence to reject the null hypothesis that the `Top_song` attribute does not have a relationship with the `Duration`, `Energy`, `Instrumentalness`, `Liveness`, `Loudness`, `Mode`, `Speechiness`, `Explicit`, and `TimeSignature` attributes. This means that the top songs cannot be predicted by looking at the values of these attributes.

- The top songs tend to have smaller values on the `Acousticness`, `Tempo`, `n_male_artists`, `n_bands`, `artist_average_years_after_first_album`, and `artist_average_number_albums` attributes.

- The songs that have greater values for the `Danceability`, `Valence`, `Artists_n_followers`, `n_female_artists` attributes tend to become top songs more often.

Of course, these patterns sound too general, and they should be; this is because they are univariate. Next, we will apply a decision tree to figure out the multivariate patterns, which may help us understand how a song becomes a top song.

The decision tree approach to finding multivariate patterns in top songs

As we discussed in *Chapter 7, Classification*, decision trees are famous for being transparent and being able to render useful multivariate patterns from the data. Here, we would like to use the decision tree algorithm to see the patterns that lead to a song raising to the top 10 list of the billboard.

The following code uses `DecisionTreeClassifier` from `sklearn.tree` to create a classification model that aims to find the relationships between the independent attributes and the dependent attribute; that is, `Top_song`. Once the model has been trained using this data, the code will use `graphviz` to visualize the trained decision tree. At the end of the code, the extracted graph will be saved in a file called `TopSongDT.pdf`. After successfully running this code, you should be able to find the file in the same folder where you have the Jupyter Notebook file.

> **Attention!**
>
> If you have never used `graphviz` on your computer before, you may have to install it first.

To install `graphviz`, all you need to do is run the following piece of code. After successfully running this code once, `graphviz` will be installed on your computer for good:

```
pip install graphviz
```

Before running the following code, note that the decision tree model that is used in the following code has already been tuned. In *Chapter 7, Classification*, we mentioned that tuning decision trees is very important. However, we have not covered how to do it in this book. The hyperparameters and their tuned values are `criterion= 'entropy'`, `max_depth= 10`, `min_samples_split= 30`, and `splitter= 'best'`:

```
from sklearn.tree import DecisionTreeClassifier, export_
graphviz
import graphviz
y = songIntegrate_df.Top_song.replace({True:'Top
Song',False:'Not Top Song'})
Xs = songIntegrate_df.drop(columns = ['Name','Artists','Top_
song','First_date_on_Billboard'])
classTree = DecisionTreeClassifier(criterion= 'entropy', max_
depth= 10, min_samples_split= 30, splitter= 'best')
classTree.fit(Xs, y)
dot_data = export_graphviz(classTree, out_file=None, feature_
names=Xs.columns, class_names=['Not Top Song', 'Top Song'],
filled=True, rounded=True, special_characters=True)
graph = graphviz.Source(dot_data)
graph.render(filename='TopSongDT')
```

Example 3 (challenges 1, 3, 5, and 6)   379

After successfully runing the preceding code, the `TopSongDT.pdf` file will be saved on your computer, which contains the visualized decision tree. This tree is shown in the following diagram. In this instance, this diagram has not be shared with you so that you can study it; as you can see, the decision tree is rather large and our space is very small. However, you can see that there are a lot of meanigful multi-variate patterns forming the data, which can help us predict the top songs:

Figure 12.19 – A decision tree that visualizes the multivariate patterns of the top songs

Open `TopSongDT.pdf` on your own and study it. For instance, you will see that the most important attribute for a distinction between top songs and non-top songs is `Artists_n_followers`. For another example, if the song does not have artists with high followings, the best shot the song has at becoming a top song is that the song is explicit, danceable, and from artists with less experience. There are many more useful patterns like this in the decision tree. Continue studying `TopSongDT.pdf` to find them.

Example summary

In this example, we performed many steps to get to a point where `songIntegrate_df` was in a state where we were able to perform analysis and find useful information. To jog our memory, these are the steps that we took:

1. Checked for duplicates in all three data sources

2. Designed the structure of the final and integrated dataset

3. Integrated the data sources in three steps

4. Checked for data redundancy

5. Performed analysis

Now, let's summarize the chapter.

Summary

Congratulations on your excellent progress in this chapter. First, we learned the difference between data fusion and data integration before becoming familiar with six common data integration challenges. Then, through three comprehensive examples, we used the programming and analytic tools that we've picked up throughout this book to face these data integration challenges and preprocess the data sources so that we were able to meet the analytic goals.

In the next chapter, we will focus on another data preprocessing concept that is crucial, especially for algorithmic data analytics due to the limitations of computational resources: data reduction.

Before you start your journey on data reduction, take some time and try out the following exercises to solidify your learning.

Exercise

1. In your own words, what is the difference between data fusion and data integration? Provides examples other than the ones given in this chapter.

2. Answer the following question about *Challenge 4 – aggregation mismatch*. Is this challenge a data fusion one, a data integration one, or both? Explain why.

3. How come *Challenge 2 – unwise data collection* is somehow both a data cleaning step and a data integration step? Do you think it is essential that we categorize an unwise data collection under data cleaning or data integration?

4. In *Example 1* of this chapter, we used multi-level indexing using `Date` and `Hour` to overcome the index mismatched formatting challenge. For this exercise, repeat this example but this time, use single-level indexing using the Python `DataTime` object instead.

5. Recreate *Figure 5.20* from *Chapter 5, Data Visualization*, but instead of using `WH Report_preprocessed.csv`, integrate the following three files yourself first: `WH Report.csv`, `populations.csv`, and `Countries.csv`. Hint: information about happiness indices come from `WH Report.csv`, information of the countries comes from `Countries.csv`, and population information comes from `populations.csv`.

6. In *Chapter 6, Prediction, Exercise 2*, we used `ToyotaCorolla_preprocessed.csv` to create a model that predicts the price of cars. In this exercise, we want to do the preprocessing ourselves. Use `ToyotaCorolla.csv` to answer the following questions:

a) Are there any concerns regarding level I data cleaning? If so, address them if necessary.

b) Are there any concerns regarding level II data cleaning? If so, address them if necessary.

c) Are there any concerns regarding level III data cleaning? If so, address them if necessary.

d) Are there any attributes in `ToyotaCorolla.csv` that can be considered redundant?

e) Apply `LinearRegression` from `sklearn.linear_model`. Did you have to remove the redundant attributes? Why/why not?

f) Apply `MLPRegressor` from `sklearn.neural_network`. Did you have to remove the redundant attributes? Why/why not?

7. We would like to use the `Universities.csv` file to put the universities into two meaningful clusters. However, the data source has many issues, including data cleaning levels I – III and data redundancy. Do the following:

a) Deal with data cleaning issues.

b) Deal with data redundancy issues.

c) Use any column necessary except for `State` and `Public (1)/ Private (2)` to find the two meaningful clusters.

d) Perform centroid analysis and name each cluster.

e) Find out if the newly created categorical attribute cluster has a relationship with either of the two categorical attributes we intentionally did not use for clustering: `State` or `Public (1)/ Private (2)`.

8. In this exercise, we will see an example of data fusion. The case study that we will use in this exercise was already introduced in the data fusion example for this chapter, so please go back and read it again before continuing with this exercise.

In this example, we would like to integrate `Yield.csv` and `Treatment.csv` to see if the amount of water can impact the amount of yield.

Do the following to make this happen:

a) Use `pd.read_csv()` to read `Yield.csv` to `yield_df`, and read `Treatment.csv` into `treatment_df`.

b) Draw a scatterplot of the points in `treatment_df`. Use the dimension of color to add the amount of water that has been dispensed from each point.

c) Draw a scatterplot of the points in `yield_df`. Use the dimension of color to add the amount of harvest that has been collected from each point.

d) Create a scatterplot that combines the visual in *Steps b* and *c*.

e) From the scatterplots in the preceding steps, we can deduce that the water stations are equidistant from one another. Based on this realization, calculate the distance between the water points, and call it `radius`. We are going to use this variable in the following set of calculations.

e) First, use the following code to create the `calculateDistance()` function:

```
import math
def calculateDistance(x1,y1,x2,y2):
    dist = math.sqrt((x2 - x1)**2 + (y2 - y1)**2)
    return dist
```

Then, using the following code and the preceding function we just created, create the `waterRecieved()` function so that we can apply it to the function for the rows of `treatment_df`:

```
def WaterReceived(r):
    w = 0
    for i, rr in treatment_df.iterrows():
        distance = calculateDistance(rr.longitude,
        rr.latitude, r.longitude, r.latitude)
        if (distance< radius):
            w= w + rr.water * ((radius-distance)/radius)
    return w
```

a) Apply `waterRecieved()` to the rows of `yield_df` and add the newly calculated value for each row to the `water` column.

b) Study the newly updated `yield_df`. You just fused these two data sources. Go back and study these steps, especially the process of creating the `waterRecieved()` function. What are the assumptions that made this data fusion possible?

c) Draw a scatterplot of the `yield_df.harvest` and `yield_df.water` attributes. Do we see any impact that `yield_df.water` has on `yield_df.harvest`?

d) Use the correlation coefficient to confirm your observation from the previous step.

13
Data Reduction

We have come to yet another important step of data preprocessing that is not concerned with data cleaning; this is known as **data reduction**. To successfully perform analytics, we need to be able to recognize situations where data reduction is necessary and know the best techniques and the *how-to* of their implementation. In this chapter, we will learn what data reduction is. Let's put this another way: we will learn what the data pre-processing steps are that we call data reduction. Furthermore, we will cover the major reasons and objectives of data preprocessing. Most importantly, we will look at a categorized list of data reduction tools and learn what they are, how they can help, and how we can use Python to implement them.

In this chapter, we are going to cover the following main topics:

- The distinction between data reduction and data redundancy
- Types of data reduction
- Performing numerosity data reduction
- Performing dimensionality data reduction

Technical requirements

You can find the code and dataset for this chapter in this book's GitHub repository at `https://github.com/PacktPublishing/Hands-On-Data-Preprocessing-in-Python`. You can find `Chapter13` in this repository and download the code and data for a better learning experience.

The distinction between data reduction and data redundancy

In the previous chapter, *Chapter 12, Data Fusion and Data Integration*, we discussed and saw an example of the **data redundancy challenge**. While data redundancy and data reduction have very similar names and their terms use words that have connected meanings, the concepts are very different. Data redundancy is about having the same information presented under more than one attribute. As we saw, this can happen when we integrate data sources. However, data reduction is about reducing the size of data due to one of the following three reasons:

- **High-Dimensional Visualizations**: When we have to pack more than three to five dimensions into one visual, we will reach the human limitation of comprehension.

- **Computational Cost**: Datasets that are too large may require too much computation. This might be the case for algorithmic approaches.

- **Curse of Dimensionality**: Some of the statistical approaches become incapable of finding meaningful patterns in the data because there are too many attributes.

In other words, data redundancy is a characteristic that a dataset may have. This characteristic is about having redundant data in the dataset, so we may have to take some actions. On the other hand, data reduction is a set of actions that we can take to reduce the size of data due to the aforementioned reasons.

When we remove some part of a dataset due to its data redundancy, can we call the removal part data reduction? After all, we are removing and *reducing* the dataset. In the general sense of the term reduction, yes, the dataset is being reduced, but in the context of data mining, the terms data reduction and data redundancy have specific meanings. And based on those specific meanings, as described previously, the answer to the question is no.

Now that we've learned about the distinction between data redundancy and data reduction, let's learn how to assess the success of a data reduction operation.

The objectives of data reduction

Successful data reduction seeks to achieve the following two objectives at the same time. First, data reduction seeks to obtain a reduced representation of the dataset that is much smaller in volume. Second, it tries to closely maintain the integrity of the original data, which means making sure that data reduction will not lead to including bias and critical information being lost in the data.

As shown in the following diagram, these two objectives can be contradictory and when performing data reduction actions, the two objectives must be taken into consideration at the same time so that one is not overshadowed by the other:

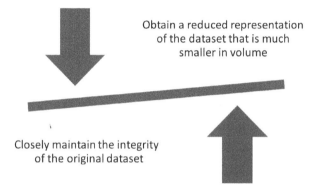

Figure 13.1 – The counterbalancing objectives of data reduction

With these two objectives in mind, we will look at examples of data reduction and how we can ensure both objectives are met. However, before we do that, let's categorize the different methods of data reduction so that we can give our content a nice structure.

Types of data reduction

There are two types of data reduction methods. They are called **numerosity data reduction** and **dimensionality data reduction**. As their names suggest, the former performs data reduction by reducing the number of data objects or rows in a dataset, while the latter performs data reduction by reducing the number of dimensions or attributes in a dataset.

In this chapter, we will cover three methods for numerosity reduction and six methods for dimensionality reduction. The following are the numerosity reduction methods we will cover:

- **Random Sampling**: Randomly selecting some of the data objects to avoid unaffordable computational costs.

- **Stratified Sampling**: Randomly selecting some of the data objects to avoid the unaffordable computational costs, all the while maintaining the ratio representation of the sub-populations in the sample.

- **Random Over/Under Sampling**: Randomly selecting some of the data objects to avoid the unaffordable computational costs, all the while creating a prescribed representation of the sub-populations in the sample.

The following are the dimensionality reduction methods we will cover:

- **Linear Regression**: Using regression analysis to investigate the predictive power of independent attributes to predict a specific dependent attribute

- **Decision Tree**: Using the decision tree algorithm to investigate the predictive power of the independent attributes to predict a specific dependent attribute

- **Random Forest**: Using the random forest algorithm to investigate the predictive power of the independent attributes to predict a specific dependent attribute

- **Brute-force Computational Dimension Reduction**: Computational experimentations to figure out the best subset of independent attributes that leads to the most successful prediction of the dependent attribute

- **Principal Component Analysis (PCA)**: Representing the data by transforming the axes in such ways that most of the variation in the data is explained by the first attributes and the attributes are orthogonal to one another

- **Functional Data Analysis (FDA)**: Representing the data using fewer points using functional representation

Some of these explanations may have gone over your head here. Don't worry; next, we will learn about each of these using analytic examples, so the context of those examples will help you understand all of these techniques.

First, we will look at the three numerosity reduction methods, after which we will cover the dimensionality reduction ones.

Performing numerosity data reduction

When we need to reduce the number of data objects (rows) as opposed to the number of attributes (columns), we have a case of numerosity reduction. In this section, we will cover three methods: **random sampling**, **stratified sampling**, and **random over/undersampling**. Let's start with random sampling.

Random sampling

Randomly selecting some of the rows to be included in the analysis is known as random sampling. The reason we are compelled to accept random sampling is when we run into computational limitations. This normally happens when the size of our data is bigger than our computational capabilities. In those situations, we may randomly select a subset of the data objects to be included in the analysis. Let's look at an example.

Example – random sampling to speed up tuning

In this example, we are using `Customer Churn.csv` to train a decision tree so that it can predict (classify) what customer will be churning in the future.

Before reading on, please go back and study *Example 2 – restructuring the table* in *Chapter 10, Cleaning Level II – Unpacking, Restructuring, and Reformulating the Table*. In that example, we used visualization – specifically, box plots – to figure out which attributes have the potential to give us an insight into the customer's future decisions regarding churning. In this example, we want to do the same thing but this time, we want to take a multi-variate approach where the interactions of these attributes are also considered. This can be done using a well-tuned decision tree algorithm.

In this book, we have not covered the techniques of algorithm tuning. But we'll get a glimpse of them here. One of the standard ways of tuning an algorithm is to take a brute-force approach where we use all the possible combinations of hyperparameters and see which one leads to the best outcome. The following code uses the `GridSearchCV()` function from `sklearn.model_selection` to experiment with all the combinations of the listed possibilities for the `criterion`, `max_depth`, `min_samples_split`, and `min_impurity_decrease` hyperparameters. These hyperparameters are the `DecisionTreeClassifier()` model's from `sklearn.tree`:

```
from sklearn.tree import DecisionTreeClassifier
from sklearn.model_selection import GridSearchCV
y=customer_df['Churn']
Xs = customer_df.drop(columns=['Churn'])
```

```
param_grid = { 'criterion':['gini','entropy'], 'max_depth':
[10,20,30,40,50,60], 'min_samples_split': [10,20,30,40,50],
'min_impurity_decrease': [0,0.001, 0.005, 0.01, 0.05, 0.1]}
gridSearch = GridSearchCV(DecisionTreeClassifier(), param_grid,
cv=3, scoring='recall',verbose=1)
gridSearch.fit(Xs, y)
print(Best score: ', gridSearch.best_score_)
print(Best parameters: ', gridSearch.best_params_)
```

Run the preceding code before reading on. Upon running this code, it will report that there are 360 candidate models, and each will be fitted three times on different subsets of the input dataset, totaling 1,080 fittings. The 360 model candidate comes from the multiplication of 2,6, 5, and 6, which are the number of possibilities that the preceding code has listed for the mentioned hyperparameters, respectively.

The code will take a while to run. It took my computer, with a CPU speed of 1.3 GHz, around *26 seconds* to finish. This may not sound like a very significant amount of time, but the dataset only contains around 3,000 customers. Imagine if the number of customers was 30 million, which is not unimaginable for today's telecommunication companies. Here, this 26 seconds would probably be 26,000 seconds, which is equivalent to 7 hours, just to tune the algorithm. That is no good.

One of the approaches we can take to reduce this amount of time is random sampling. The following code has implemented random sampling by using the pandas DataFrame .sample() function, which takes the number of random samples you'd like from the DataFrame:

```
customer_df_rs = customer_df.sample(1000, random_state=1)
y=customer_df_rs['Churn']
Xs = customer_df_rs.drop(columns=['Churn'])
gridSearch = GridSearchCV(DecisionTreeClassifier(), param_grid,
cv=3, scoring='recall',verbose=1)
gridSearch.fit(Xs, y)
print(Best score: ', gridSearch.best_score_)
print(Best parameters: ', gridSearch.best_params_)
```

As you can see, first, 1,000 of the data objects have been randomly selected and then the same tuning code has been applied. After running this code, you will see that the amount of time it takes for the code to finish will drop significantly. On my computer, it dropped from *26 seconds* to *18 seconds*.

What is `random_state=1` in the preceding code? This is the ingenious way of `sklearn` modules controlling randomness for better experimentations. What that means for us is that if you run the preceding code multiple times, even though you have included some randomness in the code, you will get the same result every time. Even better, by assigning the same number to `random_state`, you can also get the same results that I am getting, even though we are experimenting with randomness.

You won't have to include `random_state=1` in your code, but if you have, you will get the following parameters as the best ones: `{'criterion': 'entropy', 'max_depth': 10, 'min_impurity_decrease': 0.005, 'min_samples_split': 10}`.

Now that we know the optimized hyperparameters, we can use them to draw the decision tree and evaluate the multi-variate patterns that lead to customer churning in this dataset. The following code uses all the data objects to train `DecisionTreeClassifier()`, which includes the optimized hyperparameters we found earlier, to find the multi-variate relationships between the independent attributes and the dependent attribute; that is, `Churn`. Once the model has been trained using this data, the code uses `graphviz` to visualize the trained decision tree. At the end of the code, the extracted graph will be. saved in the `ChurnDT.pdf` file.

> **Attention!**
>
> If you have never used `garaphvis` on your computer before, you may have to install it first. To install `graphvis`, all you need to do is run the following one-line piece of code. After successfully running this code, `graphvis` will be installed on your computer for good.

Run the following one-line piece of code to install `graphvis` on your computer:

```
pip install graphviz
```

After successfully running the following code, you should be able to find the `ChurnDT.pdf` file in the same folder where you have your Jupyter Notebook file:

```
from sklearn.tree import export_graphviz
import graphviz
y=customer_df['Churn']
Xs = customer_df.drop(columns=['Churn'])
classTree = DecisionTreeClassifier(criterion= 'entropy', max_
depth= 10, min_samples_split= 10, min_impurity_decrease= 0.005)
classTree.fit(Xs, y)
```

```
dot_data = export_graphviz(classTree, out_file=None, feature_
names=Xs.columns,  class_names=['Not Churn', 'Churn'],
filled=True, rounded=True, special_characters=True)
graph = graphviz.Source(dot_data)
graph.render(filename='ChurnDT')
```

The following diagram shows the content of ChurnDT.pdf that will be saved on your computer after running the preceding code successfully:

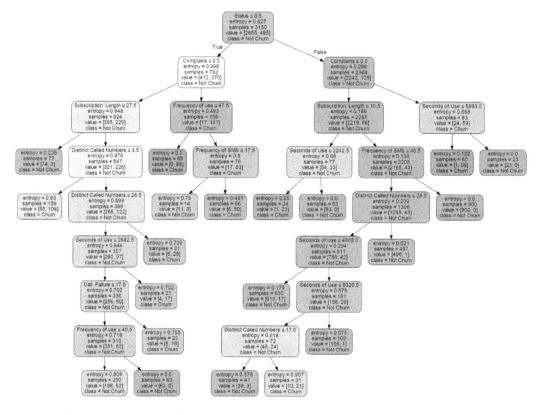

Figure 13.2 – The trained decision tree showing the multivariate patterns of customer churning in customer_df

As we can see, random sampling is useful when we don't have the computational capability to include all of the data objects. It is debatable if random sampling maintains a good balance of the two counterbalancing objectives of successful data reduction shown in *Figure 13.1*. Due to its limited computational capabilities, we do need a smaller version of the dataset. By incorporating complete randomness, we give all of the data objects the same chance to be selected, so to some extent, we are maintaining the integrity of the dataset and avoiding introducing any bias by arbitrarily selecting a subset of the dataset.

In this example, we could have maintained the integrity of the dataset better. When it comes to binary classification, most of the time, one of the classes is significantly less frequent. In the case of `churn_df`, there are 495 *Churn=1* cases and 2,655 *Churn=0* cases; that is, approximately 15.7% of cases are churn cases and 84.3% are non-churn cases. You can see this by running `customer_df.Churn.value_counts(normalize=True)`.

Now, let's see what happens to these ratios when we take samples from `customer_df`. The following screenshot shows the ratios of churn and non-churn for three experiments of sampling from `customer_df`:

```
In [7]:   ▶  for i in range(3):
                  print(customer_df.sample(1000).Churn.value_counts(normalize=True))

          0    0.865
          1    0.135
          Name: Churn, dtype: float64
          0    0.85
          1    0.15
          Name: Churn, dtype: float64
          0    0.835
          1    0.165
          Name: Churn, dtype: float64
```

Figure 13.3 – Three sampling experiments on churn_df to see the ratios of churn and non-churn in the samples

In the preceding screenshot, we can see that after every three experiments, the ratios do not match the original dataset's. This begs the question, are there sampling methods that make sure these ratios match the original dataset? The answer is yes. One such method is stratified sampling. We will look at this in the next section.

Stratified sampling

Stratified sampling, also known as proportional random sampling, is a numerosity data reduction method. The similarity between random sampling and stratified sampling is that in both samplings, all the data objects have some chance to be selected in the sample. The distinction is that stratified sampling makes sure that the selected data objects show the same representation of the groups in the original dataset. The distinction between these methods is shown in the following diagram:

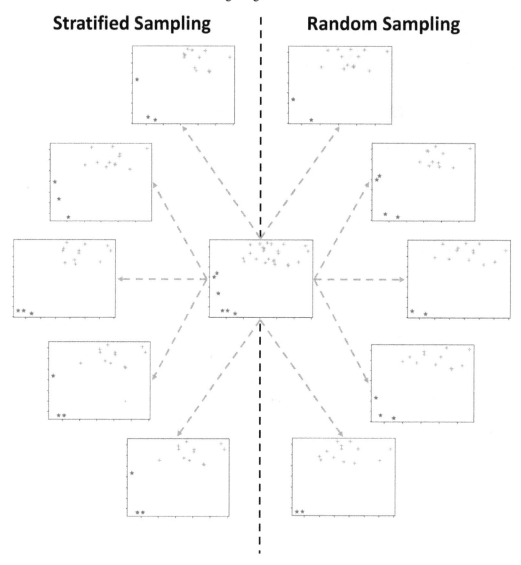

Figure 13.4 – Stratified sampling versus random sampling

The preceding diagram shows a dataset in the middle, five instances of random sampling on the right, and five instances of stratified sampling on the left. The dataset contains 30 data objects: six stars (*) and 24 pluses (+). Each of the 10 samples selects 15 data objects out of the 30 data objects. Before reading on, investigate the preceding diagram and try to figure out the difference between random sampling and stratified sampling.

What jumps out from this diagram is that while all of the stratified samplings have three stars, the instance of random sampling has stars ranging from two to four. This is because stratified sampling has maintained the ratio of the data between the groups, while random sampling does not have such restrictions; 20% (6/30) of the data objects in the original data are stars, while 20% (3/15) of the data objects in the stratified samples are stars. However, such restrictions have not been put in place for the random sampling instance.

Example – stratified sampling for an imbalanced dataset

In the previous example, we saw that `customer_df` is imbalanced as 15.7% of its cases are churn, while the rest, which is 84.3%, are non-churn. Now, we want to come up with some code that can perform stratified sampling.

The following code will be able to get a stratified sample of `customer_df` that contains `1000` data objects out of the 3,150 data objects. In the end, the code will print the ratios of churn and non-churn data objects in the sample using `.value_counts(normalize=True)`. Run the code a few times. You will see that even though the process is completely random, it will always lead to the same ratios of churn and non-churn cases:

```
n,s=len(customer_df),1000
r = s/n
sample_df = customer_df.groupby('Churn', group_keys=False)
.apply(lambda sdf: sdf.sample(round(len(sdf)*r)))
print(sample_df.Churn.value_counts(normalize=True))
```

The preceding code may have gone over your head in terms of its way of using the
.groupby() and .apply() functions. This is the first time we have had to use this
combination in this book. This is as good an opportunity as any to learn about this
combination. When we want a specific set of operations to be performed on multiple
subsets of a DataFrame, we will specify the subsets by the .groupby() function first.
After this, using the .apply() function opens the door for us to be able to perform
operations on those subsets created by .groupby(). Here, sdf stands for Subset
DataFrame.

Before moving on to the next section, let's discuss how stratified sampling approaches
the two objectives of data reduction presented in *Figure 13.1*. As we implied previously,
stratified sampling puts more effort into the objective of maintaining the integrity of the
original data. Of course, when we have different populations in the same dataset and we
want to make sure the representation ratios are intact, stratified sampling helps us achieve
this goal.

Random over/undersampling

Unlike random sampling and stratified sampling, where the chance of objects being
selected in the sample is dictated by the dataset, random over/undersampling due to the
needs of analytic gives more or less chance of being selected to certain data objects.

To understand random over/undersampling, let's compare it to stratified sampling. When
we perform stratified sampling, we calculate the ratio of the sub-populations based on the
important attribute and then perform a controlled random sampling, where the ratios are
maintained in the sample. On the other hand, in random over/undersampling, we have a
prescribed ratio that we want our sample to have; that is, we decide what ratios we want
based on our analytic needs.

To illustrate this, the following diagram compares two instances of stratified sampling
from customer_df with two instances of over/undersampling, with a 50-50% (1:1)
prescribed ratio between churning and non-churning customers. All the samples contain
500 data objects from the 3,150 data objects in the original dataset. If you study the four
samples in the following diagram, you will notice a few patterns. First, you will see that
all of them are different, which they should be due to the randomized nature of both
sampling methods. Second, you will see that the ratio of churn and non-churn customers
in the two instances of over/undersampling has been shifted, as described previously:

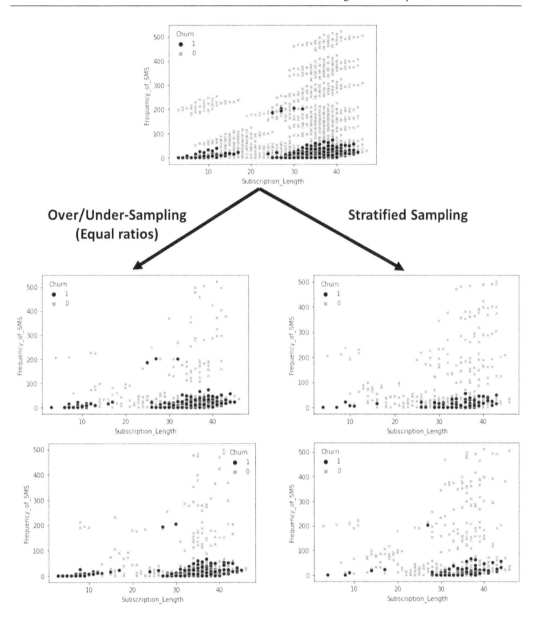

Figure 13.5 – Stratified sampling versus random over/undersampling using customer_df

The most common analytic situation that might require over/undersampling is binary classification using an **imbalanced dataset**. An imbalanced dataset is a table that has been prepared for classification and its dependent attribute has two characteristics. First, the dependent attribute is binary, meaning that it only has two class labels. Second, there are significantly more of one class label than the other. For example, the customer churn prediction that we discussed earlier in this chapter uses an imbalanced dataset. To check this, you can run `customer_df.Churn.value_counts(normalize=True).plot.bar()`, which will create a bar chart that shows the frequency of each label in the `customer_df.Churn` attribute. You will see that there are around five times more cases of *0* (non-churn customers) and cases of *1* (churn customers).

> **Too Specific to Matter?**
>
> Binary classification using an imbalanced dataset might sound too specific to matter. However, the most important classification tasks are binary, and in almost all of them, the dataset is imbalanced. To name a few very common and important examples of binary classification that have to use imbalanced datasets, we can mention online fraud detection, machinery fault detection using sensor data, and automatic disease detection using radiology images.

The reason that we might want to perform over/undersampling is that it has been seen time and again that the classification algorithm, by default, might overemphasize learning from the less frequent class label, and unfortunately, often, the case that matters more for us is the less frequent one. For example, in the example of churn prediction, it is more important for us to recognize who will be churning, rather than who will not be churning. So, when developing an algorithmic solution, we might choose to perform over/undersampling. This is done to give the algorithm a greater opportunity to learn from the less frequent cases.

The code that we use to apply randomly over/undersampling is very similar to and simpler than stratified sampling. The following code will be able to get a sample of `customer_df` that contains `500` data objects out of the 3,150 data objects. There will be `250` data objects from both the churning and non-churning customers. In the end, the code will print the ratios of the churn and non-churn data objects in the sample using `.value_counts(normalize=True)`. This code is a copy of the preceding code with a few changes; to help you see them, the updated parts are highlighted. Before running the following code, first, compare it with the preceding one to study the changes. Then, run the code a few times. You will see that even though the process is completely random, it will always lead to the same and equal ratios of churn and non-churn cases:

```
n,s=len(customer_df),500
sample_df = customer_df.groupby('Churn', group_keys=False)
.apply(lambda sdf: sdf.sample(250))
print(sample_df.Churn.value_counts(normalize=True))
```

Before switching gears from numerosity data reduction to dimensionality data reduction, let's discuss how random over/undersampling approaches the two objectives of data reduction presented in *Figure 13.1*. This approach intentionally disrupts the integrity of the original dataset due to analytic reasons. However, as the sampling is performed randomly, the randomness helps keep the integrity of the dataset to some degree. The fact that we committed to this transgression here is that, at times, random over/undersampling happens both as a data reduction strategy and as a data transformation strategy. This is the mixing that allowed us to do this. As we will learn in the next chapter, data transformation does inflict changes on the data for analytic purposes.

Over/undersampling is more of a data transformation technique, though, at times, it gets mixed with data reduction. Also, from a technical perspective, it is very similar to random sampling and stratified sampling, as we learned about here. As a data transformation technique, oversampling could also mean having repetitions of data objects with the less frequent class label or even having simulated data objects that we would predict having the less frequent class label.

> **Attention!**
> We will not discuss over/undersampling beyond this point in this book.
> This is because successful over/undersampling is highly relevant to the
> classification algorithm of choice and you could see it as a hyperparameter
> of any classification algorithm. This means that one algorithm's performance
> might improve using oversampling, while the other may suffer. Therefore,
> oversampling is the content that a book with more emphasis on teaching
> algorithms should cover. In this book, our focus is on data preprocessing.

Now, it is time to switch gear! Dimensionality data reduction, here we come!

Performing dimensionality data reduction

When we need to reduce the number of attributes (columns) as opposed to the number of data objects (rows), we have a case of dimensionality reduction. This is also known as dimension reduction. In this section, we will cover six methods: **regression**, **decision tree**, **random forest**, **computational dimension reduction**, **functional data analysis** (**FDA**), and **principal component analysis** (**PCA**).

Before we talk about each of them, we must note that there are two types of dimension reduction methods: **supervised** and **unsupervised**. Supervised dimension reduction methods aim to reduce the dimensions to help us predict or classify a dependent attribute. For instance, when we applied a decision tree algorithm to figure out which multi-variate patterns can predict customer churning, earlier in this chapter, we performed a supervised dimensionality reduction. The attributes that did not show up on the tree in *Figure 13.2* are not important for predicting (classifying) customer churn.

On the other hand, when dimension reduction is performed without paying attention to the task of prediction or classification, and data reduction is done only to reduce the data size or perhaps data transformation and massaging, then we have unsupervised dimension reduction. If the terms data transformation and data massaging are not familiar to you, don't worry. We will discuss these in the next chapter.

Now, let's look at each of the six methods. I will refrain from mentioning if each method is supervised or unsupervised so that you can think about them on your own. *Exercise 4*, at the end of this chapter, will ask you to answer that for each method.

Linear regression as a dimension reduction method

We learned about linear regression as a prediction model in *Chapter 6, Prediction*. Linear regression is a very well-researched and integrated statistical method. As such, the libraries that package this method normally come with many built-in metrics and hypothesis testings that can be very useful for analyzing the dataset. A group of such hypothesis testing is very useful in deciding if each independent attribute is playing a significant role in predicting a dependent attribute.

Therefore, linear regression can be used as a dimension reduction method by looking at the resulting p-value of those hypothesis testings. The p-values that do not show that there is a meaningful relationship between the relevant independent attributes and the dependent attribute can be used as evidence, to help remove those independent attributes from the analysis. Let's look at an example to understand this better.

Example – dimension reduction using linear regression

In this example, we would like to use amznStock.csv, which contains some calculated metrics from the historical data of Amazon stock that's was collected and computed on January 11, 2021, to predict the next day percentage of change of the Amazon stock. The dependent attribute in this dataset is today_changeP. The independent attributes are as follows:

- yes_changeP: Amazon's stock price change in the previous day
- lastweek_changeP: Amazon's stock price change in the previous week

- `dow_yes_changeP`: Dow Jones change in the previous day
- `dow_lastweek_changeP`: Dow Jones change in the previous week
- `nasdaq_yes_changeP`: NASDAQ 100 change in the previous day
- `nasdaq_lastweek_changeP`: Last week's NASDAQ 100 change in the previous week

I created this dataset on January 11, 2021, to create the YouTube video *A Taste of Prediction* (`https://youtu.be/_z0oHuTnMKc`). To find out more about this dataset and the logic behind it, please see the YouTube video.

Now that I am looking at the name of the attributes, I think the attribute names can become much more intuitive. So, let's start by doing some level I data cleaning; that is, creating concise and intuitive attribute titles. The attribute titles are concise but they can be more intuitive.

The following code reads the dataset into `amzn_df`, sets `t` as the index of `amzn_df`, and changes the attribute titles:

```
amzn_df = pd.read_csv('amznStock.csv')
amzn_df.set_index('t',drop=True,inplace=True)
amzn_df.columns = ['pd_changeP', 'pw_changeP', 'dow_pd_
changeP','dow_pw_changeP', 'nasdaq_pd_changeP', 'nasdaq_pw_
changeP', 'changeP']
```

Changing the attribute titles in the previous code followed three simple patterns. The _yes_ title segment, which was meant to represent yesterday, was updated with _pd_, which is meant to present the previous day. Moreover, the _lastweek_ title segment was updated with _pw_, which is meant to present the previous week. Lastly, the `today` title segment was eliminated from the dependent attribute.

Now, let's bring our attention to dimension reduction using linear regression. To use linear regression as a dimension reduction method, we have to perform linear regression as though we are going to train the prediction model. The following is the linear regression equation for this `amzn_df`:

$$changeP = \beta_0 + \beta_1 \times pd_{changeP} + \beta_2 \times pw_{changeP} + \beta_3 \times dow\_pd\_changeP \\ + \beta_4 \times dow\_pw\_changeP + \beta_5 \times nasdaq\ pd\ changeP \\ + \beta_6 \times nasdaq\_pw\_changeP$$

To practice and review this, before reading on, refer back to the *Example of applying linear regression to perform regression analysis* section of *Chapter 5, Data Visualization*, and estimate the values of the βs in the preceding linear regression equation using `LinearRegression()` from `sklearn.linear_model`.

Even though `LinearRegression()` is a great and stable function to use for linear regression, unfortunately, this function does not include the hypothesis testings that are necessary for applying linear regression as a dimension reduction method. That is why the following code uses the `OLS()` function, from `statsmodels.api`, to import a linear regression module that outputs the results of the hypothesis testing we discussed earlier:

```
import statsmodels.api as sm
Xs = amzn_df.drop(columns=['changeP'], index =['2021-01-12'])
Xs = sm.add_constant(Xs)
y = amzn_df.drop(index =['2021-01-12']).changeP
sm.OLS(y, Xs).fit().summary()
```

Let's go over a few things about the preceding code that might have become a question for you before we analyze its output:

- Why are we dropping the data object with an index of `2021-01-12`? If you print `amzn_df`, you will see that this data object is presented as the last row of this DataFrame and that there is no value for the dependent attribute; that is, `changeP`. Do you remember that the dataset was collected and computed on January 11, 2021? At that time, we did not know what `changeP` of January 12 will be. The dataset was put together to try to predict this value.

- What is the purpose of `Xs = sm.add_constant(Xs)`? This line of code adds a column whose value for all the rows is 1. The reason for this addition is to make sure `OLS()` will include a constant coefficient, which is what linear regression models have. Why did we not have to include this when we used `LinearRegression()` from `sklearn.linear_model`? That is a good question and the answer is that the developer of each module may choose to create their module based on what they think is a better approach. As users, we need to learn how and when we should use what module.

Now that we understand the code, let's pay attention to its output. After successfully running the preceding code, you will get the following output:

Dep. Variable:	changeP	R-squared:	0.061
Model:	OLS	Adj. R-squared:	0.044
Method:	Least Squares	F-statistic:	3.678
Date:	Fri, 27 Aug 2021	Prob (F-statistic):	0.00149
Time:	15:15:50	Log-Likelihood:	-750.72
No. Observations:	349	AIC:	1515.
Df Residuals:	342	BIC:	1542.
Df Model:	6		
Covariance Type:	nonrobust		

	coef	std err	t	P>|t|	[0.025	0.975]
const	0.2342	0.122	1.926	0.055	-0.005	0.473
pd_changeP	-0.0804	0.112	-0.719	0.473	-0.300	0.140
pw_changeP	0.0665	0.044	1.499	0.135	-0.021	0.154
dow_pd_changeP	-0.2888	0.151	-1.914	0.056	-0.586	0.008
dow_pw_changeP	0.0866	0.066	1.316	0.189	-0.043	0.216
nasdaq_pd_changeP	0.0919	0.210	0.438	0.661	-0.321	0.505
nasdaq_pw_changeP	-0.1403	0.098	-1.433	0.153	-0.333	0.052

Omnibus:	25.863	Durbin-Watson:	1.936
Prob(Omnibus):	0.000	Jarque-Bera (JB):	97.802
Skew:	-0.036	Prob(JB):	5.79e-22
Kurtosis:	5.592	Cond. No.	17.6

Figure 13.6 – The result of the OLS() function on the described linear regression model

Before reading on, go back to the βs you estimated using `LinearRegression()`. The β values must be the same as the values you can see in the preceding diagram, under the **coef** column.

In the same table, in the **P>|t|** column, you can find the p-values of the hypothesis test of the independent attribute's significance for predicting the dependent attribute. You can see that most of the p-values are way larger than the cut-off point of 0.05, except for **dow pd changeP**, which is slightly larger than the cut-off point. Based on our understanding of the p-value, we can see that we don't have enough evidence to reject the null hypothesis that most of the independent attributes are not related to the dependent attribute – that is, except for *dow_pd_changeP*, which has a rather small probability that this attribute is not related to the dependent attribute. So, if we were going to keep any attribute, we would keep *dow_pd_changeP* and remove the rest.

In this example, we used linear regression to turn a prediction model with six independent attributes into a prediction model with only one independent attribute. The following is a simplified version of the linear equation:

$$changeP = \beta_0 + \beta_1 \times dow\_pw\_changeP$$

If you modify the preceding code so that the OLS() functions will run the new model, you will get the following output:

Dep. Variable:	changeP	**R-squared:**	0.053
Model:	OLS	**Adj. R-squared:**	0.050
Method:	Least Squares	**F-statistic:**	19.40
Date:	Fri, 27 Aug 2021	**Prob (F-statistic):**	1.42e-05
Time:	15:16:47	**Log-Likelihood:**	-752.14
No. Observations:	349	**AIC:**	1508.
Df Residuals:	347	**BIC:**	1516.
Df Model:	1		
Covariance Type:	nonrobust		

	coef	std err	t	P>|t|	[0.025	0.975]
const	0.1975	0.112	1.761	0.079	-0.023	0.418
dow_pd_changeP	-0.2470	0.056	-4.404	0.000	-0.357	-0.137

Omnibus:	26.140	**Durbin-Watson:**	1.984
Prob(Omnibus):	0.000	**Jarque-Bera (JB):**	99.897
Skew:	-0.037	**Prob(JB):**	2.03e-22
Kurtosis:	5.620	**Cond. No.**	2.00

Figure 13.7 – The result of the OLS() function on the reduced linear regression model

Comparing the **adjusted R^2 (Adj. R-squared)**, which is a reliable metric for the quality of linear regression, in *Figure 13.6* and *Figure 13.7* shows that data reduction helped with the success of the model. Even though the model in *Figure 13.7* has fewer independent attributes, it is more successful than the model in *Figure 13.6*.

The shortcoming of linear regression as a dimension reduction method is that the model takes a univariate approach in deciding if an independent attribute helps predict the dependent attribute. In many situations, it might be the case that an independent attribute is not a good predictor of the dependent attribute but its interaction with other independent attributes might be helpful. That is why, when we want to perform dimension reduction before capturing multi-variate pattern recognition, linear regression is not a good method of choice. For those cases, we should use one of the other methods, such as **decision tree**, **random forest**, or **computational dimension reduction**. We will be learning about each of these methods in this section. Next up, we'll look at using a decision tree as a dimension reduction method.

Using a decision tree as a dimension reduction method

Throughout this book, we have learned that the decision tree algorithm can handle both prediction and classification data mining tasks. However, here, we want to see how a decision tree can be used as a method for dimension reduction. The logic is simple: if an attribute was a part of a tuned and trained final decision tree, then the attribute must have helped predict or classify the dependent attribute.

For example, in the tuned and trained decision tree for predicting customer churn, as shown in *Figure 13.2*, all of the eight attributes were used in the final decision tree. This shows that we would not want to remove any of the independent attributes for multi-variate pattern recognition.

The decision tree algorithm is an effective way to see if an attribute has the potential to predict or classify a dependent attribute in a multi-variate way, but it does have some shortcomings. First, the decision tree makes a binary decision about whether each attribute should be included or not, and we do not have a way to see how valuable each dependent attribute is. Second, it might be the case that an attribute is excluded – not because it does not play a role in any multivariate pattern, which can help predict the dependent attribute – but because the attribute can be beneficial but the structure and/or the logic of the decision tree fails to capture the specific patterns that the attribute plays a role in.

Next, we will learn about the random forest algorithm, which rectifies the first shortcoming of the decision tree. After that, we will learn about brute-force computational dimension reduction, which can deal with the second shortcoming.

Using random forest as a dimension reduction method

We have not been introduced to the random forest algorithm before in this book. This algorithm is similar to the decision tree algorithm and can handle both classification and prediction data mining tasks. However, its unique design makes the random forest a prime candidate to be used as a dimension reduction method.

Random forest, as the name suggests, instead of just relying on one decision tree to perform classification or prediction, uses many decision trees in a randomized way. The decision trees that the random forest uses are random and have fewer levels. These smaller decision trees are called weak predictors or classifiers. The logic behind random forest is that instead of using an opinionated decision tree (one strong predictor) to give us one prediction, we can employ multiple, more flexible, decision trees (weak predictors) and consolidate their predictions into a final class or a value.

As a dimension reduction method, we can just look at the number of times each attribute appeared in the multiple weak decision trees and arrive at a percentage of decision trees that each attribute was employed by. This will be invaluable information regarding our choice to keep or remove attributes.

Let's look at an example.

Example – dimension reduction using random forest

In this example, we would like to use random forest to come to the relative importance of each attribute in the classification of customer churn using the Customer Churn.csv file. We saw the influence that each attribute has on one tuned and trained decision tree in *Figure 13.2*. However, here, we are more interested in coming to a numerical value that shows the importance of each attribute.

The following code uses RandomForestClassifier() from sklearn.ensemble to train a random forest model that uses 1000 weak decision trees:

```
from sklearn.ensemble import RandomForestClassifier
y=customer_df['Churn']
Xs = customer_df.drop(columns=['Churn'])
rf = RandomForestClassifier(n_estimators=1000)
rf.fit(Xs, y)
```

After successfully running the preceding code, which might take a few seconds to run, nothing will happen. But don't worry – the magic has happened; we just need to access what we are looking for. Print `rf.feature_importances_` and look at the numerical values that show the importance of the independent attributes. The code shown in the following screenshot creates a pandas Series, sorts the attributes based on their importance, and then creates a bar chart that shows the relative importance of each attribute to classify customer churn:

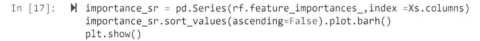

```
In [17]:  ▶  importance_sr = pd.Series(rf.feature_importances_,index =Xs.columns)
             importance_sr.sort_values(ascending=False).plot.barh()
             plt.show()
```

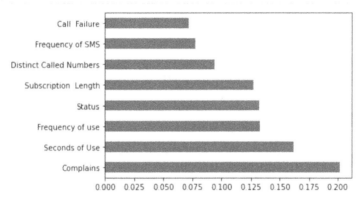

Figure 13.8 – Creating a bar chart using a pandas Series and Matplotlib to show the relative importance of independent attributes to classify customer churn in customer_df

The information shown in the preceding screenshot, other than the valuable implications for dimension reduction, may also be used for direct analysis. For instance, we can see that the `complaints` attribute has floated to the top of the list. This means that customer complaints have very important implications for customer churn and that the decision-makers of the telecommunication company that this data was collected from may be able to use that for positive change.

While random forests do not suffer from the first shortcoming of decision trees regarding dimension reduction, they do suffer from the second shortcoming. That is, we cannot be certain that if an attribute does not show enough importance through the fandom forest, it will not be valuable for predicting the dependent attribute in other algorithms. The next dimension reduction method that we will learn about, **brute-force computational dimension reduction**, does not have this shortcoming. However, this method is computationally very expensive. Let's learn more about it.

Brute-force computational dimension reduction

This method uses a brute-force approach where all the different subsets of independent attributes are used in an algorithm to predict or classify the dependent attribute. After this brute-force experimentation, we will know which combination of the independent attributes can best predict the dependent attribute.

The Achilles heel of this method is that it can become computationally very expensive, especially if the algorithm of choice is also computationally expensive. For instance, using computational dimension reduction to find the best subset of independent attributes using an **artificial neural network** (**ANN**) will probably have a higher chance of leading to the optimum predictor, but at the same time, it will probably take a significant amount of time to run.

On the other hand, this approach does not suffer from the shortcomings of the other dimension reduction methods we have learned about so far. Brute-force computational dimension reduction can be coupled with any prediction or classification algorithms, thus removing our method-specific results concern we had with the decision tree and random forest.

Now, let's look at an example and see what brute-force computational dimension reduction would look like.

Example – finding the best subset of independent attributes for a classification algorithm

In this example, we would like to find the best subset of independent attributes that would lead to the best performance of **K-Nearest Neighbors** (**KNN**) in predicting customer churn in the `Customer Churn.csv` file.

We learned about KNN in *Chapter 7, Classification,* and, as you may recall, to successfully implement KNN, we need to have tuned the number of neighbors (K). So, if we want to check which subset will lead to the best KNN performance, we will need to tune KNN once for every combination of the independent attributes. This will make the process even more computationally expensive.

The following code has put all these pieces together so that we can experiment with every combination of independent attributes after tuning KNN for them. This code has many parts and we will go over them later in the chapter.

This code has been presented in the form of a screenshot because it is rather large. If you wish to copy the code instead of typing it, please see the Chapter13 file in this book's GitHub repository:

```
In [18]:  ▶  import itertools
             from sklearn.neighbors import KNeighborsClassifier
             from sklearn.metrics import recall_score
             from sklearn.model_selection import GridSearchCV

             in_atts = ['Call  Failure', 'Complains', 'Subscription  Length',
                        'Seconds of Use', 'Frequency of use', 'Frequency of SMS',
                        'Distinct Called Numbers', 'Status']
             n_in_atts = len(in_atts)
             result_df = pd.DataFrame(columns = ['subset_candidate','best_k',
                                                 'performance'])
             customer_df_std = (customer_df - customer_df.min())/(
                 customer_df.max() - customer_df.min())

             for n in range(1,n_in_atts+1):
                 for atts in itertools.combinations(in_atts, r=n):
                     atts = list(atts)
                     Xs = customer_df_std[atts]
                     y= customer_df['Churn']

                     # Tune KNN
                     param_grid = {
                         'n_neighbors':[1,3,5,7]}
                     gridSearch = GridSearchCV(KNeighborsClassifier(),
                                     param_grid, cv=2, scoring='recall')
                     gridSearch.fit(Xs, y)
                     best_k= gridSearch.best_params_['n_neighbors']

                     # Train the tuned KNN
                     knn = KNeighborsClassifier(best_k)
                     knn.fit(Xs, y)

                     # Prediction
                     y_predict = knn.predict(Xs)

                     # Performance evaluation
                     dic_append = {'subset_candidate':atts, 'best_k': best_k,
                                   'performance': recall_score(y,y_predict)}

                     # Recording and Reporting
                     result_df = result_df.append(dic_append, ignore_index=True)
                     print(dic_append)
```

Figure 13.9   Brute force dimensionality reduction to optimize KNN's performance
when predicting customer churn

Let's go over the different parts of the code in the form of the questions you might have about it. Before reading on, try running and also understanding the code.

As the code will be computationally expensive, it might be smart to let your computer run the code while you try to understand it:

- *What is* `itertools` *and why do we need it?* It is a very useful module when we need a complex web of nested loops to get our task done. To create every possible combination of the independent attributes, we need to have various number of nested loops under the main loop, and that is not possible to do using the regular iteration functionality of Python. If the previous sentence didn't make sense and you are adamant about understanding it, try to write some code that prints all the combinations of the independent attributes; then, you will understand.

  By using itertools `.combinations()`, we were able to create all the combinations in a two-level nested loop.

- *What is* `result_df` *and why do we need it?* This is a pandas DataFrame that this code uses as a placeholder, in which we will record the records of all the `brute_force` experimentations.

- *What is* `recall` *and why are we evaluating our method using recall instead of accuracy?* Recall is a specific evaluation metric of binary classification tasks, and in this case study, having a better recall is more important than better accuracy. I'd say Google it and learn more about it, but if you are not interested in learning about what `recall` is at this point in your data analytics career, I think just looking at it as an appropriate evaluation metric would do for now.

- *Why are we only experimenting with the four possible values of* `[1,3,5,7]` *for K?* This is a measure that's used to cut the computational costs because without it, the code would take a very long time to run.

Once you have fully understood the preceding code and your computer has finished running it, you should sort the pandas DataFrame, `result_df`, by the `performance` column and see the results of your experimentation. `result_df.sort_values('performance',ascending=False)` does this, and studying its output will help you realize that the following two combinations will lead to a very successful KNN classification with recall scores of 0.99596:

- *Complains, Seconds of Use, Frequency of use, Distinct Called Numbers*
- *Seconds of Use, Frequency of SMS, Distinct Called Numbers*

Comparing the final results of this example with *Figure 13.8*, which was the final result of the random forest on the same case study, can teach us a lot about the advantages of the brute-force computational dimension reduction method:

- First, we can see that what was important for the random forest is not necessarily important for KNN. For instance, while for the random forest, *Distinct Called Numbers* was not very important, we can see that KNN can use it to get its best performance.

- Second, while the random forest gave us a good visualization about the importance of the attributes after we received these results, we will still need to make decisions as to what attributes we need to exclude or include. However, brute-force computational dimension reduction will tell us exactly what attributes to include.

While these advantages of brute-force computational dimension reduction sound very impressive, I'd hesitate to write this method up as the best. The computational cost of this method is a real concern.

So far in this chapter, we've learned about two numerosity reduction methods and four dimensionality reduction methods. The dimensionality reduction methods we've learned about so far are specific to prediction or classification. We will learn about two more dimensionality reduction methods that are more general and can be used as one of the preprocessing steps before any task, including classification and prediction. These two methods are **principal component analysis (PCA)** and **functional data analysis (FDA)**. Let's start with PCA.

PCA

This dimension reduction method is the most famous general and non-parametric dimension reduction method in the literature. There are rather complex mathematical formulas if we raise the hood of the method and take a look at how the method works. However, we are not going to get bogged down in the mathematical complexities. Instead, we are going to learn about PCA by using two examples: one containing a toy dataset and one containing a real example. So, let's dive into the first example and learn about PCA.

Example – toy dataset

In this example, we are going to use the `PCA_toy_dataset.xlsx` file. The following screenshot, which is in a dashboard-style, shows five items:

- The code to read the file into `toy_df`
- The Jupyter Notebook representation of `toy_df`

- The scatterplot of the two dimensions of `toy_df`

- The calculated variance of both attributes in `toy_df` and their summation (**Total**)

- The correlation matrix of `toy_df`:

```
In [18]:    ▶  toy_df = pd.read_excel('PCA_toy_dataset.xlsx')
               toy_df
```

Out[18]:

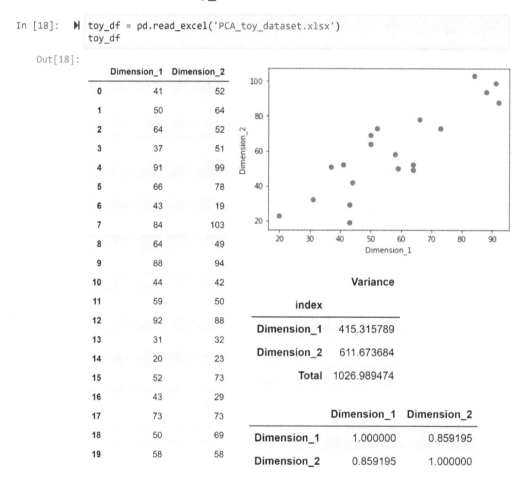

	Dimension_1	Dimension_2
0	41	52
1	50	64
2	64	52
3	37	51
4	91	99
5	66	78
6	43	19
7	84	103
8	64	49
9	88	94
10	44	42
11	59	50
12	92	88
13	31	32
14	20	23
15	52	73
16	43	29
17	73	73
18	50	69
19	58	58

Variance

index	
Dimension_1	415.315789
Dimension_2	611.673684
Total	1026.989474

	Dimension_1	Dimension_2
Dimension_1	1.000000	0.859195
Dimension_2	0.859195	1.000000

Figure 13.10 – A dashboard containing information and visuals for toy_df

Using the preceding screenshot, we can gain a lot of insight into `toy_df`. What jumps out right off the bat is that **Dimension_1** and **Dimension_2** are strongly correlated. We can see this both in the scatterplot and the correlation matrix; the correlation coefficient between **Dimension_1** and **Dimension_2** is **0.859195**. We can also see that there is a total of **1026.989474** variations in `toy_df`; **Dimension_1** contributes **415.315789** of the total variation, while **Dimension_2** contributes the rest.

The way PCA looks at any data is in terms of variations. For PCA, there is this much (1026.989474) information presented in toy_df. Yes, PCA considers variations across different data attribute information. For PCA, the way that the information is presented across the two attributes is troublesome. PCA doesn't like the fact that some of the information that is presented by **Dimension_1** is the same as some of the information presented by **Dimension_2**, and vice versa. PCA has a non-parametric view of the data. For PCA, the attributes are simply the holders of information in form of numerical variations. Thus, PCA sees it as fitting to transform the data so that the dimensions do not show similar information.

Before discussing what transformations PCA applies to a dataset, let's go ahead and apply them to toy_df and see its results. The following screenshot shows another dashboard-style visual that shows the information about the PCA-transformed toy_df. This screenshot contains five items that are similar to the ones shown in *Figure 13.11*. This screenshot also contains the code that uses the PCA() function from sklearn. decomposition to transform toy_df:

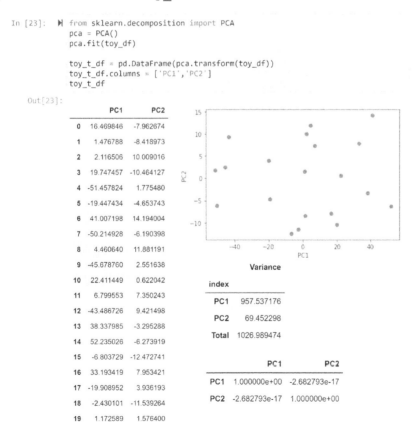

Figure 13.11 – A dashboard containing information and visuals for the PCA transformed toy_df dataset

In the preceding screenshot, we can see the information and visualizations of the PCA-transformed `toy_df`, which is called `toy_t_df`. We call the new columns of a PCA-transformed dataset **principal components (PCs)**. Here, you can see that since `toy_df` has two attributes, `toy_t_df` has two PCs called **PC1** and **PC2**.

After taking a cursory look at the preceding screenshot and comparing it with *Figure 13.11*, it might feel like there's no points of similarity between the two DataFrames: the original `toy_df` dataset and its PCA-transformed version, `toy_t_df`. However, you'll be surprised to know that there are lots of commonalities between the two. First, look at the total amount of variance in both figures. They are both exactly **1026.989474**. So, PCA does not add information to and remove information from the dataset, it just moves the variations from one attribute to the other.

A second similarity will show itself when we rotate the scatterplot of **Dimension_1** and **Dimension_2** in *Figure 13.11*. This can be seen in the following diagram, and you can see that the data presented in *Figure 13.12* is the same as that shown in *Figure 13.11* after some axis transformation:

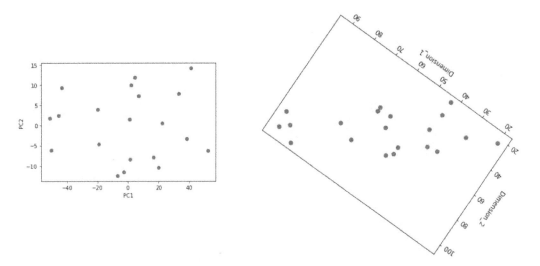

Figure 13.12 – A comparison between the PCA-transformed toy_df dataset
and the visually rotated toy_df dataset

Now, let's talk about what PCA does to a dataset. In plain English, PCA transforms the axes of a dataset in such a way that the first PC – in this example, **PC1** – carries the maximum possible variation, and the correlation between the PCs – in this example, **PC1** and **PC2** – will be zero.

Now, let's compare *Figure 13.11* and *Figure 13.12* again. While **Dimension_1** only contributes *415.315789* to the total *1026.989474* variations in *Figure 13.11*, **PC1** contributes *957.53716* to the total *1026.989474* variations in *Figure 13.12*. So, we can see that the PCA transformation has successfully pushed most of the variations into the first PC, **PC1**. Moreover, looking at the scatterplot and the correlation matrix in *Figure 13.12*, we can see that **PC1** and **PC2** have no relationship with one another and that the correlation coefficient is zero ($-2.682793e-17$). However, we do remember from *Figure 13.11* that the relationship between **Dimension_1** and **Dimension_2** was rather strong (*0.859195*). Again, we can see that PCA has been successful in making sure there is no correlation between **PC1** and **PC2** in this example. When two attributes are poised to have zero correlation with one another, it is said that they are **orthogonal** to one another.

There is more to learn about PCA, but now, you are ready to learn via a real data analytic application. Let's look at the next example.

Example – non-parametric dimension reduction

Go back to *Chapter 8*, *Clustering Analysis*, the *Using K-Means to cluster a dataset with more than two dimensions* section and review the clustering we performed there. We employed K-Means to cluster the countries in WH Report_preprocessed.csv based on their data from 2019 into three groups. In this example, instead of using only 2019 data, we want to use all of the data in the file. Also, instead of using clustering analysis, we want to use PCA to visualize the inherent patterns in the data.

In *Chapter 8*, *Clustering Analysis*, we used the following nine attributes to cluster the countries: Life_Ladder, Log_GDP_per_capita, Social_support, Healthy_life_expectancy_at_birth, Freedom_to_make_life_choices, Generosity, Perceptions_of_corruption, Positive_affect, and Negative_affect. As there are more than three attributes, we were unable to use the visualization methods to visualize a complete representation of the dataset. With the help of PCA, we can push most of the variations in the data into the first few PCs and visualize them instead, which will help us get some insight into the general trends in the dataset.

The following code reads the WH Report_preprocessed.csv file into report_df and then uses the pandas.pivot() function to create country_df:

```
report_df = pd.read_csv('WH Report_preprocessed.csv')
country_df = report_df.pivot(index='Name', columns='year',
values=['Life_Ladder','Log_GDP_per_capita', 'Social_support',
'Healthy_life_expectancy_at_birth', 'Freedom_to_make_life_
choices', 'Generosity', 'Perceptions_of_corruption', 'Positive_
affect', 'Negative_affect'])
```

After running the preceding code and studying `country_df`, you will see that the dataset has been restructured so that the definitions of the data objects are for each country, while all the happiness indices of all the 10 years from 2010 to 2019 are included. Therefore, in total, `country_df` has 90 attributes now.

After data restructuring, the following code creates `Xs` and standardizes it. To be specific, `Xs = (Xs - Xs.mean())/Xs.std()` standardizes the `Xs` DataFrame:

```
Xs = country_df
Xs = (Xs - Xs.mean())/Xs.std()
Xs
```

We already know how to **normalize** a dataset. Here, we are using another data transformation technique: **standardization**. What distinguishes these two data transformation methods is why they are used. For clustering, we use normalization as it makes sure the scale of all the attributes is the same, so each attribute will have equal weight in the clustering analysis. However, it is essential to standardize the data before applying PCA. That is because standardization transforms the attributes, so all of the transformed attributes will have an equal standard deviation: one. After successfully running the preceding code, run either `Xs.var()` or `Xs.std()` to see that standardizing the data ensures each attribute has the same variance across the data objects.

Why is standardization necessary before applying PCA? If you remember from what we have been learning about PCA, this method looks at each attribute as a carrier of some variation of the total variation. If one attribute happens to have a significantly larger variance, it will just dominate the PCA's attention. Therefore, to ensure each attribute will get fair and equal attention from PCA, we will standardize the dataset.

Now that the dataset is ready, let's apply PCA. The following code uses the `PCA()` function from `sklearn.decomposition` to PCA-transform `Xs` into `Xs_t`:

```
from sklearn.decomposition import PCA
pca = PCA()
pca.fit(Xs)
Xs_t = pd.DataFrame(pca.transform(Xs), index = Xs.index)
Xs_t.columns = ['PC{}'.format(i) for i in range(1,91)]
```

After successfully running the preceding code, print the transformed dataset, `Xs_t`, and investigate its state.

> **Attention!**
>
> You might be confused about `['PC{}'.format(i) for i in range(1,91)]` in the preceding code. The technique that was used in this line of code is called **list comprehension**. Whenever we want to fill a collection with iterable items, instead of using traditional loops, we can use list comprehensions. For instance, if you were to run this line of code separately, it would print out `['PC1', 'PC2', 'PC3', …, 'PC90']`.

The question we should be asking ourselves now is, was PCA successful? We can do better than asking – we can check. By simply running `Xs_t.var()`, we can see the amount of variations that are explained by each PC. After running this, we can see that most of the variations are explained by the first PCs, but we don't know by exactly how much. Normally, after performing PCA, we perform cumulative variance explanation analysis on the PCs.

The following screenshot shows the code for creating `explanation_df`, which is a reporting DataFrame that was created to show the variance percentage of each PC, as well as the cumulative variance percentage up until each PC, starting from PC1:

```
In [37]:   total_variance = Xs_t.var().sum()
           dic = {'variance_percentage':Xs_t.var()/total_variance,
                  'cumulative_variance_percentage':
                  Xs_t.var().cumsum()/total_variance}

           explanation_df = pd.DataFrame(dic)
           explanation_df
```

Out[37]:

	variance_percentage	cumulative_variance_percentage
PC1	4.775917e-01	0.477592
PC2	1.609550e-01	0.638547
PC3	7.197769e-02	0.710524
PC4	6.833512e-02	0.778860
PC5	5.290713e-02	0.831767
…	…	…
PC86	4.023476e-08	1.000000
PC87	6.144899e-11	1.000000
PC88	2.005157e-31	1.000000
PC89	1.969081e-33	1.000000
PC90	2.021922e-33	1.000000

90 rows × 2 columns

Figure 13.13 – Creating explanation_df from Xs_t

In the preceding screenshot, we can see that the first three PCs account for 71% of the total variation in data. We would roughly need 64 out of 90 attributes to be able to account for around 71% of the variations in a dataset with 90 attributes. However, thanks to PCA, we have transformed the dataset into a state where we can show 71% of the variations in the dataset only using three attributes.

Next, we will use our visualization skills to draw a three-dimensional scatterplot. Running `Xs_t.plot.scatter(x='PC1', y='PC2', c='PC3', sharex=False)` will ouput the following 3D scatterplot:

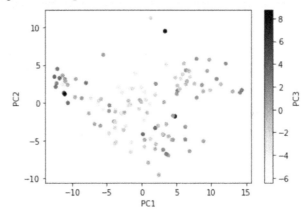

Figure 13.14 – Visualizing 71% of the variations in country_df using PC1, PC2, and PC3

The preceding visualization now has the advantage of having visualized 71% of the information in `country_df`, which is an excellent achievement. However, the disadvantage of creating visualizations using PCs is that the dimensions in the visualization will not have the intuitive meaning that they would if we were to use the original attributes for visualization. For instance, compare the preceding diagram with *Figure 8.3* of *Chapter 8, Clustering Analysis*. In *Figure 8.3*, you will see that the x-axis shows *Life_Ladder*, whereas the y-axis shows *Perception_of_corruption*, and the color shows *Generosity*. When we look at the visualization, we have an understanding of what intuitive values change while moving from one dot to the other. However, in the preceding diagram, *PC1*, *PC2* and *PC3* are simply capsules of variations; we have no intuitive understanding of what they show.

And that's not where things end. When looking at a regular scatterplot, we would intuitively assume that the x-axis and y-axis have equal weight and importance. However, we should try to beat that second nature when looking at the scatterplots of PCs. The reason for this is that the first PCs have more importance as they carry more variations. We also need to keep in mind that the representation of color only carries about 10.1% of the total variations shown by the visualization; 10.1% was calculated using the formula *7.197769e-02/0.710524*; both numbers are from *Figure 13.13*.

In any case, beating our perception by paying attention to the relevancy and ratios of PCs all at once is a tall order, especially for untrained eyes. The good news is that we can use other visualization techniques to somewhat guide our eyes. The following code uses a few strategies to help us see the relative relationship that the data points have to one another regarding the PCs:

```
Xs_t.plot.scatter(x='PC1',y='PC2',c='PC3',sharex=False, vmin=-
1/0.101, vmax=1/0.101)
x_ticks_vs = [-2.9*4 + 2.9*i for i in range(9)]
for v in x_ticks_vs:
    plt.axvline(v,c='gray',linestyle='--',linewidth=0.5)
plt.xticks(x_ticks_vs)
y_ticks_vs = [-8.7,0,8.7]
for v in y_ticks_vs:
    plt.axhline(v,c='gray',linestyle='--',linewidth=0.5)
plt.yticks(y_ticks_vs)
plt.show()
```

Before we look at how the strategies were translated into the preceding code, let's look at the result and use that as a lead-in to learning about those strategies. After running the preceding code, Python will produce the following diagram:

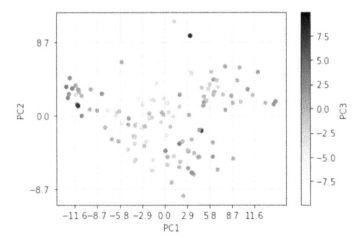

Figure 13.15 – A repeat of Figure 13.13 but with new details to guide our eyes regarding the relevance and ratios of PC1, PC2, and PC3

In the preceding diagram, you can see that two changes have been adopted. Let's go through them one by one and explain them:

- x-ticks of the plot has been updated, and vertical lines have been added accordingly. These changes are adopted using the amount of variations **PC1** offers. Likewise, y-ticks of the plot has also been updated, and horizontal lines have been added accordingly.

  The numbers 2.9 and 8.7 have been calculated by trial and error and the information taken from *Figure 13.13*; first, we can calculate 67.21682870670097% and 22.652999757925132% as the percentages that PC1 and PC2 are representing in the diagram, respectively. Then once 1 is divided by each of these values we get 2.9 and 8.7 for PC1 and PC2. Where did being divided by 1 come from? Think about it.

- The color spectrum changes as it represents **PC3**, which has been widened. We use the range of -1/0.101 to 1/0.101 here. Earlier, we calculated 11.1% as the percentage amount of variations that **PC3** carries. This change, as you can observe in the preceding diagram, helps us not give undue importance to the changes of **PC3** among the data objects.

Before we move on, let's do one last thing to enrich the visualization.

We want to annotate the dots in the preceding diagram with the names of the countries. Since annotating all of the countries would probably make the visual cluttered and unreadable, we will only add 50 countries; these 50 counties will be selected randomly using the pandas DataFrame.sample() function. We will also make the scatterplot a bit larger. The following code will do this for us. The changes that we've made to the preceding code are in bold so that you can easily find them:

```
Xs_t.plot.scatter(x='PC1',y='PC2',c='PC3',sharex=False, vmin=-1/0.101, vmax=1/0.101, figsize=(12,9))
x_ticks_vs = [-2.9*4 + 2.9*i for i in range(9)]
for v in x_ticks_vs:
    plt.axvline(v,c='gray',linestyle='--',linewidth=0.5)
plt.xticks(x_ticks_vs)
y_ticks_vs = [-8.7,0,8.7]
for v in y_ticks_vs:
    plt.axhline(v,c='gray',linestyle='--',linewidth=0.5)
plt.yticks(y_ticks_vs)
for i, row in Xs_t.sample(50).iterrows():
```

```
      plt.annotate(i, (row.PC1, row.PC2),
      rotation=50,c='gray',size=8)
plt.show()
```

The following diagram will be produced after successfully running the preceding code:

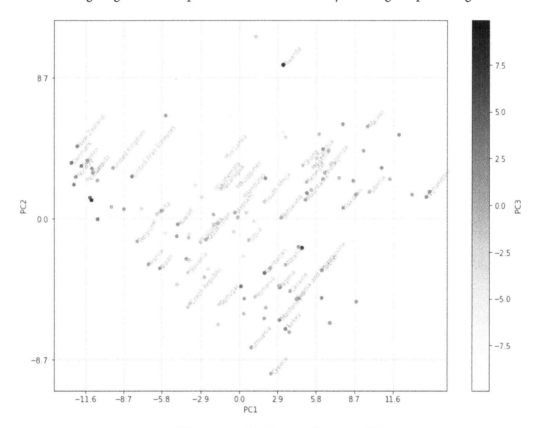

Figure 13.16 – The annotated and enlarged version of Figure 13.15

Now, instead of having to rely on a clustering algorithm to extract and give us the inherent multi-variate patterns in a dataset, we can visualize them. This visualization, to a decision-maker whose eyes have been trained, can be invaluable as 71% of the variations in the dataset are presented in this visualization.

The next dimensionality reduction method we will learn about is **functional data analysis (FDA)**; however, let's discuss the advantages and disadvantages of PCA first. As we saw in this example, PCA may be able to push most of the variations across all the attributes of a dataset into the first PCs. This is great as we can present more information using fewer dimensions.

This can have two distinct positive impacts. First, as we saw in this example, we can visualize more information using fewer visual dimensions. Second, we may use PCA as a way to help with computational costs for algorithmic decision-making. For instance, instead of having to have 90 independent attributes, we may be able to have only three attributes with only a minimal loss of information.

On the other hand, there is a very significant negative impact that comes with using PCA. By pushing the variations around, PCA effectively makes the new dimensions of the transformed data meaningless, which can deprive us of some analytical capabilities.

The next strength/weakness of PCA is also the weakness/strength of the next method we will learn about, which is FDA. PCA is a non-parametric method, which means it can be applied to any dataset and it may be able to transform the data into a new space where fewer dimensions are necessary to present much of the variations. However, FDA is not a method that can be applied to any data. FDA may be applicable or not – it all depends on if we can find a mathematical function that can imitate our data to an acceptable degree. That being said, if we do manage to find that function and apply FDA, then dimension reductionality will not transform the data into a new space where the dimensions are meaningless. However, this is what PCA does.

> **Is PCA Applicable to Any Dataset?**
>
> Actually, no. If the attributes of a dataset form non-linear relationships whose inclusion is important for the analytic goals, PCA should be avoided. However, in most everyday datasets, the assumption that attributes have a linear relationship with one another is safe. On the other hand, if capturing the non-linear relationships between data attributes is essential, you should stay away from PCA.

At this point, I hope you are very excited to learn about FDA. You should be since FDA is a very powerful and exciting method.

Functional data analysis

As the name suggests, **functional data analysis (FDA)** involves applying mathematical functions to data analytics. FDA can be a standalone analytic tool, or it can be used for dimension reduction or data transformation. Here, we will discuss how it can be used as a dimension reduction method. In the next chapter, we will discuss how FDA can be used for data transformation.

Simply put, as a dimension reduction method, FDA finds a function that can imitate the data well enough so that we can use the parameters of the function instead of the original data.

As always, let's look at an example to understand this better.

Example – parametric dimension reduction

In the preceding example, *Example – non-parametric dimension reduction*, we used PCA to transform `country_df` so that most of the variations – 71%, to be exact – were presented in only three dimensions; that is, PC1, PC2, and PC3. Here, we want to approach the same problem but use a parametric approach instead.

Before moving on, get Jupyter Notebook to show `country_df` and study its structure. Its structure is also shown in the following diagram. You can see that each country has 90 records from nine happiness indices over 10 years:

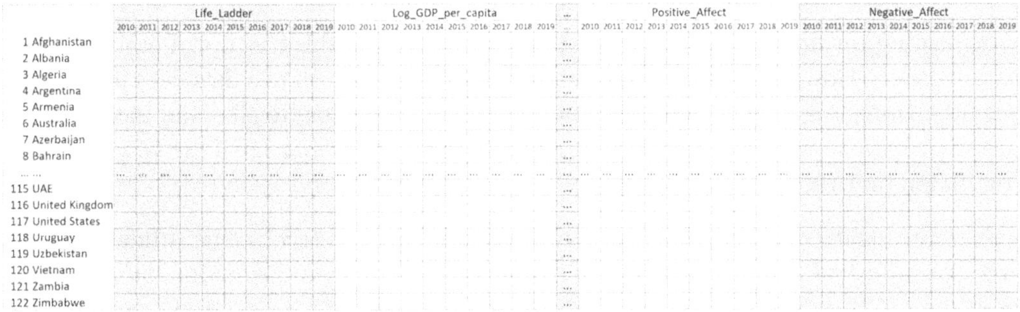

Figure 13.17 – The structure of country_df

To gauge if FDA can help us transform this dataset, let's visualize the 10-year trend of each happiness index per country.

The following code populates 1,098 (122*9) line plots. As you hit run in Jupyter Notebook, line plots will start to appear. You will not have to let your computer populate all the visuals. Once you feel like you have grasped what these plots look like, you can interrupt the kernel. If you don't know how to stop your kernel, go back to *Figure 1.2*:

```
happines_index = ['Life_Ladder', 'Log_GDP_per_capita', 'Social_
support', 'Healthy_life_expectancy_at_birth', 'Freedom_to_
make_life_choices', 'Generosity', 'Perceptions_of_corruption',
'Positive_affect', 'Negative_affect']
for i,row in country_df.iterrows():
    for h_i in happines_index:
        plt.plot(row[h_i])
        plt.title('{} - {}'.format(i,h_i))
        plt.show()
```

After this exercise, you might be convinced that a linear equation might be able to summarize the trends in all of the visualizations. The general linear equation looks like this:

$$Happiness\_index = a + b * t$$

In this equation, *t* represents time, and in this example, it can take any one of the values in the list *[0, 1, 2, 3, 4, 5, 6, 7, 8, 9]*. For each of the visualizations we saw after running the preceding code, we strive to estimate the *a* and *b* parameters so that the function shown in the preceding formula can represent all the points fairly.

Before making any final decisions, let's test the applicability of this function, both visually and statistically. However, as this is our first time fitting a function to a data, let's perform *curve fitting* for some sample data and then use loops to apply that to all of our data. The sample data we will be using will be `Life_Ladder` of *Afghanistan* – the very first visualization the preceding code created.

We will be using the `curve_fit()` function from `scipy.optimize` to estimate the *a* and *b* parameters for `Life_Ladder` of *Afghanistan*. To apply this function, other than importing it (`from scipy.optimize import curve_fit`), we need to perform the following steps:

1. First, we need to define a Python function for the mathematical function we want to use to fit the data.

    The following code creates `linearFunction()`, as we described previously:

    ```
    def linearFunction(t,a,b):
        y = a+ b*t
        return y
    ```

    We will be using `linearFunction()` shortly.

2. Second, prepare the data for the `curve_fit()` function by organizing it into `x_data` and `y_data`.

    The following code shows how this is done for `Life_Ladder` of `Afghanistan`:

    ```
    x_data = range(10)
    y_data = country_df.loc['Afghanistan','Life_Ladder']
    ```

3. Pass the function and the data into the `curve_fit()` function.

The following code shows how this can be done for the sample data:

```
from scipy.optimize import curve_fit
p, c = curve_fit(linearFunction, x_data, y_data)
```

After running the three preceding code blocks, the p variable will have the estimated a and b parameters. Printing p will show you that a is estimated to be 4.37978182, while b is estimated to be -0.19528485.

To evaluate the goodness of this estimation, we can use both visualization and statistics. The following screenshot shows the code to create the analyzing visualization, its result, the code for calculating r2, and its result:

```
In [44]:  ▶  fit_y = linearFunction(x_data,p[0],p[1])
              plt.plot(x_data,y_data,label='data' )
              plt.plot(x_data, fit_y, '--', label='fit')
              plt.xticks(x_data,y_data.index)
              plt.legend()
              plt.show()
```

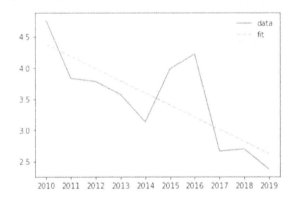

```
In [45]:  ▶  from sklearn.metrics import r2_score
              print("r2_score",r2_score(y_data,fit_y))

              r2_score 0.5954935497933329
```

Figure 13.18 – The code and the result of using visualization and statistics to evaluate the curve for fitting goodness-of_fit

Statistically speaking, r2 is the ideal metric for capturing and summarizing the goodness of fit for data one number. The metric can take any value between 0 and 1 and the higher values show a better fit. The value of 0.59 in this example is not a value that would make you say "phew! I've found the perfect fit," but it is also not terrible.

In any case, we want to combine visualization with statistics for the best interpretation and decision-making. Visually speaking, the fitted data nicely shows where the country started in 2010 (*a*) and the average slope of change the country has had over the years (*b*). Even though r2 does not show the perfect fit, the visualization shows that the function tells a perfect story of the data with only two parameters. When you're dealing with FDA, being able to capture what is essential to our analysis is more important than having a perfect fit. Sometimes, the perfect fit shows we are capturing the noise over the generalizable trend.

The Meaning behind the Parameters of a Linear Function

Similar to any other famous function, the parameters of the linear function ($y=a+b*x$) have intuitive meanings. The *a* parameter is known as an intercept or constant; in this example, the intercept represents where the country started. The *b* parameter is known as the slope, and it represents the rate and direction of change. In this example, *b* represents exactly that – the rate and direction of change a country has gone through over the years.

So, every time you perform FDA, one of the must-do activities is understanding the meaning of the parameters of the function that can capture the essential information of the dataset.

Of course, we don't stop here before finalizing the linear function – we must test how well the function can capture the essence of information for the happiness indices of each country.

The following code fits the linear function 1,098 times – one per combination of happiness indices – and the countries (122 countries and 9 happiness indices). For every curve fitting, the line plot shows the actual data and the fitted function is presented. r2 of the fit is also reported. Moreover, all calculated r2 values are recorded in rSqured_df for future analysis:

```python
happines_index = ['Life_Ladder', 'Log_GDP_per_capita', 'Social_
support', 'Healthy_life_expectancy_at_birth', 'Freedom_to_
make_life_choices', 'Generosity', 'Perceptions_of_corruption',
'Positive_affect',  'Negative_affect']

rSqured_df = pd.DataFrame(index=country_df.index,
columns=happines_index)

for i,row in country_df.iterrows():
    for h_i in happines_index:
        x_data = range(10)
        y_data = row[h_i]
        p,c= curve_fit(linearFunction, x_data, y_data)
        fit_y = linearFunction(x_data,p[0],p[1])
```

```
rS = r2_score(y_data,fit_y)
rSqured_df.at[i,h_i] = rS

plt.plot(x_data,y_data,label='data' )
plt.plot(x_data, fit_y, '--', label='fit')
plt.xticks(x_data,y_data.index)
plt.legend()
plt.title('{} - {} - r2={}'
.format(i,h_i,str(round(rS,2))))
plt.show()
```

Spend some time and review the visuals that the preceding code populates. You will see that while the r2 values of some of the visualization and the fit of the linear function are not statistically high, for almost all of the visualizations, the story about the linear function state makes sense.

To investigate this further, let's create a box plot of all of the r2 values per happiness index. The following screenshot uses the seaborn.boxplot() function to do this:

```
In [47]:  ▶  sns.boxplot(data=rSquared_df)
             plt.xticks(rotation=90)
             plt.show()
```

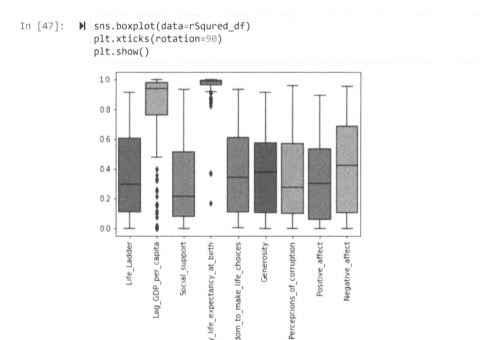

Figure 13.19 – The box plots of r2 per happiness index

After studying the box plot in the preceding screenshot, we can see that the curve fitting for **Log_GDP_per_capita** and **Healthy_life_expectancy_at_birth** have had very good fits. This shows that the trends of these two happiness indices have been the most linear.

From the preceding screenshot, we could conclude that the linear function is not the appropriate function to transform the other happiness indices and recommend going to the drawing board to find a more suitable function for them. While that is also a valid direction, continuing with the linear function for all of the happiness indices is also valid. This is because linear functions tend to capture the essence of what is important for this analysis, and having a lower goodness-of-fit does not mean the parameters will not be able to show the trends of the data.

The following code creates a code function to be applied to `country_df`. The `linearFDA()` function, when applied to a row, loops through all the hapiness indices, fits the linear function to the 10 values, and returns the estimated parameters, a and b:

```
happines_index = ['Life_Ladder', 'Log_GDP_per_capita',
'Social_support', 'Healthy_life_expectancy_at_birth',
'Freedom_to_make_life_choices','Generosity', 'Perceptions_of_
corruption','Positive_affect', 'Negative_affect']

ml_index = pd.MultiIndex.from_product([happines_index,
['a','b']], names=('Hapiness Index', 'Parameter'))

def linearFDA(row):
    output_sr = pd.Series(np.nan,index = ml_index)
    for h_i in happines_index:
        x_data = range(10)
        y_data = row[h_i]
        p,c= curve_fit(linearFunction, x_data, y_data)
        output_sr.loc[(h_i,'a')] =p[0]
        output_sr.loc[(h_i,'b')] =p[1]
    return(output_sr)
```

Once the function has been created, you can use the following code to create `country_t_df`, which is the FDA-transformed version of `country_df`.

However, there is a caveat before running the code. Once run, the code will provide a warning regarding covariance not being able to estimate. That's nothing to worry about:

```
country_df_t=country_df.apply(linearFDA,axis=1)
```

Once the code has been run, get Jupyter Notebook to show you `country_df_t` and study the transformed dataset. The following diagram shows the extent and structure of change that was applied to `country_df` to shape `country_df_t`:

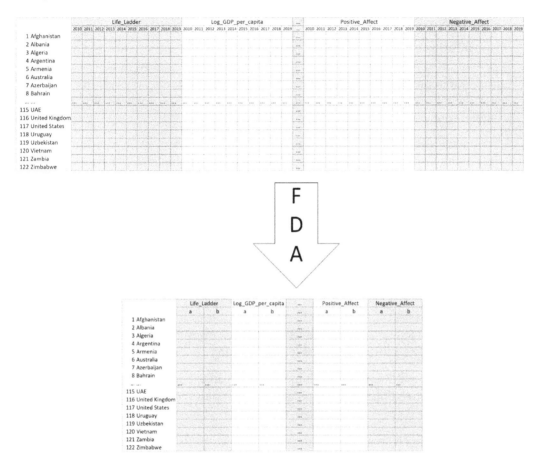

Figure 13.20 – The original structure of country_df and its FDA-transformed one

In the preceding code, we can see that `country_df_t` now only uses 18 attributes instead of the 90 attributes of `country_df`. Here, FDA has done more than just data reduction. FDA, along with the linear function, has transformed the data so that its key features – the starting point and the slope of change of the happiness indices – are massaged to the surface.

Before moving on, let's compare the FDA approach and PCA approach that we applied to the same data. There are a few key points here:

- **Extension of Reduction**: PCA was able to reduce the data into only three attributes, while FDA reduced the data into 18 attributes.

- **Loss of Information**: Both approaches removed some variations from the data. We know that PCA kept 71% of the variation, but we don't know exactly how many variations were kept by FDA. However, we did have control over what kind of variations we were interested in using with the FDA. PCA does not offer this kind of control.

- **Parametricality**: While there were fewer new dimensions for PCA, they did not have an intuitive meaning. However, FDA's reduced parameters did have meaning, and those were even more useful for analysis than the original attributes.

Next, we are going to learn about a few possible useful functions that are frequently used when transforming data sources with FDA.

Prominent functions to use for FDA

In this section, we will learn about a few functions that are frequently used for FDA.

Before we look at this list of functions, let's reiterate that the functions can be anything that has the potential to capture the trends in the data. However, the functions we will go over here are famous and frequently used for curve fitting.

When you have data and want to apply it to FDA, you can experiment with one of the four functions - **exponential**, **Fourier**, **sinusoidal**, and **Gaussian** - to see which one works best for the analytic goals.

Now, let's learn a little bit about each of them. We will start with exponential. Before moving on, please pay close attention to the following caveat.

Caveat!

There is a lot to be said about each of these functions; in a book dedicated to functional data analysis, each of these functions could take up one whole chapter. However, here, we only get a very brief introduction to each of these functions. These instructions will be enough for you to have a good guess if a function will be applicable for a dataset or not. If and when you have a function candidate for a dataset, I highly encourage you to read more about the function to understand its possible variations and the meanings of its parameters. This will be essential if you wish to succeed with functional data analysis.

Now, let's learn a little bit about these functions. We will start with the exponential function.

Exponential function

This function can capture what is characterized as exponential growth or decay. For instance, what we know as exponential growth is a growth that is slow at first but whose rate of growth rapidly increases. The following equation shows the exponential function:

$$y = a * e^{b*x}$$

The parameters of these functions are *a* and *b*. Here, *e* is a constant known as Euler's number, which is a constant that is approximately 2.71. To get an accurate value of *e*, run `np.exp(1)` in your Jupyter Notebook after having imported NumPy as np.

For example, the following code uses the `GoogleStock.csv` file, which contains the daily stock prices of Google from the day it went public until September 3, 2021, which is the day this content is being developed. This code uses everything we have learned about in this chapter on how to fit a function to a dataset:

```
def exponantial(x,a,b):
    y = a*np.exp(b*x)
    return y
price_df = pd.read_csv('GoogleStock.csv')
price_df.set_index('t',inplace=True)
y_data = price_df.Price
x_data = range(len(y_data))
p,c= curve_fit(exponantial, x_data, y_data,p0=[50,0])
fit_y = exponantial(x_data,p[0],p[1])
plt.plot(x_data,y_data,label='Google Stock Price Data')
plt.plot(x_data, fit_y, '--', label='fit')
plt.xticks(np.linspace(1,len(y_data),15),y_data.iloc[1::300].
index,rotation=90)
plt.legend()
plt.show()
```

Running the preceding code will create the following output:

r2_score 0.9448509203130201

Figure 13.21 – The output of fitting the exponential function to GoogleStock.csv

Before moving on to the next function, allow me to share with you a rather disappointing reality about the `curve_fit()` function from `scipy.optimize`. While this is a great and useful function, it is not fully integrated and the most powerful it can be. For more complex functions, for `curve_fit()` to estimate the best possible parameters, the function needs a leg-up. This small act of help must come from us as a first guess about what we think the parameters should be. For example, in the preceding code, p0=[50,0] is that leg-up. For us to be able to have good educated guesses so that we can help `curve_fit()`, we need to have a good understanding of what the parameters of the function mean. For instance, in the case of the exponential function, *a* is known as the intercept and *b* is known as the base. To get `curve_fit()` going, we have helped the function by stating that the intercept will be around the number 50. The number 50 is the price of Google stocks for the first few days.

Now, let's move at the Fourier function.

Fourier function

This function is a valid candidate for capturing vibrational signals such as noise and voice data. These vibrational signals are characterized by oscillating, reciprocating, or periodic, and the **Fourier function** can capture these periodic oscillations and reciprocations. The following equation shows the Fourier function. The parameters of the Fourier function are *a0*, *a1*, *a2*, and *w*:

$$y = a0 + a1 * cos(x * w) + b1 * sin(x * w)$$

For example, the following code uses the `Noise_data.csv` file, which contains 200 milliseconds of vibrational signals collected from a car engine for health diagnosis. Similar to the preceding code, it uses everything we have learned about in this chapter on how to fit a function to a dataset:

```
def fourier(x,a0,a1,b1,w):
    y = a0 + a1*np.cos(x*w) + b1*np.sin(x*w)
    return y
noise_df = pd.read_csv('Noise_data.csv')
noise_df.set_index('t',inplace=True)
y_data = noise_df.Signal
x_data = range(len(y_data))
p,c= curve_fit(fourier, x_data, y_data,p0=[10,1000,-400,0.3])
fit_y = fourier(x_data,p[0],p[1],p[2],p[3])
plt.figure(figsize=(15,4))
plt.plot(x_data,y_data,label='Noise Data')
plt.plot(x_data, fit_y, '--', label='fit')
plt.legend()
plt.show()
print("r2_score",r2_score(y_data,fit_y))
```

Running the preceding code will create the following output:

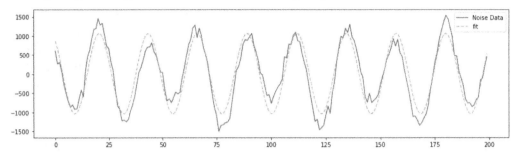

r2_score 0.8770501065480368

Figure 13.22 – The output of fitting the Fourier function to Noise_data.csv

Before moving on to the next function, Sinusoidal, note that the curve_fit() function needed even a stronger leg-up (p0=[10,1000,-400,0.3]) to be able to fit the data.

Sinusoidal function

This function, which is similar to the Fourier function, can capture oscillations and reciprocations, and similarly, the function could be a candidate for capturing noise and voice data. The following equation shows the sinusoidal function. The parameters of the sinusoidal function are *a1*, *b1*, and *c1*:

$$y = a1 * sin(b1 * x + c1)$$

For example, the following code uses the same data as in the previous example, which is contained in the Noise_data.csv file, to see whether the function can simulate the data:

```
def sinusoidal(x,a1,b1,c1):
    y =  a1*np.sin(b1*x+c1)
    return y
noise_df = pd.read_csv('Noise_data.csv')
noise_df.set_index('t',inplace=True)
y_data = noise_df.Signal
x_data = range(len(y_data))
p,c= curve_fit(sinusoidal, x_data, y_data,p0=[1000,0.25,2.5])
fit_y = sinusoidal(x_data,p[0],p[1],p[2])
plt.figure(figsize=(15,4))
plt.plot(x_data,y_data,label='Noise Data')
```

```
plt.plot(x_data, fit_y, '--', label='fit')
plt.legend()
plt.show()
print("r2_score",r2_score(y_data,fit_y))
```

Running the preceding code will create the following output:

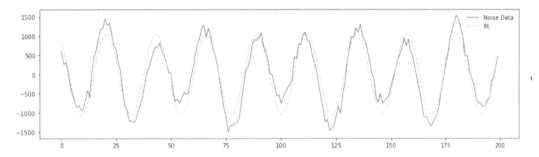

```
r2_score 0.8768630893287543
```

Figure 13.23 – The output of fitting the sinusoidal function to Noise_data.csv

Again, note that the `curve_fit()` function needed even a more significant leg-up (`p0=[1000,0.25,2.5]`) to be able to fit the data. These leg-ups can only be given to the `curve_fit()` function if we have a good understanding of the parameters of the sinusoidal function.

Gaussian function

This function is famous for Gaussian or normal distribution from probability and statistics. The functionality behind the normal distribution that we use to summarize, analyze, and compare many populations with comes from the **Gaussian function**. The general Gaussian function has three parameters called *a1*, *b1*, and *c1*. The following equation shows its formula:

$$y = a1 * e^{(x-b1)^2/2c1^2}$$

The density function of a normal distribution is a specific variation of the preceding formula with only two parameters, where $b1=\mu$ and $c1=\delta$, and *a1* is calculated as $1/\delta\sqrt{2\pi}$. If you don't know about the normal distribution, just ignore this paragraph and move on. You can just treat this function as another famous function you just became aware of.

The Gaussian function is famous for being a bell-shaped figure, and each of the three parameters shows the characteristics of the shape of a bell. Let's look at an example.

We will use the `covid19hospitalbycounty.csv` file here, which contains the daily COVID hospitalization data of all the counties in California, as collected on September 4, 2021. The following code reads the file into `covid_county_day_df` and then uses the `.groupby()` function to aggregate all of the counties' data by summing them, thus creating `covid_day_df`. The code also plots the trend of daily hospitalizations:

```
covid_county_day_df = pd.read_csv('covid19hospitalbycounty.
csv')

covid_day_df = covid_county_day_df.groupby('todays_date').
hospitalized_covid_patients.sum()

covid_day_df.plot()

plt.xticks(rotation=90)

plt.show()
```

Running the preceding code will create the following output:

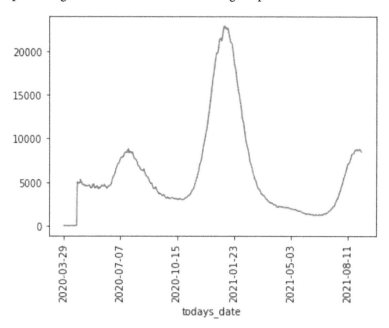

Figure 13.24 – California COVID hospitalizations until September 4, 2021

We can see a few bell-shaped figures in the trend of the data. Each of these waves can be summarized and captured using the Guassian function. For example, let's capture the one from **2020-10-15** to **2021-05-03**. The following code does that just like all the previous curve fittings do:

```
def gaussian(x,a1,b1,c1):
    y= a1*np.exp(-((x-b1)**2/2*c1**2))
    return y
y_data = covid_day_df.loc['2020-10-15':'2021-05-03']
x_data = range(len(y_data))
p,c= curve_fit(gaussian, x_data, y_data)
fit_y = gaussian(x_data,p[0],p[1],p[2])
plt.plot(x_data,y_data,label='Hospitalization Data')
plt.plot(x_data, fit_y, '--', label='fit')
plt.legend()
plt.show()
print("r2_score",r2_score(y_data,fit_y))
```

Running the preceding code will create the following output:

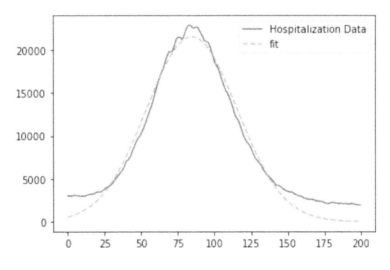

```
r2_score 0.9668373070226166
```

Figure 13.25 – The output of fitting the Gaussian function to a part of covid_day_df

While the preceding diagram shows a great fit, you may be wondering how this can be of any analytics value. This is an excellent question. Let's consider an analytics project where we want to predict the number of COVID deaths in the next month using the historical data. You could create a prediction model that connects the number of COVID deaths on any given day (the dependent attribute) to the total number of hospitalizations 2 weeks before that day (the independent attribute). Such a model can achieve a certain level of success in prediction. However, there are ways to improve that. For instance, we could add more independent attributes, such as the rate of COVID test positivity a month before that day, or the rate of vaccination 2 months before that day. This approach uses more data sources to enrich the prediction model. A second approach, which can use FDA, is to enrich the independent attributes that come from the same source of data. For instance, instead of just extracting one value from the hospitalization data from 3 weeks ago, we might be able to use the parameters of the function we used to fit the data. Doing this is certainly trickier than adding more data sources, but this might just be the improvement a model needs to reach even better predictions. See *Chapter 16, Case Study 2 – Predicting COVID 19 Hospitalization*, for great data integration/reduction examples of using FDA.

As we get closer to the end of this chapter, let us first go over a quick summary of the FDA, and after that, we will have another quick summary of the whole chapter.

Final notes on FDA

There is a lot to be said and covered in FDA. It has its own world. What we covered here should just be looked at as an introduction and a springboard for a possible deep dive into this world for more learning.

As we finish learning about FDA, we will provide a few notes and considerations:

- Any function, even one that has just been created, can be used as the function for FDA. The advantage of using these famous functions is that they are well known and there are lots of resources for them to support your learning and your data analytic projects.

- Most functions have variations and they can become more complex for more complicated datasets. If a function kind of works for a dataset but not perfectly, maybe one of its variations will. For instance, the sinusoidal function, when used with two terms, can accommodate more complex oscillations. See the following equation:

$$y = a1 * sin(b1 * x + c1) + a2 * sin(b2 * x + c2)$$

- Knowing the meaning of the parameters is essential in understanding the transformed data. Also, as we saw, you may have to tap into that knowledge in giving a leg-up to the function `curve_fit()`.

- FDA can be used as a dimension reduction method. However, FDA can be looked at as a data analytics tool. Furthermore, as we will see in the next chapter, FDA can be a data transformation method.

Now, let's summarize this chapter.

Summary

Congratulations on your excellent progress on yet another exciting and important chapter. In this chapter, we learned about the concept of data reduction, its uniqueness, the different types, and saw a few examples of how knowing about the tools and techniques we can use for data reduction can be of significant value in our data analytic projects.

First, we understood the distinction between data redundancy and data reduction and then continued to learn about the overarching categories of data reduction: numerosity data reduction and dimensionality data reduction. For numerosity data reduction, we covered two methods and an example to showcase when and where they could be of value. For dimensionality reduction, we covered two categories: supervised and unsupervised dimension reduction.

Supervised dimension reduction is when we pick and choose the independent attributes for prediction or classification data mining tasks, while unsupervised dimension reduction is when we reduce the number of dimensions with a more general outlook.

The next chapter is going to be the last one in *Part 3* of this book: *preprocessing*. We are going to learn about data transformation and massaging. In this chapter, we sometimes had to talk a little about data transformation as well. Some of the techniques that were covered in this chapter can also be used as data transformation techniques.

The next chapter is going to be another exciting chapter. However, before we learn about data transformation and data massaging, take advantage of the learning opportunities that the following exercises provide.

Exercises

1. In your own words, describe the similarities and differences between data reduction and data redundancy from the following angles: the literal meanings of the terms, their objectives, and their procedures.

2. If you decide to include or exclude independent attributes based on the correlation coefficient value of each independent attribute with the dependent attribute in a prediction task, what would you call this type of preprocessing? Data redundancy or data reduction?

3. In this example, we will be using `new_train.csv` from `https://www.kaggle.com/rashmiranu/banking-dataset-classification`. Each row of the data contains customer information, along with campaign efforts regarding each customer, to get them to subscribe for a long-term deposit at the bank. In this example, we would like to tune a decision tree that can show us the trends that lead to successful subscription campaigning. As the only tuning process we know about will be computationally very expensive, we have decided to perform one of the numerosity data reductions we've learned about in this chapter to ease the computation for the tuning process. Which method would fit this data better? Why? Once you have arrived at the data reduction method you want to use, apply the method, tune the decision tree, and draw the final decision tree. Finally, comment on a few interesting patterns you found in the final decision tree.

4. In this chapter, we learned about six dimensionality reduction methods. For each of these six methods, specify if the method is supervised or unsupervised, and why.

5. We would like to continue working on `new_train.csv` from Excercise 3. Use a decision tree and a random forest to evaluate the usefulness of the independent attributes in `new_train.csv`. Report and compare the results using both dimension reduction methods.

6. Use brute-force computational dimension reduction to figure out the optimum subset of independent attributes that the KNN algorithm needs for the classification task described in *Exercise 3*. If the task is computationally too expensive, what is one strategy that we learned about that can curb that? If you did end up using that strategy, could you say the subset you've found is still optimum?

7. In this exercise, we will use the data in `ToyotaCorolla.csv` to create a prediction model using MLP that can predict car prices. Do the following:

    a) Deal with all the data cleaning issues, if any.

    b) Apply linear regression, a decision tree, and a random forest to evaluate the usefulness of the independent attributes in the dataset. Use all the results of the evaluations to come to the top eight independent attributes that can support MLP prediction best. Which three dimension reduction methods should be given the least priority and why?

    c) Use similar code to the code we used in this chapter to tune the decision tree to tune MLP for the prediction task of connecting the top eight independent attributes from the previous step to the dependent attribute. In this tuning experiment, use the following two hyperparameters and the values given in the list:

       i.   `hidden_layer_sizes`: [5,10,15,20,(5,5),(5,10),(10,10),(5,5,5),(5,10,5)]

       ii. `max_iter`: [50, 100, 200, 500]

If the computation takes too long, feel free to use the computational cost-cutting strategy you have learned about in this chapter.

d) In this step, we would like to use brute-force computational dimension reduction to find the best subset of independent attributes out of the eight independent attributes. Can we use the tuning parameters we found from the previous step or, when using the brute-force dimension reduction method, does it have to be mixed with parameter tuning? Why/why not? Apply the best approach. Again, feel free to use the computational cost-cutting strategy you learned about in this chapter.

8. In this exercise, we would like to use the `Cereals.csv` dataset. This dataset contains rows of information about different cereal products. We would like to perform clustering analysis on this dataset, first using K-Means and then using PCA. Do the following:

a) Impute a central tendency of the attribute for all the missing values.

b) What central tendency did you choose and why?

c) Why did we impute using the central tendency? Why not use other methods? Answer by commenting on how the data will be used next.

d) Remove the categorical attribute from the data.

e) Should the data be normalized or standardized for clustering? Why?

f) Apply K-Means with K=7 and report the resulting clustering.

g) Perform centroid analysis and name each cluster.

h) Investigate the relationship between the clusters and the two categorical attributes that you removed. Which cluster has both hot and cold kinds of cereal? Which company only creates popular cereals that are not very nutritious?

i) The elementary public schools would like to choose a set of cereals to include in their cafeterias. Every day, a different cereal is offered, but all the cereals should be healthy. Which members from which cluster should be used here? Explain why.

j) Now, we want to complement this analysis using PCA. Before applying PCA, should we standardize or normalize the dataset?

k) Using the first few PCs, come up with an annotated three-dimensional scatterplot that shows most of the variation in the data. How much variation is shown? Make sure that the figure contains the necessary element to explain to the audience the importance of each PC.

l) Looking at the three-dimensional scatterplot, would you say the choice of K=7 for K-Means was good?

m) Can you spot the members of the cluster you found in *Step i* in the three-dimensional scatterplot you created in *Step k*? Are they all together?

9. In this exercise, we will use Stocks 2020.csv, which contains the daily stock prices of 4,154 companies in 2020. Remember that 2020 is the year that the COVID-19 pandemic happened. During this year, the stock market experienced a sudden crash and also a quick recovery. We want to use the data reduction methods that we know of to see if we can capture this from the data. Do the following:

a) Use the k-means algorithm to cluster the data into 27 groups. Also, use the module time to capture the amount of time it took the algorithm to run.

b) What are the outliers in the data based on the clustering results?

c) Draw line plots for all the outliers and describe the trends you see.

d) Draw line plots for all the members of the clusters where there are less than 10 members and describe the trends.

e) Apply PCA to the data and report the number of variations that the first three PCs account for. Also, draw an annotated scatterplot that includes the three PCs with all the necessary visual guides.

f) Using the visual from the previous step, count and report the outliers. Are they the same outliers that we found using k-means clustering?

g) Cluster the stocks into 27 groups again using the most significant PCs. Also, report the amount of time it took for K-means to complete the task. See how much faster K-means was compared to how fast it was in *Step a*.

h) Draw a visual that compares the clusterings in *Steps a* and *g*. Describe your observations.

i) We would like to extract the following features from the data:

- *General_Slope*: The slope of the linear regression line fitted to the data of the stock.

- *Sellout_Slope*: The slope of the linear regression line fitted to the data of the stock from Feb 14 – March 19 (stock sell-out period due to COVID).

- *Rebound_Slope*: The slope of linear regression line fitted to the data of the stock from March 21 – December 30 (Stock rebound after COVID sell-out).

We will do this in a few steps. First, create a placeholder DataFrame (fda_df) where its index is the stock symbols and its columns are the features mentioned previously.

j) Find `General_Slope` and fill the placeholder using a linear regression model.

k) Find `Sellout_Slope` and fill the placeholder using a linear regression model.

l) Find `Rebound_Slope` and fill the placeholder using a linear regression model.

m) Draw a three-dimensional scatterplot for `fda_df`. Use `x_axis` for `Sellout_Slope` and `y-axis` for `Rebound_Slope`.

n) Cluster the stocks into 27 groups again using the three attributes of `fda_df`. Then, compare the clustering outcomes with the clusterings from *Steps a* and *g* and describe your observations.

o) Among the three preprocessing approaches (no preprocessing, PCA-transformed, and FDA-transformed) you experimented with in this exercise, which one was able to help in capturing the patterns we were interested in?

10. *Figure 13.2* was created using a decision tree after random sampling. Recreate this figure but this time, use random over/undersampling, where the sample has 500 churning customers and 500 non-churning customers. Describe the differences in the final visual.

11. *Figure 13.7* shows the result of dimension reduction for the task of predicting the next day's amazon Stock prices using linear regression. Perform dimension reduction using a decision tree and compare the results. Don't forget that to do so, you will need to tune `DecisionTreeRegressor()` from `sklearn.tree`. You can use the following code for this tuning process:

```
from sklearn.tree import DecisionTreeRegressor
from sklearn.model_selection import GridSearchCV
y=amzn_df.drop(index=['2021-01-12'])['changeP']
Xs = amzn_df.drop(
columns=['changeP'],index=['2021-01-12'])
param_grid = { 'criterion':['mse','friedman_mse','mae'],
'max_depth': [2,5,10,20], 'min_samples_split':
[10,20,30,40,50,100], 'min_impurity_decrease': [0,0.001,
0.005, 0.01, 0.05, 0.1]}
gridSearch = GridSearchCV(DecisionTreeRegressor(), param_
grid, cv=2, scoring='neg_mean_squared_error', verbose=1)
gridSearch.fit(Xs, y)
print('Best score: ', gridSearch.best_score_)
print('Best parameters: ', gridSearch.best_params_)
```

14

Data Transformation and Massaging

Congratulations, you've made your way to the last chapter of the third part of the book – *The Preprocessing*. In this part of the book, we have so far covered **data cleaning**, **data integration**, and **data reduction**. In this chapter, we will add the last piece to the arsenal of our data preprocessing tools – data transformation and massaging.

Data transformation normally is the last data preprocessing that is applied to our datasets. The dataset may need to be transformed to be ready for a prescribed analysis, or a specific transformation might help a certain analytics tool to perform better, or simply without a correct data transformation, the results of our analysis might be misleading.

In this chapter, we will cover when and where we need data transformation. Furthermore, we will cover the many techniques that are needed for every data preprocessing situation. In this chapter, we're going to cover the following main topics:

- The whys of data transformation and data massaging
- Normalization and standardization
- Binary coding, ranking transformation, and discretization
- Attribute construction
- Feature extraction

- Log transformation

- Smoothing, aggregation, and binning

Technical requirements

You will be able to find all of the code and the dataset that is used in this book in a GitHub repository exclusively created for this book. To find the repository, go to: `https://github.com/PacktPublishing/Hands-On-Data-Preprocessing-in-Python`. You can find this chapter in this repository and download the code and the data for better learning.

The whys of data transformation and massaging

Data transformation comes at the very last stage of data preprocessing, right before using the analytic tools. At this stage of data preprocessing, the dataset already has the following characteristics.

- **Data cleaning**: The dataset is cleaned at all three cleaning levels (*Chapters 9–11*).

- **Data integration**: All the potentially beneficial data sources are recognized and a dataset that includes the necessary information is created (*Chapter 12, Data Fusion and Integration*).

- **Data reduction**: If needed, the size of the dataset has been reduced (*Chapter 13, Data Reduction*).

At this stage of data preprocessing, we may have to make some changes to the data before moving to the analyzing stage. The dataset will undergo the changes for one of the following reasons: we will call them *necessity*, *correctness*, and *effectiveness*. The following list provides more detail for each reason.

- **Necessity**: The analytic method cannot work with the current state of the data. For instance, many data-mining algorithms, such as **Multi-Layered Perceptron** (**MLP**) and K-means, only work with numbers; when there are categorical attributes, those attributes need to be transformed before the analysis is possible.

- **Correctness**: Without the proper data transformation, the resulting analytic will be misleading and wrong. For instance, if we use K-means clustering without normalizing the data, we think that all the attributes have equal weights in the clustering result, but that's incorrect; the attributes that happen to have a larger scale will have more weight.

- **Effectiveness**: If the data goes through some prescribed changes, the analytics will be more effective.

Now that we have a better understanding of the goals and reasons for data transformation and massaging, let's learn what is the difference between **data transformation** and **data massaging**.

Data transformation versus data massaging

There is more similarity between the two terms than difference. Therefore, using them interchangeably would not be incorrect in most situations. Both terms describe changes that a dataset undergoes before analytics for improvement. However, there are two differences that it will be good for us know.

- First, the term *data transformation* is more commonly used and known.
- Second, the literal meanings of transforming and massaging may be used for drawing a conclusive difference between the two terms.

The term transformation is more general than massaging. Any changes a dataset undergoes can be called data transformation. However, the term massaging is more specific and does not carry the neutrality of transformation, but it carries the meaning of *doing more for getting more*. Therefore, as the following figure suggests, data massaging can be interpreted as changing the data when we are trying to improve the effectiveness of data analytics, whereas data transformation is a more general term. So, some could argue that all data massaging is also data transformation, but not all data transformation is also data massaging:

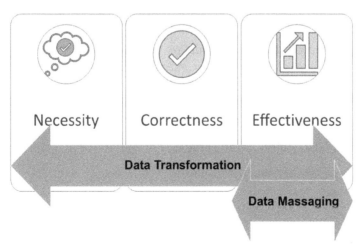

Figure 14.1 – Data transformation versus data massaging

The preceding figure shows the three reasons for data transformation that we discussed earlier: **Necessity**, **Correctness**, and **Effectiveness**. Furthermore, the figure shows that while data transformation is a more general term used to refer to the changes a dataset undergoes before the analysis, data massaging is more specific and can be used when the goal of transforming the dataset is for effectiveness.

In the rest of this chapter, we will cover some data transformation and massaging tools that are commonly used. We will start by covering normalization and standardization.

Normalization and standardization

At different points during our journey in this book, we've already talked about and used normalization and standardization. For instance, before applying **K-Nearest Neighbors (KNN)** in *Chapter 7, Classification*, and before using K-means on our dataset in *Chapter 8, Clustering Analysis*, we used normalization. Furthermore, before applying **Principal Component Analysis (PCA)** to our dataset for unsupervised dimension reduction in *Chapter 13, Data Reduction*, we used standardization.

Here is the general rule of when we need normalization or standardization. We need normalization when we need the range of all the attributes in a dataset to be equal. This will be needed especially for algorithmic data analytics that uses the distance between the data objects. Examples of such algorithms are K-means and KNN. On the other hand, we need standardization when we need the variance and/or the standard deviation of all the attributes to be equal. We saw an example of needing standardization when learning about PCA in *Chapter 13, Data Reduction*. We learned standardization was necessary because PCA essentially operates by examining the total variations in a dataset; when an attribute has more variations, it will have more say in the operation of PCA.

The following two equations show the formula we need to use to apply normalization and standardization. The following list defines the variables used in the equations:

- A: The attribute
- i: The index for the data objects
- A_i: The value of data object i in attribute A
- N_A: The normalized version of attribute A

- *SA*: The standardized version of attribute *A*

$$NA_i = \frac{A_i - \min(A)}{\max(A) - \min(A)}$$

$$SA_i = \frac{A_i - \text{mean}(A)}{\text{std}(A)}$$

Let's see an example. The following figure shows a small dataset of employees that are described by only two attributes, **Salary** and **GPA**. Naturally, the numbers we use for salary are larger than GPA, as you can see in the original attributes, **Salary** and **GPA**. The preceding two equations have been used to apply normalization and standardization transformation respectively. The middle table is the normalized version of the dataset showing **N_Salary** and **N_GPA**. You can see that after normalization, the transformed versions of the attributes have the same range from zero to one. The right table is the standardized version of the dataset featuring **S_Salary** and **S_GPA**. You can see in the standardized version that the **standard deviation** (**STD**) of the two attributes are both equal to one:

	Salary	GPA	N_Salary	N_GPA	S_Salary	S_GPA
	A	B	NA	NB	SA	SB
1	92000	3.25	0.75	0.339806	0.817616	-0.57477
2	83000	3.36	0.5	0.446602	-0.00919	-0.15882
3	83000	3.16	0.5	0.252427	-0.00919	-0.91509
4	72000	3.45	0.194444	0.533981	-1.01972	0.181506
5	101000	3.32	1	0.407767	1.644418	-0.31007
6	85000	3.57	0.555556	0.650485	0.174547	0.635271
7	74000	3.93	0.25	1	-0.83599	1.996565
8	65000	3.61	0	0.68932	-1.66279	0.786526
9	98000	3.47	0.916667	0.553398	1.368817	0.257133
10	78000	2.9	0.361111	0	-0.46852	-1.89825
Max=	101000	3.93	1	1	1.644418	1.996565
Min=	65000	2.9	0	0	-1.66279	-1.89825
Mean=	83100	3.402	0.502778	0.487379	0	0
STD=	10885.31	0.264454	0.30237	0.256752	1	1

Figure 14.2 – An example of normalization and standardization

Upon further study of the preceding figure, you may observe two interesting trends:

- First, even though the goal of normalization is equalizing the range (**Max** and **Min**), the standard deviations (**STD**) of the normalized attributes have become much closer to one another too.

- Second, even though the goal of standardization is equalizing the standard deviation (**STD**), the **Max** and **Min** values of the two standardized attributes are much closer to one another too.

These two observations are the main reason in many resources standardization and normalization are introduced as two methods that can be used interchangeably. Furthermore, I have seen all too often that the choice of applying standardization or normalization is set in a supervised tuning. That means the practitioner experiments with both normalizing the data and then standardizing it, and then selects the one that leads to better performance on the prime evaluation metric. For instance, if we want to apply KNN on the data, we might see the choice between normalization or standardization of the attribute as a tuning parameter next to K and the subset of the independent attributes (see the *Example – finding the best subset of independent attributes for a classification algorithm* subsection in the *Brute-force computational dimension reduction* section in *Chapter 13, Data Reduction*) and experiment with both to see which one works best for the case study.

Before moving to the next group of data transformation methods, let's discuss whether normalization and standardization fall under data massaging or not. Most of the time, the reason we would apply these two transformations are that without them, the results of our analysis would be misleading. So, the best way to describe the reason behind applying them is *correctness*; therefore, we cannot refer to standardization or normalization as data massaging.

In the course of this book, we have seen many examples of applying normalization and standardization, so we will skip giving a practical example on these data transformation tools and go straight to the next group of methods: binary coding, ranking transformation, and discretization.

Binary coding, ranking transformation, and discretization

In our analytics journey, there will be many instances in which we want to transform our data from numerical representation to categorical representation, or vice versa. To do these transformations, we will have to use one of three tools: binary coding, ranking transformation, and discretization.

As the following figure shows, to switch from **Categories** to **Numbers**, we either have to use **Binary Coding** or **Ranking Transformation**, and to switch from numbers to categories, we need to use **Discretization**:

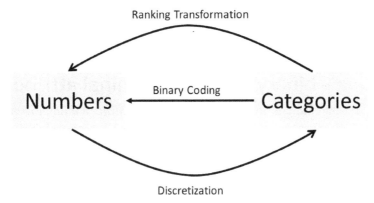

Figure 14.3 – Direction of application for binary coding, ranking transformation, and discretization

One question that the preceding figure might bring to mind is, how do we know which one we choose when we want to move from categories to numbers: binary coding or ranking transformation? The answer is simple.

If the categories are nominal, we can only use binary coding; if they are ordinal, both may be used, but each method has its pros and cons. We will talk about those using examples.

Before moving on to see examples of applying these transformations, let's discuss why we may need these data transformations, in two parts:

- First, why we would transform the data into numerical form
- Second, why we would transform data into categorical form

We generally transform categorical attributes to numerical ones when our analytics tool of choice can only work with numbers. For instance, if we would like to use MLP for prediction and some of the independent attributes are categorical, MLP will not be able to handle the prediction task unless the categorical attributes are transformed into numerical attributes.

Now, let's discuss why we would transform numerical attributes into categorical ones. Most often, this is done because the resulting analytics output will become more intuitive for our consumption. For instance, instead of having to deal with a number that shows the GPA, we may be more comfortable dealing with categories such as *excellent*, *good*, *acceptable*, and *unacceptable*. This will become the case, especially if we want to use our attention to understand the interactions between attributes. We will see an example of this in a few pages.

Furthermore, in some analytics situations, the types of attributes must be the same. For instance, when we want to examine the relationship between a numerical attribute and a categorical one, we may decide to transform the numerical attribute to a categorical attribute to be able to use a contingency table for the analysis (see *Visualizing the relationship between a numerical attribute and a categorical attribute* in *Chapter 5, Data Visualization*).

Now, let's start looking at some examples to understand these transformation tools.

Example one – binary coding of nominal attribute

In *Chapter 8, Clustering Analysis*, in the *Using K-means to cluster a dataset with more than two dimensions* section, we did not use the `Continent` categorical attribute for the clustering analysis using K-means. This attribute indeed has information that can add to the interestingness of our clustering analysis. Now that we have learned about the possibility of transforming categorical attributes into numerical ones, let's try to enrich our clustering analysis.

As the attribute continent is nominal, we only have one choice and that is to use binary coding. In the following code, we will use the `pd.get_dummies()` pandas function to binary-code the `Continent` attribute. Before doing that, we need to load the data as we did in *Chapter 8, Clustering Analysis*. The following code takes care of that:

```
report_df = pd.read_csv('WH Report_preprocessed.csv')
BM = report_df.year == 2019
report2019_df = report_df[BM]
report2019_df.set_index('Name',inplace=True)
```

After running the preceding code, we are set to give `pd.get_dummies()` a try. The following screenshot shows how this function is used and the first five rows of its output. The `bc_Continent` variable name is inspired by bc, as in binary coded:

```
In [3]:  ▶ bc_Continent = pd.get_dummies(report2019_df.Continent)
            bc_Continent.head(5)
```
```
Out[3]:
```

Name	Africa	Antarctica	Asia	Europe	North America	Oceania	South America
Afghanistan	0	0	1	0	0	0	0
Albania	0	0	0	1	0	0	0
Algeria	1	0	0	0	0	0	0
Argentina	0	0	0	0	0	0	1
Armenia	0	0	0	1	0	0	0

Figure 14.4 – Screenshot of report2019_df.Continent using pd.get_dummies() binary coding

The preceding screenshot shows exactly what binary coding does. For each possible categorical attribute, a binary attribute will be added. The combination of all the binary attributes will present the same information.

Next, we will run a very similar code to what we ran in *Chapter 8, Clustering Analysis*. Only one part of the following code has been updated, and the updated part is highlighted for your attention:

```
from sklearn.cluster import KMeans
dimensions = ['Life_Ladder', 'Log_GDP_per_capita', 'Social_
support', 'Healthy_life_expectancy_at_birth', 'Freedom_to_
make_life_choices', 'Generosity', 'Perceptions_of_corruption',
'Positive_affect', 'Negative_affect']
Xs = report2019_df[dimensions]
Xs = (Xs - Xs.min())/(Xs.max()-Xs.min())
Xs = Xs.join(bc_Continent/7)
kmeans = KMeans(n_clusters=3)
kmeans.fit(Xs)
for i in range(3):
    BM = kmeans.labels_==i
    print('Cluster {}: {}'.format(i,Xs[BM].index.values))
```

After running the preceding code successfully, you will see the result of the clustering analysis.

The only noticeable difference between the preceding code and the one we used in *Chapter 8, Clustering Analysis*, is the addition of Xs = Xs.join(bc_Continent/7), which adds the binary coded version of the Continent attribute (bc_Continent) to Xs after Xs is normalized, and before it is fed into kmeans.fit(). There is another question – why didn't we add bc_Continent without dividing it by 7?

Let's try to dispel all the confusion before moving on to centroid analysis. The reason we added bc_Continent to our code at a specific point in a specific manner is that we wanted to control how much this binary coding would affect our results. If we had added without dividing it by 7, bc_Continent would have dominated the clustering result by clustering the countries mostly based on their continent. To see this impact, remove the division by 7, run the clustering analysis, and create the heatmap of the centroid analysis to see this. Why does this happen? Isn't it obvious? The Continent attribute has information worth only one attribute, and not 7.

Furthermore, if we had added `bc_Continent/7` before the normalization, the division by 7 would not be meaningful, as the code we run for normalization, which is `Xs = (Xs - Xs.min())/(Xs.max()-Xs.min())`, would have canceled out the division by 7.

So, now we understand why we added the binary-coded data the specific way that we did. Now, let's perform the centroid analysis. The following code will create the heatmap for centroid analysis for this specific situation. The code is very similar to any other centroid analysis that we have performed so far in this book but for a small change. Instead of having one heatmap, we will have two – one for the regular numerical attributes and one for the binary-coded attribute. The reason for this twofold visual is that the normalized numerical values are between 0 and 1, and the binary-coded values are between 0 and 0.14; without the separation, the heatmap would only show the normalized numericals, as those values have a larger scale. Run the normal non-separated heatmap and see that for yourself:

```
clusters = ['Cluster {}'.format(i) for i in range(3)]
Centroids = pd.DataFrame(0.0, index = clusters, columns =
Xs.columns)
for i,clst in enumerate(clusters):
    BM = kmeans.labels_==i
    Centroids.loc[clst] = Xs[BM].mean(axis=0)
plt.figure(figsize=(10,4))
plt.subplot(1,2,1)
sns.heatmap(Centroids[dimensions], linewidths=.5, annot=True,
cmap='binary')
plt.subplot(1,2,2)
sns.heatmap(Centroids[bc_Continent.columns], linewidths=.5,
annot=True, cmap='binary')
plt.show()
```

As described, the preceding code will create a twofold heatmap. To compare the results we arrived at in *Chapter 8*, *Clustering Analysis*, with what we have arrived at here with the preceding code block, we have put these two results in the following figure for comparison:

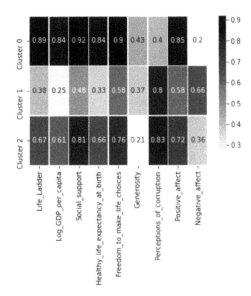

a)   Clustering Analysis without `Continent`

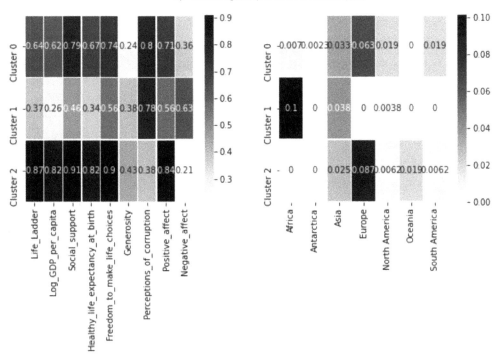

b)   Clustering Analysis with `bc_Continent`

Figure 14.5 – Clustering analysis of countries based on their happiness indices with and without the inclusion of the Continent categorical attribute

The comparison of the heatmaps from the preceding figure clearly shows the successful enrichment of the clustering analysis by the inclusion of a categorical attribute after binary coding. Note that the clustering results of **a)** and **b)** in the preceding figure are largely the same, except for **Cluster 0** and **Cluster 2** having switched places.

Next, let's see an example where our categorical attribute is not nominal but ordinal and see how we should decide between binary coding and ranking transformation.

Example two – binary coding or ranking transformation of ordinal attributes

Transforming ordinal attributes into numbers is a bit tricky. There is no perfect solution; we either have to let go of the ordinal information in the attribute, or assume some information into the data. Let's see what that means in an example.

The following figure shows the transformation of an example ordinal attribute into numbers by three methods: **Binary Coding**, **Ranking Transformation**, and **Attribute Construction**. Spend some time studying this figure before moving on to the next paragraph:

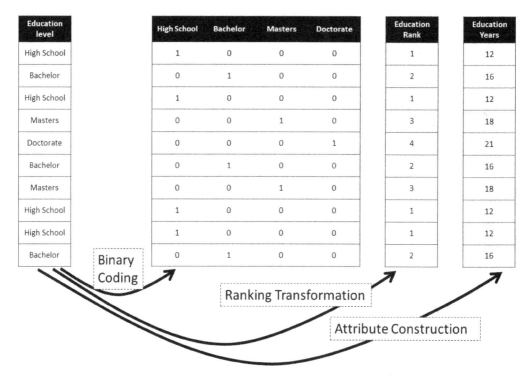

Figure 14.6 – An example showing three ways of transforming an ordinal attribute into numbers

Now, let's discuss why none of the transformations are perfect. In the case of **Binary Coding**, the transformation has not assumed any information into the result, but the transformation has stripped the attribute from its ordinal information. You see, if we were to use the binary-coded values instead of the original attribute in our analysis, the data does not show the order of the possible values of the attribute. For example, while the binary-coded values make a distinction between **High School** and **Bachelor**, the data does not show that **Bachelor** comes after **High School**, as we know it does.

The next transformation, **Ranking Transformation**, does not have this shortcoming; however, it has other cons. You see, by trying to make sure that the order of the possible values is maintained, we had to engage numbers by ranking transformation; however, this goes a little bit overboard. By engaging numbers, not only have we successfully included order in between the possible values of the attribute but we have also collaterally assumed information that does not exist in the original attribute. For example, with the ranking transformed attribute, we are assuming there is one unit difference between **Bachelors** and **High School**.

The figure has another transformation, **Attribute Construction**, which is only possible if we have a good understanding of the attribute. What **Attribute Construction** tries to fix is the gross assumptions that are added by **Ranking Transformation**; instead, **Attribute Construction** uses the knowledge about the original attribute to assume more accurate information into the transformed data. Here, for example, as we know, achieving any of the degrees in the **Education Level** attribute takes a different number of years of education. So, instead, **Attribute Construction** uses that knowledge to assume more accurate assumptions into the transformed data.

We will learn more about **Attribute Construction** in a few pages in this chapter. Now, we want to see an example of transforming numerical attributes into categories.

Example three – discretization of numerical attributes

For this example, let's start from the ending. The following figure shows what discretization can achieve for us. The top plot is a box plot that shows the interaction between three attributes, **sex**, **income**, and **hoursPerWeek**, from `adult_df` (*adult.csv*). We had to use a box plot because **hoursPerWeek** is a numerical attribute. The bottom plot, however, is a bar chart that has the interaction with the same three attributes, except that the **hoursPerWeek** numerical attribute has been discretized. You can see the magic that the discretization of this attribute has done for us. The bottom plot tells the story of the data far better than the top one:

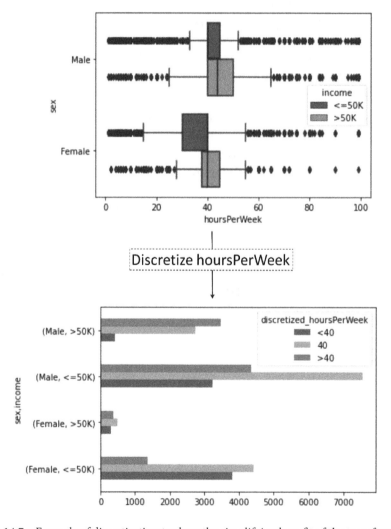

Figure 14.7 – Example of discretization to show the simplifying benefit of the transformation

Now, let's look at the code that we used to make the two plots happen. The following code creates the top plot using `sns.boxplot()`:

```
adult_df = pd.read_csv('adult.csv')
sns.boxplot(data=adult_df, y='sex', x='hoursPerWeek',
hue='income')
```

To create the bottom plot, we first need to discretize `adult_df.hoursPerWeek`. The following code uses the `.apply()` function to transform the numerical attribute to a categorical attribute with the three possibilities of `>40`, `40`, and `<=40`:

```
adult_df['discretized_hoursPerWeek']= adult_df.hoursPerWeek.
apply(lambda v: '>40' if v>40 else ('40' if v==40 else '<40'))
```

A good question here is, why are we using 40 as the cut-off point? In other words, how did we come to use this cut-off? To best answer this question and, in most cases, find the appropriate cut-off point, you'd want to study the histogram of the attribute you intend to discretize. So, you will know the answer to this question after drawing the histogram of `adult_df.hoursPerWeek`. The following screenshot shows the code and the histogram:

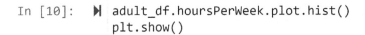

```
In [10]:  ▶  adult_df.hoursPerWeek.plot.hist()
              plt.show()
```

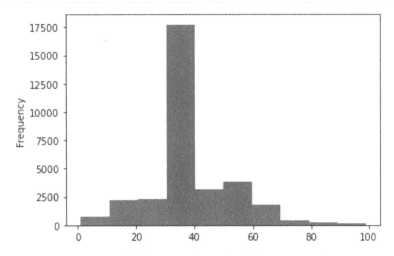

Figure 14.8   Creating the histogram for adult_df.hoursPerWeek

After discretizing `adult_df.hoursPerWeek`, running the following code will create the bottom plot in *Figure 14.7*. The following code is a modified version of the code that we learned in *Chapter 5, Data Visualization*, under *Example of comparing populations using bar charts*, which is part of the *Comparing populations* subsection; this specific code is from *The fifth way of solving* in the example. We have added `[['<40','40', '>40']]` to make sure that these values appear in the order that they make the most sense:

```
adult_df.groupby(['sex','income']).discretized_hoursPerWeek.
value_counts().unstack()[['<40','40', '>40']].plot.barh()
```

This example served well to showcase the possible benefits of discretization. However, there is more to learn about discretization. Next, we will learn about the different types of discretization.

Understanding the types of discretization

While the best tool to guide us through finding the best way to discretize an attribute is a histogram, as we saw in *Figure 14.8*, there are a few different approaches one might adopt. These approaches are called *equal width, equal frequency*, and *ad hoc*.

As the name suggests, the equal width approach makes sure that cut-off points will lead to equal intervals of the numerical attribute. For instance, the following screenshot shows the application of the `pd.cut()` function to create 5 equal-width bins from `adult_df.age`:

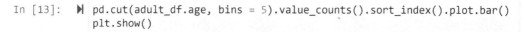

```
In [13]:  ▶  pd.cut(adult_df.age, bins = 5).value_counts().sort_index().plot.bar()
             plt.show()
```

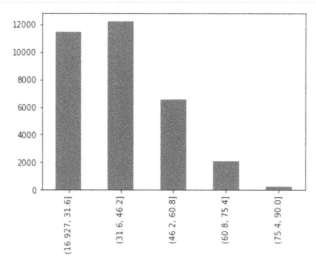

Figure 14.9 – Using pd.cut() to create equal width binning

On the other hand, the equal frequency approach aims to have an equal number of data objects in each bin. For instance, the following screenshot shows the application of the `pd.qcut()` function to create 5 equal-frequency bins from `adult_df.age`:

```
In [14]:   ▶  pd.qcut(adult_df.age,q=5).value_counts().sort_index().plot.bar()
              plt.show()
```

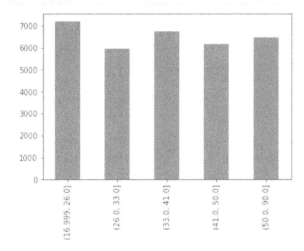

Figure 14.10 – Using pd.qcut() to create equal frequency binning

As you can see in the preceding figure, the absolute equal frequency binning may not be feasible. In these situations, `pd.qcut()` gets us as close as possible to equal frequency binning.

Lastly, the ad hoc approach prescribes the whereabouts of cut-off points based on the numerical attribute and other circumstantial knowledge about the attribute. For instance, we decided to cut `adult_df.hoursePerWeek` in *Example 3 – discretization of numerical attributes* ad hoc after having consulted the histogram of the attribute (*Figure 14.8*) and the circumstantial knowledge that most employees work 40 hours a week in the US.

In these examples, especially *Figure 14.9* and *Figure 14.10*, one matter we did not talk about is how we got to the number 5 for the number of bins. That's all right, because that is the topic of what we will cover next.

Discretization – the number of cut-off points

When we discretize a numerical attribute with one cut-off point, the discretized attribute will have two possible values. Likewise, when we discretize with two cut-off points, the discretized attribute will have three possible values. The number of possible values resulting from k cut-off points during discretization of a numerical attribute will be $k+1$.

Simply put, the question we want to answer here is how to find the optimum number for k. There is no bulletproof procedure to follow, so you will get the same answer every time. However, there are a few important guidelines that, when understood and practiced, make finding the right k less difficult. The following lists these guidelines:

- Study the histogram of the numerical attribute you intend to discretize and keep an open mind about what will be the best number of cut-off points.

- Too many cut-off points are not desirable, as one of the main reasons we would like to discretize a numerical attribute is to simplify it for our own consumption.

- Study the circumstantial facts and knowledge about the numerical attribute and see if they can lead you in the right direction.

- Experiment with a few ideas and study their pros and cons.

Before ending our exploration of discretization, I would like to remind you that we've already used discretization in our journey in this book. See the *Example of examining the relationship between a categorical attribute and a numerical attribute* section in *Chapter 5, Data Visualization*, for another example of discretization.

A summary – from numbers to categories and back

In this subsection, we learned about the techniques to transform categorical attributes into numerical ones (binary coding, ranking transformation, and attribute construction), and we also learned how to transform numerical attributes into categorical ones (discretization).

Before ending this subsection and moving to learn even more about attribute construction, let's discuss whether any of what we see could be labeled as data massaging. As we discussed in *Figure 14.1*, anything we are doing in this chapter is indeed data transformation; however, a data transformation can be labeled as data massaging when the transformation has been performed as a way to increase the effectiveness of the analysis. Most of the time when we transform an attribute from categorical to numerical or vice versa, it is done out of *necessity*; however, in the preceding few pages, there are two instances where the transformation could be labeled as data massaging because we did it for improving *effectiveness*. It will be your job to figure out which those are in *Exercise 2* at the end of the chapter.

Now, let's continue our journey of data transformation – next stop: attribute construction.

Attribute construction

We've already seen an example of this type of data transformation. We saw that we could employ it to transform categorical attributes into numerical ones. As we discussed, using attribute construction requires having a deep understanding of the environment that the data has been collected from. For instance, in *Figure 14.6*, we were able to construct the **Education Years** attribute from **Education level** because we have a pretty good idea of the working of the education system in the environment the data was collected from.

Attribute construction can also be done by combining more than one attribute. Let's see an example and learn how this could be possible.

Example – construct one transformed attribute from two attributes

Do you know what **Body Mass Index** (**BMI**) is? *BMI* is a result of attribute construction by researchers and physicians, who were looking for a healthiness index that takes both the weight and height of individuals into account.

We are going to use 500_Person_Gender_Height_Weight_Index.csv from https://www.kaggle.com/yersever/500-person-gender-height-weight-bodymassindex. Let's first read the data and do some level one data cleaning. The following code does that:

```
person_df = pd.read_csv('500_Person_Gender_Height_Weight_Index.
csv')
person_df.Index = person_df.Index.replace({0:'Extremely Weak',
1: 'Weak',2: 'Normal',3:'Overweight', 4:'Obesity',5:'Extreme
Obesity'})
person_df.columns = ['Gender', 'Height', 'Weight', 'Condition']
```

After running the preceding code, get Python to show you person_df and evaluate its state before reading on.

Next, we will leverage .scatterplot() of the seaborn module (sns) to create a 4D scatter plot. We will use the *x* axis, *y* axis, color, and marker style to respectively represent Height, Weight, Condition, and Gender. The following screenshot shows the code and the 4D scatterplot:

> **Attention**
>
> If you are reading the print version of this book, you will not see the colors, which are an essential aspect of the visualization, so make sure to create the visual before reading on.

```
In [17]:    ▶ sns.scatterplot(data = person_df, x='Height',y='Weight',
                               hue='Condition',style='Gender')
              plt.legend(bbox_to_anchor=(1.05, 1))
              plt.show()
```

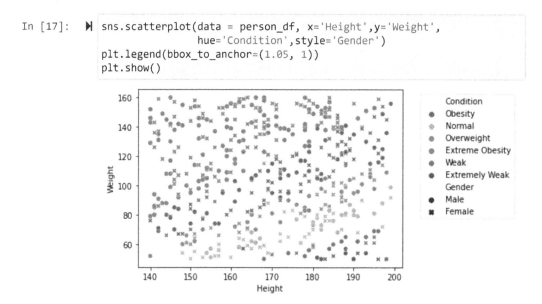

Figure 14.11 – Using sns.scatterplot() to create a 4D visualization of person_df

Our observation from the preceding plot is obvious. The two **Height** and **Weight** attributes together can determine a person's healthiness. This is what the researchers and physicians must have seen before having arrived at the *BMI* formula. *BMI* is a function that factors in both *weight* and *height* to create a healthiness index. The formula is as follows. Be careful – in this formula, weight is in kilograms and height is in meters:

$$BMI = \frac{Weight}{Height^2}$$

This begs the question, why this formula? We literally could have used an infinite number of possibilities to come up with a transformed attribute that is driven by both weight and height. So, why this one?

The answer goes back to the most important criteria of being able to apply attribute construction – deep knowledge of the environment from which the data is collected. Therefore, on this one, we have to trust that the researchers and physicians that have chosen this formula did possess such depth of knowledge and appreciation for the human body.

Let's go ahead and construct the new attribute for `person_df`. The following code uses the formula and the knowledge that the recorded *weight* and *height* in `person_df` are respectively in kilograms and meters to construct `person_df['BMI']`. Of course, this has been done using the powerful `.apply()` function:

```
person_df['BMI'] = person_df.apply(lambda r:r.Weight/((r.
Height/100)**2),axis=1)
```

After constructing the new `person_df.BMI` attribute, study it a bit, maybe create its histogram and box plot to see its variation. After that, try to create the following figure. Having reached this part of the book, you have all the skills to be able to create it. Anyhow, you have access to the code that has created the visual in the dedicated GitHub repository file of this chapter:

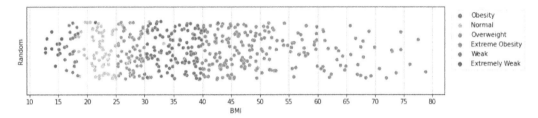

Figure 14.12 – Visualization of interaction between BMI and condition

The preceding figure shows the interaction between the constructed attribute, *BMI*, and the `Condition` attribute. The *y* axis in the preceding scatterplot has been used to disperse the data points so we can appreciate the number of data objects on the *x* axis (**BMI**). The trick to make the dispersion effect is to assign a random number to each data object.

In any case, what the interaction between the two attributes shows is the main point; that is, we can almost give out a set of cut-off points that tell us whether a person is healthy or not; *BMI* smaller than 15 indicates **Extremely Weak**, *BMI* between 15 and 19 shows **Weak**, *BMI* between 19 and 25 signifies **Normal**, *BMI* between 25 and 30 tells us the person is in the **Overweight** category, *BMI* between 30 and 40 is a case of **Obesity**, and finally, *BMI* larger than 40 is a sign that the person is **Extremely Obese**. Do a quick Google search to see whether what we've managed to find is the same as what is recommended regarding *BMI*.

In this example, we managed to construct one attribute by combining two attributes. There are cases where we can construct more than one attribute from a single attribute or source of data. However, while that can also be thought of as attribute construction, in the relevant literature, doing that is referred to as **feature extraction**. We will look into that next.

Feature extraction

This type of data transformation is very similar to attribute construction. In both, we use our deep knowledge of the original data to drive transformed attributes that are more helpful for our analysis purposes.

In attribute construction, we either come up with a completely new attribute from scratch or combine some attributes to make a transformed attribute that is more useful; however, in feature extraction, we unpack and pick apart a single attribute and only keep what is useful for our analysis.

As always, we will go for the best way to learn what we just discussed – examples! We will see some illuminative examples in this arena.

Example – extract three attributes from one attribute

The following figure shows the transformation of the **Email** attribute into three binary attributes. Every email ends with *@aWebAddress*; by looking at the website address providing the email service, we have extracted the three **Popular Free Platform**, **.edu**, and **Others** features. While **Email** may sound like just a meaningless string as regards being able to derive information about an individual, this example shows a smart feature extraction can derive valuable information from email addresses. For instance, here we can detect individuals who would like to use more popular services. Moreover, we can distinguish the individual that uses emails provided by educational institutions; this shows perhaps they work for academia or they are students:

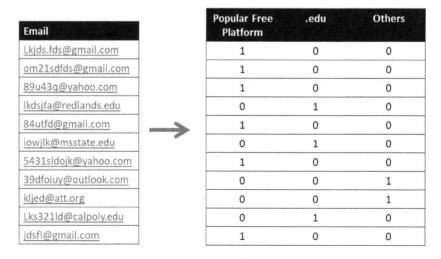

Email	Popular Free Platform	.edu	Others
Lkjds.fds@gmail.com	1	0	0
om21sdfds@gmail.com	1	0	0
89u43q@yahoo.com	1	0	0
lkdsjfa@redlands.edu	0	1	0
84utfd@gmail.com	1	0	0
iowjlk@msstate.edu	0	1	0
5431sldojk@yahoo.com	1	0	0
39dfoiuy@outlook.com	0	0	1
kljed@att.org	0	0	1
Lks321ld@calpoly.edu	0	1	0
jdsfl@gmail.com	1	0	0

Figure 14.13 – Feature extraction from the Email attribute

Let's look at another example.

Example – Morphological feature extraction

The following figure shows 100 milliseconds of vibrational signals collected from a car engine for health diagnosis. Furthermore, the figure shows the extraction of three morphological features.

Before getting more into these three features and what they are, let's discuss what the word *morphological* means. The *Oxford English Dictionary* defines it as "connected to shape and form." As a feature extraction approach, morphological feature extraction is employing the common shape and form of the data to get to new features.

The following figure serves as an excellent example. We have extracted three morphological features. Simply, in the line plot of the vibration signal, we have counted the number of peaks (**n_Peaks**), the number of valleys (**n_Valleys**), and the extent of oscillation during the 100 milliseconds (**max_Oscillate**):

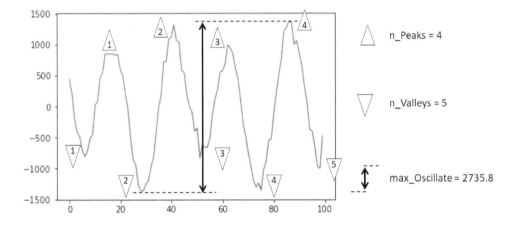

Figure 14.14 – Morphological feature extraction of vibrational signals

The value of doing such feature extraction will show itself when we see them in comparison between a few data objects. The preceding figure is the feature extraction of only one data point. However, the following figure has put together five distinct data points that are from engines with five different states: **Healthy**, **Fault 1**, **Fault 2**, **Fault 3**, and **Fault 4**:

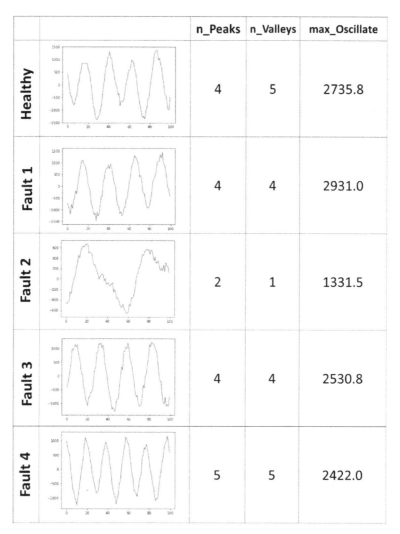

		n_Peaks	n_Valleys	max_Oscillate
Healthy		4	5	2735.8
Fault 1		4	4	2931.0
Fault 2		2	1	1331.5
Fault 3		4	4	2530.8
Fault 4		5	5	2422.0

Figure 14.15 – Morphological feature extraction of vibrational signals for five instances of data objects

Contemplating the preceding figure shows us that with simple morphological feature extraction, we might be able to accurately distinguish between different types of fault and the healthy engine. You will have the opportunity to create the classification model after doing morphological feature extraction on similar data in *Exercise 5* at the end of this chapter.

In our journey throughout this book, we have already seen other instances of feature extraction without referring to it as such. Next, we are going to discuss those instances and how we had gotten ahead of ourselves.

Feature extraction examples from the previous chapters

In this book, we have dissected data preprocessing into different stages. These stages are *Data Cleaning* (*Chapters 9–11*), *Data Fusion and Integration* (*Chapter 12*), *Data Reduction* (*Chapter 13*), and *Data Transformation* (this chapter). However, in many instances of data preprocessing, these stages may be done in parallel or at the same time. This is a great achievement from a practical perspective and we should not force ourselves to take apart these stages in practice. We've only discussed these stages separately to aid our understanding, but once you feel more comfortable with them, it is recommended to do that at the same time if it's possible and useful.

That is the reason that we've already seen feature extraction in the other stages of data preprocessing. Let's go over these examples and see why they are both feature extraction and also other things.

Examples of data cleaning and feature extraction

In *Chapter 10, Data Cleaning Level II – Unpacking, Restructuring, and Reformulating the Table*, during the solution for the *Example 1 – Unpacking columns and reformulating the table* section, which was cleaning `speech_df`, a dataset that had a few of President Trump's speeches, we unwittingly performed some feature extraction under the name of unpacking the `Content` column. The `Content` attribute had each of the speeches in text, and the solution unpacked these long texts by counting the number of times the *vote*, *tax*, *campaign*, and *economy* terms had been used.

This is both data cleaning and data transformation (feature extraction). From the perspective of data cleaning, there was so much fluff in the data that we did not need and got in the way of our visualization goals, so we removed the fluff to bring what's needed to the surface. From a data transformation perspective, we extracted four features that were needed for our analysis.

Next, let's see how data reduction and feature extraction are sometimes done at the same time.

Examples of data reduction and feature extraction

In *Chapter 13, Data Reduction*, we learned two unsupervised dimension reduction techniques. We saw how a **non-parametric method** (that is, **PCA**) and a **parametric method** (that is, **FDA**) reduced the dimension of country_df, a dataset of countries with 10 years of 9 happiness indices (90 attributes). From a data reduction perspective, the data was reduced by reducing the number of attributes. However, after learning about data transformation and feature extraction, we can see that we transformed the data by extracting a few features.

Almost always any unsupervised dimension reduction effort can also be referred to as feature extraction. More interestingly, this type of data reduction/dimension reduction can also be seen as data massaging, because we are extracting features and reducing the size of the data solely to improve the effectiveness of the analysis.

The gear shift from attribute construction to feature extraction was very smooth as the two data transformations are very similar and, in most cases, we can think of them as data massaging. These two types of data transformation are also very general and can be employed in a wide range of ways, and for their successful implementation, they require the resourcefulness of the analyst. For instance, the analyst must be able to find appropriate functions to use FDA for parametric feature extraction, which requires high-level resourcefulness.

However, the next data transformation technique we will learn is going to be very specific and is only applicable in certain situations. Next, we will learn about log transformation.

Log transformation

We should use this data transformation when an attribute experiences exponential growth and decline across the population of our data objects. When you draw a box plot of these attributes, you expect to see fliers, but those are not mistaken records, nor are they unnatural outliers. Those significantly larger or smaller values come naturally from the environment.

Attributes with exponential growth or decline may be problematic for data visualization and clustering analysis; furthermore, they can be problematic for some prediction and classification algorithms where the method uses the distance between the data objects, such as KNN, or where the method drives its performance based on collective performance metrics, such as linear regression.

These attributes may sound very hard to deal with, but there is a very easy fix for them – log transformation. In short, instead of using the attribute, you calculate the logarithms of all of the values and use them instead. The following figure shows how this transformation looks using the **Gross Domestic Product (GDP)** data of the world's countries in 2020. The data is retrieved from `https://data.worldbank.org/indicator/NY.GDP.MKTP.CD` and preprocessed into `GDP 2019 2020.csv`:

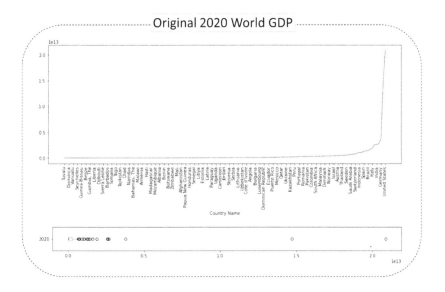

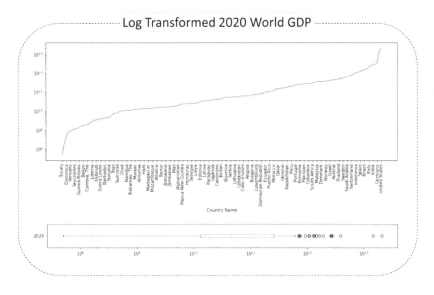

Figure 14.16 – Before and after log transformation – the GDP of the countries in the world

We can see in the preceding figure that the line plot of the original data shoots up; that is what we earlier described as exponential growth. We also see in the box plot of the original data that there are outliers with unrestrictedly high values compared to the rest of the population. You can imagine how these types of outliers can be problematic for our analytics, such as data visualization and clustering analysis.

Now, pay attention to the log-transformed version of the visualization. The data objects still have the same relationships with one another from the perspective of being more or less; however, the exponential growth has been tamped down. We can see in the box plot of the log-transformed data that we still have fliers, but those fliers' values are not unrestrictedly higher.

The preceding figures are created using GDP 2019 2020.csv, and you can find the code that created them in the dedicated GitHub repository file of this chapter.

There are two approaches in applying log transformation – doing it yourself or the working module doing it for you. Let's see these two approaches in the following section.

Implementation – doing it yourself

In this approach, you take matters into your own hands and first add a log-transformed attribute to the dataset and then use that transformed attribute. For example, the following screenshot shows doing the attribute for country_df['2020'].

Pay attention – before running the code presented in the following screenshot, you need to first run the following code that reads the GDP 2019 2020.csv file into country_df:

```
country_df = pd.read_csv('GDP 2019 2020.csv')
country_df.set_index('Country Name',inplace=True)
```

After running the preceding code, you can run the code presented in the following screenshot:

```
In [26]:    ▶  country_df['log_2020'] = np.log(country_df['2020'])
               country_df.log_2020.sort_values().plot()
               plt.xticks(rotation=90)
               plt.show()
```

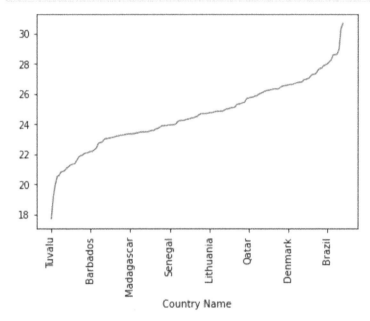

Figure 14.17 – Log transformation – doing it yourself

Next, let's cover the approach of the working module doing it for you.

Implementation – the working module doing it for you

As log transformation is a very useful and well-known data transformation, many modules provide the option for you to use the log transformation. For instance, the code in the following screenshot uses `logy=True`, which is a property of the `.plot()` Pandas Series function, to do the log transformation without having to add a new attribute to the dataset:

```
In [27]:  ▶  country_df['2020'].sort_values().plot(logy=True)
              plt.xticks(rotation=90)
              plt.show()
```

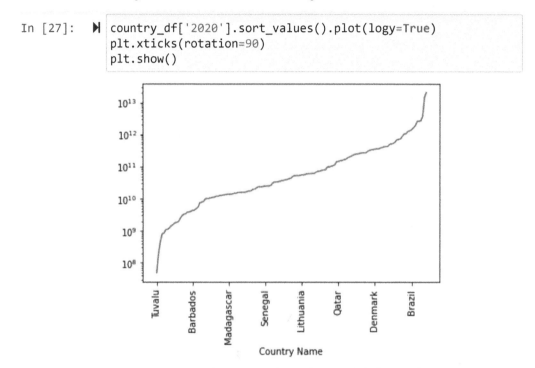

Figure 14.18 – Log transformation – the working module doing it for you

The disadvantage of this approach is that the module you are using may not have this accommodation, or you may not be aware of it. On the other hand, if such accommodation is provided, it makes your code much easier to read.

Furthermore, the result of the working module doing it for you might be even more effective. For instance, compare the *y* axis in *Figure 14.15* with that of *Figure 14.16*.

Before moving to the next data transformation tools, let me remind you that we have already used log transformation in our data analysis in the course of this book. Remember the `WH Report_preprocessed.csv` and `WH Report.csv` datasets, which are the two versions of the World Health Organization reports on the happiness indices of 122 countries? One of the attributes in these datasets is `Log_GDP_per_capita`. As `GDP_per_capita` experiences exponential growth, for clustering analysis, we used its log-transformed version.

The next group of data transformation tools is going to be used for dealing with noisy data, and sometimes to deal with missing values and outliers. They are smoothing, aggregation, and binning.

Smoothing, aggregation, and binning

In our discussion about noise in data in *Chapter 11, Data Cleaning Level III – Missing Values, Outliers, and Errors*, we learned that there are two types of errors – systematic errors and unavoidable noise. In *Chapter 11, Data Cleaning Level III – Missing Values, Outliers, and Errors*, we discussed how we deal with systematic errors, and now here we will discuss noise. This is not covered under data cleaning, because noise is an unavoidable part of any data collection, so it cannot be discussed as data cleaning. However, here we will discuss it under data transformation, as we may be able to take measures to best handle it. The three methods that can help deal with noise are smoothing, aggregation, and binning.

It might seem surprising that these methods are only applied to time-series data to deal with noise. However, there is a distinct and definitive reason for it. You see, it is only in time-series data, or any data that is collected consistently, consecutively, and with ordered intervals, that we can detect the presence of noise. It is this unique data collection that allows us to be able to detect the existence of noise. In other forms of data collection, we cannot detect the noise, and therefore there will be nothing we can do. Why is that? The answer is in the consistent, consecutive, and ordered intervals. Due to this unique data collection, we can pick apart patterns from noise.

The three methods that can help deal with noise are smoothing, aggregation, and binning. Each of these three methods to deal with noise operate under a specific set of assumptions. In the following three sections, we will first learn about these assumptions and then we will see examples of how they are implemented.

One last word before seeing the sections – strictly speaking, missing values and outliers are types of noise, and if they are non-systematic and a natural part of the data collection, either of these three methods could also be applied to deal with them.

Now, let's look at the smoothing approach in dealing with noise.

Smoothing

The following screenshot uses the `Noise_data.csv` file, which is 200 milliseconds of vibrational signals collected from a car engine for health diagnosis. The screenshot shows the line plot of these vibrational signals:

In [28]: ▶
```
signal_df = pd.read_csv('Noise_data.csv')
signal_df.drop(columns='t',inplace=True)
signal_df.Signal.plot(figsize=(15,5))
plt.show()
```

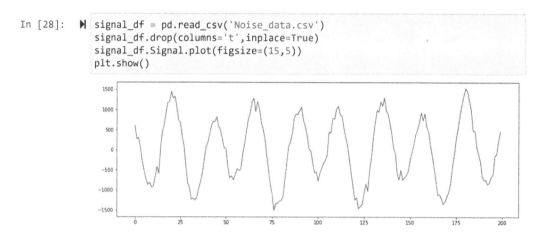

Figure 14.19 – Line plot of Noise_data.csv

In the preceding figure, you can sense what we meant by time-series data allowing us to distinguish between patterns and noise. Now, let's use this data to learn more about smoothing.

By and large, there are two types of smoothing – functional and rolling. Let's learn about each of them one by one.

Functional data smoothing

Functional smoothing is the application of **Functional Data Analysis** (**FDA**) for the purpose of smoothing the data. If you need to refresh your memory on FDA, which we covered in *Chapter 13, Data Reduction*, go back and review it before reading on.

When we used FDA to reduce the size of the data, we were interested in replacing the data with the parameters of the function that simulate the data well. However, when smoothing, we want our data with the same size, but we want to remove the noise. In other words, regarding how FDA is applied, it is very similar to both data reduction and smoothing; however, the output of FDA is different for each purpose. For smoothing, we expect to have the same size data as the output, whereas for data reduction, we expect to only have the parameters of the fitting function.

There are many functions and modules in the space of the Python data analysis environment that use FDA to smooth data. A few of them are `savgol_filter` from `scipy.signal`; `CubicSpline`, `UnivariateSpline`, `splrep`, and `splev` from `scipy.Interpolate`; and `KernelReg` from `statsmodels.nonparametric.kernel_regression`. However, none of these functions works as well as it should, and I believe there is much more room for the improvement of smoothing tools in the space of Python data analytics. For instance, the following figure shows the performance of the `.KernelReg()` function on part of the data (50 numbers) versus its performance on the whole `Noise_data.csv` file (200 numbers):

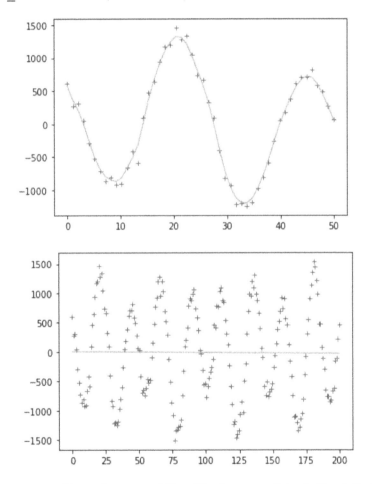

Figure 14.20 – The performance of .KernelReg() on part of signal_df and all of it

We can see in the preceding figure that the `.KernelReg()` function is successful in part of the data, but it crumbles as the complexity of the data increases.

The code to create each of the plots in the preceding figure is very similar. For instance, to create the top plot, you can use the following code. I am certain you are capable of modifying it to create the bottom one as well:

```
from statsmodels.nonparametric.kernel_regression import
KernelReg
x = np.linspace(0,50,50)
y = noise_df.Signal.iloc[:50]
plt.plot(x, y, '+')
kr = KernelReg(y,x,'c')
y_pred, y_std = kr.fit(x)
plt.plot(x, y_pred)
plt.show()
```

What was covered here in terms of functional data smoothing can only be looked at as an introduction to this complex data transformation tool. There is a lot that can be said about functional data smoothing, enough for an entire book. However, what you learned here can be a great foundation for you to go off on your own and learn more.

Now, let's bring our attention to rolling data smoothing.

Rolling data smoothing

The biggest difference between functional data smoothing and rolling data smoothing is that functional data smoothing looks at the whole data as one piece and then tries to find the function that fits the data. In contrast, rolling data smoothing works on incremental windows of the data. The following figure shows what rolling calculation and the incremental windows are using in the first 10 rows of `singnal_df`:

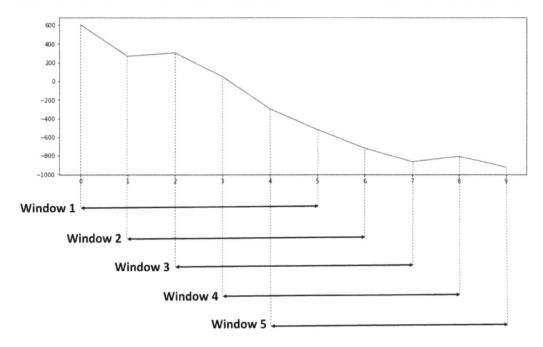

Figure 14.21 – Visual explanation of rolling calculations and the window

In the preceding figure, the width of each window is 5. As shown, the window rolling calculation happens by picking the first 5 data points. After performing the prescribed calculations, the window rolling calculation moves on to the next window by one increment jump.

For instance, the following code uses the .rolling() function of a Pandas DataFrame to calculate the mean of every window of singnal_df in a rolling window calculation where the width of each window is 5. The code also creates a line plot to show how this specific window rolling calculation manages to smooth the data:

```
signal_df.Signal.plot(figsize=(15,5),label='Signal')
signal_df.Signal.rolling(window=5).mean().plot(label='Moving
Average Smoothed')
plt.legend()
plt.show()
```

After running the preceding code successfully, the following plot will be created. Theoretically, what we just did is called **Moving Average Smoothing**, which is calculating the moving average of the time-series data:

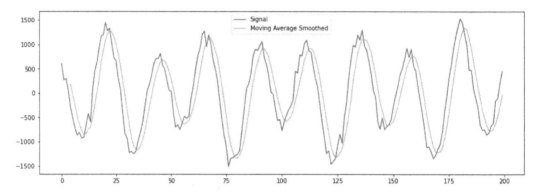

Figure 14.22 – Moving Average Smoothing using window rolling calculations

As you can see, **Moving Average Smoothing** has smoothed the data pretty nicely, but it has a distinct disadvantage – the data seems to have been shifted. Naively, you may think that you can simply shift the plot a bit to the left and all will be okay. However, the following figure, the first seven rows of **Signal** and **Moving Average Smoothed** shows you that a perfect match will never be possible:

	Signal	Moving Average Smoothed
0	605.340308	NaN
1	267.958658	NaN
2	304.652019	NaN
3	51.297364	NaN
4	-297.546288	186.340412
5	-520.492600	-38.826169
6	-719.919832	-236.401867
7	-866.546219	-470.641515
8	-807.907263	-642.482441
9	-925.817440	-768.136671

Figure 14.23 – Comparing the Signal and Moving Average Smoothed columns

It is no surprise that the first four values for **Moving Average Smoothed** are **NaN**, right? It is due to the nature of rolling window calculations. Always, when the width of windows is k, the first $k-1$ rows will have **NaN**.

Rolling window calculations provide the opportunity to use simple or complex calculations to smooth. For instance, you might want to try other time-series methods, such as **simple exponential smoothing**. The following code uses the mechanism of the rolling window calculations to apply exponential smoothing.

Before running the following code, pay attention to the way the code uses the `.rolling()` and `.apply()` functions to implement simple exponential smoothing that was first defined as a function:

```
def ExpSmoothing(v):
    a=0.2
    yhat = v.iloc[0]
    for i in range(len(v)):
        yhat = a*v.iloc[i]   + (1-a)*yhat
    return yhat


signal_df.Signal.plot(figsize=(15,5),label='Signal')
signal_df.Signal.rolling(window=5).apply(ExpSmoothing).plot(
label = 'Exponential Smoothing')
plt.legend()
plt.show()
```

Running the preceding code creates a figure similar to *Figure 14.20*, but this time, the smoothed values have used the simple exponential smoothing formulas.

Now, let's bring our attention to the next tool that we will learn to deal with noise – aggregation.

Aggregation

Data aggregation is a specific type of rolling data smoothing. With aggregation, we do not use any window's width, but we aggregate the data points from smaller data objects to wider data objects, for example, from days to weeks, or from seconds to hours.

For example, the following figure shows the line plot of daily COVID-19 cases and deaths, and then its aggregated version – weekly COVID-19 cases and deaths for California and the US:

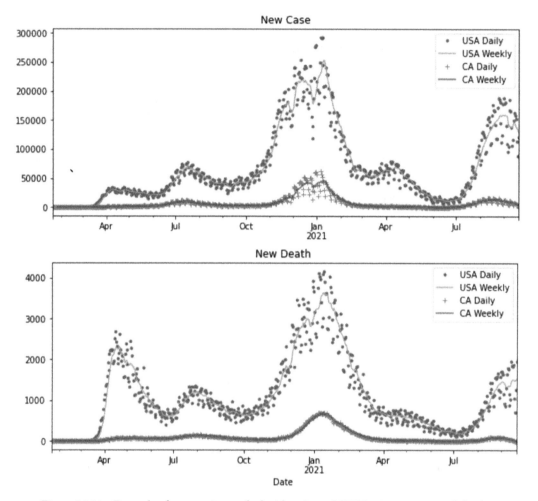

Figure 14.24 – Example of aggregation to deal with noise – COVID-19 new cases and deaths

The operation of aggregating a dataset to create a dataset with a new definition of data objects is not new to us. Through the course of this book, we've seen many examples of it. For instance, see the following items:

- *Example 1 – unpacking columns and reformulating the table* in *Chapter 10, Data Cleaning Level II – Unpacking, Restructuring, and Reformulating the Table* – in this example, `speech_df` was aggregated to create `vis_df`, whose definition of data objects is speeches in a month.

- *Example 1 (challenges 3 and 4)* in *Chapter 12, Data Fusion and Integration* – in this example, we had to aggregate `electric_df`, whose definition of a data object was the electricity consumption of half an hour, to create a new dataset whose definition of data object was hourly electricity consumption. This was done so `electric_df` could be integrated with `temp_df`.

In any case, *Exercise 12* will provide the opportunity for you to practice aggregation to deal with noise. You will be able to create *Figure 14.24* yourself.

Lastly, we will discuss binning as a method to transform the data to deal with noise.

Binning

It may seem that this is a new method, but binning and discretization are technically the same type of data preprocessing. When the process is done to transform a numerical attribute to a categorical one, it is referred to as discretization, and when it is used as a way to combat noise in numerical data, we call the same data transformation binning.

Another possibly surprising fact is that we have done binning so many times before in this book. Every time we created a histogram, binning was done under the hood. Now, let's raise that hood and see what's happening inside.

The very first histogram we ever created in this book was shown in *Figure 2.1* in *Chapter 2, Review of Another Core Module – Matplotlib*. In that figure, we created the histogram of the `adult_df.age` attribute. Go back and review the histogram.

The following screenshot shows how it would have looked if we had created the bar chart of `adult_df.age`, instead of its histogram:

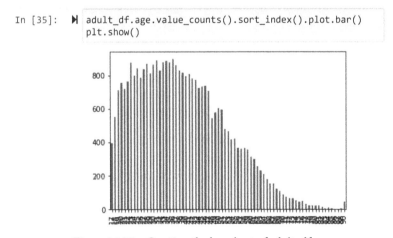

Figure 14.25 – Creating the bar chart of adult_df.age

Comparing the preceding visualization with *Figure 2.1* allows us to see the value of the histogram and how it can help us with smoothing the data so that we can get a better understanding of the variation among the population.

We can also create the same shape as the histogram by binning the attribute first and then creating the bar chart. The code in the following screenshot uses the pd.cut() pandas function to bin adult_df.age and then create its bar chart. Compare the bar chart in the following screenshot with *Figure 2.1*; they are showing the same patterns:

```
In [36]:   ▶ adult_df['age_binned']=pd.cut(adult_df.age,10)
             adult_df.age_binned.value_counts().sort_index().plot.bar()
```

```
Out[36]:   <AxesSubplot:>
```

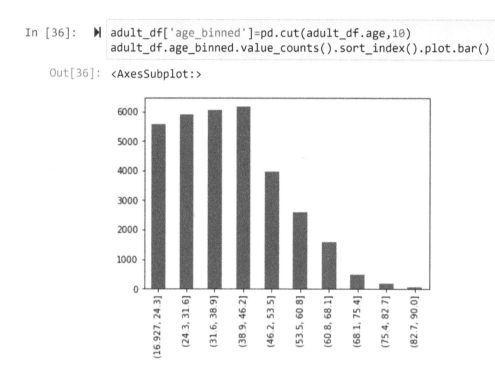

Figure 14.26 – Creating the histogram of adult_df by pd.cut() and .bar() instead of .hist()

If you are concerned about the preceding figure not looking exactly like the one in *Figure 2.1*, all you need to change is the width of the bar. Replace .bar(width=1) with .bar() in the code of the preceding screenshot and you will manage that.

In this section, we learned three ways to deal with noise in the data: smoothing, aggregation, and binning. We are getting closer to the end of this chapter. Next, we will go over a summary of the whole chapter and wrap up our learning.

Summary

Congratulations to you for completing this chapter. In this chapter, we added many useful tools to our data preprocessing armory, specifically in the data transformation area. We learned how to distinguish between data transformation and data massaging. Furthermore, we learned how to transform our data from numerical to categorical, and vice versa. We learned about attribute construction and feature extraction, which are very useful for high-level data analysis. We also learned about log transformation, which is one of the oldest and most effective tools. And lastly, we learned three methods that are very useful in our arsenal for dealing with noise in data.

By finishing this chapter successfully, you are also coming to the end of the third part of this book – *The Preprocessing*. By now, you know enough to be very successful at preprocessing data that leads to effective data analytics. In the next part of the book, we will have three case studies (*Chapters 15–17*), into which we will put our learning from across the book into use and have culminating experience of data preprocessing and effective analytics. We will end the book with *Chapter 18*, *Summary, Practice Case Studies, and Conclusions*. This chapter will provide learning opportunities for you to put what you have learned into real use and to start creating your portfolio of data preprocessing and data analytics.

Before all that real, practical, and exciting learning, do not miss out on the learning opportunity that the exercises at the end of this chapter provide.

Exercise

1. In your own words, what are the differences and similarities between normalization and standardization? How come some use them interchangeably?

2. There are two instances of data transformation done during the discussion of binary coding, ranking transformation, and discretization that can be labeled as massaging. Try to spot them and explain how come they can be labeled that way.

3. Of course, we know that one of the ways that the color of a data object is presented is by using their names. This is why we would assume color probably should be a nominal attribute. However, you can transform this usually nominal attribute to a numerical one. What are the two possible approaches? (Hint: one of them is an attribute construction using RGB coding.) Apply the two approaches to the following small dataset. The data shown in the table below is accessible in the `color_nominal.csv` file:

Index	Color	index	Color	Index	Color
1	Blue	11	White	21	Orange
2	Blue	12	Orange	22	Black
3	Black	13	White	23	Yellow
4	White	14	Black	24	Black
5	Green	15	Yellow	25	Orange
6	Orange	16	Yellow	26	White
7	White	17	Blue	27	Blue
8	Blue	18	Green	28	Orange
9	Brown	19	Orange	29	Orange
10	Yellow	20	Green	30	Yellow

Figure 14.27 – color_nominal.csv

Once after binary codding and once after RGB attribute construction, use the transformed attributes to cluster the 30 data objects into 3 clusters. Perform centroid analysis for both clusterings and share what you learned from this exercise.

4. You've seen three examples of attribute construction so far. The first one can be found in *Figure 14.6*. The other one was in the *Example – Construct one transformed attribute from two attributes* section, and the last one was the previous exercises. Use these examples to argue whether attribute construction is data massaging or not.

5. In this exercise, you will get to work on a dataset collected for research and development. The dataset was used in a recent publication titled *Misfire and valve clearance faults detection in the combustion engines based on a multi-sensor vibration signal monitoring* to show that high-accuracy detection of engine failure is possible using vibrational signals. To see this article, visit this link: `https://www.sciencedirect.com/science/article/abs/pii/S0263224118303439`.

The dataset that you have access to is `Noise_Analysis.csv`. The size of the file is too large and we were not able to include it on the GitHub Repository. Please use this link (`https://www.dropbox.com/s/1x8k0vcydfhbuub/Noise_ Analysis.csv?dl=1`) to download the file. This dataset has 7,500 rows, each showing 1 second (1,000 milliseconds) of the engine's vibrational signal and the state of the engine (*Label*). We want to use the vibrational signal to predict the state of the engine. There are five states: *H* – Healthy, *M1* – Missfire 1, *M2* – Missfire 2, *M12* – Missfire 1 and 2, and *VC* – Valve Clearance.

To predict (classify) these states, we need to first perform feature extraction from the vibrational signal. Extract the following five morphological features and then use them to create a decision tree that can classify them:

a) *n_Peaks* – the number of peaks (see *Figure 14.13*)

b) *n_Valleys* – the number of valleys (see *Figure 14.13*)

c) *Max_Oscilate* – the maximum oscillation (see *Figure 14.13*)

d) *Negative_area* – the absolute value of the total sum of negative signals

e) *Positive_area* – the total sum of the positive signals

Make sure to tune the decision tree to come to a final tree that can be used for analysis. After creating the decision tree, share your observations. (Hint: to find *n_Peaks* and *n_Valleys*, you may want to use the `scipy.signal.find_peaks` function.)

6. In this chapter, we discussed the possible distinction between data massaging and data transformation. We also saw that FDA can be used both for data reduction and data transformation. Review all of the FDA examples you have experienced in this book (*Chapter 13*, *Data Reduction*, and this chapter) and use them to make a case regarding whether FDA should be labeled as data massaging or not.

7. Review *Exercise 8* in *Chapter 12*, *Data Fusion and Integration*. In that exercise, we transformed the attribute of one of the datasets so that the fusion of the two sources became possible. How would you describe that data transformation? Could we call it data massaging?

8. In this exercise, we will use `BrainAllometry_Supplement_Data.csv` from a paper titled *The allometry of brain size in mammals*. The data can be accessed from `https://datadryad.org/stash/dataset/doi:10.5061/ dryad.2r62k7s`.

The following scatterplot tries to show the relationship between mean body mass and mean brain mass of species in nature. However, you can see that the relationship is not very well shown. What transformation could fix this? Apply it and then share your observations:

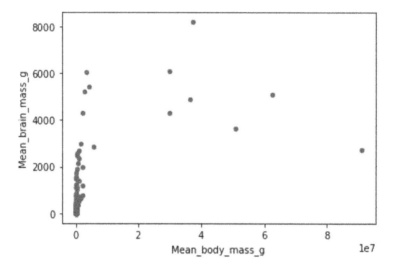

Figure 14.28 – Scatter plot of Mean_body_mass_g and Mean_brain_mass_g

9. In this chapter, we learned three techniques to deal with noise: smoothing, aggregation, and binning. Explain why these methods were covered under data transformation and not under data cleaning – level III.

10. In two chapters (*Chapter 13, Data Reduction*, and this chapter) and under three areas of data preprocessing, we have shown the applications of FDA: data reduction, feature extraction, and smoothing. Find examples of the FDA in these two chapters, and then explain how FDA manages to do all these different data preprocesses. What allows FDA to be such a multipurpose toolkit?

11. In *Figure 14.18*, we saw that .KernelReg() on all of signal_df did not perform very well, but it did perform excellently on part of it. How about trying to smooth all of signal_df with a combination of rolling data smoothing and functional data smoothing? To do this, we need to have window rolling calculations with a step size. Unfortunately, the .rolling() Pandas function only accommodates the step size of one, as shown in *Figure 14.18*. So, take matters into your hands and engineer a looping mechanism that uses .KernelReg() to smooth all of signal_df.

12. Use `United_States_COVID-19_Cases_and_Deaths_by_State_over_`
    `Time.csv` to recreate *Figure 14.24*. You may want to pull the most up-to-date data
    from `https://catalog.data.gov/dataset/united-states-covid-`
    `19-cases-and-deaths-by-state-over-time` to develop an up-to-date
    visualization. (Hint: you will need to work with the two `new_case` and
    `new_death` columns.)

13. It may seem like that binning and aggregation are the same method; however, they
    are not. Study the two examples in this chapter and explain the difference between
    aggregation and binning.

Part 4:
Case Studies

In this part, you will see three real cases of data preprocessing for analytics that you can read to shadow a real project before you pick up your own project. Some suggestions are also provided.

This part comprises the following chapters:

15
Case Study 1 – Mental Health in Tech

In this chapter and the two upcoming ones, we are going to put the skills that we have picked up in the course of this book into practice. For this case study, we are going to use data collected by **Open Sourcing Mental Illness (OSMI)** (`https://osmihelp.org/`), which is a non-profit corporation dedicated to raising awareness, educating, and providing resources to support mental wellness in the tech and open source communities. OSMI conducts yearly surveys that "aim to measure attitudes towards mental health in the tech workplace and examine the frequency of mental health disorders among tech workers." These surveys are accessible to the public for participation and can be found at `https://osmihelp.org/research`.

In this chapter, we're going to learn about mental health in tech case study by covering the following:

- Introducing the case study
- Integrating the data sources
- Cleaning the data
- Analyzing the data

Technical requirements

You will be able to find all of the code and the dataset that is used in this book in a GitHub repository exclusively created for this book. To find the repository, click on this link: `https://github.com/PacktPublishing/Hands-On-Data-Preprocessing-in-Python`. You can find this chapter's materials in this repository and can download the code and the data for better learning.

Introducing the case study

Mental health disorders such as anxiety and depression are inherently detrimental to people's well-being, lifestyles, and ability to be productive in their work. According to *Mental Health America*, over 44 million adults in the US have a mental health condition. The mental health of employees in the tech industry is of great concern due to the competitive environments often found within and among these companies. Some employees at these companies are forced to work overtime simply to keep their jobs. Managers of these types of companies have good reason to desire improved mental health for their employees because healthy minds are productive ones and distracted minds are not.

Managers and leaders of tech and non-tech companies must make difficult decisions regarding whether or not to invest in the mental health of their employees and, if so, to what degree. There is plenty of evidence that poor mental health can have a negative impact on workers' well-being and productivity. Every company has a finite amount of funds that it can invest in the physical health of its employees, let alone mental health. Knowing where to allocate resources is of great importance.

This serves as a general introduction to this case study. Next, we will discuss a very important aspect of any data analysis – who is the audience of our results?

The audience of the results of analytics

Always, the main audience of the results of any analytics is decision-makers; however, it is important to be clear about who exactly are those decision-makers. In real projects, this should be obvious, but here in this chapter of the book, as our goal is to practice, we need to imagine a specific decision-maker and tailor our analysis for them.

The decision-makers that we will focus on are the managers and the leaders of tech companies who are in charge of making decisions that can impact the mental health of their employees. While mental health should be looked at as a priority, in reality, managers have to navigate a decision-making environment that has many competing priorities, such as organizational financial health, survival, profit maximization, sales, and customer service, as well as economic growth.

For instance, the following simple visualization created by OSMI (available at `https://osmi.typeform.com/report/A7m1xC/itVHRYbNRnPqDI9C`) tells us that while mental health support in tech companies is not terrible, there remains a large gap for improvement:

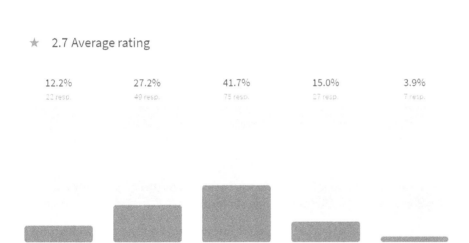

Figure 15.1 – A simple visualization from the 2020 OSMI mental health in tech survey

Our goal in this case study is to dig a bit deeper than the basic report provided by OSMI and see the interactions between more attributes, which can be informative and beneficial to the described decision-makers.

Specifically, for this case study, we will try to answer the following **Analytic Questions (AQs)** that can inform the described decision-makers about the attitude and importance of mental health in their employees:

- **AQ1**: Is there a significant difference between the mental health of employees across the attribute of gender?

- **AQ2**: Is there a significant difference between the mental health of employees across the attribute of age?

- **AQ3**: Do more supportive companies have healthier employees mentally?

- **AQ4**: Does the attitude of individuals toward mental health influence their mental health and their seeking of treatments?

Now that we are clear about how we are analyzing this data and what AQs we want to answer, let's roll up our sleeves and start getting to know the source of the data.

Introduction to the source of the data

OSMI started conducting the mental health in tech survey in 2014, and even though the rate of participation in their surveys has dwindled over the years, they have continued collecting data until now. At the time of developing this chapter, the raw data for 2014 and 2016 to 2020 is accessible at `https://osmihelp.org/research`.

> **Get to Know the Sources of Data**
>
> Go ahead and download the raw data from 2014 to the most recent version, and use the tools you've picked up in your journey in this book to get to know these files. Continue reading once you have a good grasp of these datasets.

At the time of developing this chapter, only six raw datasets from 2014, 2016, 2017, 2018, 2019, and 2020 were collected and available. Only the five datasets from 2016 to 2020 are used in this chapter, so there is continuity in the data.

As we move along in this chapter, feel free to add the most recent versions, if they are available at the listed address, and update the code accordingly.

Now, let's get started. We will have to start with **data integration** and then **data cleaning**.

> **Attention!**
>
> You are going to experience a shift in the way code is represented in this chapter. From Chapter 1 to Chapter 14, almost all of the code that was used for analytics and preprocessing was shared both during the chapter and also in a dedicated file in the GitHub repository. However, in this chapter, and in the following two chapters, *Chapters 16, Case Study 2 – Predicting COVID Hospitalization,* and *Chapter 17, Case Study 3 – United States Counties Clustering Analysis,* the code will be presented mainly in the dedicated file for this chapter in the GitHub repository. So, while studying this chapter, make sure you also have the code in the GitHub repository handy so that you can go back and forth and learn.

Integrating the data sources

As discussed, five different datasets need to be integrated. After having seen these five datasets that collected data of OSMI mental health in tech surveys across five different years, you will realize that the survey throughout the years has undergone many changes. Also, while the collected datasets are about mental health in tech, the wordings of the questions and sometimes the nature of these questions have changed. Therefore, the figurative funnel in the following figure serves two purposes. First, it lets the parts of the data from each dataset come through that are common among all six datasets. Second, the funnel also filters out the data that is not relevant to our AQs:

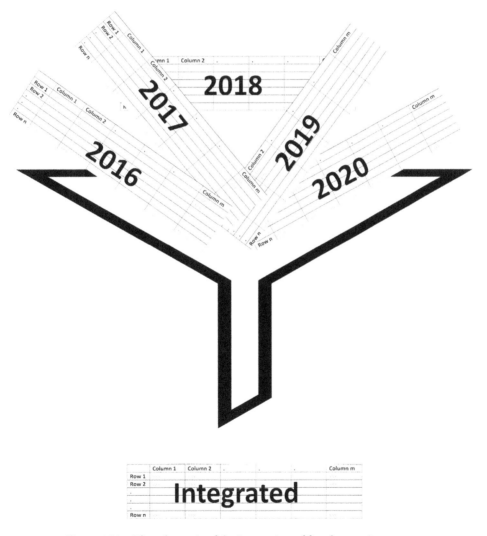

Figure 15.2 – The schematic of the integration of five datasets into one

While the preceding figure makes the integration of these five datasets seem simple, there are meaningful challenges ahead of us. The very first one is knowing what the common attributes are among all these five datasets if there is no consistent wording among them. Do we need to do it manually? While that is certainly one way of doing it, it would be a very long process. We can use `SequenceMatcher` from the `difflib` module to find the attributes that are similar to one another.

After doing the filtering based on what is common among all five datasets, we still need to only keep the attributes that are relevant to our AQs. The following list is the collection of the attributes that are both common among all five datasets and are relevant to our AQs. To make cleaner-looking data, each long attribute name that is a question on the survey has been assigned a name. These names are used to create an attribute dictionary, `Column_dict`, so the attribute names are codable and intuitive, and the complete questions are also accessible:

- `SupportQ1`: Does your employer provide mental health benefits as part of healthcare coverage?

- `SupportQ2`: Has your employer ever formally discussed mental health (for example, as part of a wellness campaign or other official communication)?

- `SupportQ3`: Does your employer offer resources to learn more about mental health disorders and options for seeking help?

- `SupportQ4`: Is your anonymity protected if you choose to take advantage of mental health or substance abuse treatment resources provided by your employer?

- `SupportQ5`: If a mental health issue prompted you to request medical leave from work, how easy or difficult would it be to ask for that leave?

- `AttitudeQ1`: Would you feel comfortable discussing a mental health issue with your direct supervisor(s)?

- `AttitudeQ2`: Would you feel comfortable discussing a mental health issue with your coworkers?

- `AttitudeQ3`: How willing would you be to share with friends and family that you have a mental illness?

- `SupportEx1`: If you have revealed a mental health disorder to a client or business contact, how has this affected you or the relationship?

- `SupportEx2`: If you have revealed a mental health disorder to a coworker or employee, how has this impacted you or the relationship?

- `Age`: What is your age?

- `Gender`: What is your gender?

- `ResidingCountry`: What country do you live in?

- `WorkingCountry`: What country do you work in?

- `Mental Illness`: Have you ever been diagnosed with a mental health disorder?

- `Treatment`: Have you ever sought treatment for a mental health disorder from a mental health professional?

- `Year`: The year that the data was collected.

After removing the other attributes, renaming the long attribute names with their key in the dictionary, the five datasets can be easily joined using the `pd.concat()` pandas function. I have named the integrated DataFrame `in_df`.

Cleaning the data

While going about data integration, we took care of some level I data cleaning as well, such as the data being in one standard data structure and the attributes having codable and intuitive titles. However, because `in_df` is integrated from five different sources, the chances are that different data recording practices may have been used, which may lead to inconsistency across `in_df`.

For instance, the following figure shows how varied data collection for the `Gender` attribute has been:

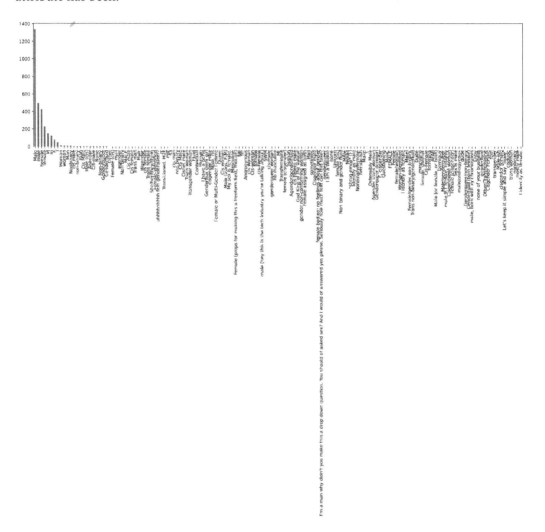

Figure 15.3 – The state of the Gender attribute before cleaning

We need to go over every attribute and make sure that there is no repetition of the same possibilities in a slightly different wording due to varying data collection or misspellings.

Detecting and dealing with outliers and errors

As our AQs are only going to rely on data visualization for answers, we don't need to detect outliers, as our addressing them would be adopting the *"do nothing"* strategy. However, as we use outlier detection to also find possible systematic errors in the data, we can visualize all of the attributes in the data and spot inconsistencies, and then fix them.

The following figure shows the box plot and histogram of the Age attribute, and we can see there are some mistaken data entries. The two unreasonably high values and the one unreasonably low value were changed to *NaN*:

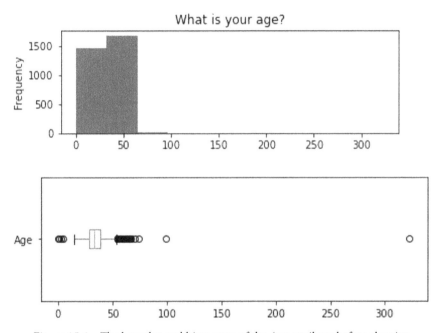

Figure 15.4 – The box plot and histogram of the Age attribute before cleaning

After the prescribed transformation, the box plot changed to more healthy-looking data distribution, as shown in the following figure. There are still some fliers in the data, but, after further investigation of these entries, it was concluded these values are correct, and the individuals who responded to the survey just happened to be older than the rest of the respondent population:

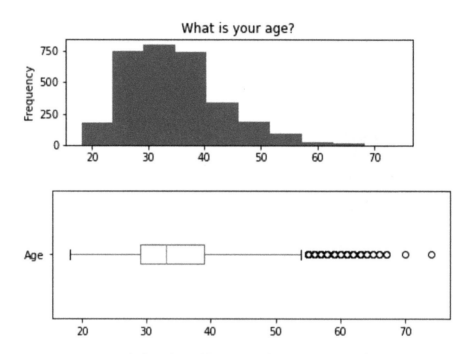

Figure 15.5 – The box plot and histogram of the Age attribute after cleaning

The visualization of another two attributes showed that they need our attention – ResidingCountry and WorkingCountry. The following figure shows the bar chart of the WorkingCountry attribute. The visuals of the two attributes are very similar, which is why we have shown only one of them:

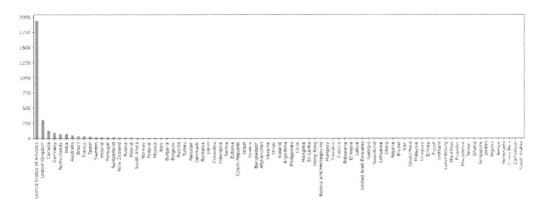

Figure 15.6 – The box plot and histogram of the WorkingCountry attribute before transformation

Considering the bar charts of these two attributes, we do know that the issue with this data is not mistaken data entries; however, the fact that there are just more data entries from the US than the other countries is not because the US only has tech companies, but, at a guess, because the survey participation was more encouraged in the US. To deal with this situation, the best way is to focus our analysis on the US respondents instead of the whole data. Therefore, we remove all the rows, except for the ones that have United States of America under both WorkingCountry and ResidingCountry.

After implementing this data transformation, the values under WorkingCountry and ResidingCountry will only have one possible value; therefore, they are not adding any information to the population of the transformed dataset. The best way to move forward would be to remove these two attributes.

Next, let's deal with the missing values in the dataset.

Detecting and dealing with missing values

After investigation, we realize that except for `AttitudeQ3`, `Age`, `Gender`, `Mental Illness`, `Treatment`, and `Year`, the rest of the attributes do have missing values. The first thing we check is to make sure the missing values are all from the same data objects. The following figure was created so that we can see the assortment of missing values across the population of the dataset:

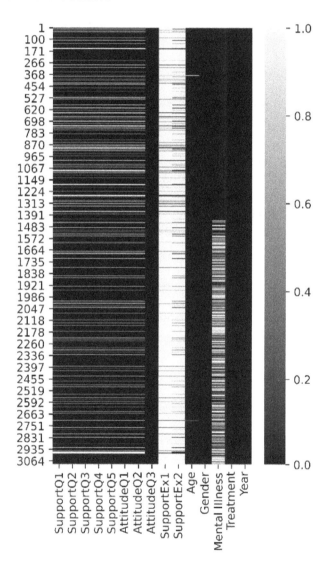

Figure 15.7 – Assortment of missing values across the population of the dataset

Considering the preceding figure, the answer to our wondering is yes, some data objects have missing values on more than one attribute. The missing values for the attributes from **SupportQ1** to **AttitudeQ3** are from the same data objects. However, the preceding figure brings our attention to the fact that the missing values under **SupportEx1** and **SupportEx2** are much more troublesome, as the majority of the data objects have missing values under these two attributes. The best way of moving forward in these situations is to forego having these attributes. So these two attributes have been removed from the analysis.

Now, let's bring our attention back to the common missing values among the data objects for the attributes from **SupportQ1** to **AttitudeQ3**.

The common missing values in attributes from SupportQ1 to AttitudeQ3

We need to diagnose these missing values to figure out what type they are before we can deal with them. After running the diagnosis, we can see these missing values have a relationship with the Age attribute. Specifically, the older population in the dataset has left these questions unanswered. Therefore, we can conclude that these missing values are of the **Missing At Random** (**MAR**) type. We will not deal with these missing values here because our decision regarding them depends on the analysis. However, we'll keep in mind that these missing values are of the MAR type.

Next, let's diagnose the missing values on the other attributes – next stop: the Mental Illness attribute.

The missing values in the MentalIllness attribute

The Mental Illness attribute has 536 missing values. The missing value ratio is significant at 28%. To investigate why these missing values happen, we compare the pattern of the occurrence of these missing values with the distribution of the whole data. In other words, we diagnose these missing values, and after the diagnosis, it will become apparent that missing values under this attribute are closely connected with the Age, Treatment, and Year attributes. It is apparent that these missing values are also of the MAR type, and we will not deal with them before the analysis.

Lastly, we need to address the three missing values in the Age attribute.

The missing values in the Age attribute

The Age attribute has three missing values. These are missing values that were imputed from the extreme point analysis. We decided these attributes were mistake data entries. As we know where they come from and that there are only three of them, we can assume that they are of the **Missing Completely At Random** (**MCAR**) type.

Now that the dataset is clean and integrated, let's move our attention to the analysis part.

Analyzing the data

As we have seen in our journey in this book, data preprocessing is not an island and the best data preprocessing is done by being informed about the analytics goals. So we will continue preprocessing the data as we go about answering the four questions in this case study. Let's progress in this subsection one AQ at a time.

Analysis question one – is there a significant difference between the mental health of employees across the attribute of gender?

To answer this question, we need to visualize the interaction between three attributes: Gender, Mental Illness, and Treatment. We are aware that the Mental Illness attribute has 536 missing MAR values and those missing values have a relationship with the Treatment attribute. However, as the goal of the analysis is to see the mental health across Gender, we can avoid interacting with Treatment and Mental Illness and bring the focus of our analysis to the interaction of the Gender attribute with both of these two attributes. With this strategy, we can adopt the do-nothing approach for the missing values in Mental Illness.

Using the skills that we have picked up in the course of our learning in this book, we can come up with the following two bar charts that meaningfully show the interactions in the data that can help us answer this AQ:

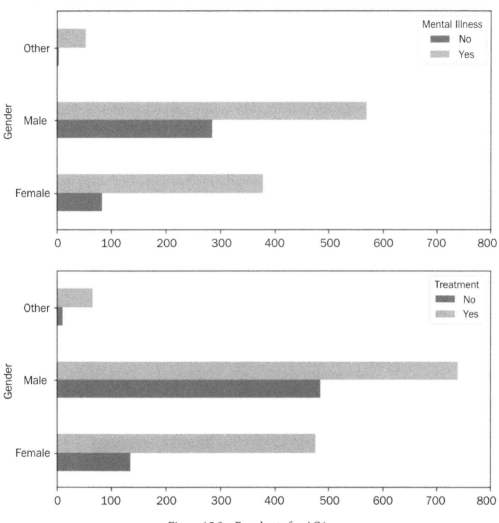

Figure 15.8 – Bar charts for AQ1

The preceding figure shows that the **Gender** attribute does have a meaningful impact on the mental health of tech employees. So the answer to this question is yes. However, while the ratio of not having a mental illness compared to having a mental illness is higher for **Male** than **Female**, there is also a much higher *"never having sought professional mental health help" ratio* among **Male**. These observations suggest that there is a population of male employees in tech that are not aware of their mental health and have never sought professional help. Based on these observations, it should be recommended to target male employees for mental health awareness.

Another important observation from the preceding figure is that there seem to be many more mental health concerns for the individuals who have not chosen **Male** or **Female** for their gender. However, the preceding figure does not show what the difference is because this segment of the population has much smaller data objects than **Male** and **Female**. Therefore, to tease out the portion of these individuals with mental health concerns and compare them with the other two subpopulations, the following two heat maps were created:

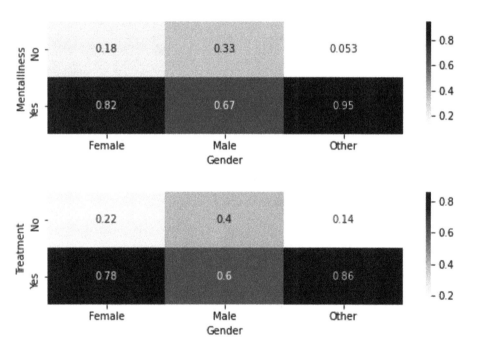

Figure 15.9 – Heat maps for AQ1

In the preceding figure, we can see that indeed the subpopulation that did not identify as **Male** or **Female** has a much larger percentage of people with mental illnesses than the other two populations. However, we can that see this population, similar to the population of **Female**, has a higher percentage of having sought treatment.

Now, let's discuss AQ2.

Analysis question two – is there a significant difference between the mental health of employees across the Age attribute?

To answer this question, we need to visualize the interaction between three attributes: Age, Mental Illness, and Treatment. We are aware that the Mental Illness attribute has 536 missing MAR values and those missing values have a relationship with the Treatment and Age attributes. Moreover, we are aware that Age has three missing MCAR values.

Dealing with the missing MCAR values is simple, as we know these missing values are completely random. However, we cannot adopt the approach of leaving them as they are because to be able to visualize these relationships, we need to transform the Age attribute from categorical to numerical. Therefore, for this analysis, we have removed the data objects with missing values under the Age attribute.

We cannot take the same approach we took in AQ1 to deal with the missing MAR values of Mental Illness because this attribute has a relationship with both the Age and Treatment attributes. Therefore here we have added a third category to Mental Illness – **MV-MAR**. The following figure shows the bar charts that visualize the relationships that we are interested in investigating:

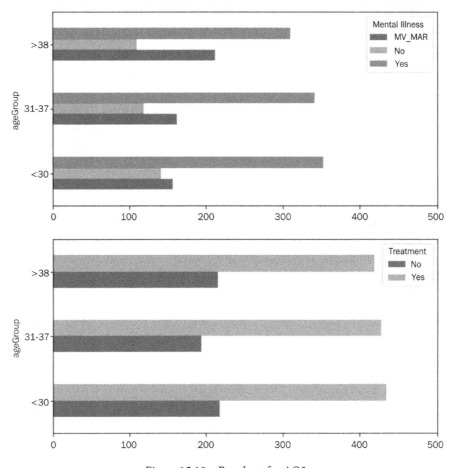

Figure 15.10 – Bar chart for AQ2

Studying the preceding figure, we can see that there seem to be some patterns in the data; however, they are not as pronounced as they were under AQ1, so before discussing these patterns, let's see whether these patterns are significant statistically. We can use the chi-square test of association for this purpose. As seen in *Chapter 11, Data Cleaning Level III – Missing Values, Outliers, and Errors*, the scipy.stats module has this test packaged in the chi2_contingency function.

After calculating the p-values of the test for both bar charts in the preceding figure, we come to 0.0022 and 0.5497 respectively. This tells us that there are no significant patterns in the second bar chart, but the patterns in the first bar chart are significant. Using this information, we can conclude that while age does have an impact on mental health concerns, it does not impact the behavior of individuals in seeking treatment.

Moreover, the significant pattern in the first bar chart tells us that as the Age attribute increases, the answer *no* to the question *"Have you ever been diagnosed with a mental health disorder?"* also increases. Surprisingly, the answer *yes* to the same question also increases. It is surprising because we would expect these two to counteract with one another. The reason for this surprising observation is also shown in this bar chart; as the age increases, the number of individuals who have not answered the question has also increased. This could be because older individuals do not have as much trust in the confidentiality of the data collection.

The conclusion that is drawn from this observation is that older tech employees may need to build more trust for them to open up about their mental health concerns than younger employees.

Next, we will discuss AQ3.

Analysis question three – do more supportive companies have mentally healthier employees?

To answer this question, we first need to perform some data transformation, specifically attribute construction. We have constructed the PerceivedSupportScore attribute, which is a column that indicates how supportive the participant's employer is of mental health. The SupportQ1, SupportQ2, SupportQ3, SupportQ4, and SupportQ5 attributes were used to calculate SupportScore. The $+1$ or $+0.5$ values were added to PerceivedSupportScore where the answers to these attributes indicated support, whereas the -1 or -0.5 values were subtracted from PerceivedSupportScore where the answers to these attributes indicated a lack of support. For instance, for SupportQ5, the $+1$, $+0.5$, -0.5, -0.75, and -1 values were added/subtracted respectively for *Very easy*, *Somewhat easy*, *Somewhat difficult*, *Somewhat difficult*, and *Very difficult*. The question that SupportQ5 asked was *"If a mental health issue prompted you to request medical leave from work, how easy or difficult would it be to ask for that leave?"*

The following figure shows the histogram of the newly constructed column:

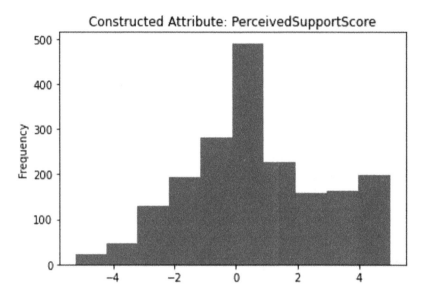

Figure 15.11 – Histogram of the newly constructed attribute for AQ3

We certainly do not forget that all of the ingredients of the newly constructed SupportQ1 and SupportQ2 attributes have 228 missing MAR values. These missing MAR values showed a relationship with the Age attribute. As for answering AQ3, we need to visualize the relationship between the newly constructed attribute and the Mental Illness and Treatment attributes; we can adapt the approach of "leaving as is" for these missing values. The reason is that neither the Mental Illness attribute nor the Treatment attribute influenced the missing values on the ingredient attributes.

Before doing the visualization, as the newly constructed attribute is numerical and both Mental Illness and Treatment are categorical, we need to first discretize the attribute. Scores higher than 1 were labeled as **Supportive** and scores lower than -0.5 were labeled as **Unsupportive**. The results are presented in the following bar chart:

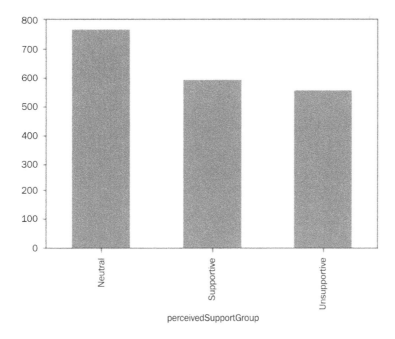

Figure 15.12 – Bar chart of the newly constructed attribute after discretization for AQ3

The following figure shows the interaction between the three **Mental Illness**, **Treatment**, and **pereceivedSupportGroup** attributes. As a visualization with three dimensions is going to be somewhat overwhelming, we can make a strategic decision to only include the two extreme categories, **Supportive** and **Unsupportive**, and leave out **Neutral**:

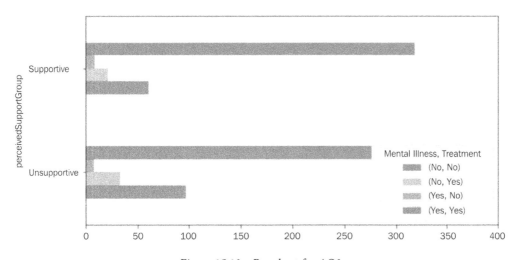

Figure 15.13 – Bar chart for AQ3

Studying the patterns shown in the preceding figure, we realize that `perceivedSupportScore` influences the employee's behavior in seeking professional help for mental health concerns. The number of respondents that have answered **Yes** to both *"Have you ever been diagnosed with a mental health disorder?"* and *"Have you ever sought treatment for a mental health disorder from a mental health professional?"* questions is significantly higher in the **Supportive** category. Likewise, the number of respondents that have answered **No** to both questions is significantly lower in the **Supportive** category.

Based on these observations, we can recommend investing in creating trust and employees' perception of support in tech companies.

Next, we will address the last AQ.

Analysis question four – does the attitude of individuals toward mental health influence their mental health and their seeking of treatments?

Similar to AQ3, to answer this question, we first need to construct a new attribute; `AttitudeScore` will be a column that indicates the participant's attitude toward sharing mental health issues. The `AttitudeQ1`, `AttitudeQ2`, and `AttitudeQ3` attributes are used to construct `AttitudeScore`. The +1 or +0.5 values were added to `AttitudeScore` where the answers to these attributes indicated openness, whereas the -1 or -0.5 values were subtracted from `AttitudeScore` where the answers to these attributes indicated a lack of openness. For instance, for `AttitudeQ3`, the +1, +0.5, -0.5, and -1 values were added/subtracted respectively for *Very open, Somewhat open, Somewhat not open,* and *Not open at all*; the question that `AttitudeQ3` asked was *"Would you feel comfortable discussing a mental health issue with your coworkers?"*

The following figure shows the histogram of the newly constructed attribute:

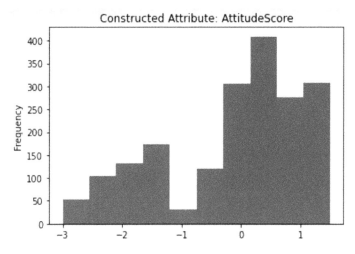

Figure 15.14 – Histogram of the newly constructed attribute for AQ4

Similar to `perceivedSupportScore` in AQ3, before doing the visualization, as the newly constructed attribute is numerical and both `Mental Illness` and `Treatment` are categorical, we need to first discretize the attribute. Scores higher than `0.5` were labeled as **OpenAttitude**, scores lower than `-0.5` were labeled as **ClosedAttitude**, and scores between `-0.5` and `0.5` were labeled as **Neutral**. The results are presented in the following bar chart:

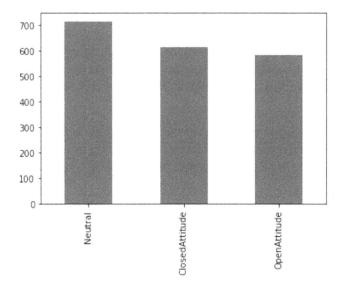

Figure 15.15 – Bar chart of the newly constructed attributes after discretization for AQ4

The following stacked bar chart is created to show the interaction between the three **MentalIllness**, **Treatment**, and **attitudeGroup** attributes. We use a similar strategy to the one used in *Figure 15.13* to avoid overwhelming our sensory faculty:

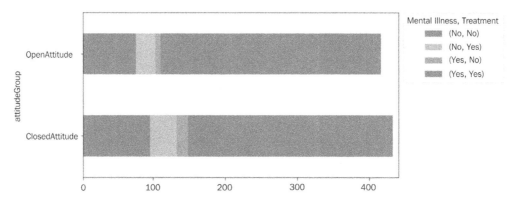

Figure 15.16 – Stacked bar chart for AQ4

The preceding visualization provides an answer for AQ4. There seems to be a meaningful improvement in employees seeking treatment if they have an open attitude toward sharing mental health issues. These observations suggest that tech companies should see the education of employees in their attitude toward mental health as a sensible investment option.

Summary

In this chapter, we got to practice what we have learned during our journey in this book. We did some challenging data integration and data cleaning to prepare a dataset for analysis. Furthermore, based on our analytics goals, we performed specific data transformations so that the visualization that answers our AQs becomes possible and, at times, more effective.

In the next chapter, we will practice data preprocessing on another case study. In this case study, the general goal of the analysis was data visualization; however, the preprocessing in the next case study will be done to enable predictive modeling.

16

Case Study 2 – Predicting COVID-19 Hospitalizations

This chapter is going to provide an excellent learning opportunity to perform a predictive analysis from scratch. By the end of this chapter, you will have learned a valuable lesson about preprocessing. We will take the COVID-19 pandemic as an example. This is a good case study because there is lots of data available about different aspects of the pandemic such as covid hospitalizations, cases, deaths, and vaccinations.

In this chapter, we're going to cover the following:

- Introducing the case study
- Preprocessing the data
- Analyzing the data

Technical requirements

You will be able to find all of the code examples and the dataset that is used in this chapter in this book's GitHub repository at `https://github.com/PacktPublishing/Hands-On-Data-Preprocessing-in-Python/tree/main/Chapter16`.

Introducing the case study

As the world started grappling with the ramifications of COVID-19, healthcare systems across the globe started dealing with the new overwhelming burden of caring for the people infected with the disease. For instance, in the US governments, all levels – Federal, State, and local, had to make decisions so they can help the hospitals as they struggled to shoulder the crisis. The good news is that database and data analytics technologies were able to create real value for these decision-makers. For instance, the following figure shows a dashboard that monitors the COVID-19 situation for Los Angeles County in the State of California in the United States. The figure was collected from `http://publichealth.lacounty.gov/media/coronavirus/data/index.htm` on October 4, 2021.

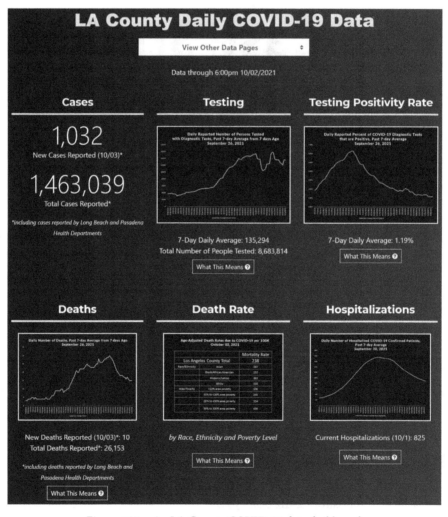

Figure 16.1 – An LA County COVID-19 data dashboard

In this case study, we are going to see an example of data analytics that can be of meaningful value to a local government department. We are going to focus on the government of Los Angeles County (LA), California. This county is the most populated in the US, with approximately 10 million residents. We are going to use historical data to predict the number of patients that will need hospitalization in the near future; specifically, we will create a model that can predict the number of hospitalizations in LA County two weeks from the present moment.

Now that we have a general understanding of this case study, let's get to know the datasets that we will use for our prediction model.

Introducing the source of the data

When we create a prediction model, one of the first things we need to do is to imagine what kind of data can be useful for predicting our target. In this example, our *target* is the *number of hospitalizations*. In other words, we want to imagine what the independent attributes could be for predicting this specific dependent attribute.

Go back to *Chapter 3*, *Data – What Is It Really?*, and study the DDPA pyramid in *Figure 3.2*. When we imagine what data resources could be useful for the prediction of our target, we are exploring the base of the DDPA pyramid. The base of the pyramid represents all of the data that is available to us. Not everything is going to be useful at this point, but that is the beginning of the data preprocessing journey. We start by considering what could be useful, and by the end of the process, we should have a suitable dataset that can be useful for pattern recognition.

The following list shows four sources of data that can be useful for predicting hospitalizations:

- Historical data of LA County COVID-19 hospitalizations (`https://data.chhs.ca.gov/dataset/covid-19-hospital-data`)

- Historical data of COVID-19 Cases and Deaths in LA County (`https://data.chhs.ca.gov/dataset/covid-19-time-series-metrics-by-county-and-state`)

- Historical data of COVID-19 Vaccinations in LA County (`https://data.chhs.ca.gov/dataset/covid-19-vaccine-progress-dashboard-data-by-zip-code`)

- The dates of US public holidays (these can be accessed via **Google**)

You can download the latest versions of these datasets from the provided links. The three datasets that we use in this chapter, `covid19hospitalbycounty.csv`, `covid19cases_test.csv`, and `covid19vaccinesbyzipcode_test.csv`, were collected on October 3, 2021. You must keep this date in mind as you go through this chapter, as the time range of our prediction is an important feature. I strongly encourage you to download the latest version of these files and update the analysis and do some actual predictions. Better yet, if the same datasets are available where you live, do the predictive analysis for your local government.

The fourth data source is a simple one – the US public holidays are, well, public knowledge, and some simple Googling can provide these.

> **Attention!**
> I strongly encourage you to open each of these datasets on your own and scroll through them to get to know them before continuing. This will enhance your learning.

Now that we have the datasets, we need to perform some data preprocessing before we get to the data analytics. So, let's dive in.

Preprocessing the data

The very first step in preprocessing data for prediction and classification models is to be clear about how far in the future you are planning to make predictions. As discussed, our goal in this case study is to make a prediction for two full weeks (that is, 14 days) in the future. This is critical to know before we start the preprocessing.

The next step is to design a dataset that has two characteristics:

- First, it must support our prediction needs. For instance, in this case, we want to use historical data to predict hospitalizations in two weeks.

- Second, the dataset must be filled with all of the data we have collected. In this example, the data includes `covid19hospitalbycounty.csv`, `covid19cases_test.csv`, `covid19vaccinesbyzipcode_test.csv`, and the dates of US public holidays.

One of the very first things we will do codewise, of course, is to read these datasets into pandas DataFrames. The following list shows the name we used for the pandas DataFrames:

- `covid19hospitalbycounty.csv`: `day_hosp_df`

- `covid19cases_test.csv`: `day_case_df`

- `covid19vaccinesbyzipcode_test.csv`: `day_vax_df`

Now, let's discuss the steps for designing the dataset, which needs to have the two characteristics we previously described.

Designing the dataset to support the prediction

While designing this dataset to possess the two characteristics that were mentioned earlier, we basically try to come up with possible independent attributes that can have meaningful predictive values for our dependent attribute. The following list shows the independent attributes that we may come up with for this prediction task.

In defining the attributes in the following list, we have used the t variable to represent time. For instance, `t0` shows $t=0$, and the attribute shows information about the same day as the row:

- `n_Hosp_t0`: The number of hospitalizations at $t=0$

- `s_Hosp_tn7_0`: The slope of the curve of hospitalizations for the period $t=-7$ to $t=0$

- `Bn_days_MajHol`: The number of days from the previous major holiday

- `av7_Case_tn6_0`: The seven-day average of the number of cases for the period $t=-6$ to $t=0$

- `s_Case_tn14_0`: The slope of the curve of cases for the period $t=-14$ to $t=0$

- `av7_Death_tn6_0`: The seven-day average of the number of deaths for the period $t=-6$ to $t=0$

- `s_Death_tn14_0`: The slope of the curve of deaths for the period $t=-14$ to $t=0$

- `p_FullVax_t0`: The percentage of fully vaccinated people at $t=0$

- `s_FullVax_tn14_0`: The slope of the curve of the percentage of fully vaccinated people for the period $t=-14$ to $t=0$

> **Note!**
>
> A great question to ask about these suggested independent attributes is how did we come up with them. There is no step-by-step process that can guarantee the perfect set of independent attributes, but you can learn the relevant skills to position you for more success.
>
> These independent attributes are the byproduct of the creative mind of a person that has the following characteristics: 1) they understand the prediction algorithms, 2) they know the types of data that are collected, 3) they are knowledgeable about the target attribute and the factors that can influence it, and 4) they are equipped with data preprocessing tools such as data integration and transformation that enable effective data preprocessing.

After reviewing these potential attributes, you realize the importance of **functional data analysis (FDA)**, which we learned about in different parts of this book. Most of these attributes will be the outcome of the FDA for data integration, data reduction, and data transformation.

The dependent attribute (or our target) is also coded similarly as `n_Hosp_t14`, which is the number of hospitalizations at *t=14*.

The following figure shows the placeholder dataset that we have designed so that we can fill it up using the data resources we have identified:

	t0	n_Hosp_t0	s_Hosp_tn7_0	n_days_MajHol	av7_Case_tn6_0	s_Case_tn14_0	av7_Death_tn6_0	s_Death_tn14_0	p_FullVax_t0	s_FullVax_tn14_0	n_Hosp_t14
0	2020-03-29	NaN	NaN	NaN	NaN	NaN	NaN	NaN	NaN	NaN	NaN
1	2020-03-30	NaN	NaN	NaN	NaN	NaN	NaN	NaN	NaN	NaN	NaN
2	2020-03-31	NaN	NaN	NaN	NaN	NaN	NaN	NaN	NaN	NaN	NaN
3	2020-04-01	NaN	NaN	NaN	NaN	NaN	NaN	NaN	NaN	NaN	NaN
4	2020-04-02	NaN	NaN	NaN	NaN	NaN	NaN	NaN	NaN	NaN	NaN
...	...	...	...	...	...	...	...	...	...	...	...
549	2021-09-29	NaN	NaN	NaN	NaN	NaN	NaN	NaN	NaN	NaN	NaN
550	2021-09-30	NaN	NaN	NaN	NaN	NaN	NaN	NaN	NaN	NaN	NaN
551	2021-10-01	NaN	NaN	NaN	NaN	NaN	NaN	NaN	NaN	NaN	NaN
552	2021-10-02	NaN	NaN	NaN	NaN	NaN	NaN	NaN	NaN	NaN	NaN
553	2021-10-03	NaN	NaN	NaN	NaN	NaN	NaN	NaN	NaN	NaN	NaN

554 rows × 11 columns

Figure 16.2 – The placeholder for the designed dataset

Filling up the placeholder dataset

The following figure tells a simple story of how we will be filling up the placeholder dataset. Of course, the data comes from the four data sources that we have identified; however, the ingenuity and the skills that we need to integrate, transform, reduce, and clean the data so it can fill up the placeholder will come from our knowledge and creativity.

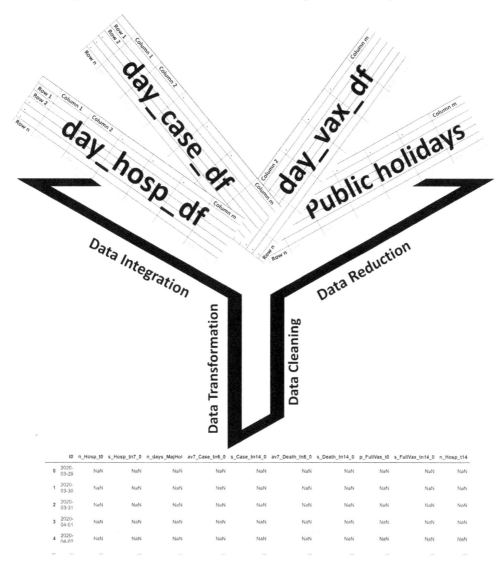

Figure 16.3 – A schematic of filling up the placeholder dataset

> **Attention!**
>
> It is important to remember that we learned about each of the data preprocessing steps in isolation. We first learned about *data cleaning*, then *data integration*, and after that *data reduction*, and at the end came *data transformation*. However, now that we are starting to feel more comfortable with these stages, there is no need to do these in isolation. In real practice, they can and should be done at the same time very regularly. In this case study, you are seeing an example of this.

So, as shown in the preceding figure, we will be using the data from the four sources to fill the columns, one by one, in the designed placeholder dataset. However, to make the connections between the data sources, some data cleaning is needed. The main priority is to make sure all of the rows in day_hosp_df, day_case_df, day_vax_df, and even the placeholder day_df are indexed with the datetime version of the dates. These dates will provide seamless connections between the data sources. After that, we will use what we have learned in this book to fill the columns in the placeholder day_df DataFrame. The following figure shows the day_df DataFrame rows after having been filled:

	t0	n_Hosp_t0	s_Hosp_tn7_0	n_days_MajHol	av7_Case_tn6_0	s_Case_tn14_0	av7_Death_tn6_0	s_Death_tn14_0	p_FullVax_t0	s_FullVax_tn14_0	n_Hosp_t14
t0											
2020-03-29	2020-03-29	489.0	NaN	67	NaN	NaN	NaN	NaN	0.000000	0.000000	1433.0
2020-03-30	2020-03-30	601.0	NaN	68	NaN	NaN	NaN	NaN	0.000000	0.000000	1501.0
2020-03-31	2020-03-31	713.0	NaN	69	NaN	NaN	NaN	NaN	0.000000	0.000000	1587.0
2020-04-01	2020-04-01	739.0	NaN	70	NaN	NaN	NaN	NaN	0.000000	0.000000	1624.0
2020-04-02	2020-04-02	818.0	NaN	71	NaN	NaN	NaN	NaN	0.000000	0.000000	1679.0
...	...	...	...	...	...	...	...	...	...	...	...
2021-09-29	2021-09-29	872.0	-16.928571	21	970.285714	-34.732143	13.000000	-0.528571	0.712213	0.000669	NaN
2021-09-30	2021-09-30	862.0	-13.773810	22	954.142857	-21.414284	11.857143	-0.814286	0.712213	0.000623	NaN
2021-10-01	2021-10-01	825.0	-14.380952	23	897.857143	-25.339285	9.714286	-1.021429	0.712213	0.000566	NaN
2021-10-02	2021-10-02	790.0	-15.750000	24	804.571429	-42.971429	7.857143	-1.078571	0.712213	0.000503	NaN
2021-10-03	2021-10-03	768.0	-19.500000	25	737.285714	-67.714286	6.000000	-1.228571	0.712213	0.000437	NaN

554 rows × 11 columns

Figure 16.4 – The placeholder dataset after being filled

You may be wondering why some of the rows still contain NaN. That's a great question and I am confident you can figure out the answer on your own. Just go back to the definition of each of these independent attributes we designed earlier. Give this some thought before reading on.

The answer to the question is simple. The reason that there are still NaN values on some of the rows is that we did not have the information in our data sources to calculate them. For instance, let's consider why s_Hosp_tn7_0 is NaN in the 2020-03-29 row. We have to go back to the definition of s_Hosp_tn7_0, which is *the slope of the curve of hospitalizations for the period t=-7 to t=0*. As 2020-03-29 is t=0 for this row, we will need to have the data of the following dates to calculate s_Hosp_tn7_0, and we don't have them in our data sources:

- t=-1: 2020-03-28
- t=-2: 2020-03-27
- t=-3: 2020-03-26
- t=-4: 2020-03-25
- t=-5: 2020-03-24
- t=-6: 2020-03-23
- t=-7: 2020-03-22

The dataset that we are using in this case study has data from 2020-03-29. This almost always happens when creating a dataset for future prediction with a decision-making gap. The reason we included the 14 days' difference between the sources of data we use for calculating the independent attributes and computing the dependent attribute is for our prediction to have decision-making values. Of course, we can have a more accurate prediction if the decision-making gap is shorter, but at the same time, these predictions will have fewer decision-making values, as they may not allow for the decision-maker to process the situation and make the decision that can have a positive impact.

As you will see in the following sections, we will have to eliminate the rows that contain NaN. But that's okay, as we have enough data for our algorithm to still be capable of finding patterns.

Next, let's see whether the independent attribute we imagined would have predictive values has them. We will do that with supervised dimension reduction during our data preprocessing.

Supervised dimension reduction

In *Chapter 13, Data Reduction*, we learned a few **supervised dimension reduction** methods. Here, we want to apply three of them before moving to the data analysis part of the case study. These three methods are **linear regression**, **random forests**, and **decision trees**. Before reading on, make sure to revisit *Chapter 13, Data Reduction*, to freshen up your understanding of the strengths and weaknesses of each of these methods. The following figures show the results of each of these three methods.

In the following figure, we see that linear regression deems all of the independent attributes significant for the prediction of n_Hosp_t14, except for n_days_MajHol and s_FullVax_tn14_0. Pay attention to the P>|t| column, which shows with the p-value of the test on the null hypothesis that the relevant dependent attribute is not capable of predicting the target in this model. The p-values for all of the other independent attributes – except n_days_MajHol and s_FullVax_tn14_0 – are very small, indicating the rejection of the null hypothesis.

OLS Regression Results

Dep. Variable:	n_Hosp_t14	R-squared:	0.981
Model:	OLS	Adj. R-squared:	0.981
Method:	Least Squares	F-statistic:	2937.
Date:	Mon, 04 Oct 2021	Prob (F-statistic):	0.00
Time:	10:03:07	Log-Likelihood:	-3653.5
No. Observations:	525	AIC:	7327.
Df Residuals:	515	BIC:	7370.
Df Model:	9		
Covariance Type:	nonrobust		

	coef	std err	t	P>|t|	[0.025	0.975]
const	316.7108	35.260	8.982	0.000	247.439	385.983
n_Hosp_t0	0.6368	0.053	12.043	0.000	0.533	0.741
s_Hosp_tn7_0	8.7896	0.643	13.672	0.000	7.527	10.053
n_days_MajHol	0.6326	0.422	1.499	0.135	-0.197	1.462
av7_Case_tn6_0	0.2514	0.017	14.956	0.000	0.218	0.284
s_Case_tn14_0	0.5128	0.130	3.932	0.000	0.257	0.769
av7_Death_tn6_0	-5.3348	1.324	-4.030	0.000	-7.935	-2.734
s_Death_tn14_0	-132.9086	12.351	-10.761	0.000	-157.172	-108.645
p_FullVax_t0	-496.0640	57.139	-8.682	0.000	-608.319	-383.809
s_FullVax_tn14_0	-7834.8102	8950.211	-0.875	0.382	-2.54e+04	9748.603

Omnibus:	27.076	Durbin-Watson:	0.168
Prob(Omnibus):	0.000	Jarque-Bera (JB):	67.116
Skew:	0.213	Prob(JB):	2.67e-15
Kurtosis:	4.699	Cond. No.	4.00e+06

Figure 16.5 – The output of linear regression for supervised dimension reduction

We should remember to take the conclusion from the preceding figure with the caveat that linear regression is only capable of checking the linear relationships for us, and that these two attributes may have non-linear relationships that could be useful in a more complex model.

This is shown in the second supervised dimension reduction method: the **random forest**. The following figure visualizes the importance that the Random Forest has given to each independent attribute, and we do see, unlike our conclusion we arrive at under Linear Regression, only four independent attributes are among the most important attributes, and the rest has not given any sizable share of importance.

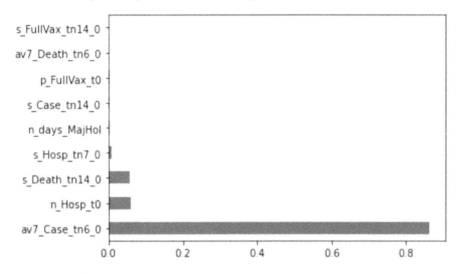

Figure 16.6 – The output of a random forest for supervised dimension reduction

The following figure shows the final decision tree after being tuned for the successful prediction of n_Hosp_t14. The resulting decision tree has many levels, and you will not be able to see the splitting attributes. However, you can see the complete decision tree via the HospDT.pdf file in this book's GitHub repository, or you can create it yourself to investigate it.

Figure 16.7 – The output of a decision tree for supervised dimension reduction

The data preprocessing is almost done. However, because we are going to use different algorithms in the next section, we will leave some of the last preprocessing steps to be performed immediately before applying each prediction algorithm.

Analyzing the data

Now that the data is almost ready, we get to reap the rewards of our hard work by being able to do what some may consider magic – *predict the future*. However, our prediction is going to be even better than magic. Our prediction will be *reliable*, as it is driven by meaningful patterns within historical data.

Throughout this book, we have got to know three algorithms that can handle prediction: linear regression, **multilayer perceptrons** (**MLPs**), and decision trees.

To be able to see the applicability of the prediction models, we need to have a meaningful validation mechanism. We haven't covered this in this book, but there is a well-known and simple method normally called the *hold-out mechanism* or the *train-test procedure*. Simply put, a small part of the data will not be used in the training of the model, and instead, that small part will be used to evaluate how well the model makes predictions.

Specifically, in this case study, after removing the rows that have any missing values, we have 525 data objects that can be used for prediction. We will use 511 of these data objects for training, specifically, the data objects from 2020-04-12 to 2021-09-04 (which would include 507 data objects). The rest, which are 14 data objects from two weeks of the data (that is, the data objects from 2021-09-05 to 2021-09-18), will be used for testing our models. Using these dates, we will separate our data into *train* and *test* sets. We will then train the algorithms using the train set and evaluate them using the test set.

The following figure shows how well the three models – namely linear regression, the decision tree, and the MLP – were able to fit themselves to the training data. With the decision tree and MLP, we should not trust a good fit between the training data and the model, as these algorithms can easily overfit the training data. Therefore, it is important to also see the performance of these algorithms on the test data.

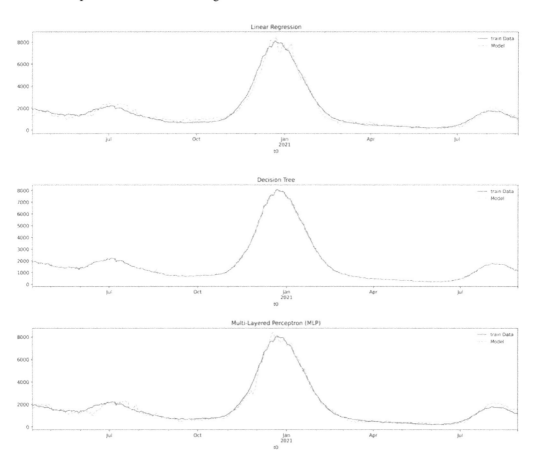

Figure 16.8 – The train dataset versus the fitted model for the linear regression, decision tree, and MLP models

The following figure shows how the trained models were able to predict the test data. The figure also shows what the prediction of actual future values looks like. Remember that this content was created on October 3, 2021.

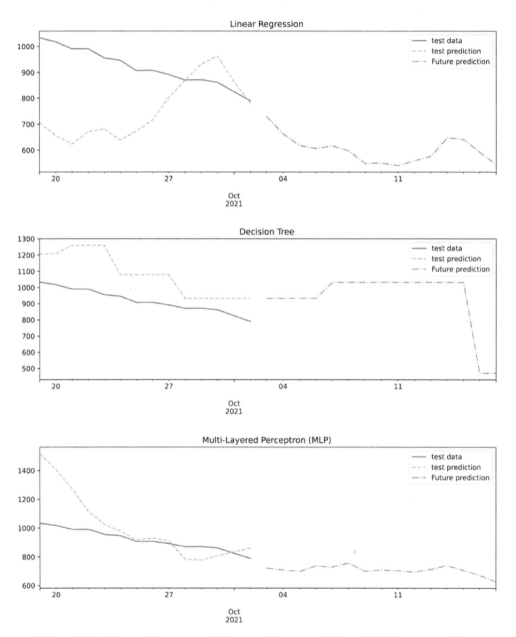

Figure 16.9 – The test data, test prediction, and future prediction of the linear regression, decision tree, and MLP models

Comparing the performance of these three models on the test data is rather difficult due to the way the preceding figure is set up. The following figure shows the prediction of all three models on the test data and also the test data itself in one chart. The following visualization will allow us to find the best algorithm for the job:

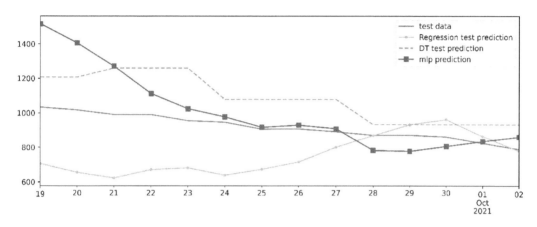

Figure 16.10 – Comparing the performance of the linear regression, decision tree, and MLP models on the test set

In the preceding figure, we can see that while the MLP model performs slightly better than the other two, the three models are largely comparable in performance, and they are all successful.

Well done, we were able to complete the prediction task and also validate it. Let's wrap up this chapter with a summary.

Summary

In this chapter, we got to see the real value of data preprocessing in enabling us to perform predictive analytics. As you saw in this chapter, what empowered our prediction was not an all-singing, all-dancing algorithm – it was our creativity in using what we learned during this chapter to come to a dataset that could be used by standard prediction algorithms for prediction. Furthermore, we got to practice different kinds of data cleaning, data reduction, data integration, and data transformation.

In the next chapter, we will get to practice data preprocessing on another case study. In this case study, the general goal of the analysis was prediction; however, the preprocessing in the next case study will be done to enable **clustering analysis**.

17

Case Study 3: United States Counties Clustering Analysis

This chapter is going to provide another excellent learning opportunity to showcase the process of data preprocessing for high-stakes clustering analysis. We will practice all the four major steps of data preprocessing in this chapter—namely, **data integration**, **data reduction**, **data transformation**, and **data cleaning**. In a nutshell, in this part of the book, we are going to form meaningful groups of **United States** (**US**) counties based on different sources of information and data. By the end of this chapter, we are going to have a much better understanding of the different types of counties that are in the US.

In this chapter, we're going to extract information from this case study using the following main subchapters:

- Introducing the case study
- Preprocessing the data
- Analyzing the data

Technical requirements

You will be able to find all of the code and the dataset that is used in this book in a GitHub repository exclusively created for this book. To find the repository, click on this link: https://github.com/PacktPublishing/Hands-On-Data-Preprocessing-in-Python/tree/main/Chapter17. In this repository, you will find Chapter17 folder from which you can download the code and the data for better learning.

Introducing the case study

During the 2020 US presidential election, the world and America alike were reminded that where an individual lives can best predict what they will decide for their future (that is, how they vote). This may be a sobering realization at an individual level, but this is a billion-dollar understanding for national businesses such as Starbucks, Walmart, and Amazon. Furthermore, for federal, state, and local politicians, this realization can be monumentally useful both at election time and when drafting legislation.

All these benefits may be available to these entities if they are capable of doing meaningful locational analyses of groups of people. In this case study, we are going to analyze the differences and the similarities between US counties. In the following screenshot, we can see that the US has many counties; there are 3,006, to be exact. The color-coded map shows the county-level relative population density:

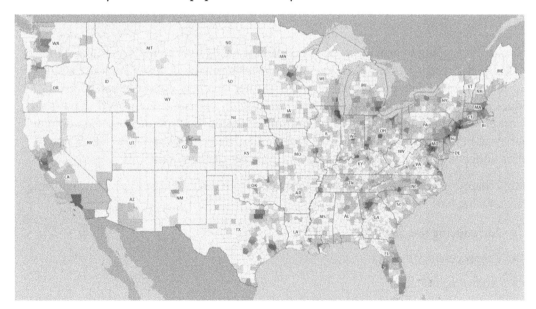

Figure 17.1 – US demographic data map at a county level

> **Note!**
>
> The source of the US demographic data map at a county level can
> be found at the following link: `https://mtgis-portal.`
> `geo.census.gov/arcgis/apps/MapSeries/index.`
> `html?appid=2566121a73de463995ed2b2fd7ff6eb7`.

What is the first step in being able to meaningfully analyze the differences and similarities between all the counties shown in the preceding screenshot? The answer is, of course, data preprocessing. I hope you didn't hesitate to give this answer at this point in the book.

In this chapter, specifically, we are going to integrate a few sources of data, and then perform the necessary data reduction and data transformation before the analysis. There will be lots of data cleaning that needs to be done across different steps of data preprocessing; however, at this point in your learning about data preprocessing, your skillset for data cleaning should have sufficiently developed that you will not need reminding to recognize these steps.

Now that we have a general understanding of this case study, let's get to know the datasets that will be used for this clustering analysis.

Introduction to the source of the data

We will use the following two sources of data to create a dataset that allows us to perform county clustering analysis:

- The four files `Education.xls`, `PopulationEstimates.xls`, `PovertyEstimates.xls`, and `Unemployment.xlsx` from the **US Department of Agriculture Economic Research Service** (**USDA ERS**) (`https://www.ers.usda.gov/data-products/county-level-data-sets/`)

- US election results from **Massachusetts Institute of Technology** (**MIT**) election data (`https://dataverse.harvard.edu/dataset.xhtml?persistentId=doi:10.7910/DVN/VOQCHQ`)

Across the preceding two sources, we've got five different files that we need to integrate. The files from the first source are easily downloaded; however, the one file from the second source will need to be unzipped after being downloaded. After downloading `dataverse_files.zip` file from the second source, and unzipping it, you will get `countypres_2000-2020.csv`, which is the file we want to use.

We will eventually integrate all this data into a `county_df` pandas DataFrame; however, we will need to read them into their own Pandas DataFrames first and then go about the data preprocessing. The following list shows the names we will use for those Pandas DataFrames per file:

- `Education.xls`: `edu_df`
- `PopulationEstimates.xls`: `pop_df`
- `PovertyEstimates.xls`: `pov_df`
- `Unemployment.xlsx`: `employ_df`
- `countypres_2000-2020.csv`: `election_df`

> **Attention!**
> I highly encourage you to open each of these datasets on your own and scroll through them to get to know them before continuing to read on, as this will enhance your learning.

Now that we know the data sources, we need to go through some meaningful data preprocessing before we get to the data analytics part. Let's dive in.

Preprocessing the data

The very first step in preprocessing for clustering analysis is to be clear about which data objects will be clustered, and that is clear here: counties. So, at the end of the data preprocessing, we will need to have a dataset whose rows are counties, and with columns based on how we want to group the counties. As shown in the following screenshot, which is a summary of the data preprocessing that we will perform during this chapter, we will get to `county_df`, which has the characteristics that were just described.

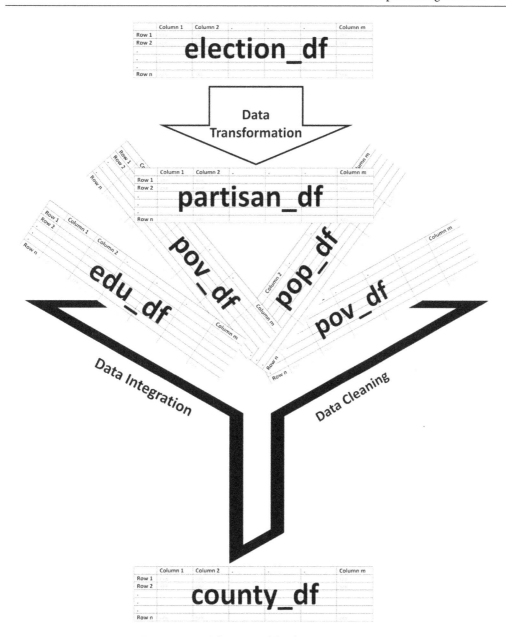

Figure 17.2 – Schematic of the data preprocessing

As shown in the preceding summarizing screenshot, we will first transform `election_df` into `partisan_df`, and then integrate the `partisan_df`, `edu_df`, `pov_df`, `pop_df`, and `employ_df` DataFrames. Of course, there will be more detail to all of these steps than the preceding screenshot shows; however, this serves as a great summary and a general map for our understanding.

Let's roll up our sleeves, then. We will start by transforming `election_df` into `partisan_df`.

Transforming election_df to partisan_df

With a first glance at the `election_df` dataset, we should realize that the definition of data objects for this dataset is not counties, and instead, it is the *county-candidate-election-mode* in each presidential election. While counties are indeed a part of the definition, we only need to have *county* as the definition of the data object. This very fact can be our guiding principle in the data transformation process.

Let's work our way back from *mode* to *county*. Mode refers to the different ways that individuals had been able to participate in the election. By recognizing the fact that `election_df` also has the mode of `'TOTAL'`, which is the sum of all the other modes, we can simply drop all the other rows that have modes other than `'TOTAL'` to simplify the definition of data objects to *county-candidate-election*.

To simplify from *county-candidate-election* to *county* for the definition of data objects, we will first use **attribute construction**, and then **functional data analysis (FDA)**.

Constructing the partisanism attribute

The `partisanism` attribute is meant to capture the level of uniformity in individuals' votes in electing a democrat or a republican in each election. The following formula shows how this constructed attribute can be calculated:

$$partisanism = \frac{votes\ for\ Republicans - votes\ for\ Democrats}{votes\ for\ Republicans + votes\ for\ Democrats}$$

If a county in an election has a large positive partisanism value, it shows the county in that election has swung largely toward republicans; if it has a large negative value, it shows a great swing toward democrats.

The following screenshot shows a small portion of the `partisanElection_df` DataFrame, which is the result of calculating a partisan value for each election and county:

			partisanism
state_po	county_name	year	
AK	DISTRICT 1	2000	0.510367
		2004	0.253528
		2008	0.222669
		2012	0.56734
		2016	0.0914432
...	...	...	...
WY	WESTON	2004	0.636498
		2008	0.574107
		2012	0.714201
		2016	0.775383
		2020	0.771629

18050 rows × 1 columns

Figure 17.3 – A portion of partisanElection_df

By constructing the new `partisanism` attribute and calculating it for every county and election, we managed to move from the definition of data objects being *county-candidate-election* to *county-election*. Next, we will use FDA to have the definition of data objects as only *county*.

FDA to calculate the mean and slope of partisanism

Looking at *Figure 17.3*, you may notice that we have the `partisanism` value of presidential elections 2000, 2004, 2008, 2012, 2016, and 2020 for every county—in other words, for every county, we have a time series of `partisanism` values. Therefore, instead of having to deal with 6 values, we can use FDA to calculate the mean and slope of `partisanism` across elections over 20 years.

After doing this FDA transformation and creating a `partisan_df` DataFrame whose definition of data objects is *county*, we will make sure to also perform a necessary data cleaning step. Specifically, we will transform the `County_Name` column so that its characters are presented in lowercase. This data cleaning is performed for future data integration purposes. As the name of counties may have been written in different formats that are understandable for human comprehension but not for a computer, we thus need to make sure the county names are all in lowercase in all of the data sources so that the data integration will go smoothly.

The following screenshot shows the `partisan_df` attribute:

State	County_Name	Mean_Partisanism	Slope_Partisanism
AK	district 1	0.274999	-0.0762906
	district 10	0.404606	0.0388433
	district 11	0.429907	0.00906478
	district 12	0.417909	0.0196095
	district 13	0.28947	0.00391493
...	...	...	...
WY	sweetwater	0.379123	0.0557874
	teton	-0.155271	-0.086146
	uinta	0.540841	0.0254894
	washakie	0.573747	0.0170218
	weston	0.69149	0.0294079

3151 rows × 2 columns

Figure 17.4 – A portion of partisan_df

Note that the definition of data objects for the DataFrame shown in *Figure 17.4* is *county*. If you go back to the beginning of this subchapter (*Transforming election_df to partisan_df*), our goal was to transform the `election_df` dataset, whose definition of data objects is *county-candidate-election-mode*, into `partisan_df`. We saw that the definition of data objects for `partisan_df` is *county*.

Next, we will perform the necessary data cleaning on `edu_df`, `employ_df`, `pop_df`, and `pov_df`.

Cleaning edu_df, employ_df, pop_df, and pov_df

To take another step toward the preprocessed `county_df` dataset, we will need to perform some data cleaning on `edu_df`, `employ_df`, `pop_df`, and `pov_df`. The steps will be very similar for all these datasets. These include removing unwanted columns, transforming the index attributes, and renaming the attribute titles for brevity and intuitiveness.

Data integration

By the time we arrive at this step, the hardest part of data integration—preparing the DataFrames for integration—has already been done. Because we took our time preparing each one of the DataFrames, doing the data integration is as simple as one line of code, as shown in the following snippet:

```
county_df = pop_df.join(edu_df).join(pov_df).join(employment_
df).join(partisan_df)
```

Once the code is successfully run, we will get the following DataFrame that is almost ready for analysis:

State	County_Name	Population	HigherEdPercent	PovertyPercentage	MedianHHIncome	UnemploymentRate	MedHHIncome_Percent_of_State_Total	Mean_Partisanism	Slope_Partisanism
	autauga	54571	26.5716	12.1	58233	2.7	112.482	0.467068	0.00184533
	baldwin	182265	31.8625	10.1	59871	2.8	115.646	0.532724	0.0128458
AL	barbour	27457	11.5787	27.1	35972	3.8	69.4829	0.0342589	0.00718466
	bibb	22915	10.3785	20.3	47918	3.1	92.5576	0.453212	0.0603812
	blount	57322	13.0934	16.3	52902	2.7	102.185	0.683058	0.0702235
...	...	...	...	...	...	...	...	...	...
	sweetwater	43806	22.4984	8.3	80639	4	121.9	0.379123	0.0557874
	teton	21294	57.0051	6	98837	2.8	149.409	-0.155271	-0.086146
WY	uinta	21118	16.029	8.5	70756	4	106.96	0.540841	0.0254894
	washakie	8533	23.3862	11.1	55122	4.1	83.3263	0.573747	0.0170218
	weston	7208	19.9725	10.5	59410	3	89.8083	0.69149	0.0294079

3007 rows × 8 columns

Figure 17.5 – A portion of preprocessed county_df

Now, we need to perform the next important data preprocessing steps: Level III data cleaning—missing values, errors, and outliers.

Data cleaning level III – missing values, errors, and outliers

After investigation, we realize that there are a handful of missing values under seven out of eight of the attributes in county_df. If this were a real government project, these missing values would need to be tracked down before we moved forward with the analysis; however, as this is practice analysis and there are not too many missing values, we adopt a strategy of dropping the missing values.

Furthermore, when investigating outliers, we will see that all of the attributes in county_df have fliers in their boxplots. However, the extreme values under the Population and UnemploymentRate attributes are too different than the rest of the population, so much so that the extreme values can easily impact the clustering analysis. To mitigate their impact, we will use log transformation on these two attributes.

Regarding the possibility of having errors in the data, there are two matters we need to pay attention to, as follows:

- First, as all of the attributes do have actual extreme values, our tools for possibly detecting univariate errors become ineffective.

- Second, the clustering analysis that we will be doing eventually will show us the outliers, and at that point, we can investigate whether those outliers are possible errors.

One last data preprocessing step and we will then be set for the analysis—we need to check for data redundancy.

Checking for data redundancy

Data redundancy is very possible for county_df as we have brought together different sources of data to create this dataset. As clustering analysis is very prone to be heavily impacted by data redundancy, this step becomes very important. We will use two effective tools for this goal: a **scatter matrix** and **correlation analysis**.

The following screenshot shows a scatter matrix, which is very useful for seeing the possible relationship between the attributes and assessing whether the assuming linear relationship between the attributes is reasonable:

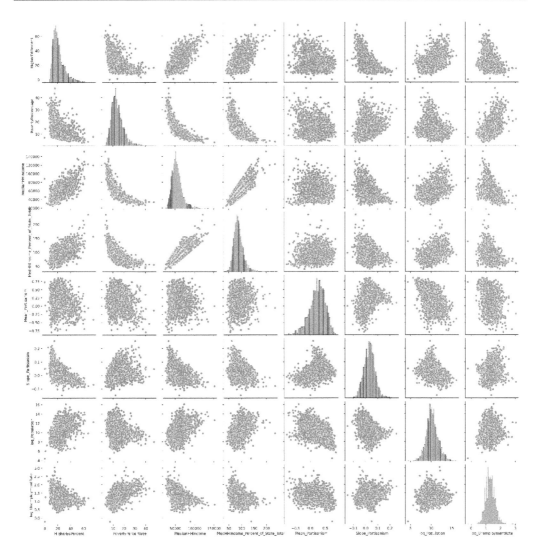

Figure 17.6 – Scatter matrix of county_df

In the preceding screenshot, we can see that while there is somewhat of a non-linear relationship between `PovertyPercentage` and `MedianHHIncome`, assuming a linear relationship between the rest of the attributes does sound reasonable.

The following screenshot shows a correlation matrix of `county_df`:

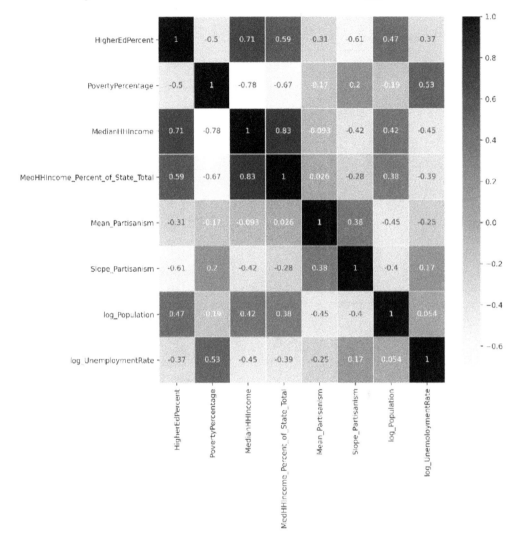

Figure 17.7 – Correlation matrix of county_df

We can see in the preceding screenshot that `MedianHHIncome` has a strong relationship with `PovertyPercentage` and `MedianHHIncome_Percent_of_State_Total`. This is a concerning data redundancy for clustering analysis as there seems to be a repetition of information in these three attributes. To rectify this, we will remove `MedianHHIncome` from the clustering analysis.

Now, we are set to begin the analysis part of this case study.

Analyzing the data

In this part, we will do two types of unsupervised data analysis. We first use **principal component analysis** (**PCA**) to create a high-level visualization of the whole data. Next, after having been informed how many clusters are possibly among the data objects, we will use K-Means to form the clusters and study them. Let's start with PCA.

Using PCA to visualize the dataset

As we already know, PCA can transform the dataset, so most of the information is presented in the first few **principal components** (**PCs**). Our investigation showed that the majority of relationships between the attributes, including `county_df`, is linear, which is allowing us to be able to use PCA; however, we won't forget about the few non-linear relationships as we move ahead with PCA, and we will not rely too much on the results of the PCA.

The following screenshot shows a **three-dimensional** (**3D**) scatterplot of **PC1**, **PC2**, and **PC3**. **PC1** and **PC2** are visualized using the *x* and *y* axes, whereas **PC3** is visualized using color. From the PCA analysis, we learned that **PC1** to **PC3** account for almost 80% of the variations in the whole data, so the following screenshot is illustrating 80% of the information in the data. To get a better insight into what we see in this scatterplot, the counties that are at the extreme end of **PC1** and **PC2** are annotated.

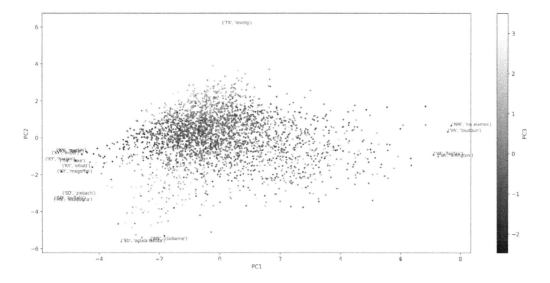

Figure 17.8 – 3D scatterplot of PC1, PC2, PC3 PCA for transformed county_df

Now, let's look at our K-Means clustering analysis. Pay attention to the fact that we standardize the data before performing PCA and normalize the data before performing clustering analysis.

K-Means clustering analysis

After our investigation of *Figure 17.8*, which shows a 3D scatterplot of the PCs and some computational experimentations, we will conclude that the best *K* value for K-Means clustering is 5. The computational experimentation method to find *K* is not covered in this book; however, the code that is used for this step is included in the file dedicated to this chapter in the book's GitHub repository.

The following screenshot shows the result of the K-Means clustering (*K=5*) using **PC1** and **PC2**. This screenshot is advantageous for two reasons—first, we can see the relationship between the clusters, and second, the dispersion between the members of the clusters is depicted.

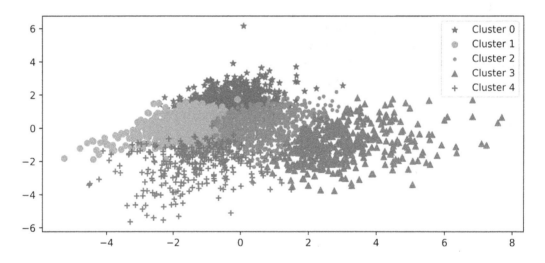

Figure 17.9 – Visualization of the result of clustering county_df using PC1 and PC2

To understand the patterns among the data objects and also know more about the relationship between the clusters, we can view the following centroid analysis using heatmaps:

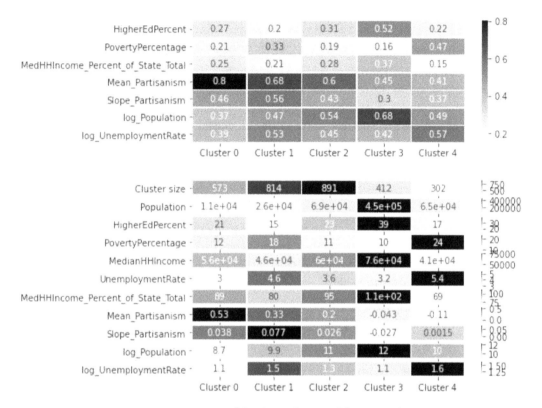

Figure 17.10 – Heatmaps of the clusters' centroid for centroid analysis

From studying *Figure 17.9* and *Figure 17.10*, we can see the following patterns and relationships:

- *Clusters 0, 1, and 2* are Republican-leaning, and *clusters 3 and 4* are Democrat-leaning.

- *Cluster 2* is the one that has the most in common with all the rest of the clusters. This cluster is the best characterized to be the most moderate and affluent among all the Republican-leaning counties.

- *Cluster 0* only has a relationship with *clusters 2 and 3* and is completely cut off from *clusters 4 and 5*, which are the only Democrat-leaning clusters. This cluster is best characterized by the most Republican-leaning cluster with the lowest *unemployment rate* and *population* among all the clusters.

- *Cluster 1* has a relationship with all the clusters except *cluster 3*. This cluster is best characterized as having the lowest `HigherEdPercent` value among all the clusters, and the lowest `MedianHHIncome` and highest `PovertyPercentage` and `UnemploymentRate` values among the Republican-leaning clusters.

- Another interesting pattern about *cluster 1* is that this cluster has the fastest movement toward becoming more Republican-leaning among all the clusters.

- *Cluster 4*, which is a Democrat-learning cluster, has more in common with two Republican-leaning clusters, *clusters 1 and 2*. This cluster is best characterized as having the highest `PovertyPercentage` and `UnemploymentRate` values and the lowest `MedianHHIncome` value among all clusters.

- Another interesting pattern about *cluster 4* is that while this cluster is the most Democrat-leaning cluster, it is the only cluster that has been moving in the opposite direction in terms of partisanism.

- *Cluster 3* has more of a relationship with *cluster 2*, which is a Republican-leaning cluster, than *cluster 4*, which is the only other Democrat-leaning cluster. Among all the clusters, this cluster seems to be a unique one. This cluster is best characterized by the highest `Population` and `HigherEdPercent` values and the lowest `PovertyPercentage` value.

- Another interesting pattern about *cluster 3* is that it is the only cluster that has a movement toward becoming more Democrat-leaning; however, its movement is the slowest among all the clusters:

Well done! We were able to complete the clustering analysis and visualize very interesting and meaningful patterns. What enabled this visualization was partly the existence of great tools such as PCA and K-Means; however, what made this analysis happen was our ingenuity during the data preprocessing step that allowed us to create a dataset that would lead to the presented meaningful outcome.

Summary

In this chapter, we got to experience the essential role of effective data preprocessing in enabling us to perform meaningful clustering analytics. Furthermore, we got to practice different kinds and types of data cleaning, data reduction, data integration, and data transformation situations.

This was the last case study that we have in this book. The next and final chapter will provide some directions for more learning and some practice case studies.

18
Summary, Practice Case Studies, and Conclusions

This chapter will provide a summary of the book, some practice case studies, and lastly offer some concluding remarks.

In this chapter, we're going to cover the following main subchapters:

- A summary of the book
- Practice case studies
- Conclusions

A summary of the book

Congratulations on your excellent journey of learning through the course of this book; you've acquired invaluable skills. You learned various skills in the four parts of this book. In the following subchapter, we will go over what we learned in each part of this book.

Part 1 – Technical requirements

In this part of the book, which lasted from *Chapter 1, Review of the Core Modules of NumPy and Pandas* through *Chapter 4, Databases*, we covered all the technical and foundational concepts, techniques, and technologies that you will need for effective data preprocessing. Specifically, in *Chapter 1, Review of the Core Modules of NumPy and Pandas*, and *Chapter 2, Review of Another Core Module – Matplotlib*, we picked up all the foundation Python programming skills that we will need for data preprocessing. In *Chapter 3, Data – What Is It Really?* we acquired a fundamental understanding of data and the different analytics paths that have implications for our data preprocessing. Finally, in *Chapter 4, Databases*, we learned about the technological backbone of data analytics, which is databases, and got to understand their role in effective analytics and preprocessing.

Part 2 – Analytics goals

While the first part of the book was meant to give you a technological and foundational background for effective data preprocessing, the second part of the book, which we will cover next, was meant to provide a deep enough understanding of data analytics goals.

It may sound counterintuitive for *The preprocessing*, which is the third part of the book to come after *Analytics goals*, but that is actually a common misunderstanding regarding data preprocessing and data cleaning. In many resources, data cleaning is presented as a stage of data analytics that can be done in isolation; however, as you have experienced in this book, most of the data cleaning and the rest of the data preprocessing steps must be done to support the analytics. That is to say, without a proper understanding of what the analytics goals are, we cannot prepare the data through effective data preprocessing.

To best prepare you for your hands-on learning of data preprocessing, this part of the book provided learning opportunities for you to know the four most data analytics goals: *data visualization, prediction, classification*, and *clustering analysis*. These goals are the titles of *Chapters 5* through *8*. Under each chapter and through examples, we formed a deeper understanding of each of these analytics goals and we got to employ various analytics tools to realize these goals.

In this stage of your learning, the datasets that you worked on were mostly cleaned and prepared to best support your learning. However, the datasets you used after that had different issues and challenges that you learned how to deal with. You learned most of this in *Part 3* and *Part 4* of the book. Let's now go over our learning in *Part 3*.

Part 3 – The preprocessing

This part of the book is indeed the meat of our learning. Our learning happened in six chapters. The first three chapters, *Chapters 9* through *11*, covered data cleaning. Specifically, in these three chapters, we learned about three different levels of data cleaning. In *Chapter 12, Data Fusion and Data Integration*, we covered data integration. As you experienced, data integration is one of the simplest data preprocessing steps to understand but one of the most challenging parts to implement. In *Chapter 13, Data Reduction*, we got to learn about data reduction, which is a necessary step for many analytics projects, for many reasons. Lastly, *Chapter 14, Data Transformation and Massaging* provided a learning opportunity about data transformation, which can be thought of as the very last step of data preprocessing.

So, the four major data preprocessing steps that we learned during the course of this part of the book are *data cleaning*, *data integration*, *data reduction*, and *data transformation*. While we went about learning them in isolation in these six chapters, in real practice, you will more often perform some of them at once.

Let me use an analogy to explain that better. Imagine we wanted to learn how to effectively play soccer. In this scenario, we would have to know how to kick the ball, pass the ball, control the ball, and so on; our coach would probably give us lessons and let us practice each skill. However, when you are put to play in a real soccer game, you would not be allowed to just show your competence in one skill but would have to be relatively good at all skills to be considered a decent soccer player. Moreover, at some points during a game, you might have to combine skills and perform them either at the same time or one after the other in a split second.

The same is true regarding data preprocessing skills: *data cleaning*, *data integration*, *data reduction*, and *data transformation*. We learned them first in isolation, but real learning happens when you can perform them at the same time, in tandem, or in a smooth sequence. The next part of the book, *Part 4 – Case studies*, provides just that learning opportunity.

Part 4 – Case studies

In this part of the book, including the current chapter, we have culminating experiences so that we can see how the data preprocessing tools that we picked up in the previous parts of the book are used in concert with each other.

Specifically, the first three chapters, *Chapters 15* through *17*, were three complete case studies that showcased three real analytics examples that required significant data preprocessing. As you experienced in these three chapters, the order in which we performed the preprocessing steps was very different. Not only that—the steps were not done in complete isolation, and some data preprocessing was performed at the same time too.

In this current chapter, which is the last chapter of *Part 4* of the book, besides a book summary and conclusion, you will also be provided with more culminating experiences and learning opportunities. In the next subchapter, you will be introduced to 10 case studies that can be used for more practice. As we discussed, learning each skill in isolation is great but your data preprocessing will become more effective when they are performed in tandem with one another.

Practice case studies

This subchapter introduces 10 practice case studies. Each case study introduces a dataset and provides an analytics goal that can be achieved by preprocessing and analyzing the dataset. While each case study comes with a few **analytics questions** (**AQs**), don't allow them to close your mind to other possibilities. The suggested AQs are only meant to get you started.

We will start with a very meaningful and valuable case study that can provide real value to many levels of decision makers.

Google Covid-19 mobility dataset

Since the beginning of the recent COVID 19 pandemic, the **United States** (**US**) had various responses to combat Covid-19, varying from state to state. Each state implemented different health and safety precautions and followed different timeframes when shutting down the state. Many factors contributed to each state's health regulations, such as the number of Covid-19 cases, population density, and healthcare systems; however, most states issued stay-at-home orders, asking citizens to stay in their houses.

To aid public health officials in combating the virus and learn whether techniques such as social distancing were working, Google put forth a database called the **Global Mobility Report**. The data was put together to give insights into how different regions of the world were responding to the Covid-19 crisis. The report breaks down changes in people's movements in parks, grocery stores, and pharmacies; retail and recreation; and workplaces. For instance, the following screenshot portrays changes in people's behavior in San Luis Obispo County, California from the baseline during September 12 to October 24, 2021, for each movement category:

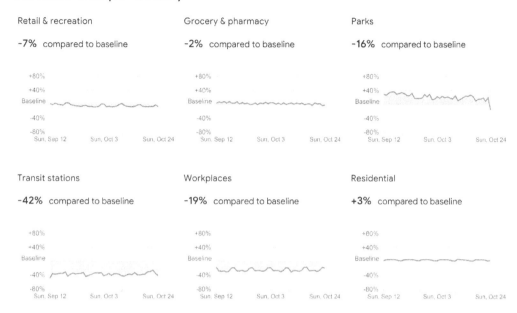

Figure 18.1 – Sample from Global Mobility Report: San Luis Obispo County, California

This data was collected from the users of **Google Maps** by using aggregated, anonymized data, and seeing how frequently people traveled around during the ongoing pandemic. To ensure the privacy of all users of Google Maps, the company used an **anonymization technology** called **differential privacy**. This technology adds artificial noise to datasets to not allow the system to identify an individual.

The latest version of the dataset can be accessed at `https://www.google.com/covid19/mobility/`. We could define many analytics questions that can be answered using this rich dataset; however, to get you started, please see the following two AQs:

- **AQ1**: Did people's behavior change after the government's stay-at-home order? This can be answered at different levels: counties, state, country.

- **AQ2**: Was the degree of change to stay-at-home orders different state by state and county by county?

The next practice case study is also going to be very meaningful for federal, state, and even individual decision makers.

Police killings in the US

There are a lot of debates, discussions, dialogues, and protests happening in the US surrounding police killings. In the past 5 years, *The Washington Post* has been collecting the data of all fatal police shootings in the US. The dataset available to the government and the public alike has data regarding age, gender, race, location, and other situational information of these fatal police shootings. You can download the dataset from `https://github.com/washingtonpost/data-police-shootings`.

Again, while the dataset has the potential to answer many valuable questions, the following two AQs are provided to get you started:

- **AQ1**: Would the suspect's race increase the chance of being fatally shot at?

- **AQ2**: Can wearing a body camera help decrease the number of fatal police shootings?

The next case study will feature a dataset regarding automobile accidents in the US.

US accidents

Not all roads are the same; there is a much higher risk of weather conditions causing an accident during winter in Chicago versus a summer in San Jose. Data analysis can shed so much light on hazardous roads and weather conditions—for instance, in the following screenshot, we can see that the frequency of accidents varies significantly across states. However, we must pay attention to the fact that the population of the states might be causing this variation more than the difference in driving habits and road conditions:

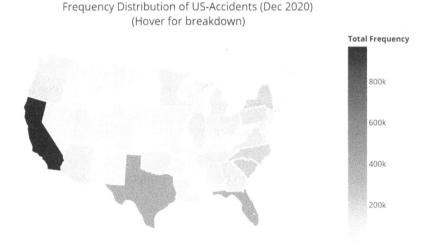

Figure 18.2 – Sample visualization from the US-Accidents dataset

> **Note**
>
> The preceding screenshot is sourced from `https://smoosavi.org/datasets/us_accidents`.

You can download the dataset from the following link: `https://www.kaggle.com/sobhanmoosavi/us-accidents`. The following list provides two possible AQs that can get you started:

- **AQ1**: Is there a discernable difference between the frequency of accidents per capita across different states?

- **AQ2**: Does a specific type of road become more prone to a fatal accident in rainy weather conditions?

The next case study will be another form of data analytics for the greater good; we will use the power of data analytics to investigate crime patterns.

San Francisco crime

San Francisco experiences a somewhat higher crime rate than other parts of the US. On average, 19 crimes happen per 100,000 people, and in a year, every person has a 1 in 15 chance of being mugged. While these statistics are staggering, data analytics might be able to help by showing crime patterns. These patterns can help decision makers to first understand the cause of the much higher crime rate and then try to address them using sustainable measures.

The following screenshot shows that data analytics is already being used in the *San Francisco Police Department*. It is greatly encouraging to see that the tools you know are being actively used and that you could be contributing to these efforts.

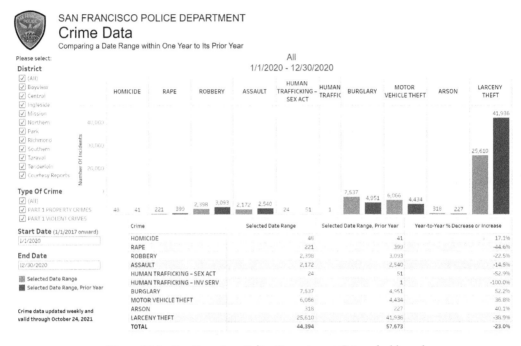

Figure 18.3 – San Francisco Police Department Crime dashboard

> **Note**
>
> The preceding screenshot is sourced from `https://www.sanfranciscopolice.org/stay-safe/crime-data/crime-dashboard`.

You can access a rather large dataset that is ripe for data preprocessing practice via `https://www.kaggle.com/roshansharma/sanfranciso-crime-dataset`. This dataset includes the records of crimes in San Francisco in 2016. The following two AQs can get you started:

- **AQ1**: Are there times of the day during which the frequency of assaults increases?
- **AQ2**: Are there locations in the city that see more theft?

In the last four case studies, we focused on the greater good by studying cases that can benefit society. Let's shift gear and look at a case study that can empower an individual—in this case, to become smarter in the data analytics job market.

Data analytics job market

The job market for data analysts and data science has not yet taken a stable shape. There is a wide range of variations experienced by people who try to find jobs in this market. This dataset provides an opportunity to discover some of the patterns in the job market. The dataset can be downloaded via `https://www.kaggle.com/andrewmvd/data-analyst-jobs`. The following two AQs can get you started:

- **AQ1**: Does the location of the data analytics job influence the amount of compensation?

- **AQ2**: Does the company rating influence the amount of compensation?

The next two practice case studies relate to sports analytics. I am glad you are already excited.

FIFA 2018 player of the match

20 minutes after each international soccer game, the player of the match is recognized. For instance, the following screenshot shows a YouTube video honoring Antoine Greizmann who was recognized as the player of the match for the 2018 FIFA World Cup™ final after helping his team to beat Croatia and become the 2018 FIFA World Cup champions:

Figure 18.4 – Player of the Match: 2018 FIFA World Cup™ final

> **Note**
>
> The preceding screenshot is sourced from `https://youtu.be/-5k-vgqHO2I`.

While knowing the player of the match is peripheral to the main soccer competition, knowing who will be the winner beforehand can be of much value to gambling professionals. This dataset contains the data of all of the games in FIFA 2018. You can access the data via `https://www.kaggle.com/mathan/fifa-2018-match-statistics`. The following two AQs can get you started to preprocess and analyze this exciting dataset:

- **AQ1**: Can the ball position predict the team from which the man of the match will be selected?

- **AQ2**: Can a combination of the number of attempts and passing accuracy predict the team from which the man of the match will be selected?

The next practice case study is going to relate to sports analytics too, but this time, the sport is going to be basketball.

Hot hands in basketball

Basketball is a very exciting game in that the winning and losing teams may switch places in a matter of seconds, and there is a lot of common sense and theories around this captivating game. One of them is the *Hot Hand* theory, which is about a successful sequence of three-point shots. As the theory goes, if a player has a hot hand, if they have made some consecutive successful shots, they will continue to make more successful shots. While behavioral economists have long rejected the Hot Hand theory, citing representativeness heuristic bias, I bet it will be fun to let the data speak and see whether the historical data supports the theory. I am more excited for you to do an analysis using the dataset on this Kaggle page: `https://www.kaggle.com/dansbecker/nba-shot-logs`. The following two AQs can get you started on preprocessing and analyzing this dataset:

- **AQ1**: Does the historical data support the Hot Hand theory?

- **AQ2**: Does being against a "good" defender dampen the success rate of a "good" shooter?

After having some fun with sports analytics, let's turn our attention to more high-stakes analysis. The next case study is going to have both environmental and societal analysis value. We are going to analyze wildfires in California.

Wildfires in California

California saw two of its worst wildfire seasons in 2020 and 2021, and the ecological predictions all point to the hypothesis that these are not just some outliers in the historical data but are long-term shifts in trend. This dataset provides the opportunity for you to analyze firsthand the pattern of California wildfires from 2013 to 2020. You can access this dataset from the Kaggle web page: `https://www.kaggle.com/ananthu017/california-wildfire-incidents-20132020`.

This dataset can both support **data visualization** and **clustering analysis**. An example of data visualization is used by *BLM California Wildfire Dashboard (Public)*, and the following screenshot shows the dashboard information collected on October 28, 2021:

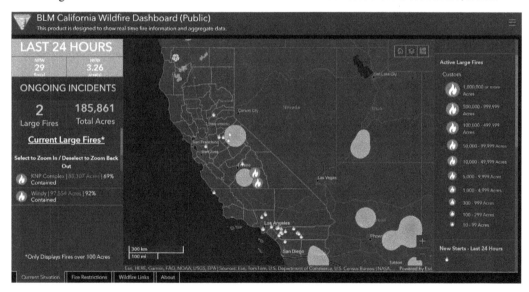

Figure 18.5 – BLM California Wildfire Dashboard (Public)

> **Note**
>
> The preceding screenshot was sourced from `https://www.arcgis.com/apps/dashboards/1c4565c092da44478befc12722cf0486` on October 28, 2021.

I highly suggest practicing data preprocessing for the purpose of clustering analysis on this dataset first, and then turn your attention to more data visualization. The first AQ listed here can only be answered using clustering analysis:

- **AQ1**: Do the fires from 2013 to 2020 form meaningful clusters? What are their patterns?

- **AQ2**: Are there more large fires in specific years?

We are going to see some more societally meaningful data analysis next. The following case study is going to provide an opportunity to analyze the diversity profile of 23 top tech companies in Silicon Valley.

Silicon Valley diversity profile

This Kaggle web page, `https://www.kaggle.com/rtatman/silicon-valley-diversity-data`, has three datasets, and you want to focus on `Reveal_EEO1_for_2016.csv` for this case study. Many meaningful AQs can be designed that this dataset can help provide an answer to; however, the following two AQs are meant to get you started.

The first AQ listed here can only be answered using clustering analysis:

- **AQ1**: Is there a relationship between the attribute gender and job category? In other words, does the gender of an individual influence their job category?

- **AQ2**: Is there a noticeable difference between the Silicon Valley companies concerning employee diversity profiles?

In the next case study, we are going to have an opportunity to practice our preprocessing for prediction models.

Recognizing fake job posting

There is nothing worse than spending hours on a job application only to realize the job posting is fake. In this practice case study, you will get to see whether prediction models can help us weed out fake job postings. Furthermore, we can see which characteristics tend to give away a fake posting.

The dataset that provides this learning opportunity is accessible on the Kaggle web page at `https://www.kaggle.com/shivamb/real-or-fake-fake-jobposting-prediction`. This dataset supports many possible AQs; however, the following will get you started:

- **AQ1**: Can Decision Tree meaningfully predict fake postings?

- **AQ2**: What are the characteristics that fake posts share?

The 10 listed practice case studies in this chapter of the book are excellent sources to continue learning; however, there are more potential learning opportunities out on the internet that you can find on your own. Before ending this subchapter, we will go over a list of possible resources that you may use to hunt for more datasets.

Hunting more practice case studies

The following two resources are excellent for finding datasets to practice your newly acquired data preprocessing and analytics skills.

Kaggle.com

This website is the best resource for finding more case study projects. Throughout this book, you may have noticed that most of the datasets we used were sourced from this website. The Kaggle website has done a great job of creating a community of developers with different skill levels who have come together to share knowledge and datasets. I highly encourage you to join this community to find more learning and practice resources.

The next resource is not as vibrant a community as Kaggle; however, it is the oldest most well-known **machine learning** (**ML**) dataset repository.

University of California Irvine Machine Learning Repository

Very well known by the term *UCI ML Repository*, this repository has been collecting datasets for research purposes since 1987. A great feature of this repository is that you can see datasets based on the analytics goals; all the datasets are filterable by four associated tasks: classification, regression (prediction), clustering, and others. You can access this repository at `https://archive.ics.uci.edu/ml/index.php`.

In this subchapter, you were introduced to 10 possible case studies and 2 sources that have many more possible practice case studies. The next subchapter offers some conclusions to this chapter and the whole book.

Conclusions

Allow me to start concluding this book by congratulating you on having gone through this journey of learning about data analytics and data preprocessing. I am confident that your learning about data analytics and data preprocessing does not end here, and you are already planning to learn more useful tools and pick up valuable skills. So, how about we conclude this book by examining a few routes for learning and improvement?

My first suggestion would be to cover your base and take advantage of all of the learning resources that this book has to offer so that you can deepen your learning and bring your skill level closer to second nature. The end of most chapters provides exercises for exactly this purpose. Furthermore, the three case studies in *Chapters 15* through *17* can be expanded upon and improved; doing that would be a great way to improve your learning. Lastly, this current chapter provided many starting points and case studies to practice the skills you've picked up during your journey in this book and make them second nature.

Besides solidifying what you learned in this book, there are a few distinct learning routes you may consider. For organization, I call these routes *data visualization and storytelling*, *algorithms*, *technology*, and *mathematics*. Let's go over these routes one by one.

Chapter 5, Data Visualization, provided a brief but fundamental understanding of data visualization. The material was provided to support our learning for data preprocessing. There is much more to learn about data visualization as far as techniques and technology go, but also from the perspective of storytelling. You might be good at the technical aspect of coming up with visualization, but this visualization must be prescribed before you can create it. In other words, if you are the one deciding what kind of visualization is needed to convince an audience, you might not be the best person to go to. If that's the case, I'd highly recommend that you consider reading *Storytelling with Data: A Data Visualization Guide for Business Professionals*, by Cole Nussbaumer Knaflic, and *Effective Data Visualization: The Right Chart for the Right Data*, by Stephanie Evergreen. Not only do these books help to kindle your curiosity and creativity regarding data visualization, but they will also guide you through the actual storytelling part that is bound to come with effective data visualization.

In this book, we only scratched the surface of algorithmic analytics. In *Chapters 6* through *8*, we briefly learned about some classification, prediction, and clustering algorithms. Not only are there more algorithms for each of the three mentioned data analytics tasks, but there are also more analytics tasks that need an algorithmic approach for effective solutions. You may want to invest in these to deepen your learning and pick up more skills in this area, and if you become proficient with all these algorithms, you'd become a highly attractive hire for ML engineer roles.

While this route of learning sounds very promising, I would like to offer a few notes of caution. First, for this route, you want to have good programming skills or at least enjoy programming; I am not talking about the type of programming we did during this book. In this book, we only learned enough programming to use modules and functions created by real programmers. I mean that you need enough programming skills so that you would be able to create those modules and functions. My second note of caution regards the future of algorithmic analytics. I surmise that out of all the four routes of learning that I am discussing here, this route is the one that is the most automatable. That means in the near future, the cost of hiring an ML engineer to develop an algorithmic solution becomes higher than subscribing to **Artificial Intelligence as a Service** (**AIaaS**) or **Machine Learning as a Service** (**MLaaS**) solutions provided by tech giants such as Amazon (**Amazon Web Services** (**AWS**)), Microsoft (Azure), and Google (**Google Cloud Platform** (**GCP**)). Unless you are the best of the best in these areas and hirable by these companies, you might end up needing to reskill.

Next, let's talk about the *technology* route of learning and improvement. For better or worse, many organizations and companies think of effective data analytics as visualization dashboards that are effectively connected to their relevant databases. For these organizations, the skill in drafting effective queries that pull the appropriate data from the databases that create and enliven the graphics on the dashboard is what they will look for in their analytics professionals. This is the simple reality of the data analytics job market: companies are not looking for hires that have more technical and conceptual knowledge, but they are looking to hire people who can work most effectively with the technologies that they have already adopted. Granted—being able to work with those technologies requires its own specific knowledge and skillset, but they may be rather different.

If today's most adopted technology that allows survival and competitiveness is databases, in the near future, it is my humble prediction that most companies will take the next technological leap and adopt **cloud computing**. This exciting trend in technological improvement is a world in itself. Not only has it streamlined and improved database technologies and the current mass technological adoption, but it also has a lot more to offer, including **Platform as Service** (**PaaS**), **Supply Chain as Service** (**SCaaS**), MLaaS, AIaaS technologies, and more.

While cloud computing platforms such as Amazon's AWS, Microsoft's Azure, and Google's GCP will provide all these solutions under various payment schemes, these services will have many variations that are designed for different needs and companies. Knowing these variations and being able to select the correct one for a company can save a meaningful amount of money for companies. Not only that—to be able to adopt AIaaS solutions such as natural language translators, the solution needs to be appropriately linked to the databases of the companies. Being able to effectively put together these pieces of technologies and cater them to the needs of a company will be a very valuable skill.

We are already seeing pioneer companies having developed roles such as **development-operations** (**DevOps**) engineer, cloud engineer, and cloud architect whose responsibilities are to recognize and adapt different pieces of cloud technology and streamline them for their needs. It is my humble prediction that for a good while, we will see a rise in the demand for these roles, while we will see a decline in demand for roles that were meant to develop analytics, AI, and ML solutions from scratch, such as data scientists and ML engineers. This trend will continue until the cloud computing adoption rate becomes high enough that companies cannot remain competitive and survive just by being able to use this technology, and they will need to adopt the new hot one. So, right now, it lays before us as a golden opportunity to break into a high-paying future tech role. Granted—you would still need to understand the business, computer programing, data preprocessing, and algorithmic data analytics to some extent, but in these roles, you would most contribute by knowing the ins and outs of the solutions that cloud computing has to offer.

Last but not least, let's talk about the learning route of *mathematics*. Toward the end of this book—specifically, in *Chapter 13, Data Reduction*, and *Chapter 14, Data Transformation and Massaging*—we started to talk about **functional data Analysis** (**FDA**). As you experienced during these two chapters, FDA can be a very powerful analytics and preprocessing tool if you have a solid mathematical understanding of various functions. Improving your understanding of various mathematical functions can give you an untouchable edge when it comes to the effectiveness of data preprocessing. After all, if other analysts don't know the mathematical function that can capture the most important information in the data, they are reduced to using a noisy dataset whose patterns are not brought to the surface and hope the algorithm will be able to pick up on them.

All of the four learning routes that I have provided here could be the right one for you, and the correct decision as to which one hinges on your personality and the types of daily activities you would enjoy doing. If you are more interested in inspiring people and would like to be more effective at persuading people, *data visualization and storytelling* may be the right route for you. If you enjoy computer programming and take pleasure from the thrill of zoning out into the third or fourth nested loop, the *algorithms* route might be it. If you enjoy being up to date with technology and enjoy debating what will happen if a new piece of technology is adopted, the *technology* route could be for you. Lastly, if you are good at math and can envision functions in your mind, and are fast at simulating data with various functions, the *FDA* route could help you in your tech career.

Lastly, I would like to say that I hope you learned many things of value in this book. I enjoyed the journey of writing this book, and I hope you enjoyed it as much as I did. Happy learning, everyone!

Index

O

P

`Packt.com`

Subscribe to our online digital library for full access to over 7,000 books and videos, as well as industry leading tools to help you plan your personal development and advance your career. For more information, please visit our website.

Why subscribe?

- Spend less time learning and more time coding with practical eBooks and Videos from over 4,000 industry professionals

- Improve your learning with Skill Plans built especially for you

- Get a free eBook or video every month

- Fully searchable for easy access to vital information

- Copy and paste, print, and bookmark content

Did you know that Packt offers eBook versions of every book published, with PDF and ePub files available? You can upgrade to the eBook version at `packt.com` and as a print book customer, you are entitled to a discount on the eBook copy. Get in touch with us at `customercare@packtpub.com` for more details.

At `www.packt.com`, you can also read a collection of free technical articles, sign up for a range of free newsletters, and receive exclusive discounts and offers on Packt books and eBooks.

Other Books You May Enjoy

If you enjoyed this book, you may be interested in these other books by Packt:

Learn Amazon SageMaker - Second Edition

Julien Simon

ISBN: 978-1-80181-795-0

- Become well-versed with data annotation and preparation techniques
- Use AutoML features to build and train machine learning models with AutoPilot
- Create models using built-in algorithms and frameworks and your own code
- Train computer vision and natural language processing (NLP) models using real-world examples
- Cover training techniques for scaling, model optimization, model debugging, and cost optimization
- Automate deployment tasks in a variety of configurations using SDK and several automation tools

The Data Science Workshop - Second Edition

Anthony So, Thomas V. Joseph, Robert Thas John, Andrew Worsley, Dr. Samuel Asare

ISBN: 978-1-80056-692-7

- Explore the key differences between supervised learning and unsupervised learning
- Manipulate and analyze data using scikit-learn and pandas libraries
- Understand key concepts such as regression, classification, and clustering
- Discover advanced techniques to improve the accuracy of your model
- Understand how to speed up the process of adding new features
- Simplify your machine learning workflow for production

Packt is searching for authors like you

If you're interested in becoming an author for Packt, please visit `authors.packtpub.com` and apply today. We have worked with thousands of developers and tech professionals, just like you, to help them share their insight with the global tech community. You can make a general application, apply for a specific hot topic that we are recruiting an author for, or submit your own idea.

Share Your Thoughts

Now you've finished *Hands-On Data Preprocessing in Python*, we'd love to hear your thoughts! Scan the QR code below to go straight to the Amazon review page for this book and share your feedback or leave a review on the site that you purchased it from.

`https://packt.link/r/1-801-07213-2`

Your review is important to us and the tech community and will help us make sure we're delivering excellent quality content.

www.ingramcontent.com/pod-product-compliance
Lightning Source LLC
Chambersburg PA
CBHW081449050326
40690CB00015B/2734